THE BEGINNING
Berkeley, 1964

berkeley campus 1965

The main section of the Berkeley campus, as it looked in 1965. In the foreground is the student union complex (1), completed in the early 1960s. Sproul Hall (2), the administration building, rises behind it. The tall building immediately behind Sproul is Barrows Hall (3), for the social sciences. Sather Gate (4) lies to the left of Sproul Hall, at the end of tree-lined Sproul Plaza (5). Dwinelle (6) and Wheeler (7), classroom buildings for the humanities and social sciences, lie just beyond Sather Gate, across Strawberry Creek. The multi-chimneyed former student union (8), used until 1960, stands to the right of the Campanile tower (9), immediately adjacent to the physical science buildings (10) rising up the hill behind the Campanile.

University of California Archives

berkeley campus
1948

To see how the campus had changed by
1965, compare this air view, taken in
1948, with the one taken in 1965. The
Free Speech controversy began over the
strip of brick pavement shown below and
at (11) on the 1965 air view. This
pavement marks a formal entrance to
the campus, where Bancroft Way is
intersected by Telegraph Street. Although
the white posts, low wall, and flagpoles
appear to mark the edge of University
property, the border actually lies twenty-
six feet nearer to the street. One of the
small plaques in the sidewalk which mark
the edge of the campus is shown on these
photographs. Student "off-campus
political activity" was forbidden in that
area in the autumn of 1964.

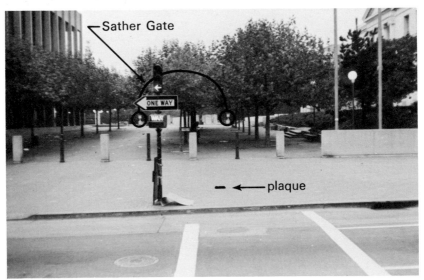

Sather Gate

ONE WAY

plaque

John and Lynn Lofland

University of California Archives

UNIVERSITY OF CALIFORNIA
PROPERTY OF THE REGENTS OF
THE UNIVERSITY OF CALIFORNIA
PERMISSION TO ENTER OR PASS
OVER IS REVOCABLE AT ANY TIME

John and Lynn Lofland

MAX HEIRICH

THE BEGINNING

BERKELEY
1964

columbia university press   new york and london

TO JANE

*whose practical expressions of love have
been evident in so many ways during the
field work and the preparation of this
book*

ACKNOWLEDGMENTS

Were it not for the remarkable openness of the Berkeley community and its willingness to be studied in detail, this report could not have been written. Literally hundreds of persons have cooperated with this project, sharing not only their behavior but also their perceptions, their motives, their private records and correspondence, and in some cases even their own carefully gathered research data. In footnotes I have mentioned 46 persons who granted interviews ranging from an hour to several days in length. A number of other persons, occupying less central roles in the controversy, also gave interviews "on the scene" of various events. In addition, more than 125 students wrote essays describing their recruitment into the controversy, their participation in a variety of events, and their perceptions of a number of issues in dispute. I regret that I cannot give more specific credit to these anonymous contributions.

A few persons should be singled out for special thanks. William Nichols made available to me three carefully sampled surveys of the student body, which are used in Chapter 1.

John Clausen and Carl Werthman lent tape recorders at critical moments. Eleanor Langlois was of invaluable assistance in helping to locate statistical records showing changes in the University of California at Berkeley over time, and University Archivist J. R. K. Kantor was a constant source of information.

I am particularly grateful to the following persons, who made available records and documents detailing daily events: Edward Strong, chancellor at Berkeley during the fall of 1964; Nathan Glazer, a faculty member active in several key phases of the dispute; Marston Schultz and Ron

Anastasi, who furnished a wide range of documents concerning the Free Speech Movement organization; Bernardo Garcia, who offered me his careful statistical records of participation in the strike of December, 1964; Siegfried Hesse of the University of California's Center for Continuing Education at the Bar, who furnished court transcripts of the trial of students arrested in December, 1964; and Burton White of radio station KPFA, Berkeley, who generously allowed me to transcribe tape recordings made during various Free Speech Movement events of the fall of 1964.

Aerial photographs of the campus appear by courtesy of University Archives, the University of California at Berkeley. Andrew Pierovich, editor of the *California Monthly,* the magazine for alumni of the University of California at Berkeley, made available its records of events and also photographs, taken by Don Kechely, which appear in this book. John and Lynn Lofland photographed the Bancroft and Telegraph entrance to the campus, and plaque. The Oakland *Tribune,* San Francisco *Chronicle,* and *The Police Chief* magazine furnished additional pictures of the arrests of December, 1964.

I have appreciated the help, encouragement, and freedom that Herbert Blumer, Neil Smelser, and Dwight Waldo provided while I developed a portion of this manuscript as a doctoral dissertation at Berkeley. Since then, Richard Flacks, William Gamson, David Goldberg, Kurt Lang, John and Lynn Lofland, Albert J. Reiss, Martin Roysher, Marvin Scott, Paul Seabury, David Segal, Anselm Strauss, Guy E. Swanson, and Ralph Turner have given useful advice after reading earlier drafts of portions of the manuscript.

John D. Moore of Columbia University Press gave me perceptive editorial advice, Sue Bishop designed the book, and Ruth Flohn did wonders with my sometimes mangled prose. My thanks to them all.

Judy Dal Corso, Andrea Foote, and Emilie Schmeidler served as research assistants at various stages of this study and added a great deal to it. My thanks go also to the people who typed tape transcripts and the massive document itself: Pat Lang did the bulk of tape transcribing; Flora Ayers typed most of the manuscript.

Finally I should like to thank those who provided the funds that made this work possible. A fellowship from the Danforth Foundation enabled me to spend a year "in the field" while the controversy was taking place. The late Joseph Lohman secured a University of California contract with the United States Department of Health, Education, and Welfare (Contract JD-66-03) which covered the costs of analyzing the data.

In summary, I greatly appreciate the help that has come from so many sources. It goes without saying that the responsibility for any errors or other shortcomings is mine alone.

June, 1970   *Max Heirich*

CONTENTS

Surrounding a University police car on Sproul Plaza on October 1, 1964, demonstrators listen to Mario Savio (standing on car roof) protest the arrest of Jack Weinberg. Student body president, Charlie Powell, is climbing down from the car.

Weinberg remained in the stranded police car for 32 hours, until an agreement between University President Clark Kerr and protest leaders ended the demonstration.

Don Kechcly

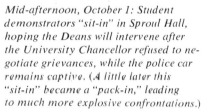

Mid-afternoon, October 1: Student demonstrators "sit-in" in Sproul Hall, hoping the Deans will intervene after the University Chancellor refused to negotiate grievances, while the police car remains captive. (A little later this "sit-in" became a "pack-in," leading to much more explosive confrontations.)

As night falls, curious students line the roofs and porches of the Student Union complex, watching the police car.

October 2: Demonstrators lock arms and prepare for arrest as police gather nearby.

Don Kechely

November 20: Supporters of the "Free Speech" position, carrying the American flag, march through Sather Gate to a vigil outside the Board of Regents Meeting. FSM Steering Committee members Ron Anastasi and Mike Rossman carry the "Free Speech" banner. Mario Savio walks beside Rossman. Faculty-supporter John Leggett, in dark glasses, walks immediately behind the banner next to Anastasi. At least 2,000 students joined the march and vigil.

December 2: Joan Baez sings "We Shall Overcome" as students march into Sproul Hall to "stop the machine."

Don Kechely

A solemn Mario Savio leads singing supporters inside Sproul Hall, December 2.

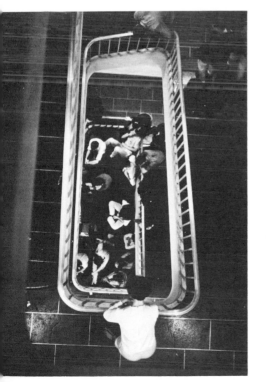

Sproul Hall stairwell frames a "Freedom School" class conducted during the evening of December 2. This class discussed civil disobedience as a tool for social reform. Other classes reviewed legal and social aspects of the national civil rights movement.

While demonstrators were being arrested and removed from Sproul Hall, a large crowd filled Sproul Plaza, trying to see what was happening. Police cordons prevent the curious from approaching the building from any other direction.

Don Kechely

Mario Savio, using a bull horn, instructs Sproul Hall demonstrators during December 2 sit-in.

Many of the Free Speech demonstrators arrested in Sproul Hall, December 3, went limp, forcing the police to carry or drag them out of the building. It took police twelve hours to clear the building.

San Francisco *Chronicle*

Don Kechely

December 7: Student pickets support the student-faculty strike
protesting the mass arrest of FSM demonstrators on December 3.

*December 7: University President Clark Kerr addresses a crowd of
approximately 13,000 in the Greek Theater, promising "a new era of freedom
under law." Moments later, police seized Mario Savio as he walked toward
the microphone.*

The FSM rally in Sproul Plaza after the Greek Theater meeting,
December 7.

Don Kechely

Spring 1965: A student sells Spider *magazine on city-owned portion of sidewalk at Bancroft and Telegraph after the magazine was banned on campus. A plaque marking the border of the campus is visible in the right foreground.*

THE BEGINNING

Berkeley, 1964

INTRODUCTION

On October 1 and 2, 1964, several hundred students at the University of California's Berkeley campus held a police car captive for thirty-two hours, until administrative leaders of the university agreed to negotiate a series of grievances. The prolonged conflict that emerged from the encounter of the newly formed "Free Speech Movement" with the university administration convulsed the campus for most of the year, leading to mass arrest of students, a general strike, the involvement of the entire faculty in the dispute, the removal of some administrative officers, and a continuing atmosphere of crisis and distrust. Perhaps more significantly, it saw the emergence in student circles of massive civil disobedience as a strategy for carrying on conflict, making the "philosophic" problem of the basis of law and order a matter of practical, daily concern to the entire university community.

As a dramatic, historic episode, the Berkeley conflict holds much fascination. It gains additional interest, however, because of what followed. As the first of a new genre of conflicts on American campuses, the Free Speech controversy set the tone for an entire college generation's confrontation with authority. Some of the conflicts that ensued grew directly from the influence of Berkeley; others arose independently but adopted (and eventually came to adapt) the Berkeley style. So pervasive was this influence that by 1968—only four years, but an entire college generation later—"freedom," "anarchy," "law and order," "student power," and similar themes had become burning issues on scores of campuses across the country. The radical activist had become the symbol of a college generation.

A few years earlier the University of California had set the pace in developing a new kind of educational system, which has come to characterize a large section of American higher education. Not surprisingly, the student style that emerged in this new setting has been copied on campuses across the country. As an "ideal type"—an extreme example of the clustering of influences that have also been at work elsewhere in American higher education—the Berkeley experience bears close examination. The shifts in outlook and style now pervading much of the American university scene are visible in relatively clear outline at Berkeley, so that one can begin to sense how they arose and why they spread so widely.

The Free Speech controversy at Berkeley took place over a period of nine months. It grew from a relatively small dispute involving a few hundred persons to a major confrontation enlisting the active participation of more than ten thousand. Twenty-six dramatic events occurred, each involving anywhere from fifty to several thousand persons who acted collectively in ways that were, for most, a major departure from normal activity. The participants ranged from political activists at one extreme, to students violently opposed to them at the other, and included several hundred faculty members and a variety of other persons from the surrounding community. Most of the incidents were so well documented that one can examine in retrospect the dynamics of an encounter, as well as the planning and communications on the part of students, faculty, and university administration that preceded it.

I was a graduate student at Berkeley, just beginning a dissertation in sociology at the time the Free Speech controversy began. The events of the conflict were so dramatic that they led me to spend a year "in the field," documenting developments on the campus as part of my dissertation.

This report uses the Berkeley events as raw material for studying the genesis of collective action in a conflict setting. Many of its pages reflect the drama of the immediate situation, as captured in tape recordings, confidential memoranda and diaries, or other records of the time. But its focus is on the organizational trends that spin a web of conflict, ensnaring actors and giving each action choice a logic of its own. The account describes conditions for observation and judgment that impart to ambiguous acts a threatening or heroic cast, and then presents the actions that proved most crucial at Berkeley for the ensuing events.

This, then, will be a peculiar kind of history. Readers who pore through the detail in an effort to identify heroes and villains may find themselves confused. In much the same way, readers who look for an analysis of a political movement will find this book only occasionally illuminating, for it focuses on the problem of explaining conflict encounters rather than on strategies, plottings, and the rivalries of elites. To the extent that organizational visions of the present or future, efforts to mobilize followers, or internal dissensions and reorganizations affected the conflict encounters, this book chronicles the Free Speech Movement and its leadership. It does not try to analyze the emergence of a political movement, however; rather, its aim is to examine the emergence of a political conflict. The selection of detail has been affected accordingly.

There is another peculiarity to this kind of approach. Some readers, noting the book's focus on perceptions, processes, and conditions, may wonder uneasily whether the author is trying to argue that moral issues, exploitation, opportunism, right and wrong do not exist—or at least that they were irrelevant to the Free Speech controversy. Not at all. The underlying argument of the book, in fact, is the opposite: ethical issues and conditions of disadvantage, discrimination, and exploitation of the gullible exist so universally and are so infrequently challenged that their presence does not explain adequately why people take common corrective action. Indeed, such conditions are created and perpetuated by persons with lofty ideals as well as by the self-centered or by crass manipulators of power. If this is so, the person who wants to explain why collective action occurred in a specific situation must show how perceptions of such conditions became viable bases of action. And the problem remains the same whether these perceptions are based on fact or error.

The opening paragraph of this introduction referred to the capture of a police car. As is often true of crowd behavior, the spontaneous events of that October drama left the actors surprised, but in no sense shocked or overwhelmed, by their action; to most of these students the act of capturing a police car *in that situation* seemed a perfectly logical, and indeed a *moral,* response to a series of events they had just encountered. How did they come to perceive the situation in ways that could make this action an appropriate response? Who was drawn into the demonstrations? What conditions structured the conflict and gave direction to the exchanges that preceded this act? How did the encounter then snowball into the kind of controversy that could bring the very nature of the university into question? What made the University of California susceptible to this kind of internal strife?

When the Berkeley campus opened for enrollment in the fall of 1964, the ingredients for a serious controversy were ready and waiting. "Faultlines" of distrust and suspicion had already formed. Beginning in midsummer of 1964, a series of exchanges had set in motion a process that slowly, but with increasing momentum, began to shake various levels of the community, leaving first administrators, then students, and finally faculty deeply divided about what should be done. Yet the explosion that rocked the Berkeley campus and reverberated across the country was triggered by actions so innocuous, in themselves, as to leave the uninitiated totally perplexed. How could such trival events shake a university to its core?

Many observers rushed in with theories. Some saw the university (and American universities in general) at the mercy of a small band of Communist and other radical plotters, who almost magically gained the confidence of the gullible young and led them in a twentieth-century version of the Pied Piper. Some others theorized that what happened was less a conspiracy than a contagion, beginning accidentally but sweeping through the population mercilessly once it began, almost like the plagues of medieval Europe. Critics of recent trends in higher education, with its teeming campuses and research-oriented faculties, saw events as an outburst of frustration on the part of alienated, atomized students who, treated as numbers by a machine-like system, responded with massive rebellion against those who operate the large educational "factories." All these theories had in common a tendency to dismiss the claims of demonstrators as irrelevant. In contrast to such approaches, supporters of the students tended to view the triggering events as a "moment of truth" when the exploitive nature of power alliances in higher education became visible—and intolerable to anyone with a sensitive conscience.

Each of these explanations has a certain dramatic appeal. What is more, each has an initial plausibility unique to itself because it focuses on some aspect of social behavior that rival accounts ignore, yet which we instinctively sense to be important.

The conspiracy theorists, for example—whatever the merits or shortcomings of their conclusions—sense that little is explained in a conflict situation until the *actions* and *goals* of various key actors in the dispute are examined. In addition, they look for unique *patterns of association* that can make sense out of apparently random occurrences. Similarly, those who support the student position realize that little can be explained until the *beliefs* and *perceptions* of the actors are taken seriously and are examined in relation to the social conditions they describe.

Those who opt for a theory of animal contagion note that conditions for perceiving and acting become altered systematically in a conflict situation, particularly when people respond in crowds. Thus they focus on the immediate *context of interaction,* which sets unique *conditions* for perceiving and acting.

"Alienation" theorists realize that *organizational structures* create their own conflicts of interest. They are also aware that experiences growing from organizationally created encounters can become a basis for viewing the world and responding to it.

Yet each of these approaches fails to deal with some important aspects of the Berkeley controversy. Consequently the account of events presented in this book will borrow none of these explanations for what happened. It will, however, consider their varied analytic questions, in an attempt to produce a fuller picture of what transpired.

Readers who have a scholarly interest in collective behavior, a professional concern for the organizational problems of modern American universities, or who are skeptical about the objectivity of the account which follows may wish to read a longer work that I have written. It will repeat the history of events given here but will also include a discussion of the way facts were gathered and a sociological analysis of conflict dynamics in this controversy. That more technical study, to be entitled *The Spiral of Conflict: Berkeley 1964,* will also be published by Columbia University Press.

part i

THE CONFLICT SETTING

one

STRUCTURING THE CONFLICT

The Free Speech controversy made Berkeley a pacesetter across the country for student confrontations with authority. But for at least a decade before this conflict erupted, the Berkeley campus had been a pacesetter of another kind, establishing by its own phenomenally successful example patterns of organization that began to change higher education in the mid-twentieth century. Berkeley's political conflict and its changes in organizational structure are not unrelated, and the same may prove to be true of other campuses as well.

To understand the explosion of student protest that rocked Berkeley and then triggered far wider movement elsewhere, we need to take a careful look at some changes that had developed in the organization of university life and to consider how these helped to facilitate the mobilization of students for political activity. We will note ways that these university changes encouraged innovation in student political organizations and the types of activities that became practical for them to conduct. Then we will ask how these developments combined with the sweep of national events to make political activism relevant to a mass of students, so that expressive pranks, which earlier constituted the greater part of crowd activity by students, began to give way to deliberate confrontations with power interests in the larger community. Finally we shall see how this dynamic affected the larger university organization, and how organizational formulas for dealing with students began to generate a conflict dynamic of their own.

The specifics of this account are peculiar to Berkeley. But many of the same kinds of things were happening elsewhere, as well.

ISOLATING A SUBGROUP: TRENDS IN THE UNIVERSITY
COMMUNITY THAT MADE STUDENTS MORE AVAILABLE FOR
RECRUITMENT INTO MASS POLITICAL ACTION

Three long-range trends in the university community at Berkeley have
increased the ease with which students could be recruited for collective
action with a political focus. In themselves, these trends are insufficient
to account for the phenomenon; but they have helped to make the campus *structurally conducive* to recruitment of this sort, once more immediately dynamic factors entered the picture. These three trends—in the
size and distribution of the campus population, in university policy that
altered the composition of the student body and the nature of student-
faculty and student-administration relationships, and in the ecological
organization of the campus and adjacent community—encouraged the
formation of "radical" networks of communication and isolated politically oriented segments of the student body from informal contacts with
those who might be expected to disagree with them.

There is nothing *inherently* politicizing about the trends we shall describe. Their effect, rather, was to alter the significance of other traditional patterns at the university and to make a large number of students
easily accessible for political mobilization once more dynamic changes
were introduced.

Changes in campus population
1. *Size.* The University of California at Berkeley has been a "big"
school for several decades. By 1940 campus enrollment had passed
16,000. Enrollment dropped during World War II but surged again
with the influx of veterans to a peak of 25,325 students in the fall of
1947. Almost 50% of these were veterans.[1] *

Campus enrollment gradually approached prewar levels again, drop-
ping to a low of 17,363 students in 1953, when young people born in
the low-birth-rate period of the depression had replaced the earlier group
of students. Within 10 years, however, the Berkeley student population
grew again by 10,000 persons, and by the fall of 1963 the university
had an enrollment of 26,757. In contrast to the earlier upswing, however, this increase was expected to be permanent.

* Superior numbers indicate notes beginning on page 286.

2. *Distribution.* There were major shifts in the *number* of students on the campus between 1940 and 1953; except for the period during World War II when the campus adapted its program to include specialized military training, however, the *proportions* of students at various stages of their education remained fairly constant. In 1940, for example, undergraduates made up 85% of the student body. This proportion did not vary by more than 5 or 6% during the next 15 years, and the distribution within major fields remained fairly stable.[2] Thus, although the university had to accommodate major shifts in numbers of students, the problems required quantitative rather than qualitative solutions.

About 1957, however, this traditional balance of students began to shift. As enrollment increased, the number of new graduate students matched almost exactly the number of new undergraduates added to the student body. Even at the undergraduate level the additions favored juniors and seniors over freshmen and sophomores by a proportion of almost 2 to 1. In 1953 freshmen and sophomores made up 40% of the student body; by 1964 they accounted for 28% of it. Thus the new increase in population called for a change in the entire organization of the university to accommodate not only greater numbers of students but also students with quite different relationships to the university itself.

University policies that affected the recruitment of students into mass political action

Several policies developed by the university to cope with these changes in size, age, and status of the student body worked together in the long run to make mass political mobilization more likely. Only one of these decisions was made with this aspect of student life in mind. The net effects of these policies, however, were to relocate large groups of students in ways that exposed them to politicizing influences, and to create strain between students and faculty and between part of the students and the administration, so that counterinfluences were minimal.

Most social organizations have several points of strain—arrangements that inhibit easy communication, that encourage distance or hostility among certain members, or that provide unequal conditions for competition among rival segments of the organization. These need not disrupt day-to-day operations; but when actions by some segments of the community shatter the balance that has been maintained between groups, cleavages often follow the "fault lines" most affected.

The policies that created new "fault lines" in the Berkeley campus organization did not, in themselves, produce a social protest movement. Rather, they created a setting that changed the impact of other exchanges between groups.

1. *The master plan for higher education in California.* Adopted in 1959 to coordinate planning for the surge of college-age students expected to inundate the various state campuses, the Master Plan created a new admissions policy for the Berkeley undergraduate student body and channeled graduate students in increasing numbers to the campus.[3] The State University system, of which the Berkeley campus was the largest and most prestigious member, was to get the cream of the high school crop, leaving less gifted students to the state or the junior colleges. For admittance to Berkeley a student now had to be in the upper one eighth of his graduating class. Because of the Master Plan, Berkeley was able to double its enrollment by attracting a high proportion of intellectually committed students, including a much greater number already in young adulthood.

The significance of this change for recruitment into political action becomes more apparent when we note which departments reaped the harvest of new students. In 1953 36% of the juniors and seniors at Berkeley were enrolled in the humanities and social sciences; by 1962 this proportion had increased to 50%.[4] The departments of political science, history, and English each showed an enrollment gain of about 500 junior and senior majors during the period from 1953 to 1964. And the six longer-term graduate programs that in the past had a solid core of liberal to radical political students (mathematics, economics, political science, sociology, English, and history) together increased their graduate enrollment by 1156 students.[4]

Lists of officers of militant and/or radical student organizations, filed with the office of the dean of students between 1957 and 1964, show a preponderance of students from the departments listed above.[5] Newspaper accounts and reminiscences by informants suggest that "radical" leadership had come from these six departments for at least two or three decades.

Thus these shifts in student enrollment brought a disproportionate increase to the academic areas that not only provided the leadership for student political causes, but also traditionally have had a liberal to radicalizing influence on their students more generally. Surveys at Berkeley over the preceding fifteen years consistently showed students in the social sciences and the humanities taking more liberal political positions and being more concerned about questions of civil liberties than their counterparts in other departments.

When S.M. Lipset surveyed Berkeley student attitudes toward a proposed loyalty oath for faculty members in 1950, for example, he found students in the social sciences and the humanities most strongly opposed to the oath.[6] A 1957 survey of Berkeley student attitudes toward a variety of civil liberties issues (conducted by Hanan Selvin and Warren Hagstrom)[7] disclosed that men in the social sciences and the humanities were much more likely than other students to take a highly civil libertarian position. Selvin and Hagstrom also found that juniors and seniors with very high grade-point averages (the group increasingly recruited under the Master Plan) were twice as likely to hold liberal views on such questions as were high-achieving freshmen and sophomores.

If these tendencies were present before the major shifts in student population occurred at Berkeley, the admissions policies of the California Master Plan should have created an increasingly large reservoir of students with sentiments at least sympathetic to liberal political causes and positions. A survey of the Berkeley student body, conducted in November, 1964, by Robert Somers, repeated several of the same questions asked by Selvin and Hagstrom. The findings indeed show an increase in sentiment favoring civil libertarian positions, much as the shifts in population trends would predict.[8] Although the changing population distribution on the Berkeley campus hardly accounts for the growth of mass political behavior there, it suggests one reason why recruiting may have become easier.

There are sound reasons why students in the humanities and the social sciences should become more liberal in their political attitudes. First, the subject matter emphasized in many of their courses brings these students to consider moral and social issues, and should to some degree attract those already sensitive to such nuances.

Second, the subject matter of undergraduate programs in the humanities and the social sciences offers no clear avenue to specific occupations when students graduate. Their futures thus are relatively unpredictable. It should not be surprising that many such students do not develop a career-oriented approach to college, but instead remain detached and critical of established arrangements.

Third, for reasons that will become clear shortly, undergraduates in these courses at Berkeley, more than in other departments of the university, interacted with the faculty primarily in the persons of graduate teaching assistants and visiting professors. Graduate students in the social sciences and the humanities took longer to complete their degrees than did those in other academic areas, consequently remaining longer in the Berkeley community in marginal economic and social roles. These graduate students as a group probably were more sensitive to political and civil libertarian currents (just as are the undergraduates who decide to major in these fields). Since they spent a good period of their young adult lives at Berkeley, it should not be surprising that a number of them became involved in the controversies and issues of the immediate community (campus and town), nor should it be surprising that their marginal social position often limited them to "meaningful roles" in the fringe social, artistic, and/or political groups of the community. The net result was that undergraduates majoring in the social sciences and the humanities had a much greater chance of exposure to minority viewpoints on the social issues confronting the campus or communities about them.

Why did students in the humanities and the social science graduate programs stay longer at the university, and why was a large part of the teaching of undergraduates in their hands rather than in those of senior faculty members? The answers to these questions will be clear when we consider policies concerning financial support for graduate students and ways of enlarging the size of departmental faculties to meet increasing enrollments.

2. *Programs for the financial support of graduate students.* Fields of graduate study at Berkeley varied considerably in the length of time required to complete a doctoral program. Students in the larger social science and humanities departments averaged from 6 to 9 years "in process," and about 40–50% of those who entered dropped out without earning their degrees. Students in the larger natural science departments, in contrast, averaged 4–6 years for their doctoral programs, and with the exception of mathematics (where about half of the students dropped out) the natural science departments had an average drop-out rate of approximately 30%.[9]

One important reason for this difference in the time required to complete a program of study (and in the proportion of those entering who actually completed it) lay in the extent to which departments assumed responsibility for the economic support of their graduate students. A study of several of the larger departments at Berkeley, made in 1964–1965, showed 68% of graduate students in the natural sciences, 46% of those in the social sciences, and 41% of those in the humanities receiving financial support. More significant than these differences in total percentages of supported students was the type of support available by field. Twenty-five per cent of the students in the natural sciences were on fellowships allowing them to study full time. Twenty per cent of the students in the social sciences, 11% of those in English and history, and 2% of those in foreign languages were receiving fellowships in 1964–1965. The remainder of students receiving financial support worked part time for the university. Students in the natural sciences were twice as likely as those in the social sciences to have research assistantships, which sometimes provide support for work on one's own research problem. Research assistantships were almost totally lacking in the humanities. The other supported students served on the teaching staff of the university.[10]

With this variety in degree and type of financial commitment to graduate students by departments, it is not surprising that the programs varied in the length of time required to complete them and in the number of students who gave up along the way.

3. *Policies for increasing the staff in "high-growth" departments.* After Clark Kerr became president of the University of California,[11] Berkeley began a systematic strengthening of departments outside the natural sciences, which produced a more uniform reputation for quality among the various fields and departments within the university. The mathematics and statistics departments recruited aggressively in the early years of the decade, with salaries and recruitment practices designed to attract the nation's leading scholars in these fields. Their aspirations were supported by the university on the assumption that their growth was essential to the qualitative development of other scientific areas. They were quickly followed by a variety of departments in the humanities and social sciences, which sought to upgrade their graduate programs by bringing to the campus eminent scholars in developing fields. These fields generally had a quantitative, statistical orientation and were com-

patible in interest with the scholarly work of much of the rest of the university.[12] So successful were the Berkeley departments in their efforts at self-improvement that ten years later the campus was rated by academicians across the country as the best graduate school in the United States, holding top rank in most fields when judged by the reputations of university faculty.[13]

How could Berkeley achieve this eminence? It had a natural head start, in some respects, with its beautiful location near the San Francisco Bay and its already stellar reputation in the physical sciences. The university developed strong research centers for the social sciences and the humanities and offered famous scholars great encouragement to develop their own specialized programs of research. In addition to having available a large number of bright graduate students who could serve as research assistants, Berkeley frequently offered star scholars lighter teaching loads, through part-time appointments in research centers. By 1963, almost one sixth of the tenured faculty at Berkeley had half-time teaching appointments, which in many fields meant that they would teach no more than one course per term.[14] The rest of their normal teaching load was assumed by temporary or irregular staff.

This upgrading of specific departments at a time when junior, senior, and graduate student enrollments were increasing rapidly encouraged the influx of new students to head disproportionately toward a few fields, rather than to spread evenly across the university. Thus, while the university as a whole was doubling its student load, enrollment in highly reputed departments in the humanities and social sciences tripled.[15]

The result was serious staffing problems in a number of fields. Many departments found it impossible to recruit as many new faculty members with sufficient academic stature as there were openings. As a result positions often were left vacant, even when funds were on hand, because the scholars these departments wished to attract were not currently available.[12] (This practice is common, of course, at prestige universities across the nation.)

Moreover, the increase in departmental "eminence" occurring generally in the social sciences and the humanities tended to create additional strains in regard to staffing. Faculty "leaves of absence" became a major headache for some departments. Normally, sabbatical leaves available to faculty after six years of service would lead to about 15% of the senior faculty being away from campus each year. The recruitment impetus of the late 1950's, the growing demand for public service from prominent scholars, and the availability of research grants for study in other parts of the world, however, combined to produce fewer senior faculty on campus than might otherwise be expected. The problem was less acute in the natural sciences, perhaps because of differences in the timing of staff additions or because of the superb research facilities available on the Berkeley campus and at nearby research centers, which tempted more professors to remain at home. But for the larger departments in the humanities and the social sciences, every year during the period from 1954 to 1964, about one fourth of the tenured faculty members were absent from their teaching duties on campus for at least half of the year.[16] Thus the list of staff members on departmental rolls indicated only approximately the number of persons or the amount of their time actually available for teaching students in any given year.

The problem can be comprehended by comparing changes in the ratios of faculty members actually present for the year to the number of graduate students and undergraduate majors enrolled in the various departments between 1953 and 1964. For the largest social science departments, the ratio of faculty present for the year to majors and graduate students changed from 1 : 10 to 1 : 20. For the largest humanities departments, the change was from 1 : 12 to 1 : 20. For the largest natural science departments, however, the change was much less: from 1 : 8 to 1 : 12.[17]

With these staffing problems, the enlarged enrollment in courses in the humanities and the social sciences was handled by increasing the size of classes and relying more and more on graduate teaching assistants for face-to-face contacts with the undergraduates. Hence these growing student faculty ratios meant that the senior teaching staff became even less accessible than before for direct conversation with students. In the social sciences and the humanities, the members of the teaching staff who had the most opportunity for person-to-person encounter (i.e., graduate teaching assistants and visiting lecturers) had the least access to accurate day-to-day information about inner university policies or the "inside" decisions made by leaders in the surrounding community. Another result of the lack of direct contact was that the senior faculty, administrators, and local community leadership were less privy to the rumors, the concerns, and the world of discourse developing among the growing body of intellectually sophisticated and mature students flocking to the campus.

What were the consequences of these developments for political mobilization? First, the policy of the humanities and the social science departments for handling the increase in students meant that their potentially radicalizable student populations (as judged from earlier attitude surveys) were increasingly *isolated from* communication links to *persons whose social positions* were most likely to lead them to disagree with the more politically active students.

Second, this break in natural communication channels provided a source of potential strain, in that situations of misunderstanding and differences of interest were more likely to be handled through formal "negotiations" between interest groups, with the relatively rigid positions such encounters entail, simply because of the lack of procedures for communicating differences before they sharpened. In short, the earlier function of senior faculty members as informal links between administrators, junior faculty, and students was largely vacated. Senior faculty members were less likely to know many students well and, because of the growing size of the faculty and administration, were also less likely to know one another or the administrators very well. Although friendship and communication networks that crossed these interest groupings still existed, they were less likely to include persons in touch with numerous students.

A third consequence for the political mobilization of students was that such cutting of natural communication links lessened the number of student information sources about what was "really going on" in the university or the community. With fewer accredited sources of rumor, the persuasive impact of a single cogent explanation of the cause of current strains in student life or in the lives of persons these young people cared about (such as members of poor minority groups in the community) could be far greater. The ideological political groups were most likely to have a consistent, plausible explanation for the numerous twists and turns of local policies. Whether their explanations were correct or incorrect in a given instance, students who heard their claims were much less likely to listen to an attempt to refute them on the basis of "inside facts."

In summary, the effect of such isolation of interest groupings on the campus, through the erosion of natural communication links, was to strengthen the persuasive power of persons who had access to each group and to increase the possibility of tension by forcing communication between groups to become formal and relatively rigid.

4. *Spatial rearrangements of the campus.* As the Berkeley enrollment grew, additional buildings and facilities resulted in a rearrangement of student traffic patterns and the location of informal meeting centers. One effect of these changes was to isolate the segments of the campus most subject to politically radicalizing influences from the kinds of informal conversations that might challenge the "world view" of their academic associates.

CHANGES IN CAMPUS LAYOUT.[18] Before World War II the campus centered around a square-block area of terraces, lawns, and benches, dominated by a bell tower called "the Campanile." The library and most classrooms either clustered around this central space or were within a block of it. The Student Union and Student Activities buildings bordered it on the south. Since the campus has a fairly steep slope from east to west, and some deep ravines divide it from north to south, it is reasonable to suppose that most people organized their physical movement both to save steps and to minimize climbing. The way the main campus buildings fed into this quadrangle should have encouraged considerable mingling of many segments of the student body, for it was an easy walk from the facilities of many disciplines to the library, or to the Student Union and its Eshleman Court or the adjacent "Faculty Glade."

Actually, this description of classroom layout as a quadrangle plan is an oversimplification. Even before World War II the campus had stretched beyond a quadrangle plan of organization. Nevertheless, the greater number of students were centered in that area, and their unscheduled campus time was likely to be spent in the general vicinity. The campus maps at the beginning of the book show the specific locations of various areas and facilities.

With the growth in enrollment and the subsequent expansion of the physical plant during the nineteen fifties and sixties, the entire relationship of parts of the campus to one another began to shift. Old campus drives were broken by huge new buildings that forced pedestrian traffic patterns to readjust. As departments enlarged their facilities, the various discipline areas began to move away from each other. They tended to be separated not only by greater distances but also by noticeable differences in elevation as the campus expanded up and down the steep slope of its territory. Some new buildings were placed on the far side of deep ravines, which should effectively have discouraged casual wandering back and forth. The physical sciences and applied sciences expanded in directions that took them increasingly out of the main pathways for the rest of the student body. Although these kinds of changes in campus layout were common on many rapidly expanding campuses, they probably have more extreme impact on interaction at Berkeley because of the steep terrain.

More specifically, four spatial changes of the twelve-year period from 1952 to 1964 seem to have made a major difference in the way people interacted with one another on the campus. Dwinelle Hall, a mammoth labyrinth of classrooms, large lecture halls, a theater, and offices devoted primarily to the humanities, was built just west and north of Sather Gate in 1952. Also, as the University Library collection continued to expand, several branch libraries were developed for specialized academic subjects, so that the main library became more and more the meeting ground for students in the humanities and the social sciences and for freshmen and sophomores, but not for persons majoring in the natural sciences or the professions.

In 1960 and 1961 the cafeteria, book store, Student Union, and general common leisure area were moved to what had been a block of stores adjoining the university just south and west of Sather Gate. This shifted the gathering point for coffee and conversation downhill to the natural territory of the humanities and the social science students, adjacent to an area traditionally set aside for political recruiting. The new Student Union contained four restaurant areas catering to different eating styles; these four areas quickly became identified with specific subcultures of student life. One of the largest seating areas, called "the Terrace," is outdoors and adjacent to a sandwich and coffee area. It had a magnificent view of San Francisco and the bay on sunny days (until the completion of the university theater in the late 1960's blocked the outlook) and a large, rather fluid space for diners; also, its outdoor location makes it psychologically "public ground" in a way that the indoor eating areas are not. The Terrace, the only area that welcomed persons carrying their own bag lunches, was quickly appropriated by graduate students and by persons in the adjoining classrooms (i.e., the humanities and the social sciences). Soon it was dubbed as the homeground of graduate students and the campus radicals. Its street-level convenience to the south entrance to the campus encouraged neighbors and friends of students, as well as registered students themselves, to meet there.

Telegraph Avenue, the principal business street near the campus, was converted to a mall for the block between the new Student Union and the administration building, Sproul Hall. Renamed Sproul Plaza, this mall provides a large open space for clusters of people to gather and talk. Sproul Plaza and the Terrace, which adjoins it on the same level, came to have the social uses accorded the old student union's plaza in earlier days. But now these were "home territory" for only one segment of the campus, humanities and social science students. Sproul Plaza joined this leisure area of the campus to a street along which were several coffee shops and a large low-rent apartment area frequented by students. This architectural treatment made the border between campus and community less marked and encouraged nonstudents to use the area as well.

It is difficult to overstress the extent to which relocating the humanities students and the Student Union complex made these students more available for political recruitment. Berkeley students had been accustomed since the nineteen thirties to the "Sather Gate tradition," which limited political proselyting to a technically "off-campus" area just outside Sather Gate. The 1952 relocation of humanities students brought them into fairly steady contact with the political activists, for relatively few journeys on campus took them far from the orbit of these recruiters. In 1960 the relocation of the Student Union complex served to bring the students, in their hours of leisure or recreation, even more within this area of influence. Equally important, it effectively broke up the quadrangle plan of the campus, for the addition of new buildings and the gradual focusing on "centers" of academic discipline turned major subject areas *away* from the Campanile area rather than toward it. This meant that students beyond the freshman and sophomore levels had few natural meeting places with persons from other fields. Students in the humanities and the social sciences had less chance for leisure-time mingling with those in the more politically conservative disciplines but were placed in close proximity to the proselyters on the edge of campus. The creation of four eating areas in the Student Union further encouraged this segregation, while the relocation of the Student Union itself guaranteed maximum exposure of students with free time to the political harangues of the day.

In one sense the capstone of this construction of a separate locale for humanities and social science students occurred in the summer of 1964, when Barrows Hall, a starkly modern, eight-story social sciences building, was built east of the new Student Union, on the same general level. The administration building, Sproul Hall, built adjacent to the university proper in 1940, just south and east of Sather Gate, now was surrounded by Barrows Hall on the east, the political hawkers on the south, the Student Union complex to the west, and Dwinelle and Wheeler Halls, classroom buildings for the humanities and the social sciences, immediately through Sather Gate to the north.

With the relocation of classroom buildings and leisure areas to adjoin the political proselyting area, it is little wonder that many students at Berkeley began to think of the "marketplace of ideas" where political recruiting took place as the unique and wonderful trademark of the campus. Such recruiting was, in fact, the most noticeable activity of extracurricular campus life, given the rerouting of student traffic patterns. This was particularly true for students in the humanities and the social sciences, who had little reason to wander far from the area.

SHIFTS IN HOUSING PATTERNS. In 1947, when housing shortages were severe and campus enrollment high, 40% of the student body lived at home. By 1953, however, when the campus was at its lowest enrollment since the end of World War II, only 25% of the single students lived with their parents. The trend for students to leave home to attend the university has continued. By 1964 the total number of students living at home had declined by 900, and their proportion of the single student population had dropped to 10%.[19]

Large numbers of students were coming to live in areas immediately adjacent to the university. In 1956, 9900 students lived within 10 blocks of the university. By 1964, the number had risen to 16,700. New dormitories accommodated 2600 of the influx, and the fraternities and sororities added facilities for about 200 additional students. Boarding houses and private homes accommodated approximately 600 more. But about 7200 single students were living in apartments near the campus.[19]

Sharing an apartment with friends was no more expensive than living in a dormitory or other group accommodations. It offered the advantages of freedom from supervision, flexible hours for meals, quiet conditions for study, and a guarantee of congenial associates. Small wonder, then, that an increasingly adult student population shifted to apartment life as places became available.

Apartments became popular with students of all types—those in the fraternities and sororities, the vocationally oriented, and the growing intellectual and political subgroups. Part of their appeal lay in the fact that no one style of student life was imposed on apartment dwellers. Each could pick his own associates and activities and need adapt his pace only minimally to those around him.

With an older and more academically oriented student body living near the campus, tastes in leisure activities began to change. Attendance at athletic events declined, and Big Game riots became a memory of the past. Bookstores and coffee houses for conversation began to do a lively business near the campus. Art theaters showing foreign and old American films expanded in number. Clothing, accents, and the atmosphere in general had taken on a noticeably cosmopolitan aura in contrast to the "collegiate" tone of earlier years. With about 7200 single students living in apartments, as contrasted with roughly 2700 in the Greek system houses and 3300 in the dormitories, the campus style began to shift from organized group activities to much more independent activity.[20]

This shift from family or group living situations to private apartments accelerated the isolation and regrouping of students that administrative policies had created on the campus itself. Students in apartments can avoid personal contact with persons who disagree with their views. They are not provided with automatic and semiobligatory group activities whereby they meet persons outside their intimate circle, except in the relatively impersonal setting of the lecture hall. The persuasive power of a circle of friends can become very great when one does not interact directly with others who might challenge them.

The apartment dweller is uniquely available for recruitment into mass activities. His time schedule is much more flexible than that of a student living in a group or family accommodations. Since he lives free of supervision, direct or indirect, few pressures can be placed on him.

Under these circumstances we would expect apartment dwellers in the social sciences and the humanities to be the most politically liberal, because they should have the greatest exposure to the politicizing influences we have enumerated thus far. Three surveys, made in 1960, 1961, and 1962, provide evidence with which to test these claims. William Nichols gathered descriptive samples of the Berkeley undergraduate student population in each of these years.[21]

During the three-year period covered by these samples, as shown in Table 1, undergraduate political preference did not shift very much for the student body as a whole. Apartment dwellers, however, moved to the left in their preferences. At every point apartment dwellers majoring in the social sciences and the humanities were more than twice as likely as the average student to have liberal to radical political preferences.

TABLE 1 | **percentages of students stating a preference for liberal democratic or more radical political policies—by residence**

			Ap't dwellers	
Time of study	All students	Ap't dwellers	Planning to major in humanities and social sciences	Other ap't dwellers
Spring 1960	23	27	52	12
Spring 1961	20	35	42	29
Spring 1962	24	40	54	27

Mere exposure to the humanities and the social sciences had a somewhat liberalizing influence. The combination of these fields of study and isolated living conditions, however, was much more powerful, as indicated in Table 2.

TABLE 2 | **percentages of students stating a preference for liberal democratic or more radical political policies—by major**

			Humanities and social science majors		
Time of study	All students	Humanities and social science majors	In ap'ts	In group living situations	At home
Spring 1960	23	36	52	35	29
Spring 1961	20	26	42	25	34
Spring 1962	24	32	54	22	34

The proportion of undergraduate apartment dwellers in the social sciences and the humanities increased steadily during this three-year period, rising from 40% of the apartment residents surveyed in 1960 to 49% in 1962. Thus there was an increasing reservoir of students subject to the combination of influences most likely to have a politicizing effect at Berkeley. That these young people were moving beyond general liberal sentiments to increasingly radical outlooks is suggested by the rise in proportions of students expressing a preference for a political party other than the major parties, Republican and Democratic. (At Berkeley the most noticeable competing parties were to the left of the Democrats.) The results in Table 3 confirm this shift.

TABLE 3 | percentages of students stating a preference for a political party other than the Republicans or Democrats

| | | | | Ap't dwellers | |
Time of study	All students	Humanities and social science majors	Ap't dwellers	Humanities and social science majors	Other majors
Spring 1960	2	2	0	0	0
Spring 1961	3	4	6	6	6
Spring 1962	4	4	9	13	6

Student sentiment as a whole was not becoming more politically radical (although the growth in student population meant that the gross *number* of political radicals was increasing for the school as a whole). But, as the tables indicate, apartment dwellers in the humanities and the social sciences *were* becoming politically radicalized. In absolute numbers, single undergraduate students majoring in humanities and social sciences and living in apartments had increased from about 800 (in 1960) to about 1650 two years later. By 1962 about 200 of these students were identifying themselves with minority political parties; it is probable that the majority considered themselves to be some kind of Socialist.[22]

The changing size and composition of the student body, a variety of administrative policies designed to take advantage of these changes or to accommodate to them, and ecological shifts in campus layout and in the nature and size of student residential arrangements, then, made students more available for political mobilization. These factors interacted to isolate one growing group of students from conservative influences and to increase its contact with the politically radical areas of campus life.

Nevertheless, these structural pushes toward a liberal-to-radical political *outlook* for some of the students did not make what occurred inevitable. Possession of a generalized *attitude* does not necessarily lead persons to *act* in terms of it. The effect of these influences, rather, was to create an increasingly large reservoir of students living near the campus who possessed sentiments generally sympathetic to the goals of radical political action and who were structurally unimpeded (by problems of schedule coordination or sanctions that could be imposed by other persons) from joining in such action if they wished to do so.

Two ingredients important for mobilizing large numbers of students for direct political action still are missing. First, the would-be mobilizers must develop some form of social organization for including this vast but isolated throng in their programs. Second, something must happen to focus the attention of large numbers of these students on the programs being proposed, and to focus it in ways likely to lead to a positive response. Other changes in university policy affected the ease with which this could be done.

5. *Policies concerning the limits of appropriate political activity by students.* For many years the University of California has been plagued by a set of unresolved—and perhaps unresolvable—issues pertaining to the political rights of students, faculty members, and the public at large. Disputes involving these unresolved issues have tended to boil over about every eight years for the last few decades, whenever a political campaign moves beyond competition between personalities to a major confrontation of differing political values. At such times, or at other times when political issues arose that threatened to split the public, the University of California usually found itself redefining its basic policy to accommodate the new situation.

A tax-supported university stands uneasily between its heritages—on the one hand, it inherits the academic tradition of free inquiry and free expression of the truth as one perceives it; on the other hand, it inherits the American political tradition of balance of powers, which implies that a public institution should not give unfair political advantage to any interest group at the expense of the general public. When the search for truth involves political value judgments, maintaining a balance between these two positions becomes extremely awkward.

In principle, the problem was resolved for the University of California by the state constitution, which prohibited political or religious proselyting on campus, and which placed policy-making for the University in the hands of a Board of Regents not subject to political pressures through the state legislature. In *fact,* however, the arrangements for accomplishing this created several points of organizational strain that made a final resolution of the problem extremely difficult.

POINTS OF STRAIN IN THE ORGANIZATION OF THE UNIVERSITY AT THE STATE LEVEL. According to the state constitution, the university is autonomous, governed directly by a Board of Regents, which establishes the general policy to be carried out by the university administration, and is supposed to act as a buffer between the university and the political pressures of various interest groups within the state. The state legislature appropriates funds for the overall university budget but is enjoined by the constitution from meddling in the internal operations of the university.

This decree of political independence for the university breaks down, however, at two points. First, the state constitution provides that the governor make appointments to the Board of Regents and that four ex-officio members of the board be elected officials (the governor, the lieutenant governor, the majority leader of the state senate, and the superintendent of public instruction in the state). The presence of these elected officials may guarantee that public concerns are considered by the board, but it also guarantees that its controversial deliberations will carry a political tenor. Furthermore, although the sixteen-year terms of the members of the Board of Regents ensure that no single governor can control its composition, their appointment by the chief political officer of the state in fact guarantees that the board will consist of "prominent public citizens" connected with various powerful interests in California.

In the 1964–1965 school year, for example, the twenty-four members of the University of California's Board of Regents had various connections with larger interests in the state and the nation. The board chairman was president of the largest chain of department stores in the West. Other members included the chairman of the Bank of America, the chairman of the nation's largest gold-mining corporation, a vice-president of Lockheed Aviation active in the California Manufacturer's Association, the board chairmen of two oil companies, the president of one of California's largest food-processing concerns, a past chairman of the Republican State Central Committee, a Democratic Party career woman, the wives of two of the state's leading newspaper publishers, a past president of the state bar association, a government official active in the American Civil Liberties Union, a national labor leader, two corporation lawyers, and a former advertising executive. Members of the Board of Regents either headed or served on the boards of directors of thirty-eight major corporations in the state and the nation.[23] Thus, although the existence of the board protected the university from such gross political pressures as inclusion in the patronage system of the state, it hardly provided freedom from the political currents of the day.

Second, the state legislature, theoretically deprived of authority over university policies, in practice tends to express its attitude by reducing the university budget by amounts identical to subunit budget items that have the disapproval of legislators.[24] This means that members of the appropriations committees have unusual leverage for criticizing university policies of which they disapprove. In short, the independence of the university from political pressure is only partial and is invariably of unstable equilibrium.

By balancing powerful interest groups in the state as represented on the Board of Regents, by cultivating key legislators in the state capital, and by employing a public relations staff to furnish favorable publicity for the university, the administration sought to minimize outside pressures. These extraconstitutional practices developed as administrative responses to the failure of the constitutional mechanism to protect the university system from intervention by special interest groups, as was intended in the university charter.

RULES FOR POLITICAL ACTIVITY. If student or faculty actions threaten the special interests of some group of organized and powerful citizens, the vulnerability of the university organization to political pressure can threaten the financial stability of the institution, at minimum, and perhaps even the tenure of administrative officers considered responsible for the state of affairs. How can administrators balance this political vulnerability against academic traditions of free inquiry and expression?

The classic Berkeley solution, delineated most clearly during the nineteen thirties, defined the university as a controlled "marketplace of ideas." The function of the university was to examine controversial ideas critically, rather than to propagate or oppose them. A series of regulations, which eventually came to be summarized as Rule 17, spelled out the details of this policy.[25] Faculty members were expected to analyze controversial political positions in the classroom, but not to take stands in favor of them or against them. Partisans for political or religious causes were not allowed to speak on campus in advocacy of their positions, except when approved by the administration with explicit representation of opposing viewpoints at the same meeting. Funds for off-campus causes could be collected on campus only with explicit permission from the administration.

On the other hand, the off-campus activities of students and faculty were their own business so long as they did not implicate the university in their political actions. Thus the academic and political purity of the institution was to be safeguarded at the same time that the rights of citizens were preserved for off-campus action.

Technical implication of the university and practical implication, however, are two different things. The public prominence of faculty members meant that their names inevitably were associated with the university whether or not they proclaimed the affiliation. And the participation of a group of young citizens who all happened to be attending the university in a controversial political action frequently meant that in terms of social (as contrasted with legal) definitions "students at the university" were taking part in various political conflicts. Since the university was "home territory" for resident students, they often found the technical distinction between their relationship on one side of the university gates and that on the other side a difficult one to accept. And so did the public. If large numbers of students or faculty members behaved in noticeably controversial ways off campus, there was frequent suspicion that the rule was being violated on campus. During the nineteen thirties the American Legion recruited fraternity members to report un-American comments made in the classrooms.[26] Moreover, this decade provides a record of constant struggle between student organizations and/or the student government on the one hand, and the campus administration on the other, over proper limits to the examination of ideas and the judgment of their validity.[27] The faculty, too, was under pressure. The Board of Regents, in 1940 and again after a period of legislative reaction to the controversial Presidential campaign of 1948 (in which the Progressive Party was an issue), laid down additional loyalty requirements for the faculty.[28]

Although the campus was technically virginal in terms of political and religious activity, its borders were besieged by efforts to convert. A student solution to the on-campus/off-campus technicality was to develop the "Sather Gate tradition." Persons who wished to express controversial political views would speak just outside the main entrance to the campus, with their audience sometimes remaining on university property because of space limits. This compromise in fact allowed proselyters access to a voluntary audience of university personnel but without the overt concurrence of the administration or faculty. At several points during the nineteen thirties University President Robert Gordon Sproul made it clear that students had a right to attend meetings at Sather Gate if they chose to do so, but that the university was not involved in the proceedings.[29] After 1938, when collection of funds was added to the list of prohibited political activities (to counter a student attempt to raise funds for medical relief in the Spanish Civil War), fund raising also became assigned to the Sather Gate area.[30]

Thus the administrative solution to the dilemma of conflicting values inherent in academic and American political traditions was to allow a dual system to grow up. The formal legal code, delineated in increasing detail as Rule 17 of the university, forbade any kind of partisan advocacy of political or religious ideas. The common-law amendment, which came to be known as the "Sather Gate tradition," allowed genuine freedom of expression so long as the university technically could not be held responsible for what was said.

AMENDING THE RULES. This legally neat but practically awkward solution became obviously absurd in 1956, when Presidential candidate Adlai Stevenson addressed a crowd of several thousand members of the university community. Stevenson spoke from a truck parked at the sidewalk, on city of Berkeley property. Loudspeakers were set up so that a crowd of several thousand people, sitting on the campus lawn, could hear him.[31]

Modification of Rule 17. With this episode a student campaign to change Rule 17 began. After a year of negotiation, Rule 17 was amended to allow partisan speakers to appear individually on campus, rather than always to speak in tandem with their opponents; a proviso was added, however, to the effect that advocates of opposing viewpoints also must appear on the campus "within a reasonable time limit." [32]

This modification of political rules had direct implications for recruiting students for massive political action. First, it made it possible for student organizations to sponsor prolonged public events (such as evening lecture programs or noon meetings) in which an intellectually plausible and emotionally appealing presentation could be made for only one side of a question, in a setting that minimized distraction, accommodated large numbers of people, and was located in the regular pathways of many students. Second, the separation of controversial viewpoints meant that students were free to hear only one side of the issue if they chose to do so; in fact, extra effort would be required to hear both sides. Third, such presentations made it logical for the audience to move beyond detached criticism of the merits of each position to a consideration of the implications for action of an argument that appealed to it.

Relocation of the Sather Gate tradition. After Rule 17 was modified to allow partisan speakers to address the campus when their opposition was not present, the university administration assumed that the Sather Gate tradition gradually would die.[33] In 1958, however, when the university boundaries were moved a block beyond Sather Gate to allow the new Student Union to be built, the tradition associated with the gate also moved a block, to the edge of Bancroft and Telegraph streets, the new campus boundary. Student political groups gathered at the new "gate," which for architectural reasons actually was set back 36 feet onto campus property. It did not occur to many that the proselyting activity now was technically illegal: those who noted the small plaques set in the paving to mark the edge of university property considered the technical violation to be in the spirit of the old rules; most people assumed that the brick sidewalk was the property of the city of Berkeley.

By concentrating all political advocacy at the university entrance in the nineteen thirties, the university unwittingly increased the visibility of political activists. With the relocation of the Sather Gate tradition to Bancroft and Telegraph, this visibility was retained. The new architectural treatment of the campus entrance, moreover, provided much more space for political activities.

DEVELOPING DISTINCT SUBGROUP GOALS: ORGANIZATIONAL INNOVATION THAT ENCOURAGED MASS POLITICAL ACTION

In 1957 a group of students at Berkeley whose political beliefs ranged from liberal to radical abandoned their ideological differences to form an issue-oriented coalition. Originally named TASC (Toward an Active Student Community), the new group decided to run a slate of candidates in the student government elections that fall. Within a few months these students changed the name of their party to Slate, and within a year they had won control of the student government and elected a student body president. In the years that followed, Slate's strength waxed and waned. Its style of organization—an ideologically argumentative but nondogmatic, issue-oriented coalition—however, came to characterize effective political groups on the Berkeley campus. Hence it is worth examining in some detail.

Slate was to a considerable extent the creation of an undergraduate student in sociology named Mike Miller. Because he had been active in the campus YMCA, he had entree to a wide range of student "liberal" groups; his background as a boy reared in public housing projects in New York City previously had brought him into contact with radical political expression on the East Coast. His special contribution was to bring together potential student leaders from a variety of political persuasions and to develop a coalition that was dominated by no one group but that, despite constant internal dissension about ideological matters, could focus common energies on goals held in common by all the groups.[34] Thus Slate directed its attention to taking control of the student government away from the traditionally better organized fraternities and sororities, and on pressuring student government to deal with controversial issues of the campus and state: discrimination in the Greek system (which became a campaign issue in the 1958 gubernatorial race between Patrick Brown and William Knowland); the abolition of compulsory military training on campus; the housing problems of the growing influx of students; the improvement of teaching (a particular problem for intellectually curious students in large, impersonal lecture courses); the expression of student opinion in such current statewide controversies as the abolition of capital punishment; the harassment of radicals and other politically deviant minorities; the escalation of the arms race through the development of nuclear weapons; *de facto* segregation in housing, which affected the composition of student bodies in the public schools; and the access of minorities (including the rural minority of agricultural laborers) to jobs in the immediate community.[35]

For several reasons Slate was ideally designed to appeal to the growing subgroups already described. First, although it was intensely critical of established arrangements, Slate did not engage in partisan ideological rantings, which might be derided by the growing numbers of intellectually sophisticated students coming to the campus. Second, it had an informality of structure that allowed these students to come and go—to join it for projects in which they personally were interested, and to ignore it for others. Third, because of its early leadership by a coalition no one political organization dominated Slate, though many tried. Thus it became an intellectually exciting meeting ground for political theory and debate, without requiring the listeners finally to take ideological sides; this made it attractive to a wide range of independent students who shied away from the political parties and sectarian divisions on campus. At the same time, its exclusion of political conservatives from the coalition limited the range of political debate that occurred.

Finally, Slate's specific action programs focused on goals common to persons of many political persuasions; thus it brought large numbers of vaguely liberal students into dialogue with committed radical students from a variety of party backgrounds. The net effect was less to recruit the former into radical party membership (although this occurred to some extent) than to make radical political positions and acts more nearly *respectable*. In short, Slate redrew the boundaries of informal contact between political groupings on the campus. And because it united a concern with recognizable problems on the campus and action programs to deal with issues affecting the state and the nation, it challenged the traditional distinction between on-campus and off-campus political issues. This in itself was enough to guarantee a long series of conflicts with the university administration, which often seemed to place the latter more nearly in an antagonist than in a neutral role with the student groups.

Without the unique perspective of Mike Miller and his ability to bring potentially hostile factions together to work on common goals, such an organization as Slate might not have become a viable arrangement. Once established, however, it became the working model for several other student organizations that sprang up in the nineteen sixties, both locally in the Bay area and nationwide. Thus the "New Left," as it has come to be known, argued endlessly about political ideology but carefully avoided imposing a political creed on its followers; it called for their commitment, not to particular statements or organizations, but to direct pressure tactics to try to ensure the achievement of commonly held goals.

What Slate managed was a revival of the old "United Front" idea of the nineteen thirties, but because of the interests of its founders it focused more on being "united" than on being a "front." Beginning with picket projects and other "militant" ways of registering *opinion* on such matters as capital punishment, the criticism of political minorities, and racial discrimination, it gradually shifted attention toward direct imposition of "what is right" by massive *intervention.*

By the late nineteen fifties Berkeley had, then, a setting increasingly ripe for the recruitment of students into the direct expression of political beliefs. It also had a growing number of students, disproportionately representative of the independent intellectual minority found on most campuses. The new students were moving into the humanities and the social sciences, where a strong body of liberal to radical political sentiment already existed, and many of them were living in isolated apartments where they could ignore outlooks different from their own and where restraining pressures were missing. The campus was shifting the location of classroom buildings and social centers, bringing students in the humanities and social sciences into more casual contact with political proselyters and reducing their informal contact with the more conservative segments of the campus. The same things, of course, were occurring at other campuses across the country. But Berkeley had developed an action-centered coalition of liberal and radical politicos, providing a flexible base for joint projects and an exchange of participants for various activities.

CREATING EXPECTATIONS OF HOSTILITY OR TRUST: POLICIES AFFECTING STUDENT-ADMINISTRATION RELATIONSHIPS

While all these developments were taking place, two campus decisions aimed at simplifying relationships between students and the administration worked instead to provide additional strain, because they made direct communication with this politically active segment of the campus more difficult.

Reorganization in the chancellor's office

In July, 1958, the relationship of the dean of students to the chancellor was altered by the appointment of a vice-chancellor for student affairs, who coordinated all student-centered programs and recommended policy to the chancellor.[36] This move was designed to increase the day-to-day efficiency of programs concerned with student services. One result of this administrative reorganization, however, was a practical de-motion of the post of dean of students, which removed a direct link between the chancellor and any student groups involved in nonroutine activities. The change resulted in a three-step communication process for policy decisions on controversial student matters. Thus no matter what the motivations or reactions of the university administration might be, the number of levels involved in making a decision added an overtone of bureaucracy and of indecision to contacts between the administration and student leaders. The more active, politically oriented students came to see the dean's office as a necessary inconvenience to be faced in order to speak with people in a position to make real policy decisions.[37]

This indirectness of communication was increased by the presence of the statewide university administrative offices a few blocks away. Controversial questions such as Slate tended to raise often were referred to the university president before decisions were made. The involved system of communication encouraged wide speculation about motives for decisions and led to many rumors about how various decisions were reached. Moreover, it encouraged more stereotyped exchanges than might otherwise have occurred. Representatives of student political groups recognized correctly that they were talking to middle-level bureaucrats rather than to policy-makers. This in turn made meetings with representatives of the student political groups a less than pleasant task for members of the dean's staff on many occasions. The elaboration of a formal communication and decision network thus made response to crises and to innovations more difficult by removing direct channels and by preventing simple responses to questions in the early stages of a developing controversy.

Removal of graduate students from student government

In the fall of 1958 the vice-chancellor for student affairs decided to make a survey of graduate student desires for continued representation in the student government, whose concerns and activities were primarily directed toward undergraduate, collegiate interests. This decision received impetus from at least two student sources. For the first time in many years a student political party had been formed that had considerable support from graduate students; this party, Slate, announced its intention to make student government a serious force and began making basic criticisms of current procedures. A second, apolitical group, the

Committee for the Disassociation of Graduate Students from the ASUC (student government), was circulating a petition for graduate students to be removed from student government and to be refunded the fees levied against them for its activities.

Already the graduate enrollment had increased by about 2000, and the campus administration felt that some reassessment of graduate students' relationship to student government was in order. Consequently, graduate students who filed study lists for the spring semester of 1959 were handed a survey asking their preference, in regard both to form of representation and amount of fee to be paid, among five possible resolutions of the current student representation debate. The questionnaire offered choices ranging from leaving student government (with fees cut in half), through forming a separate organization (with fees depending on the cost of the new operation), to remaining in student government with strengthened graduate representation (at current fee levels). Sixty-nine per cent of the graduate students (3778 out of 5420) returned the questionnaires. No alternative got more than 30% of the "vote." The two most popular, however, were those involving a reduction in fees, either by leaving student government or by forming a separate organization.[38]

On April 26, 1959, Arleigh Williams, director of activities in the office of the dean of students, brought the results of the poll to the Executive Committee of the student government. He stated that the survey results were inconclusive regarding the type of organization desired, but that "the graduate students should be given the chance to decide for themselves what kind of association they want." The Executive Committee then formally approved a separate graduate association.[39]

The suggestion, however, was not followed. Instead, a new administrative policy was announced in a public release from the chancellor's office, which appeared in the student newspaper on May 4, 1959. The release stated that, as a result of the poll and of a petition for disassociation signed by 1300 graduate students,[40] it was clear that

. . . a majority of graduate students wish to be separated from the undergraduate student government. The Berkeley administration accepts this preference, recognizing that graduate students have different needs because of such factors as age, concentration of intellectual interests, and previous experience as undergraduate students. . . .

The statement announced that the chancellor's office would recommend to the university president and the Board of Regents that graduate students be disassociated from the student government. It stated also that financial commitments undertaken to build a new Student Union building would require a compulsory fee of $8.75, which was $3.25 *more* than was being charged at the time.[41]

This interpretation of the results of the poll led to removal of the graduate students from student government, but to no reduction in fees and no proposal for alternative action. No major opposition movement was organized, however, and the recommendation was forwarded to the policy-making body of the university. In the summer of 1959 graduate students were formally disaffiliated from participation in the student government.[42]

This development increased the strain inherent in administrative-student relations in at least three ways. First, it removed any direct communication link between graduate students and the administration, at a time when these students were becoming a third of the student body. There were no official communication links for three and a half years after the 1959 action, and the procedure that eventually emerged did not fill this gap.[43]

Second, the removal of graduate students from student government elections effectively kept the student government in the hands of the collegiate subculture of the university, represented most typically in the fraternities and sororities. Slate won control of the student government only once (by a margin of 33 votes) [44] in the spring of 1959, just before the graduate students were removed from the voting rolls. Their removal guaranteed that undergraduate members of the political and intellectual subcultures could take only a "minority opposition" stance within the student government. Furthermore it removed them from daily policy-making within the student government and from roles within the university that would bring them into natural, informal, working contact with members of the administration. Thus it effectively isolated the growing political and intellectual subcultures from the administration and forced them to rely on formal "negotiations" when they were concerned about university policies.

Third, the timing and procedures used to disfranchise graduate students led to widespread rumors about the motivation of the administration in taking this action. A graduate representative of the student government charged that the action was a political maneuver designed to neutralize the graduate student vote in the coming ASUC elections:

It is designed to put the ASUC even more under the dominance of the Chancellor's office and to reduce student government to an even greater farce than in the past. The graduate students did not express any preference for relinquishing all rights while still paying $8.75 a semester.[45]

The failure to replace graduate representation in student government with an equivalent graduate association led many observers among the students to accept such accusations as true. I have no information about how this decision was reached. But whether the assessment of administrative motivation quoted was correct or not is unimportant in terms of its *structural* consequences. Because the accusations were given credence by a large number of students, however, they affected future dealings between the student groups "on the fringe" and the campus administration. Ambiguous events in the future were more likely to be interpreted as further evidence of "administrative duplicity."

These two innovations—the reorganization of student services personnel within the administration and the removal of graduate students from the student government—had similar results: they enlarged the social distance between interest groups on the campus and increased the difficulty of simple and direct communication about differences that arose. Thus they increased the possibility of student "crises," at the same time that they made response to crisis more difficult.

FOCUSING ENERGY TOWARD NEW GOALS

The Kerr Directives

In October, 1959, the one school year in which Slate controlled the student government, President Clark Kerr announced a new set of directives to replace earlier rules for student political conduct. The Kerr Directives included these points: (1) the preamble of the student government constitution on each campus shall be changed to make it clear that the student governments are directly responsible to the appropriate chancellor's office; (2) student governments are forbidden to speak on off-campus issues; (3) amendments to student government constitutions are subject to the prior approval of campus officials; (4) to be recognized, student organizations must have an active adviser who is a faculty member or a senior staff member, must declare their purposes to be compatible with the educational objectives of the university, must not be affiliated with any partisan political or religious group, and must not have as one of their purposes the advocacy of positions on off-campus issues.[46]

One effect of this clear statement of administrative policy was to eliminate student government as an effective vehicle for the partisan expression of student concerns. It was not that the policies were more repressive, for they allowed liberalizations of former rules. But coming as they did after the election of a student body president pledged to revamp student government, they made clear the administration's determination to maintain control over student political expression on campus. After removal of the graduate students and presentation of the Kerr Directives, the student newspaper began increasingly to refer to the student government as "the sandbox."

The juxtaposition of a Slate-dominated student government and the reiterated administrative position against the taking of public positions by this government meant that public debate of political events was certain to take place in meetings of the student government and that student attention was sure to be focused on these events, but that formal ways of registering widespread student feelings, through resolutions or the like, could not be used. Expression of student sentiments in less traditional ways would be necessary if students wished to act in concert.

Focusing student attention on off-campus political issues

During 1958 and 1959 a variety of Slate actions focused a fair amount of attention on the question of whether students on the campus had the right to band together to work directly on controversial questions. Nevertheless, although Slate received an increasing proportion of the vote in student body elections, it felt pleased if as many as 50 students turned out for one of its picket lines. During this early period mass behavior was not present.

Then, in the spring of 1960, two events occurred that caught the attention of hundreds of students at Berkeley and moved them toward the programs being proposed by the various groups operating under the Slate umbrella. In February of that year Negro students in the southern states began marching to segregated lunch counters and demanding to be served. The "sit-in movement," as it came to be called, gave birth to one of the most militant civil rights organizations to work in the South. The experiences of southern Negro students, arrested in large numbers and sometimes beaten or attacked by dogs, cattle prods, and fire hoses, enlisted the sympathies of thousands of college students throughout the North and the West. Sympathy picket lines outside the local outlets of segregating chain stores were manned by large numbers of students in many cities across the country. The Congress of Racial Equality, until that time a little-known organization urging nonviolent direct action to desegregate public facilities, became a prominent national organization as chapters sprang up in many communities. Berkeley was no exception to this trend. Moreover, the university already possessed a working coalition of student political organizations that could direct this enthusiasm into an on-going program.

Within about a month of the height of these activities, the House Un-American Activities Committee (HUAC) conducted a series of hearings in San Francisco's City Hall, at which many persons with experience in radical politics were questioned. On many campuses HUAC was unpopular because it was associated with "McCarthyist" efforts to force political conformity on universities across the country in the early nineteen fifties, and because many of its current members were known for their segregationist sympathies and had attempted to demonstrate a link between the Communist Party and civil rights agitation in the South. Hence the appearance of HUAC for a full-scale series of hearings might have produced picketing in almost any northern or western college area that spring, given the widespread student activity in support of southern students. Its appearance in San Francisco became particularly explosive because of two local developments.

First, the two-year-old coalition of political groups on the Berkeley campus, and the recent enlargement of this informal network by the infusion of students demonstrating in support of their southern fellows, meant that witnesses being called to testify were persons known to a growing number of students on the campus. One, in fact, was a sophomore at the university. These witnesses claimed they were being subjected to trial without benefit of judicial protections.[47] To a larger extent than would have been true at other places or in earlier times, those being "harassed" by the committee were linked to persons who could vouch for their integrity to large numbers of students.

Second (and more crucial for the large-scale mobilization of students), a Berkeley public school teacher's contract was not renewed after the school board learned she had been subpoenaed to appear before HUAC. In fact, despite widespread protest by several hundred people in Berkeley who went to the meeting of the school board, decision not to renew her contract was made *before* she even appeared as a witness for HUAC. The student newspaper, the *Daily Californian,* carried the story in detail and stressed the fact that no one was allowed to speak on behalf of the accused teacher before the decision was made. Thus, to large numbers of students the claims against HUAC as a star-chamber proceeding seemed verified by the action taken by the Berkeley school board.[48] (This was exactly the kind of thing the opponents of HUAC were predicting would happen.)

Finally, several prominent leaders of religious and civic groups in the Bay area denounced the coming of HUAC as a threat to democratic principles of fair play. A group affiliated with Slate helped to organize public meetings and marches, at which prominent civic leaders spoke, to protest the presence of HUAC in San Francisco.[49]

On the day that a University of California student was called to testify before HUAC, several hundred students arrived at the hearings. The student newspaper and signs in the Sather Gate area announced that rides to San Francisco would be available from Stiles Hall (the campus YMCA). Little coordination was needed: persons with cars drove past the designated corner and picked up anyone who wanted a ride.[50]

By now all the ingredients for conflict were in place: a core of 800 students (apartment dwellers in the humanities and the social sciences) structurally exposed to conditions that would maximize politicizing influences already present and able to furnish from their ranks a nucleus to draw in other students; a well-organized but ideologically vague coalition of political organizations; and two dramatic events that seemed to challenge American values of fair play in a context of crisis.

The City Hall demonstration in San Francisco in May, 1960, marked a major shift in crowd behavior at Berkeley. The number of persons who tried to attend the HUAC session at which a university student testified exceeded the capacity of the hearing chamber by several hundred. After a morning session in which students applauded HUAC's "defendants," the committee's chief investigator issued white passes to persons who would receive preferential seating. These went predominantly to older, well-dressed persons who showed sympathy to HUAC; rumors passed among the waiting students that these persons were members of the Daughters of the American Revolution and other conservative groups. One hundred fifty white passes, each of which was good for the admittance of six persons, were issued. Students who were not allowed in the hearing chamber because there was little room after the holders of white passes had filed past their waiting line decided that the hearings were being rigged against them. They began beating on the doors and shouting, "Let us in!" They then sang "The Battle Hymn of the Republic."

At this point a group of witnesses, led by Archie Brown, a longshoremen's union officer and long-time Communist political candidate, rushed to the stand. They shouted, "Open the doors! Let our families in!" [51] Pandemonium broke out in the hearing room. According to newspaper reports, police dragged the shouting witnesses away, while middle-aged members of the audience kicked and hit the men being dragged down the aisle by the police. After a period of general excitement and shouting, a group of students standing in the back of the hearing chamber began singing "The Star-Spangled Banner." Individual students scattered through the chamber stood up and sang also; the white-card spectators remained seated, and some muttered angrily that the national anthem was not being sung respectfully. The students in the room then recited the pledge of allegiance.

These events were reported with sympathy and in great detail in the student newspaper the next morning. Not surprisingly, several hundred students returned that afternoon and tried to attend the hearings. The white-card bearers again were admitted first, and only a handful of students got inside the chambers. A man shouted, "First come, first served!"

Police told the crowd to move back and be quiet. (During the morning a judge had complained that noise from the demonstrators had forced him to recess a trial being held two floors above.) A Stiles Hall staff member feared that the crowd might lose its self-control. He hurried away to obtain orders from the chief of police to admit students to the hearings.[52] Before he could return, an inspector from the police intelligence unit ordered fire hoses unrolled. He pointed the hose at the crowd. "You want this?" he demanded.

"Go ahead!" somebody cried.

While the hoses were being turned on, the crowd surged against the rope barricades and there were more cries for admission to the hearings. An officer standing behind the rope barricade was knocked down by the surge. Some persons began hitting police officers as the fire hoses were turned on, and many people were arrested. Students washed down the steps to a landing, braced themselves there and began singing again. After City Hall had been cleared of demonstrating students, many of the young people formed a picket line outside the building.[53]

The parallel here to treatment of southern Negro students when they attempted to protest racial injustice produced widespread sympathy for the demonstrators on the Berkeley campus itself. When conservative political groups produced a movie of the "San Francisco riots" purporting to show that "Operation Abolition" was Communist-inspired, supporters of the students answered with another film, "Operation Correction," showing that scenes in the original film were not in sequence and produced inaccurate impressions of what had occurred.[54] A year later all charges had been dropped against students, except for one student who had been acquitted in court.[55] But things were not the same, for two important changes came out of the HUAC affair.

First, out of the experience of being washed down the steps and/or arrested, developed a core of students who considered themselves to have "become committed" to direct action for civil rights. They saw themselves as unjustly harassed for acting as good citizens, as unfairly condemned by right-wing propagandists but vindicated by local courts. Around this traumatic experience they then organized their leisure activity. Civil rights picket lines and demonstrations, antiwar demonstrations—in short, "good causes" in the Bay area—drew an increasing number of demonstrators.

Second, and equally important, public response after the events led the students to consider their actions vindicated, whereas the San Francisco police became equated in their eyes with southern police, who treated in similar fashion the Negroes seeking equal rights. That is, these students regarded the police not as men controlling a potential riot, but as the agents of a prejudiced power group (HUAC) who would not allow the expression of dissent.[56] Since the students did not see themselves as about to riot (though clearly other observers had a different impression), they talked less about *why* the police decided to act than about the *effects* of the police action on the expression of dissent.

The students' equating of San Francisco police with "corrupt southern cops" meant that large numbers of liberal, idealistic young people watching these two groups of law enforcement agents came to question the impartiality and legitimate authority of the police. To be arrested "for civil rights" became a sign of virtue, calling forth pride perhaps similar to that with which Christian missionaries describe being jailed in foreign lands for their faith.[57] These students did not become anarchists in the sense of believing there is no legitimate power or social order; rather, large numbers of young people came to accept the claims of their more radical friends about the corruptibility of power and of agents of power and no longer saw the police as a symbol of *legitimate* authority. They believed people were arrested because they challenged vested interests, rather than because of the particular *means* they used.

Thus, out of an encounter between a "righteous crowd," which the police saw as essentially no different from a "football crowd" in its potential for violence, came experiences that led increasing numbers of students to define police as "agents of the power structure" rather than as "upholders of law and order." The significance of this shift in attitude for events that followed cannot be overemphasized.

In the next three years the civil rights, direct-action organizations grew slowly in numbers and activities. They did not attract massive support but could count on a solid core of persons who had taken part in the San Francisco demonstrations, as well as on a small percentage of growth in adherents from newcomers to the campus community. Equally important, the bonds created by these earlier experiences led a number of alumni of radical persuasion to remain in the Berkeley community among the apartment-dwelling, coffee-house set. As drop-outs from the current campus population joined them, a radicalized, "nonstudent" group with links to current students began to appear on the fringes of the campus and to visit on the Terrace of the Student Union, imparting an increasingly political tone to the small talk of informal social life.

It is hard to measure the growth in numbers of "nonstudents" (to a considerable extent consisting of recent alumni and of drop-outs from the university) who remained in Berkeley on the edge of campus and in touch with current students, but, by 1962 the *Daily Californian* was running feature stories on this phenomenon. These ex-members of the university continued to frequent their old haunts on and off campus. Many had time for voluntary work with the political action groups, which gained new vigor. Although this is hard to document, the growing group of such young persons who lived among the apartment-dwelling students seems to have furnished an important source of manpower and a conversational focus that generated interest in "direct-action" projects. Campus organizations promoting direct action often did not consider the current legal status of their "student" members. Memoranda in the office of the dean of students attest to the growing problem the university faced in ensuring that the officers of "student" organizations were all *currently* enrolled students.

During this period a number of special interest groups sprang up which gathered under the general Slate umbrella. Two that became centrally important at Berkeley abandoned any pretense at political ideology and focused on the civil rights of minorities as their central concern. As a graduate student, Mike Miller formed Friends of SNCC, an organization to educate about the southern civil rights movement, to raise funds for it, and eventually to recruit students to work in the South during the summer. Two years later CORE began a major student organization, devoted to direct action against discrimination in the Bay area. Both of these organizations followed the Slate format of welcoming students of all political persuasions in the service of concrete, specific, and common goals. In the fall of 1963 a sort of super-Slate for several campuses in the area was formed, the Ad Hoc Committee Against Discrimination.[58] It mounted a series of large-scale demonstrations during 1963–1964, and suddenly hundreds of students were in the streets again. But unlike the 1960 protest against HUAC, these demonstrations took place over many months and increased in size. Why?

The answer is fairly simple. At the same time that the reorganization of the campus and trends in off-campus political organization were rising to new heights, a series of local and national events made a great emotional impact. These events particularly drew the attention of students at Berkeley.

In April, 1963, the city of Berkeley narrowly defeated a fair-housing ordinance after an emotional campaign in which a university professor ran for mayor on a fair-housing platform.[59] In May, demonstrating Negroes in Birmingham, Alabama, were met with attacks by police dogs and hundreds of children (as well as adults) were arrested.[60] James Baldwin, the Negro writer, had an audience of 9000 students for his talk on campus shortly after the Birmingham demonstrations began.[61]

In June, Medgar Evers, NAACP leader in Mississippi, was murdered as he was entering his home.[62] All through the summer demonstrations swept the cities of the South, some remaining nonviolent and others becoming riotous. In August the various civil rights organizations jointly conducted a march on Washington, in which about two hundred and fifty thousand persons participated to urge the passage of a civil rights bill.[63] Then, just after students had returned to campus—and the day before classes were scheduled to begin—the nation was stunned by the bombing of a church in Birmingham, in which four children were killed.[64] The following day James Farmer, the national head of CORE, appeared on the Berkeley campus to give a scheduled series of addresses.[65]

A week later a minor local crisis again alerted the campus community to the prevalence of radical prejudice in its midst: the Berkeley Junior Chamber of Commerce abandoned its traditional Festival of Football Queens. This action was taken after the University of California student government protested a request from festival officials that a Negro student leader not escort a white football queen (from another campus) in the ceremony.[66]

A few weeks later Malcolm X, then chief spokesman for the Black Nationalists (militant Negro separatist movement) spoke to a crowd of about 8000 students on the Berkeley campus. His speech gave effective expression to his sense of rage and his judgment that whites were complacent about racial discrimination.[67]

The campus newspaper for the fall of 1963 gave major front-page space to race controversies on an average of three out of five days in the week that semester (as compared with nine times during the entire semester of the preceding year); student attention was focused sharply on racial issues, and there was a sense of impending crisis. When President Kennedy was assassinated in November, many students attended a candlelight ceremony on campus led by the unsuccessful mayoralty candidate, in which they dedicated themselves to fight for the things for which Kennedy stood.[68]

That same fall a number of students picketed a drive-in restaurant chain, whose owner was running for mayor of San Francisco, charging that the chain discriminated in the hiring and promotion of Negro employees. At Christmas students picketed Berkeley merchants who refused to sign a nondiscriminatory hiring agreement or to report the number of minority employees on their payroll each month.

In February, 1964, the Berkeley campus chapter of CORE joined a Bay-wide "shop-in" campaign proposed by San Francisco CORE. On March 2, 1964, the grocery chain involved signed an agreement with CORE. That evening a hundred persons ignored a restraining order against picketing San Francisco's Sheraton-Palace Hotel, which had refused to sign an agreement to employ a quota of minority personnel. With the arrest of comedian Dick Gregory, some NAACP officials in San Francisco, and a number of students, a major campaign began. In the next few weeks literally thousands of students took part. More than nine hundred persons were arrested in the various Sheraton-Palace demonstrations, including about two hundred students enrolled at the Berkeley campus. With this momentum—and the existence of hundreds of martyrs for a popular cause—the campaign swept on toward "Automobile Row" in San Francisco and toward the Bank of America. More arrests followed.[69]

Horrified citizens demanded a return to respect for law and order. The massive arrests from these two campaigns led to prolonged court cases costing the county thousands of dollars and resulting in judgments ranging from acquittal to prolonged jail sentences for the same offense. The severity of sentence depended on the judge or jury to which the defendant was assigned, as well as on the facts in the individual case.[70]

The net effect on the new band of "student radicals," as they increasingly called themselves, was to cement their sense of "rightness" in taking action. Criticisms of their use of force were shrugged aside. They could point to concrete gains in numbers of minority persons employed in the community. They could also cite the inconsistent application of penalties by the courts as evidence that the judicial system was not infallible and that statements of prejudice come from judges as well as from common citizens.[71]

A moral crisis was developing, in which the basis of legitimacy for police and other agents of common order in the community was called increasingly into question. Students recognized the "fact" of arrest and its consequences, but not the "legitimacy" of such action in their cases. They stated willingness to pay fines, and some were even ready to go to jail for the causes in which they believed.

CONFLICT OVER DIVERGENT GOALS: THE UNIVERSITY BECOMES "AN ENEMY"

During the series of moral crusades that students had launched in the preceding five years, the university administration had taken pains to avoid linkage to their actions and to prohibit the student government from acting officially on behalf of the student body as a whole. This attitude came under considerable student criticism, and a few cases caused particular controversy.

In 1959, for example, the dean of students had ruled that Slate could not hold a rally to support the Berkeley fair-housing election, because an on-campus organization could not take a stand on off-campus issues. [72] (When the state attorney-general gave an opposite opinion, [73] the administration reversed its ruling, but its motives were publicly questioned.) In 1960 the administration prevented the student government from sending a letter of censure to the University of Illinois for dismissing a professor who had made controversial remarks about sex in class. [74] In 1962, the university refused permission for Slate to conduct a vigil protesting continued atomic testing by America. Students were quick to note that the university itself took part in the production and testing of atomic weapons. [75]

In addition, several rulings had worked to the severe disadvantage of the politically active students in their competition with the fraternity/sorority-dominated group for control of the student government. The 1959 ruling that removed graduate students from the voting rolls and effectively cost Slate the possibility of winning elections for several years has already been mentioned. In 1960 the editor of the student newspaper was removed from his job for endorsing Slate candidates in the fall election; [76] in the heated controversy that followed, few students seemed to distinguish between the student government elite that had taken this action and the university administration, which had remained neutral on the sidelines. At any rate, the rules of procedure for the student newspaper were revised to prohibit partisan campaigning in the future. In the summer of 1961 Slate was stripped of its on-campus status for a violation of university regulations prohibiting a group that took an off-campus stand from identifying itself with the university. [77] Since this action coincided in timing with the state legislature's consideration of the university budget, and the legislative session had been marked by considerable criticism of the university for allowing Slate to bring a controversial speaker to campus, many students interpreted the action as an administrative "sell-out" to conservative pressure.[78] President Kerr's public praise of students' active concern for social justice, in a speech given at the time the suspension was announced,[79] did little to mitigate this judgment.

This loss of recognition marked the beginning of a serious decline for Slate that encouraged its former leaders to turn their attention to the larger community. As we have noted, new Slate-format organizations in the civil rights field began to spring up. Thus one side effect of this administratively aided decline as a political organization *on campus* was the growth of more extensive organization off campus; a second effect was a deepened distrust of the university administration.

The administrative policies that removed the growing "political" body of students from access to working relationships with the administration produced a serious strain in the operation of the university organization. In the absence of straightforward access to policy-makers at Berkeley, politically active student leaders interpreted administrative motives in terms of their *consequences* for their own student-led activities and assumed that these consequences were a major consideration in administrative action. Hence a growing hostility began to emerge between the student politicos and "the administration"—a term referring, in student speech, to a generalized group rather than a particular collection of personalities. Although the antipathy may have been mutual, the administrators, in striking contrast to the students, seldom stated their feelings publicly.[80]

And so the situation was ripe for conflict. With the increase in coercive student activity off campus in the name of a righteous cause, and the growing expression by politically active students of distrust for the legal authority being exercised by the university administration, the police, and the courts, a potentially explosive situation was at hand. It was an election year with an emotion-laden civil rights amendment to the state constitution on the ballot, and a campaign between Presidential candidates that cut to the core of value differences within the electorate. If past history was any indication, the external pressure upon the university could be expected to increase in such an election year.[81] But at the same time greater student activism also could be anticipated.

part ii

THE CONFLICT BEGINS: ROUND ONE

two

OPENING

MOVES

It started in the spring, when several persons complained to Alex C. Sherriffs, vice-chancellor for student affairs, that noise from the bongo drums in the Student Union Plaza was disruptive. Looking into the matter, Sherriffs found not only bongo players in the plaza but also bicycle riders in pedestrian areas and political hawkers at Bancroft and Telegraph. Increased political activity during the spring, he noted, was producing a littered plaza, since students dropped leaflets thrust upon them as they entered the campus. More seriously, persons with permits to set up tables on city of Berkeley property at the edge of the campus were moving back onto the more spacious "no man's land"—a 26-foot-wide strip of brick pavement that resembled the public sidewalk but actually belonged to the University of California. Since the university forbade all political proselyting, such activity at this location technically was illegal. [1]

Sherriffs concluded that the office of the dean of students was not taking its policing functions seriously enough, and that something should be done before increased enrollment and the election campaign in the fall brought still greater activity in the area. He scheduled for July 22 a meeting of administrative staff concerned with student affairs and included three items on the agenda: bicycle riding, bongo drums, and use of the area at Bancroft and Telegraph. The "Ad Hoc Committee" asked to deal with these matters included Elizabeth Neely (dean of women), Arleigh Williams (dean of men), Captain Frank E. Woodward and Lieutenant Merrill F. Chandler of the campus police department,

Alex Sherriffs himself, and Richard P. Hafner, the campus public affairs officer, who had made some suggestions about how bicycle traffic might be handled.

In July, before the meeting was held, the Republican Convention met in San Francisco to choose a Presidential candidate; it was an emotional convention with open displays of hostility between conservative advocates of Barry Goldwater and the more moderate Republicans who supported the candidacy of William Scranton. Berkeley students had formed two Republican clubs, reflecting the divisions felt more generally within the party, and a number of Berkeley students (along with students from other campuses in the Bay area) demonstrated at the convention—for Scranton, for Goldwater, or as part of a CORE picket line demanding a strong statement on civil rights.

The Oakland *Tribune* city desk got a phone tip that the W.E.B. Du-Bois Club on the Berkeley campus was recruiting demonstrators for Scranton. If the DuBois Club (which was accused of being a Communist front, nationally) should be found working for Scranton, city editor Roy Grimm sensed that a good story might result. (The phone tip may have come to the *Tribune* because the paper editorially was supporting the candidacy of Barry Goldwater.)

A *Tribune* reporter checked over the permits to set up tables on city property that had been filed at the Berkeley City Hall. Meanwhile Carl Irving, who covered the university as part of his regular beat, was asked by Grimm to check with the Berkeley campus public information office as to whether recruiting demonstrators for the GOP convention was permissible on university property. Such recruiting was taking place at the edge of the campus, at the intersection of Telegraph Avenue and Bancroft Way.

Irving called on Richard Hafner and asked whether the recruiting violated university rules. Hafner replied that he did not believe the recruiters were on university property but that he would inquire.[2]

When Hafner checked, he discovered to his surprise that the concrete wall that seemed to form an entrance gate to the campus actually was set back onto university property. Inserted into the brick pavement between the concrete wall and the street were small plaques, about twenty feet out from the wall, which read: "Property of the Regents, University of California. Permission to enter or pass over is revokable at any time." The tables from which students were distributing political literature, though appearing to be on public sidewalk, actually were located behind the plaques and thus were on University property.

Hafner then informed Alex Sherriffs of the phone call from the *Tribune* and of his own discovery that students were in technical violation of the university rule. The campus public information office subsequently informed Irving that the area in question *was* campus property. Shortly thereafter, Irving and other reporters were informed that the area was out of bounds to such recruiting activities.

Incidentally, the newspaper story about Scranton supporters never was printed. The lead proved false, for the W. E. B. DuBois Club did not have a table set up during the period in question.[3] Though the newspapers lost interest in the recruiting situation, the campus administrators involved did not.

A few days later the July 22 meeting to consider stricter regulation of bongo drums, bicycle traffic, and political activity at Bancroft and Telegraph was held in the office of the dean of students. Hafner repeated his account of the *Tribune* phone call and his discovery that the present location for student political activity was in technical violation of university regulations. After the meeting Vice-Chancellor Sherriffs dictated the following as part of the minutes:

Item 3: Area by Bancroft and Telegraph—We noted that the area outside the posts at Bancroft and Telegraph was being misused according to University policy and that we could not turn our heads. We will continue to discuss this item on our Wednesday, July 29, meeting.[4]

So far as Alex Sherriffs was concerned, the issue at stake was whether the office of the dean of students and the campus police department were going to accept what he saw as their disciplinary responsibilities. He said later,

Had there never been a Tribune, *the thing would have gone exactly as it did. . . . I was not upset by the* Tribune *report. The* Tribune *is no power. . . . Frankly I had been exasperated with this excessive permissiveness. . . .*

So far as I was concerned it was not a matter of clearing the area: the ninety permits that student organizations had gotten from the city of Berkeley were "peachey-keen." It was a matter of the dean of students office going down more often [to enforce the rules].[5]

For some of the other participants in the meeting, who did not share Alex Sherriffs' judgment of the way enforcement of rules had deteriorated, the information about the *Tribune* phone call changed the nature of the problem. It no longer was a question of differences in philosophy about dealing with students, as they saw it, but a question of the consistency of university policy.[6] On May 5, 1964, following public criticism of the university for not dismissing students arrested in the San Francisco civil rights demonstrations, University President Clark Kerr had said at Charter Day ceremonies on Davis campus:

I say again, as I have said before, that the activities of students acting as private citizens off-campus on non-University matters are outside the sphere of the University. (1) The student is an individual and his individuality should be respected by the University. The University should seek to govern him and discipline him only in areas of direct University concern. (2) The student is also an independent citizen. As student, the University assumes certain responsibilities for his conduct. As citizen, the state assumes certain responsibilities. (3) The punishment, for students and citizens, should fit the crime. One punishment, not two, should fit one crime. A citizen because he is a student should not be penalized more than his fellow citizen who is not a student. There should be equal treatment under the law.

There is another side to this coin. Just as the University cannot and should not follow the student into his family life or his church life or his activities as a citizen off the campus, so also the students, individually or collectively, should not and cannot take the name of the University with them as they move into religious or political or other non-University activities; nor should they or can they use University facilities in connection with such affairs. . . . The University will not allow students or others connected with it to use it to further their non-University political or social or religious causes, nor will it allow those outside the University to use it for non-University purposes. . . .

At a second meeting, scheduled a week later on July 29, the controversial item was deferred until Katherine Towle, dean of students, returned from her vacation. (Aware that an *ultimatum* about the use of the area was not consistent with Dean Towle's philosophy of the proper way to work with student groups, Arleigh Williams requested that she have a part in the decision.) When Dean Towle returned, both Williams and Sherriffs were on vacation, so the matter was not brought up again until they returned.

On September 4, 1964, following another meeting at which this problem was discussed, Alex Sherriffs dictated for the records a memorandum that included these items: [7]

Re: Bancroft and Telegraph Area

History. At the time Sather Gate became well within the campus by the closing of Telegraph Avenue and the substituting of the Mall, there was considerable concern about maintaining a free speech area. Temporarily, we allowed the "Ivy Patch" as a place for students to stand while off-campus speakers addressed them from Berkeley sidewalk.

Construction went on, and for a while we considered building a podium in concrete at the southeast corner of the Union. In several committees we discussed turning over the small area concerned as a gift to the City of Berkeley. This somewhat wild idea was discarded . . . because it was believed embarrassing to ask Berkeley to allow a function that we could not allow. . . . In the months and years that followed, individuals and groups have utilized this bricked space outside the posts at Bancroft for card tables, handing out materials, posters, as well as for speeches.

. . . What is done on the 10 feet between the curb and the bronze plaque is none of our business. . . .

Dean Towle, Dean Williams, Dean Neely, Mr. Tregea, Captain Woodward, Dick Hafner, and I met for a second time and discussed this at length. Our alternatives as we saw them were: (1) to ignore the misuse. We agreed that we would never be able to get through the semester; (2) *to negotiate with Berkeley about taking over the area as previously proposed. This we all rejected and in any event,* it could not be done in time; (3) *to make the area a poster area. We decided that Sather Gate serves the same purpose and is not a sore in the public's eye and, further, it would have to be a limited area because of the "traffic." The only other alternative was (4) to treat the area, as stated above, like any other area on campus, and enforce it.* (Emphasis added.)

Berkeley Chancellor Edward Strong penciled a comment to alternative 4, also dated September 4, 1964: "If this is to be done, the reason should be made clear in advance. Do the posts mark off a boundary not identical with the plaque? If so, this is really awkward. What can be done to clearly mark off the line of demarcation for purposes of campus control?"

Enforcement was placed in the hands of Katherine Towle, dean of students. She was not particularly happy with the decision that had been made, though she agreed with the judgment that something had to be done. In a conversation several months after the events, Dean Towle said: [8]

We never had any trouble with this area before, though I knew perfectly well that that was university property. Many people since then have claimed that they didn't know it, and I assume that they didn't, but I find it a little hard to understand that no one seemed to recognize the fact that that was university property except myself. . . . When I became dean of students in July of 1961, I inherited, more or less, the area out there, and the students did use it for their political action and social action activities, collecting funds and setting their tables up and handing out literature, and it didn't seem to pose any particular problem at that time. In fact, if I thought about it at all, which I think was not very often, I—it seemed to me as sort of a safety valve, and there was no harm in what they were doing. . . .

Katherine Towle herself had decided in the spring, however, that litter from dropped leaflets at the university entrance and traffic congestion from too many tables being set up at once might require some kind of corrective action.

When I came back in August . . . Dean Williams had left a memorandum saying that Vice-Chancellor Sherriffs would be calling a meeting probably to discuss further the use of the area out here at Bancroft-Telegraph, and that he had asked that I think about what we might do to control a little bit more. And that was that. . . . Dr. Sherriffs had gone on vacation, and so had Dean Williams . . . and, in fact, so had everybody else. Up to this time I never had done anything without consulting students who were going to get involved in the matter, and I knew that the students were away—most of them at least— who were primarily concerned with the use of the area out here—and so, I'll just have to confess, I just dragged my heels, I just left the memorandum over there, kind of in a pile of papers on my desk, put it aside.

I should say that in the interim . . . Mr. Hafner had an inquiry from a reporter on the Oakland Tribune *. . . I think this reporter asked Mr. Hafner if this was not university property, and how come the university didn't have the same rules applying out there as applied on the rest of the campus. Well, that was really the question, I suppose, that put everybody's mind on this. And this was also indicated to me in the memorandum I found on my desk. . . .*

. . . In September, after everyone was back from their vacation, we had another meeting to be sure that everything was planned about the bicycle riding on the campus . . . and there was this discussion again of what we'd do out here. And it was decided . . . that a letter should be gotten out to the students informing them that the regulations which pertained to the rest of the campus would now pertain to the Bancroft-Telegraph area. *From the start—and I can say this without any equivocation—I was not in favor of doing it this way. I had wanted to work with the student groups first, and talk to them about it. . . . I suggested it, but the feeling was that we shouldn't wait any longer, that this should be done now.*

. . . I wrote the memorandum according to my understanding of what was wanted by the chancellor's office, and it went out over my signature. One thing that I did insist upon, however, was that it not go into effect until classes began, and students were at least back on campus—I thought they ought to have a chance that week there to get used to the idea.

. . . I felt that by sending it out on the 14th—that was the week of registration—I'd have students coming to see me . . . because I knew this meant a great deal to some of the students. . . . I must confess I was not prepared for the high feeling that it engendered among the groups. . . .[8] (Emphasis added.)

What had happened?

1. A report—that political activists on the edge of the campus were violating university rules—became a common focus of attention for several campus administrators, meeting as a committee to consider student activity in the plaza area.

2. The vice-chancellor for student affairs, who had scheduled the meeting, claimed that leniency in enforcing campus rules created a critical situation that must be resolved before the students returned in the

fall. He claimed that a general principle was at work which would change conditions for accomplishing desired goals: university administrators were allowing students to ignore campus rules and thus throwing into question the integrity of the university's position.

3. The persons on this committee recognized that the university administration (of which they all were members) would be placed in an embarrassing position if such a state of affairs were true and became public knowledge.

4. The claims, which apparently had not been taken too seriously before that time, suddenly became plausible when they were reinforced by information of a recent event (the *Tribune* reporter's phone call) which seemed to provide independent confirmation that the general principle was indeed at work. Information about the phone call was provided by an independent witness of unquestioned reliability. The group's immediate experience (with massive student pressure campaigns in the spring, public attacks by state legislators, and problems during the summer with violations of the rules for off-campus organizations on the part of radical student groups) made claims of a challenge arising during the fall highly credible. The phone call directed the group's attention to the discrepancy between architectural and legal boundaries to the campus, which appeared serious because the discussion linked it with President Kerr's policy statement of late spring of the same year, thus showing inconsistency in the university's position. If the threatening situation were caused by the discrepancy between actual and apparent boundaries (which seemed likely to become public knowledge), some solution to this problem must be found.

5. Four proposals were made for meeting the situation. (*a*) It could be ignored. (But the group present "agreed we would never be able to get through the semester.") (*b*) The technical violation could be avoided by turning the area over to the city of Berkeley. (This would be embarrassing, and "it could not be done in time.") (*c*) It could be made a poster area, with no tables. (It would remain in the public eye, and numerous posters could impede traffic.) (*d*) The area could be treated "as any other area on campus," and the rule enforced. The fourth alternative was selected as that which most simply and reliably would maintain the pre-existing commitments of the acting group (i.e., "the administration of the university"). There were no immediately measurable costs for acting.

The move in response to the newly "critical" situation was timed to minimize so far as possible its appearing arbitrary. No letters were sent until students were expected to be back on campus.[9] When the letters went out, they announced that the policy would be enforced beginning the first week of classes—a week after their receipt by the students. Dean Towle intended, through this move, to give students time to react and to consult with her about the regulation.

In the meantime, by coincidence, two student statements were published that changed the context in which the new administrative statement would be viewed. The first did not have immediate impact on very many students, but it established boundaries within which some administrators viewed succeeding events. The second statement provided boundaries within which students viewed administrative pronouncements.

On September 10, 1964, Slate published a "Supplement to the General Catalogue." This was an effort to pressure the faculty to improve the quality of teaching, by publishing student evaluations of the performances of individual teachers, along with general advice on "how to get an education in spite of the system." This publication had first been issued the preceding fall. In order to avoid paying a sales tax, it was to be printed five times a year. Since course evaluations were of interest primarily at the beginning of a semester, the issues appearing at other times were open to anyone who had something he wanted to say about problems of education or educational reform. The "summer supplement," so called for tax purposes, was not printed until the fall course evaluations came out and was included with the latter booklet. This "summer" issue was a "letter to undergraduates," written by a former student and active Slate member named Brad Cleveland. It was a long (twelve printed pages), rather vituperative indictment of undergraduate education as "training for obedience" under the guise of "training for leadership." Its message can perhaps be revealed in these quotes:

This institution . . . does not deserve a response of loyalty and allegiance from you. There is only one proper response to Berkeley from undergraduates: that you organize and split this campus wide open!

FROM THIS POINT ON, DO NOT MISUNDERSTAND ME, MY INTENTION IS TO CONVINCE YOU THAT YOU DO NOTHING LESS THAN BEGIN AN OPEN, FIERCE, AND THOROUGHGOING REBELLION ON THIS CAMPUS. . . .

TRAINING IN THE CAPACITY FOR UNQUESTIONING OBEDIENCE TO A COMPLEX FLOOD OF TRIVIAL BUREAUCRATIC RULES. IN THE NAME OF HUMAN LEARNING YOU ACQUIRE THE CAPACITY TO BE DOCILE IN THE FACE OF RULES. WHILE YOU ARE TRAINING, THE RULES WHICH TELL YOU HOW TO GO ABOUT YOUR TRAINING ARE DISPLACING YOUR FREEDOM TO THINK. . . . SKILL AND OBEDIENCE ARE WHAT YOU ACQUIRE. . . .

THE MULTIVERSITY IS NOT AN EDUCATIONAL CENTER, BUT A HIGHLY EFFICIENT INDUSTRY: IT PRODUCES BOMBS, OTHER WAR MACHINES, A FEW TOKEN "PEACEFUL" MACHINES, AND ENORMOUS NUMBERS OF SAFE, HIGHLY SKILLED, AND RESPECTABLE AUTOMATONS TO MEET THE IMMEDIATE NEEDS OF BUSINESS AND GOVERNMENT. . . .

The letter then lists the members of the Board of Regents and their connections with major industries and banking and goes on to say:

In these men you find substantial ownership and control of the vital raw materials and service industries in the West . . . virtually enough power to make or break five governors and ten university presidents. . . . I would like you to think for a moment about the "public" character of these men. In the first place, who even knows them? . . . except a few of us who are aware that they are "famous" or "very wealthy men." What do they do? AND WHY? FOR WHOSE INTEREST? . . .

FROM TIME IMMEMORIAL, MEN OF POWER HAVE CONSIDERED IT WISE TO KEEP THEIR CONSTITUENTS AT A LEVEL OF IGNORANCE WHEREBY THE PROCESS OF RULING THEM IS MORE EASILY ACCOMPLISHED.

The Brad Cleveland letter closed by suggesting eight demands the students should make. These included the elimination of the course-grade-unit system for undergraduates in the humanities and the social sciences, the disbanding of all university dormitory and living-group rules, the establishment of a permanent student voice in university decision-making, the recruitment of an undergraduate *teaching faculty* in the humanities and the social sciences, greater flexibility in designing undergraduate study programs, and the immediate establishment of a university committee to deal with these demands on the Berkeley campus.

Go to the top. Make your demands to the Regents. If they refuse to give you an audience: start a program of agitation, petitioning, rallies, etc., in which the final resort will be CIVIL DISOBEDIENCE. *In the long run there is the possibility that you will find it necessary to perform civil disobedience at a couple of major University public ceremonies.*

Depending on the resistance, you might consider adding the following two demands:

RESIGNATION OF CLARK KERR. RESIGNATION OF TOP ADMINISTRATORS WHO MIGHT EMPLOY SLICK DIVERTING TACTICS.

RECONSTITUTION OF THE BOARD OF REGENTS, EITHER THROUGH FIRING OR EXPANSION, PERHAPS BOTH.[10]

The letter did not create much stir in student circles, perhaps because its length and style of presentation discouraged many students from reading it in its entirety.[11] It created sufficient uneasiness among some administrators, however, that a copy of the letter was sent to President Kerr.[12] Its importance for later events was twofold.

First, when student rebellion developed within a few weeks, some administrators remembered the letter and wondered whether events had been planned in advance by an organized group of agitators. Second, some of its accusations against the university and its governing board eventually became incorporated in the public rhetoric of the Free Speech Movement. Thus it became a "resource document" for later public debate. In short, although the immediate impact of the letter seems to have been slight, its appearance shortly before the beginning of exchanges between students and administrators provided material for each side to use later to its own advantage.

Of more immediate significance in the creation of "meaning" for ambiguous events was the public announcement, on September 15, 1964, that the Ad Hoc Committee to End Discrimination planned to picket the Oakland *Tribune.* The Ad Hoc Committee, which had conducted the San Francisco demonstrations in the spring, accused the paper of discriminatory employment policies. This pressure campaign actually had been under way for a period of three weeks, through word-of-mouth recruitment among previous activists. It was absorbing the energy of a number of student "radical" leaders, who were affiliated with the Ad Hoc Committee and were expecting repercussions for their activities. Jacqueline Goldberg, head of the campus Women for Peace organization and therefore a member of the Ad Hoc Committee, had this to say about the *Tribune* campaign:

I didn't figure we'd win on the Oakland Tribune. . . . *I knew that no one would ever sign the agreement, ever.* . . . [*William Knowland, who owns the paper*] *was too strong, too powerful. He can't be frightened,*

*and he can't be hurt. He could simply quit; he's so wealthy and power-
ful. He owns too much of the city, controls too much of the city. . . .*

*I think pretty much everybody agreed. See, there are certain ways
you decide on what project to hit. In certain areas you do it to get an
agreement and win. In certain areas you do it for the . . . side effects.
The side effects were things like Negro awareness of what kind of
paper the* Tribune *was, Negro community awareness of the . . . loosely
organized but very detrimental boycott of downtown Oakland stores
which advertised in the* Tribune. . . .

*We had never at any time considered a mass sit-in because we know
what Oakland is. You'd go to jail for a long time if you sat-in on the*
Tribune—*a long time, and there isn't going to be any hung juries there,
boy! You're going to get one conviction after another as fast as they can
convict you, because that's the way the white population is down there,
scared.*

*. . . So you see we grew up a little from the Sheraton-Palace, and we
knew what was facing us.*[13]

On the day after the Ad Hoc Committee to End Discrimination made
public its project against the Oakland *Tribune,* Dean Towle's letters arrived for the president of each off-campus political organization at the
university. The following is a copy of this communication: [14]

Office of the Dean of Students   Berkeley, California
                                                          September 14, 1964

TO: Presidents or Chairmen and Advisers of All Student Organizations

Beginning September 21, 1964, provisions of the policy of The Regents
concerning "Use of University Facilities" will be strictly enforced in all
areas designated as property of The Regents of the University of California,
including the 26-foot strip of brick walkway at the campus entrance on Bancroft Way and Telegraph Avenue between the concrete posts and the in-
dented copper plaques on Bancroft Way which read "Property of The Regents, University of California. Permission to enter or pass over is revocable
at any time."

Specifically, Section III of the policy referred to above prohibits the use
of University facilities "for the purpose of soliciting party membership or
supporting or opposing particular candidates or propositions in local, state
or national elections," except that Chief Campus Officers "shall establish
rules under which candidates for public office (or their designated represen-

tatives) may be afforded like opportunity to speak upon the campuses at meetings where the audience is limited to the campus community." Similarly, Chief Campus Officers "shall establish rules under which persons supporting or opposing propositions in state or local elections may be afforded like opportunity to speak upon the campuses at meetings where the audience is limited to the campus community."

Section III also prohibits the use of University facilities "for the purpose of religious worship, exercise or conversion." Section IV of the policy states further that University facilities "may not be used for the purpose of raising money to aid projects not directly connected with some activity of the University . . . ."

Now that the so-called "speaker ban" is gone and the open forum is a reality, student organizations have ample opportunity to present to campus audiences on a "special event" basis an unlimited number of speakers on a variety of subjects, provided the few basic rules concerning notification and sponsorship are observed. These are outlined in detail in the booklet, "Information for Student Organizations," distributed to all organizations and their advisers. The "Hyde Park" area in the Student Union Plaza is also available for impromptu, unscheduled speeches by students and staff.

It should be noted also that this area on Bancroft Way described above has now been added to the list of designated areas for the distribution of handbills, circulars or pamphlets by University students and staff in accordance with Berkeley Campus policy. Posters, easels and card tables will not be permitted in this area because of interference with the flow of traffic. University facilities may not, of course, be used to support or advocate off-campus political or social action.

We ask for the cooperation of every student and student organization in observing the full implementation of these policies. If you have any questions, please do not hesitate to come to the Office of the Dean of Students, 201 Sproul Hall.

KATHERINE A. TOWLE

KAT:mh   Dean of Students

Jackie Goldberg said later, "I knew [Dean Towle] from before, and I knew darn well that there was something up, here, because she wouldn't have formulated that rule. That wasn't her rule. That's just not her operating procedure. . . ." [15]

Arthur Goldberg, Jackie's brother, also received one of the letters as the out-going chairman of Slate. Art and Jackie Goldberg compared notes and then called a meeting of representatives from all the organizations that would be affected by the new ruling. The "United Front," as it was soon called, met at Art Goldberg's apartment. The reactions of many of the people who came are summed up by Brian Turner, who accompanied his roommate, Mario Savio. (Both were representing University Friends of SNCC, which raised funds for the southern civil rights movement through tables placed on the Bancroft-Telegraph strip.) Said Brian Turner:

Obviously, this ruling was directed against the civil rights movement, no matter what kind of language it was clothed in. . . . The only groups that were doing any kind of effective proselytizing or fund raising were the civil rights groups and the socialist groups; the civil rights groups have impact. . . .[16]

There was no "proof" that this was the motive for the ruling, though a number of people at the meeting made this claim. Whatever its cause, however, Dean Towle's letter marked a change of conditions for the conservative political organizations as well. Said Jackie Goldberg, "From the beginning we all knew that the only way we would have any chance at all would be if we were all in it together. . . ."

The Goldbergs seemed to have set the tone for the early meetings of the United Front. They hoped to force the administration to reconsider the ruling because of the effect it would have on *all* political activity, including that of conservative groups.[17] Thus a coalition of radicals and conservatives was imperative. Art Goldberg recalls:

Our first meetings were these huge meetings with almost always consensus. I would work, when I chaired the meeting, to get agreement from the right and agreement from a substantial segment of the left, and didn't give a shit about what the rest of the left thought, as long as I had enough to swing it, so we could keep both parties together. . . .[18]

In short, the traditional Slate format—of an issue-oriented coalition of ideologically divergent groups—now was being extended to include groups with conservative ideologies as well. Jo Freeman, who attended the meetings as a representative of two different student organizations, recalls:

. . . Most of the radical groups were there in force—and very little of the nonradical groups. . . . The poor Republicans—they tried to respect them, and they did a pretty good job. They tried to settle things by consensus and tried to come up with programs in which, if the Re-

publicans couldn't participate, they could at least abstain. We were trying to keep them with us. . . .[19]

Although the *reasons* for the letter from Dean Towle's office were not established, it created a critical situation for the entire assembled group, for all of the persons who came to the Goldberg meetings were using the forbidden strip for their major organizational activity. Moreover, there was a limited time period in which to protect their traditional "rights" to this territory: the prohibition would go into effect on September 21.

Jackie Goldberg had made an appointment to see Dean Towle on September 17:

I was selected as spokesman, unofficially by that group, largely because I was the most palatable to the right wing. . . . I don't lose my temper often, and I also speak in pear-shaped tones and give a very dignified impression while holding a hard line. They liked that style better than some of the lefties. . . . That's mostly the reason. Besides some of them knew me a little bit as being fairly even-tempered.

So we went to see Dean Towle on the 17th. . . . All she said was that it was traffic, and we said we would submit to a traffic study. And she said, "No, that's the way it's going to be," blah, blah, blah. And I said, "Look, can we give you proposals?" She said, "Yes," which is what I expected her to say. Sandor Fuchs (the in-coming chairman of Slate) and I drew them up and brought them back to her that afternoon.[20]

The *Daily Californian*, student newspaper on the Berkeley campus, reported that Dean Towle informed the group that further use of the Bancroft area was "almost out of the question." She suggested that they use the "Hyde Park" area for their activity instead. (This is an area in the Student Union Plaza, one floor below the Sproul Hall Plaza level and farther west; student groups had objected to the location in the past because it is not in the regular pathway of students.) [21]

So far as the student spokesman, Jackie Goldberg, was concerned, the important outcome from the conference was Dean Towle's willingness to receive counterproposals from them. The eighteen student organizations involved in the controversy [22] then formally petitioned for the use of the Bancroft-Telegraph area under the following conditions:

1. *Tables for student organizations at Bancroft and Telegraph will be manned at all times.*
2. *The organizations shall provide their own tables and chairs; no university property shall be borrowed.*
3. *There shall be no more than one table in front of each pillar and one at each side of the entrance way. No tables shall be placed in front of the entrance posts.*
4. *No posters shall be attached to posts or pillars. Posters shall be attached to tables only.*
5. *We [students] shall make every effort to see that provisions 1–4 are carried out and shall publish such rules and distribute them to the various student organizations.*
6. *The tables at Bancroft and Telegraph may be used to distribute literature advocating action on current issues with the understanding that the student organizations do not represent the University of California—thus these organizations will not use the name of the university and will dissociate themselves from the university as an institution.*
7. *Donations may be accepted at the tables.*[23]

The first five conditions were drawn up to answer objections raised in the conference with Dean Towle on the morning of September 17. Conditions 6 and 7 contained the heart of the matter, so far as student interests were concerned.

When Jackie Goldberg took the petition back to Dean Towle, she thought she obtained final confirmation of her suspicion about the source of the new ruling. In Jackie Goldberg's own words:

The only way [William Knowland] was suspected was because of . . . an intimation that Dean Towle made to me. . . . Also the timing, but especially the initmation directly. It tied them up. . . . After everybody left I was standing talking to her for a second. She said something to the effect of somehow or another tying Knowland—I don't know what it was, but it was very clear who she meant—to the whole picture.[24]

(This conversation with the dean of students cannot be reconstructed accurately. Jackie Goldberg may have asked whether the ruling had anything to do with the Oakland *Tribune,* or Dean Towle may have alluded to general pressures or even to a *Tribune* call. The important fact is this: an ambiguous statement was interpreted in the context of an unstated claim, which already had been made privately by these students. Within this context it seemed to provide independent and authoritative confirmation of their theory.)

At any rate, Jackie Goldberg reported back to the United Front that Dean Towle had admitted the university was acting because of pressure from Knowland.[25] If the university were under pressure from a person who seemed so powerful, these students had little reason to expect their petition to be received favorably. They would meet with Dean Towle at 10:30 A.M. on Monday, September 21, the morning that the regulations were to go into effect, but they would be prepared for a denial of their request.

three

CONFRONTATIONS

In a meeting held on Sunday night, September 20, the United Front voted to picket and to conduct vigils and rallies, and most groups agreed also to act in civil disobedience if the university stood firm on the Bancroft-Telegraph ban.[1] The Republican groups did not agree to participate in civil disobedience but pledge themselves not to undercut other groups that did.[2] The main tactic, however, was to mobilize counterpressure, in the form of public sentiment, to balance the forces students believed were being exerted by powerful, conservative politicians.

Already the United Front had been in close touch with the *Daily Californian.* Monday morning's paper, which came out before the administration announced its reaction to the petition, carried two front-page stories on the matter, plus an editorial and a letter headlined, "The Fight for Free Speech Begins." One article, entitled "Bancroft Controversy Grows," reported disagreement within the student government over the appropriateness of the activity ban, some student representatives supporting the administrative announcement and others disagreeing with it. A second article, headed "Off-Campus Political Groups Prepare for Dean's Response," announced a series of tactics to be taken if the dean's office did not approve the petition:

1. A press conference was scheduled for 11:30 A.M. on September 21 if the 10:30 meeting with Dean Towle brought a rejection of the United Front petition. (The conference included television cameramen as well as newspaper reporters.)

2. If the university made no retraction of its ruling, tables would be set up as usual at noon and pickets would march in front of Sproul Hall. (In a word, the students would make public their refusal to ratify the ruling or to conform to it.)

3. A rally would be held on the Sproul Hall steps at 7:00 P.M. of that same day, so that protesting groups could explain to students what was happening.

4. The United Front would begin an all-night vigil on the Sproul Hall steps at 10:00 P.M.

In the meantime, Katherine Towle had been busy reaching various members of the Berkeley campus administration and the university statewide administration to see what kind of response could be given to the students.

On September 18, Vice-Chancellor Sherriffs sent a copy of the student petition to Vice-President and General Counsel Thomas Cunningham (the Board of Regents' lawyer) with a covering letter and carbon copy to President Kerr. The letter noted that the petition had been received that morning and represented "demands by the political and social action groups on the campus." It continued:

The area at Bancroft and Telegraph has developed into an area of wholesale misuse of University facilities in the opinion of the Chancellor, myself, and the Dean of Students. In any event, to clean up this area, especially for this emotional period before the November elections, the Chancellor has designated the 26 feet of University property, between the Berkeley sidewalk and the cement posts, as an area for the distribution of legitimate literature, but he insists that the University rules be strictly enforced on posters, fund-collecting for off-campus purposes, and speakers. This, you will realize, is not an area which has been previously designated as one of those available for any of the above. We are clearly in for some demonstrations, but so far, the press and the student body seem to be with us. I am informing you of the particular demands attached just in case we should be cautioned on any matter of law, or any misinterpretation of University policy.

We have just received these demands and demonstrations are apparently scheduled for Monday. I apologize for sending you a rush item.[3]

Later that day, at President Kerr's request, Kerr, Chancellor Strong, Vice-Chancellor Sherriffs, Dean Towle, and Dick Hafner discussed the student petition. Afterward, Mrs. Kitty Malloy, Chancellor Strong's administrative assistant, wrote the following memorandum summarizing her understanding of what Strong reported had taken place:

The President said there is to be no distribution of action literature on the campus anywhere. This means no supporting one candidate or another, one issue or another, no literature on such things as a call for a meeting to organize a picket or stage a demonstration. Speakers can advocate causes and take stands on issues but cannot distribute literature such as bumper strips.

There is to be no fund raising or receiving of donations for causes (except, of course, for those approved by the Chancellor).

The area on Bancroft and Telegraph between the posts and the plaques is University property and there are to be no speakers there— no literature distributed which can be claimed to be propaganda—no tables except that the Dean of Students will permit a number of tables which are to be manned at all times. A poster may be affixed to the table. Otherwise no posters.

On an experimental basis we will extend Hyde Park area on the steps of Sproul Hall as long as the crowd does not interfere with the flow of traffic. Speakers must be students or members of the faculty—not the public.

Kerr wants Cunningham [the Regents' counsel] to see the paper which Towle will hand to the students at her meeting with the group on Monday morning—to check for freedom of speech and assembly points.

Cunningham and CK do not agree on the place of the University. Cunningham sees it as public property and Kerr does not.

Kerr understands that we are in an awkward position since we didn't crack down on the area before, when we knew that it was University property. Therefore it is essential that the explanation be given very carefully to the students and to the faculty. Namely, that no rule has been modified—that the boundary between city and university property was thought to be the posts and this is not the case, it is the plaques. Students got their permits from the City believing it was City property

—now it is clear that it is not City property, we must follow University regulations. Sherriffs—E.S. wants the statement made just like the above.

KCM [4]

Clark Kerr's memory of the meeting is different. Although he kept no detailed memoranda on day-to-day conversations, as did the Berkeley chancellor's office, he reports that he called the Berkeley administrators together and told them that he thought they were making a great mistake, that a substitute for Sather Gate was needed, and that they ought not to take back the area. He reports that the reasons they gave him for taking the action originally were not convincing to him, but that finally Strong said if they reversed the ruling he would lose face. How was it possible to pull back? Kerr reports he then suggested that they pull back gradually.[4]

Katherine Towle remembers that she was not in favor of the decision to keep students off the Bancroft-Telegraph area strip, but that she did not say anything at this meeting. She does not recall that Kerr objected to the ruling, though she had the impression that he thought the action had been precipitous in that it was taken without consulting with students first. (This, of course, was her own reaction at the time to the decision.) She remembers that Kerr wanted to lessen the strains caused by the ruling, if at all possible. The decision to allow the use of Sproul Hall steps was taken with this desire in mind. Katherine Towle thinks she may have left before Kerr and Strong finished talking together.[4]

There is no way now to establish which version of the conversation is correct, nor is there any real need to do so. Although memoranda and memories each can reflect the personal interests of those who create them (and can be accordingly distorted or selective), the *fact* of what was said is less important than what was *remembered* by each party to the conversation. The particular differences of recall noted here led to much mistrust and recrimination in the months that followed. What is crucial for understanding what happened next is that Chancellor Strong's version of the conversation, as written down later by Mrs. Malloy, became the permanent record and guided the actions of the Berkeley campus administration.

Two days later, on Sunday, September 20, Sherriffs called President Kerr to discuss the matter further. After the call Sherriffs wrote this memorandum:

Towle and Sherriffs et al. had worked on a draft of statement to be made to the students in Dean Towle's office at 10:30 Monday morning. Dean Towle then took it to Cunningham who said he would have to have more time to decide on the issue. I called Clark Kerr. He said Cunningham would like to have time to consider the stand. I said we couldn't put it off. He said Cunningham would like to have time to consider the stand. I said we couldn't put it off. He said he would call Tom Cunningham after I told him I did not want to desert a position because we might lose in the courts. Cunningham agreed then to stand by our rules—a couple of changes were needed however—(1) making clear by the Dean that having been promised cooperation by the users—the situation is to be kept under control and that the rules were under this condition; (2) making clear that it is a condition to use of Sproul as Hyde Park—a trial basis.

The President wants to see the wording of the final statement to be made by Miss Towle.[5]

On Monday morning Sherriffs again called President Kerr to ask whether bumper strips and buttons could be given away at tables. A memorandum in the chancellor's office reports that Kerr said no— distributing bumper strips and buttons is regarded as political action and therefore must be carried out on land owned by the city of Berkeley.[6]

Consequently, when Dean Towle met with the students that morning, she accepted the first five points of their petition (which had been their concession to her in the first place) and informed them that she could not accept points 5 and 6. She would, however, allow them to distribute "informative—as opposed to advocative" literature from a regulated number of tables, which could have posters attached to them and could be set up in the disputed area. She further offered, "on an experimental basis," a second Hyde Park free-speech area at the entrance to Sproul Hall, provided there was no voice amplification or interference with traffic or the conduct of university business. Bumper strips and buttons could not be distributed from the informational tables.[7]

The next morning's *Daily Californian* reported that Dean Towle admitted the question arose in the first place because of the frequent announcement of and recruitment for picket lines and demonstrations going on in the area in the past. The story implied that the dean made this admission during the Monday conference, though it did not say so explicitly.[8] Anyone reading the *Daily Californian* story would assume that the administration's motive for announcing the ban was a concern about civil rights demonstrations rather than about political activity per se.

The press conference, rally, picketing, and vigil went on as scheduled. Few trustworthy data about the persons who took part in these public pressure activities during the first week of classes are available. The *Daily Californian* estimated that about 200 students joined the picket line on Monday, including "a surprising number of nonactivists."[9] It reported that approximately 100 people watched the picketers. A graduate student in sociology, who was actively campaigning against an attempted repeal of fair-housing laws and who was picketing the *Tribune,* explained his reason for joining the picket line in these words:

Friends . . . told me there would be picketing. As a civil libertarian I wanted to participate. The administration was shutting down on rights of advocacy. . . . A non-elite which allows an elite to take away rights without opposition will continue to lose rights. Friends who had been around Cal before, generally felt the same as I did and were out there from the start. . . . I felt the situation demanded immediate protest, and a picket had been organized. . . .

Peaceful protest seemed quite reasonable. I don't know what is meant by "normal procedures" where this university is concerned. I do know that if no stink is made, nothing will be done, and that counterpressure to that of rightists has to be applied. . . . I knew there were leftists involved with different reasons than my own, but that is always the case and is no excuse for getting out. Some of these leftists are close friends of mine—nice people, as much as we disagree.[10]

A freshman girl who left her dormitory to take part in the all-night vigil described her motivation in this way:

This is my first year at Cal; I was highly impressed by the concern, activity, and cross section of opinions displayed at the Bancroft-Telegraph area—and was highly shocked and infuriated when for, it seemed, absolutely no reason at all the school administration decided to eliminate this. [It was] a wonderful area for bantering ideas around, in-

*forming people, and keeping them aware of the world around them.
. . . If the administration's rules were followed it would seriously sti-
fle the means of communication in this area, perhaps resulting in Cal
becoming more apathetic like other colleges. . . . [The restriction of
activity there would leave me confused] as to how I should believe and
thus act.*

*At the first vigil [there] were about 100 [people]. . . . Perhaps if
no one else had responded I would have grumbled, been sorry for the
end of the Bancroft-Telly type area at Cal and done nothing except perhaps argue with friends on the matter; I am not a leader.*[10]

Meanwhile, opposition to the announced policy began to grow. The
Daily Californian, which previously had defended the administration's
stand, editorialized on Tuesday, September 22, that the university had
"made a basic mistake." It defended the *right* of students to picket and
vigil, while questioning the wisdom of applying pressure tactics in a
controversy.[11] Also, the Student Senate, meeting on Tuesday night,
asked for an end to the ban and began circulating a student petition to
this effect.[12]

Meanwhile, the United Front was acting as though Dean Towle's letter had never been sent. Tables continued to be set up in the forbidden
zone, and activity went on much as usual. Although the campus administration took no restrictive action, by Tuesday night the members of
the United Front were becoming uneasy. "We seemed to have won,"
Jackie Goldberg said. "Then we came to the decision that what they
could do was let us have our tables all semester and then start action
against us before finals. That would really be nasty." [13] (Some of these
students had been arrested in the Sheraton-Palace demonstrations in San
Francisco during the spring and had experienced great difficulty in com-
pleting their semester's work because the trials had been scheduled for a
period when term papers were due and final examinations given. They
assumed the timing of the trials was deliberate, an effort by the "power
structure" to make their opposition as inconvenient as possible.) [13]
Jackie Goldberg continued as follows:

*We decided we'd have to make them agree to change the rules back.
And that's when we decided to have the vigil on Wednesday, the 23, on
the steps. Because we were afraid they were going to let us get away*

with it until it was more convenient for them and less convenient for us to fight. . . . We publicized this greatly, and we had pretty good response.[13]

A hand-out announcing the vigil urged,

Act before the administration succeeds in its efforts to silence you. At this moment Cal students are being denied their inalienable rights to persuade and to call for action corresponding to their social mood and political principles. . . . Come to the Vigil and support Freedom of Speech NOW!

Wednesday morning's *Daily Californian* carried three items concerning the controversy: news of the ASUC Senate action supporting the position of the United Front, an announcement of the vigil, and a statement by Chancellor Strong defending the university decision announced the day before:

The open forum policy of the University is being fully maintained. Any student or staff member is free to address a campus audience in the "Hyde Park" areas in the heart of the campus. Printed materials on issues and candidates can be distributed by bona fide student groups in nine places on campus, including the Telegraph-Bancroft location. A full spectrum of political and social views can be heard on campus, and candidates themselves can be invited to speak on campus.

The University rightly, as an educational institution, maintains an open forum for the free discussion of ideas and issues. Its facilities are not to be used for the mounting of social and political action directed to the surrounding community. The University has held firmly to the principle set forth by President Kerr in his Charter Day Address on the Davis Campus, May 5, 1964. . . .[14]

According to an account in the *Daily Californian*, the vigil began about 9:00 P.M., with nearly 300 members of various organizations taking part. Participants read, talked, or sang. The theme song of SNCC, "We Shall Overcome," was a popular choice,[15] and new verses were added: "We Shall All Speak Out" and "We Shall Advocate." (By symbolic linking, the controversy was being treated as part of the civil rights movement.)

When Art Goldberg arrived, he told demonstrators that the Board of Regents was meeting at University House. After a fifteen-minute discussion the group marched in single file over to the site, singing "Left and Right Together, We Shall Not Be Moved," only to find that the Regents had left for the night.[16] Thereupon Art Goldberg and Paul Cahill of the Young Republicans wrote a letter that Marjorie Woolman, secretary of the Regents, agreed to convey to the members the next day. Then the group returned to the Sproul Hall steps for the night. By 6:30 A.M., 75–100 persons were left. The vigil ended at 9:00 A.M.[17]

If the *Daily Californian's* estimates of crowd size were consistent from event to event, the Wednesday night vigil evidently brought new people into the controversy. One student who became active at this point reported he joined a friend taking part in the vigil: "I joined him because of both the events on campus prior to that and a vague hope to establish freedom on campus. All I expected to do was to show the administration that there was objection to their policies. Five hundred people are hard to completely ignore." [18]

A student who never had been active in political demonstrations before joined the vigil because he was shocked to hear, on returning from a year in Europe, that the Bancroft-Telegraph area was out of bounds to political activity. Another youth, an unaffiliated, "radical" graduate student who had taken part in occasional demonstrations over the past seven years, joined this vigil also. Both reported that they were offended by the vigil, however, and left. They described it as dominated by "the Pepe's Pizza crowd"—a term referring to a clique of ostentatiously nonconforming young radicals who used as their social base a pizza shop on Telegraph Avenue. (Both of the young men who left the vigil later became leaders in the Free Speech Movement.) [19]

Such labeling of the core of vigilers may have been quite inaccurate. Of more interest is the fact that the situation had become sufficiently defined by this time to begin attracting people outside the social networks that furnished its original participants.

The United Front received no personal reply to its letter from the Board of Regents. In fact, the only administrative responses that week were ones challenging the group's definition of the situation. In addition to Strong's statement, President Kerr said on Friday, at a press conference following the Regents meeting:

The Dean of Students has met many requests of the students. The line the University draws will be an acceptable one. . . . I don't think you have to have action to have intellectual opportunity. Their actions —collecting money and picketing—are not high intellectual activity. . . . These actions are not necessary for the intellectual development of the students. If that were so, why teach history? We can't live in ancient Greece.

The University is an educational institution that has been given to the Regents as a trust to administer for educational reasons, and not to be used for direct political action. It wouldn't be proper. . . . It is not right to use the University as a basis from which people organize and undertake direct action in the surrounding community.[20]

At this point the United Front decided it was time to increase the pressure and to force a clarification of the situation.[21] At a meeting held on Friday night, the group voted to picket the university convocation, scheduled for September 28, in the Student Union Plaza, with Chancellor Strong as the principal speaker. On Monday morning the *Daily Californian* announced both the convocation and the planned picketing to protest the university's position on the Bancroft-Telegraph controversy. It also carried, under the headline "Kerr Condemns Politicking," the statements by President Kerr just quoted.

On the morning of September 28, before the convocation started, the United Front conducted an unauthorized rally from "the Rally Tree," which had been the traditional "Hyde Park area" until 1961, when it was declared off limits because the noise from speeches interfered with classes in adjacent buildings. The Rally Tree was directly on the path of students leaving their social science and humanities classes either to attend the convocation, to go to the Student Union, or to leave the campus. The most eloquent speaker at the rally turned out to be a junior in philosophy, a hitherto unknown student named Mario Savio.[22] Afterward a sizable picket line formed. Estimates have put the number of demonstrating students as high as a thousand, though this may be an exaggeration. The picketers moved down the stairs from the Sproul Hall Plaza into the Student Union Plaza, where the convocation was being held, and circled in a serpentine pattern through the aisles that had been set up.

One of the students who first became active in the controversy by joining this picket line was a freshman, who lived in a rented room at the time, the son of a biochemist at a university in another part of the country. The student reports that he was approached by the chairman of the Young People's Socialist League and invited to join the picket line. "I found the table ban an inconvenience, because I had not found the right political group to join yet. I considered the picketing exciting, and thought perhaps 200 people might join in. I believed normal procedures would be futile." [23]

A fifth-year student in architecture, married and living in an apartment off campus, expressed his feelings as follows:

The world is so fucked up that we must be directly concerned with changing it. There was gross injustice here. Rights had been taken away. I first noticed the situation by reading the newspaper and seeing posters; then I saw people picketing and read their leaflets. This was a threatening, despicable, frightening situation. Radical groups would not have tables on campus; I would not be able to find out about these groups. I had to act at that time. It appeared that "normal" procedures wouldn't produce a "just" result. I didn't know who the leaders were, but I respected the picketers. I expected many others to join in.[23]

The administration's stand, when judged by its public statements during the preceding week, had appeared intransigent. Behind the scenes, however, there had been considerable re-examination of the university's position.

On September 21, 1964, in a letter that never became public, Berkeley's legal counsel, Thomas Cunningham, pointed out to Alex Sherriffs that "neither University-wide rules nor the Berkeley campus Regulation in point make any distinction as to the forms of non-commercial literature which may be . . . distributed." [24] Because of this difference of judgment between Cunningham and Kerr regarding appropriate limits on student expression, the matter had been taken to the Regents Committee on Educational Policy.[25] The members took no official action at this point, but a confidential memorandum was circulated to all chancellors reporting the position that the Regents informally endorsed. This essentially reiterated the Kerr position banning social or political action on university property but incorporated the Cunningham reservations: thus "yes" or "no" advocacy on specific voting propositions and candidates was to be allowed, and bumper strips could be distributed.[25]

Chancellor Strong based his convocation address to the students on Monday, September 28, on the memorandum just mentioned, which he understood was the Regents' new policy. Thus, as the pickets milled through the audience, they were startled to hear the chancellor announce two major concessions to their position—the right to advocate "yes" or "no" votes and to endorse specific candidates, and the right to distribute campaign literature such as bumper strips and lapel buttons. Strong continued:

I have received from the ASUC Senate the text of a motion passed by that body on September 22 requesting freedom (1) to solicit political party membership, (2) to mount political and social action on the campus, (3) to solicit funds on campus for such action, and (4) to receive funds to aid projects not directly concerned with an authorized activity of the University. This petition has received the attention of the President and the Regents of the University. University facilities are not to be used for any of these four purposes. Any student or group of students seeking to recruit members for social or political action, or to solicit funds for such action, is free to do so off campus, but is prohibited from doing so on campus. . . .[26]

Perhaps the milling of the picketers made it difficult for the audience to hear. At any rate, few people caught Chancellor Strong's reference to the president and the Board of Regents. The next day's *Daily Californian* headlined the story, "Strong Yields to Political Groups." The article said:

Another substantial concession was made by the University yesterday to the political groups protesting the Bancroft-Telegraph ban. . . . This new "reinterpretation of Regents policy" was publicly announced by Chancellor Edward Strong at the University meeting held at 11:00 A.M. yesterday. . . . Chancellor Strong has made a partial concession to both Senate and political group demands. . . .

Other issues may also be brought up by the protesting groups. . . . "The Bancroft-Telegraph issue has alerted us to the free speech issue all over campus," said one spokesman for the protesting groups. "We won't stop now until we've made the entire campus a bastion of free speech."

The Chancellor's statement was in direct contradiction to statements made in earlier stages of the dispute by Dean of Students Katherine A. Towle.[27]

Art Goldberg's delighted response to Chancellor Strong's speech was this: "And you're asking me if picketing is effective?" [28]

That night the United Front had a meeting to decide on further action. Their initial elation at their "victory" had dimmed during the afternoon, because of a conversation Jackie Goldberg had with a reporter from one of the Bay area papers. She had become friendly with him during their press conferences of the preceding week. After the picketing that day he called her over and said he had something that might interest her. He told her that the university had just sent out a general mailing that urged the passage of Proposition 2 (a university bond issue) in the fall election and had made the apparent concession so that the administration would not appear inconsistent in applying university rules to students and staff.

The United Front leaders immediately checked out this information. When they discovered that the university had indeed made such a mailing, they decided students had not wrested anything from the administration. The apparent "concession," in fact, had been something else. [29]

In their meeting that night, the members of the United Front decided to "escalate." As they saw it, the university had admitted that its position was invalid but had acted only enough to "save face."

Several persons who later became leaders in the Free Speech Movement look back on this meeting as a major turning point in the controversy. [30] Jack Weinberg, who was representing Campus CORE, described the Monday night meeting in these terms:

[This meeting] actually formulated a policy statement, which after some debate was passed. And the policy was that from that point on the purpose of the United Front was no longer to regain as much of what had been taken away as was possible. At that point the purpose of the United Front was to secure freedom for student groups, with the only limitation being things which would interfere with the effective function of the University. . . . [31]

Jo Freeman described the meeting in this way:

The administration refused to negotiate. We'd tried picketing . . . so we thought we'd press a little harder and see what happened. After all, if we put up tables—if they did something, that would give us a basis for arguing; and if they didn't do anything, we had what we wanted, anyway.

. . . This was when our thinking was beginning to jell . . . not just that we wanted our area back, but that this was really part of the University, and the whole situation was wrong. . . .

We'd tried everything else we could think of. We'd talk to the administration—we'd been good little boys and girls and gone to talk to the administration four or five times—we'd picketed, we'd held a rally, we got this fantastic petition out during the rally; there was totally no response, so the next step—look, these are civil rights people, they know civil rights action and they also know that you escalate—put on your pressure a little bit more, and a little bit more. . . . So we thought we'd put on a little more pressure.[32]

Mario Savio described the rationale behind the United Front decision in these terms:

You see, they told us there were about eight areas on campus where we could do the kind of thing that we wanted to do at Bancroft and Telegraph, minus politics. In other words, tables. . . . They included Sather Gate. And seeing as we didn't recognize their right to restrict what we wanted to do at Bancroft and Telegraph, likewise it was perfectly consistent to do those things at Sather Gate. . . . They couldn't get us for having tables at Sather Gate; they could only get us for doing certain things at those tables. . . .

The emotional force of it was moving 100 yards inward, you know, so you put the damn tables right out where they can see them.[33]

Brian Turner added this argument:

We decided to set up the tables, express our right to collect money on the campus, because the campus—in our view—was public property. We knew that we could collect money, say, on the steps of the post office, so we wanted to not just have the privilege . . . [to] collect at a little corner on Telegraph and Bancroft. We wanted to establish the right to collect money on any piece of public property, whether it was at Sather Gate, or under the Campanile, or whatever.[34]

Accordingly, on Tuesday, September 29, 1964, several tables were set up on campus both at Bancroft and Telegraph and in front of Sather Gate. Only a few of the tables were authorized by permits from Dean Towle's office, for these permits required a promise that there would be

no solicitation of money or members or any advocacy of off-campus activity other than voting. The Young Republicans decided that they
could not break the university regulations in this way, but, as they put
it, "We won't fink out." [32] Instead of obtaining a permit for their table,
they decided not to set one up at all during this period of testing. Thus,
although there was a division of opinion about tactics, the front remained united.

Chancellor Strong called a meeting of his staff, including Dean
Towle, Dean of Men Arleigh Williams, and Vice-Chancellor O. W.
Campbell, who was responsible for university police. In Katherine
Towle's words,

*This was something we hadn't faced before: we couldn't allow them
to continue to violate the rules without some kind of university action.
. . . After the tables were set up, we decided to send someone out, and
I think two of the assistant deans went out from this office. . . . We decided that we would take their names, tell them that they were commit-
ting illegal acts, so to speak, bring them in. Dean Williams . . . went
out himself, with one of his assistants. . . .*

*Police officers [accompanied] Dean Williams. . . . There was a
question of whether there were people on campus who were not students. This had already arisen. And so I think the idea was that if they
refused to give their name or identify themselves, the police would step
in and quote whatever the statutes were, or something of this sort. . . .
This was not a new thing, this matter of people on the campus using
university facilities who were not students.*

*. . . I think they [went out] each time someone new would come
up.*[35]

Dean of Men Arleigh Williams and university police officers informed students at each of the tables that some of the activities being
conducted were illegal. They asked a few of the persons manning tables
to show their registration cards, to prove that they were bona fide students. The *Daily Californian* quoted Dean Williams as saying, "Every
effort will be made to remove those tables." It was not clear to the reporter, however, whether such efforts would involve use of the university police or not. Art Goldberg was asked to make an appointment
with Dean Williams.[36]

That afternoon the dean's office, sensing that a crisis might be imminent, set up a conference with the student organizations involved in the United Front and their faculty advisers. This meeting was to be held in Sproul Hall at 4:00 P.M. on Wednesday.[37]

On Tuesday evening a number of persons active in the United Front, including Jack Weinberg and Brian Turner, went to hear a talk Hal Draper was giving at Stiles Hall to one of the socialist organizations.[38] There was a fair-sized crowd, perhaps because Draper's topic was "Clark Kerr's View of the University as a Factory." The talk was a critical review of Clark Kerr's book, *The Uses of the University,* and vividly impressed some of the students.[39]

At 10:30 that night the United Front met again to discuss plans. Students who had manned tables that day were encouraged to do so again on Wednesday.

four
SIT-IN

It was noon on Wednesday before tables went up again. Within ten minutes members of the dean's office staff and the campus police were at Sather Gate. Brian Turner reported the scene in these words:

The Deans went by the YSA table, I think it was. . . . And they went down. Then they moved on to what must have been the Slate table, and they moved on from there. Apparently, the Slate table said they would leave, or something like that. And then they came over to the SNCC table. . . . We'd dreamed up funny questions, like they said, "May I ask you for some identification?" and I said, "Where's your identification?"

The one dean was just whispering. He was mortified. It was terrific. . . . Well, they said, "Will you leave?" And at that point I went over to talk to Mario. I asked him two questions. One was, if he were there, would he stop, because I had great respect for his philosophical judgment. And then I asked him if I got canned, would there be any support among the students, in his opinion. He didn't know, but he said that he would try to bring that about. So I went back and told the deans that I wasn't going to leave, and they told me to come and see the deans at 3:00.[1]

Another student immediately took Turner's place. This student also was cited, only to be replaced by another student and then by still a fourth. After the deans had cited five students, they left.[2] In the meantime, however, the encounter had become transformed into a public "event." Here is Jack Weinberg's description of how this happened:

. . . *When I saw the first citations being made to students at the tables—it was at Sather Gate— . . . I got up on that wall (by the* gate), *and I started pointing out what was happening. . . . I was feeling very self-conscious in doing it, because* [*I was not enrolled that semester*]. . . . *I think someone else took my place. While this was going on, Mario took a chair from the table, got up on the chair, and began speaking in front of the table. . . . This was when the deans had first come, while they were citing people. . . . All I remember is—the deans are there, and what they were doing, and I tried to gather a crowd—I guess my aims were general agitation. It was partly spontaneous, but partly a conscious act to try to get something going. To get a group together. I was mad about what was happening. . . . Mario spoke for a while pointing out what was happening. This was the first speech of the Free Speech Movement. When Mario got down, I was the second person that spoke. . . . I remember my speech at the time—two things I recall; the night before, Hal Draper had given a talk at Stiles on "Clark Kerr's View of the University at a Factory." . . . I was at this talk, and Mario was also there for at least part of his talk—at the time I felt I was greatly influenced by this speech. I talked about the university factory.* I was essentially trying to fit some of what was happening into the theoretical framework—explaining it in terms of this framework that had been exposited the night before. *At the time I felt I was very heavily dependent on the speech.*

. . . *I remember the first time I ever spoke publicly—about a month before that—I had written everything up and read it. Now I was saying things I had never thought through carefully before. . . and there was this huge group around me, and I really felt I was communicating directly to everybody.*

This was around noon, I think. People were coming through Sather Gate. I really expected people to stop and hear what I said. . . .[3] (Emphasis added.)

While all this was going on someone wrote on a piece of notebook paper, "WE HAVE JOINTLY MANNED THE TABLES AT SATHER GATE. DEAN

OF STUDENTS OFFICE 3:00 P.M." This was passed around for signatures.[4]

Additional sheets with this claim at the top were circulated through the crowd while the speeches continued. Someone ran down to the Bancroft and Telegraph entrance a block away, where other tables had been set up, and asked for signatures there. By 3 o'clock, 415 names had been signed to these sheets. Some people signed more than one sheet, but at least 365 individual students were involved.[5]

At 3:00 P.M. a crowd of students began marching into Sproul Hall to keep their "disciplinary appointment" with Dean Williams. The *Daily Californian* claimed that almost 500 students entered Sproul Hall at this point. If this was an actual head count (as it could have been, since they remained inside for several hours), the marchers picked up additional sympathizers as they went in. At any rate they must have included a good proportion of the persons who signed the "petition of complicity," as it came to be called. The United Front leaders were amazed and delighted at the size of their following as they led the march inside.

Who joined them? Here are brief excerpts from essays [6] by several students who first became involved that afternoon.

A freshman boy who planned to major in philosophy heard about the incident at the noon rally, went on to class, and then stood outside Sproul Hall while the demonstrating students went inside. After awhile someone inside exhorted those standing around outside to come in with them or leave. "I didn't want to leave," this boy wrote, "so I went in. . . . I felt it was the least I could do, because the action was necessary. I felt that this was the only possible way to be effective." [6]

One of Mario Savio's teaching assistants joined the demonstration after he heard Savio speak from the wall outside Sproul Hall just before they marched in. He said:

Since the first crack-down . . . I was on the look-out for a way to channel my outrage. . . . It was an opportunity to reveal the American drift toward elitism and possibly change its course in this instance. . . . The majority aren't alive to their situation: the activists who are . . . need support. It meant that students were at the point where nothing more by way of controllable policy decisions would be respected. I found the situation humorous, inflammatory, exciting, and ennobling— asking people to attempt something equal to their potential.[6]

A senior art major joined the demonstrating crowd at Sather Gate because she felt guilty for having signed a loyalty oath in order to get a student loan. She saw this as an opportunity to take a stand for a principle in which she believed.

A law student, who was having coffee on the terrace, assumed the students would face trespass arrests after he heard Weinberg and Savio explain the citations. He reports he decided that "this time the university probably went too far with its subtle reign of terror. Our trespass arrests would inform the public and the university that free speech was being abridged on our campus." He states that he expected to be arrested and to be given a $25 court fine plus a warning from the university. He noticed that many of the demonstrators "were mainly having a good time." [6]

One student hadn't planned to join the demonstration at all:

I got off the elevator on the second floor of Sproul Hall to get a loan from the dean's office, and saw the demonstration. I had made up my mind before on the issues and felt morally obliged to join. I had no idea at first what had happened except that it was related to the political freedom issue. I thought there was a good chance they would be arrested. I talked to the people around me. After I found out what was happening at the dean's office I counted 220 people—and decided to join them. I had decided to be arrested then, but I didn't think we could rally support if we were expelled. But it seemed the only way this could be done. I admired the leaders' courage and devotion to good principles.[6]

There is no way to tell how typical these perceptions are for the several hundred students involved. It is clear from these accounts, however, that a variety of explicit impressions motivated the actors to join this venture. What they shared in common was an agreement about the basic nature of the crisis confronting them and a sense that the response being taken was necessary and was the only thing that had a chance of working at this time.

The students' activities to gather support before they kept the appointment with Dean Williams had not gone unnoticed by members of the administrative staff. About 1:30 P.M. Alex Sherriffs dictated the following memorandum to the records:

Talked with Arleigh about the fact that he was possibly / probably going to be invaded by 100's of "confessed" violators demanding to be

*interviewed. He was thinking of moving the meeting to the old Regents'
room and see them one at a time, and setting up appointments for others. I insisted that someone else, an assistant dean of men, request that
they simply leave their names and ways to reach them: the dean would
decide whether or not he wished to call them in; they should then be informed that they have communicated their information and should go
away and stop blocking the corridor. I told AW to stay in the dean of
students office and put the burden on them for interfering with university business. I suggested that he might wish police to aid in dispersal
and to keep them out of his office proper. He thought that this was a
good idea and asked that I provide police in his office before the group
arrived so that they would be available and at a point when needed. I
told him under no circumstances to start setting up a series of appointments. He could not meet with 300 people and "confessions" would be
insufficient evidence and insecure evidence at best. I told him it was his
job to continue carrying out action on the cases with which we were
dealing. It is 1:30 and I am trying reach Hump Campbell to clear details on police action. Television is here.*

ACS:jh

*1:45   AW tele. asking if police were going out to break up the mass
meeting at Sather Gate. I told him that this was the business of the dean
of students—send out an assistant dean to inform the group, etc., and I
said that I thought it had been done an hour ago.*[7]

At 3:00 P.M., as the petitioners were beginning to march into Sproul
Hall, Alex Sherriffs dictated this memorandum to the records:

*3 P.M.   Meeting (2:20 P.M.) with Hump Campbell and UCPD [uni-
versity campus police department]. Hump Campbell and I met with
Chandler, Woodward, and four members of the UCPD. We are agreed
on their instructions (in which we caucused them): (1) Four will be
within 201 Sproul Hall and out of sight. (2) AW will man the door;
will accept the signatures; and don't call us, we will call you. At request
of leaders of your group, there is a meeting at 4 P.M. so you add nothing by being here. "I can count you," please leave and let the Sproul
Hall business continue—*

*(1) If they crash the office, the police immediately go into action in
terms of keeping order and security, (2) the police do not remove anyone from Sproul Hall at this time, but in a quiet way insist that there be*

passageway into the office, and quiet. At 7 P.M. when building closes,
if they are still there, they will be arrested entirely and removed (with
Chancellor's permission).

. . .

A W will be the one to say who can enter the office since he has 5
critical appointments. If there is violence, police will handle this in "po-
lice ways." A W is to tell the leaders in the 4 P.M. group that if there is
continuing disturbance, that this meeting was at their request; that they
get their followers out of Sproul onto the steps outside where they be-
long or the meeting is canceled. A W was reminded once again that his
only real job for today is to have the faculty cases ready for tomorrow.[8]

Thus, as the encounter between students and members of the dean's
staff began, the script for the latter had already been written. Although
there does not seem to have been any serious difference of judgment at
this point between the dean's staff members and the chancellor's office,
no latitude in possible responses to the crisis was permitted to the actors who represented the administration. Thus the encounter quickly became stereotyped, in the directions already envisioned by the administration.

The students entering Sproul Hall were met at the door of the dean
of students office by Arleigh Williams, who responded as he had been
instructed. Mario Savio quickly became the spokesman for the students
and tried to argue the case with Dean Williams. When the student leaders got nowhere, they announced that they would remain inside the
building until all of them were granted a disciplinary hearing. No one
would go into the dean's office unless all of them could be heard. Arleigh Williams announced that the 4 o'clock meeting was canceled
under these circumstances. Angered, the students voted to remain in
Sproul Hall until the administration would agree to deal with them.
When the building closed at 7:00 P.M. they were still inside. Sometime
later that evening a reporter from radio station KPFA [9] joined the students inside Sproul Hall, so that a verbatim record of their proceedings
is available from this point on.

Meanwhile, Alex Sherriffs continued to dictate his summaries of
events to the files. Between 3 and 3:30 o'clock both Dean Fretter of
the College of Letters and Science and Dean Elberg of the Graduate Division called Sherriffs, concerned about what was happening in the hall.

At 3:55 P.M. Campbell called to say that Arleigh Williams again was talking to the waiting students. He discussed fire dangers, safety problems with so many people inside the building, and complaints from the Graduate Division and the College of Letters and Science about the noise in the hall. [Sherriffs?] "told him of 4 P.M. meeting being called off; am against closing building until 7 (at this point). There comes a time when riot act should be read; 'I am ordering you to leave' type that AW should use with group."

The memoranda continue:

First response to dismissal: five students didn't come in and therefore sending a notice to Chancellor for their dismissal, or other action. Discussion of this going to Daily Californian, *for tonight or tomorrow paper.*

Report during this period that Parkinson [10] *and some other faculty member would talk to these students at 4 P.M.—defend them against any discipline, render any support for them. Implied faculty behind them.*

. . .

Later report that Goldberg [?], someone on balcony of Sproul, had opened windows, and telling outside students to come in the building.

3:40–4 P.M. Tele. discussion with AW and Hump Campbell— discussed closing building; I requested do not do until 7 P.M., and only with permission of Chancellor.

With respect to the signatures of the 400—perhaps might have to accept their guilt and then let them come in and explain.

The 4 P.M. meeting has been called off because the leaders and some of the faculty advisers are no longer interested in it.

4–5 P.M. Talks with President Kerr and Chancellor Strong—during conversations, also talked with AW on telephone, Hump Campbell, Degnan. [11]

AW is to sit down and write a brief and get it here by 8 A.M. at this office tomorrow morning. On basis of brief, 8 students will be expelled. This will be given to press. At the same time, if asked in the morning, tell students there is no clear stand to sit-ins of right and wrong way of dealing with them. Won't force students to leave, request that they do leave, at 7 lock building (police will have to have somebody there at all times), if students wish to remain, O.K., if wish to leave locked building, must do so thru only open entrance, police department. [12]

It is clear from interviews conducted with several members of the university administration after the events that administrators were united in considering this sit-in a crisis of authority. Both the setting up of tables in the Sather Gate area the day before and the mass appearance for discipline were perceived, first and foremost, as challenges to the authority of the chancellor's office, ones that could not be ignored.[13]

In contrast, the students saw these events as a crisis of legitimacy. They were claiming the regulation that precipitated them was unconstitutional and therefore not one to be observed.

Unfortunately for documentation, Alex Sherriff's memoranda to the files for September 30 stop at this point. A meeting was held after supper, attended by President Kerr, Chancellor Strong, Vice-Chancellor Sherriffs, Dean Towle, and others. Administrative officers were highly annoyed by the student action. Had the students reported to the dean's office, as ordered, they would have been informed that their cases had been referred to the Faculty Committee on Student Conduct. In the administrators' view, the students cited had refused to appear for disciplinary hearing when they refused to enter the dean's office unless their friends could enter also.

There is a long-standing university regulation dealing with this kind of situation: students who refuse to respond to appropriate requests from the dean of students or other administrative officers may be forthwith dismissed. A proposal was made that the rule be applied to this situation. President Kerr requested that the eight cited students [14] be notified that they had been "indefinitely suspended." Chancellor Strong asked whether there was such a status in the university regulations. When told that the president had authority to invoke whatever penalties he deemed appropriate, Strong replied he was willing to act on Kerr's recommendation but that he wanted a written memorandum by the president. Strong then asked Arleigh Williams to present documentation on each case, since the chancellor acts on the dean's recommendation.[15] Williams spent the rest of the night in his office drawing up the charges against the eight students.[16]

Meanwhile the demonstrators were continuing their sit-in. As supper time approached, money was collected for food and Slate announced a sizable contribution for this purpose. By 5:00 P.M. women students were preparing sandwiches in a second-floor alcove. After supper Thomas Barnes, an associate professor of history and a member of the dean's staff, began to debate with the students concerning the legitimacy of their action.

About midnight, Chancellor Edward Strong issued the following statement:

Students and student organizations today enjoy the fullest privileges in the history of the University, including discussing and advocating on a broad spectrum of political and social issues. Some students demand on-campus solicitation of funds and planning and recruitment of off-campus social and political action. The University cannot allow its facilities to be so used without endangering its future as an independent educational institution. The issue now has been carried far beyond the bounds of discussion by a small minority of students. These students should recognize the fullness of the privileges extended to them by the University, and ask themselves whether they wish to take further actions damaging to the University.

The University cannot and will not allow students to engage in deliberate violation of law and order on campus. The Slate Supplement Report this fall urged "open, fierce and thorough-going rebellion on this campus . . . in which the final resort will be Civil Disobedience." Individual students must ask themselves whether they wish to be a part of such action.

When violations occur, the University must then take disciplinary steps. Such action is being taken. Eight students were informed individually by a representative of the Office of the Dean of Students that they were in violation of University regulations and were asked to desist. Each of the eight students refused to do so. I regret that these eight students by their willful misconduct in deliberately violating rules of the University have made it necessary for me to suspend them indefinitely from the University. I stand ready as always to meet with the officers of any student organization to discuss the policies of the University.[17]

The *Daily Californian* quoted Mario Savio as making this response: "I don't really know what to say. If you won't take this as the official statement of the group, I think they're all a bunch of bastards." [17]

It is about here that KPFA began tape-recording the discussion in Sproul Hall. On the tapes there is an excited pitch to voices, and most people speak very rapidly. The students sound angry. Professor Barnes is speaking quickly, trying to interpret the university policy and to argue that the student action is inappropriate. The students contend that their constitutional right to free speech has been denied by the university.

The debate is of special interest because all of the arguments that became important at later stages of the conflict emerged that evening. Thus it is worth following in detail.[18]

Barnes argued that students may hold political meetings off campus at Stiles Hall. He went on to state his personal impression that anyone was allowed to speak, to set up tables, or to advocate positions at nine "Hyde Park" areas on campus, including the one at Bancroft and Telegraph:[19]

This, it does not seem to me, is a restriction of free speech. It may be a restriction of political action, and I can't argue that, it obviously is. But it is not a restriction of free speech. The distinction is essentially a legal one. A legalistic one, if you wish, sure. . . . But by this distinction, quibble though it may be, legalistic though it may be, the university places itself in a posture where it can honestly say to those who would pressure it, that this university is not a forum for political action. And you who would attempt—I don't mean you, I mean the outside pressures, the outside forces—who would like to turn it into your own political bailiwick, have to stay out. We stay out of your action. You stay out of ours.

Barnes's speech was met with some scattered applause and a chorus of boos. Voices began to call out, "What about the eight?" Barnes replied that he had no information about the action taken against them. He went on to say, "What I fear is that, if there is continued disobedience of the rules and regulations concerning this policy, . . . further suspensions may in fact result."

There was some applause at this point. Barnes continued as follows:

. . . What worries me precisely, is this: that much of the best will power and manpower in this university is up here tonight. I have no doubt about that. I think that you can, within this existing framework of policy announced on Monday, work effectively for the political ends you want. I have no doubt about this. I think that if you disobey these rules, then you are in jeopardy as individuals and the organizations that you are working with are in jeopardy as organizations.

A student interrupted to shout, "We're selling out the people that have gone before us—that's why we are in jeopardy!"

A new student, Martin Roysher, shouted, "If this university is so rotten and so corrupt at its base that a simple demonstration by students asking for free speech will cause this university to collapse from outside pressure, I ask you if you can stand there and solicit my support for it? How can you?" Applause, cheers, and whistles resounded for twenty-two seconds after this challenge.

Barnes tried to continue. "It is not a demonstration that is involved," he said. "It is the continued, and I fear willful, breaking and violation of regulations."

Students began to shout objections to this definition of the occasion. Finally a voice cut through the uproar: "You have stated that the university must withstand the outside pressure. I maintain that the university is walking hand in hand with the outside pressure [loud applause]. With its participation in the cold war manufacture of weapons—"

At this point some persons shouted objections while others answered, "Let him speak!" The same voice went on: "in the Giannini Institute over here that has made a decision that the bracero program is O.K. for the growers. Isn't that, isn't that using the university, the university's name for the outside community that it's supposed to be withstanding from?"

The debate continued, with loud audience reaction. Finally a shout went up: "Let Savio speak!" Savio's speech directly challenged Barnes' claims:

There are three main things. . . . First, the remarks of Chancellor Strong that the open-forum policy will be maintained and that that policy will include no acceptance of donations and no recruitment of people to take part in direct action, nor recruitment of, you know, of people to join off-campus political organizations. Oh, yes! Now let's for a moment try to clear our minds of legal cobwebs and try to see just what that means in terms of facts. Most of the groups affected are of such a character that if they couldn't do these things, they just might as well do nothing at those tables. Now that's a fact we ought to consider. . . .

But I understand that it does not address . . . the legal questions involved. So I'd like to move very quickly to what Professor Barnes said concerning the neutrality of the University of California. The university wants to maintain itself, he said at one point, politically neutral. And then he amended that—I was very careful in my notes—to legally neutral, and there is a very big distinction. Because I agree it is legally neutral. Now let's see how politically neutral it is. . . .

He said the university is run as a trust by the Board of Regents. O.K. They have quite a bit of control over what goes on at the university. We ought to ask who they are. You know, who are the Board of Regents? Well, they are a pretty damned reactionary bunch of people!

Savio went on to point out that the Board of Regents included major power interests in the state, heavily representing big business.

. . . There are groups in this country, like laborers, for example, like Negroes—laborers usually—like educators, sometimes, when they don't act as Uncle Toms for administrations [laughter]. These people, see, I don't think have a community of interest with the Bank of California. . . .

On the Board of Regents, please note, the only academic representative —and it's questionable in what sense he's an academic representative—is President Clark Kerr. The only one. There are no representatives, you know, explicitly, of faculty—because they don't need it. They don't need it, you know. So [the] question is, is the university in fact neutral politically? And it obviously is false. Obviously. . . .

Savio continued as follows:

. . . When someone brought up the issue of the kinds of things we do here, like the building of newer and better atom bombs, there was a lot of booing. . . . The people here don't want to discuss this matter. I think that it should be discussed. . . . Let's consider for a second the degree to which in this country we have democratic control over our foreign policy. I'd like you to consider this, please. I think it is extremely important.

One day after that Tonkin Bay incident,[20] the very next day—remember this was an action of a Democratic administration—one day after this action was taken the two representatives of the Republican Party, Miller and Goldwater, said, "As of now, Vietnam is not an issue in the campaign."

What did that mean to you as voters and to me as a voter? It means that when we go to vote in November, we can't choose on what kind of foreign policy we want because they both [the two major parties] have the same kind of foreign policy. Part of that foreign policy involves doing various things like building newer and better atom bombs. . . . We have no say in choosing . . . between that foreign policy and some other policy that someone else may want.

Now note—extremely important—the University of California is directly involved in making newer and better atom bombs. Whether this is good or bad, don't you think . . . in the spirit of political neutrality, either they should not be involved or there should be some democratic control over the way they're being involved?

His point was greeted by applause and shouts of delight. Savio went on:

I would like to raise now some genuinely legal issues, to which maybe some people will want to respond. There are several ways in which we can look at a university from a legal point of view. We can look at it as a private organization run by a small group of people. And in the past, on occasion, the Regents have taken a position that they have virtually unlimited control over the private property which is the University of California. That's one way.

Another way is, we can look at the university as [a] kind of little city . . . and then we could ask ourselves is there any part of this so-called open-forum policy which contradicts the ways in which we do things in little cities. O.K.? I say there certainly is.

. . . Let's say that the mayor of Berkeley announced that citizens of Berkeley could speak on any issue they wanted from the steps of the fire building. . . . But let's say that they placed the following restriction upon nonresidents from Berkeley, that they could not do so unless they obtained permission from the city of Berkeley and did so 72 hours before they wanted to speak. You know there'd be a hue and cry going up: "Incredible violation of the First Amendment! Unbelievable violation of the 14th!" . . .

Well now, look at the university here not as the private property of Edward Carter [Chairman of the Board of Regents]. . . . Let's say, instead, that we look upon it as a little city. Well, then, how come I—before I was expended [laughter]— . . . all right, before I was expelled—suspended —I could get on the steps of Sproul Hall and say anything I wanted as long as I didn't start giving arms to people. You know, I could say anything I wanted without notifying anybody. But a nonstudent would have to obtain permission from the university and do that 72 hours before he wanted to speak, and the university might just not like what he had to say and might well deny the permission.

Now, consider the analogy with the city. Consider how gross—how gross a violation of the spirit of the First and Fourteenth Amendments that is! Here's the legal principle. I think it's more a moral principle.

We hold . . . that there ought to be no arbitrary restrictions upon the right of freedom of speech. Now what does an arbitrary restriction mean? An arbitrary restriction is one based upon an arbitrary distinction. For example, as between students and nonstudents.

Now, note . . . sometimes the distinction is very material: if, for example, you consider classrooms . . . perfectly reasonable, material distinction. . . . But now the issue is freedom of speech. We have people out in Sproul Hall. There's not a class going on there. . . . What therefore is the material basis for the distinction in this instance between students and nonstudents?

. . . Why 72 hours for nonstudents and no time for students? Let's say, for example—and this touches me very deeply—let's say that in McComb, Mississippi, some children are killed in the bombing of a church. . . . Let's say that we have someone who's come up from Mississippi . . . and he wanted to speak here and he had to wait 72 hours in order to speak. And everybody will have completely forgotten about those little children because, you know, when you're black and in Mississippi, nobody gives a damn . . . 72 hours later and . . . the whole issue would have been dead.

Or let's say that some organization here . . . objects to some action of the administration in Vietnam . . . and has to wait 72 hours to object. By that time it's all over. You know, we could all be dead.

. . . I'm suggesting legally, therefore, that the distinction that they make between students and nonstudents has no basis except harassment. . . . Furthermore, they claim that the university is neutral. A lot of hogwash! It's *legally* neutral. It's the most un-politically-neutral organization that I've had personal contact with. It's really an institution that serves the interests and represents the establishment of the United States. And we have Clark Kerr's word on it in his book on the multiversity.

As I said before, the purpose of the university is simple: it's to create a product. The product is to fit into certain factories. You go out and take part in the Establishment and that's why there is a university!

. . . Anybody who wants to say anything on this campus, just like anybody on the city street, should have the right to do so—and no concessions by the bureaucracy should be acceded to by us, should be considered by us, until they include complete freedom of speech!

When the applause died, Marty Roysher said:

For just a minute, I think we should get just a little bit nitty-gritty. . . . There is one issue here, and that issue is whether we are going to be able to function politically on this campus. That is the issue.

Now it was suggested before, by a previous speaker, that we will be able to function politically as before, although not legally; and this is wrong on two counts. It's wrong because, if you look at the civil rights movement, the only tie that the civil rights movement has . . . with our college community—is, . . . for example, the group that was involved today, the University Friends of SNCC. They are raising the money to send to the South. If we . . . cannot advocate joining SNCC, cannot raise money for SNCC, it doesn't make a damn bit of difference what we do on this campus, we're not going to be any use to the people in Mississippi. . . .

Now this is an election year, and it is particularly important to be able to endorse or not endorse various political candidates. All that we would be allowed to do is display bumper stickers, and so on, once every four years.

. . . There are those of us who can risk getting expelled, and there are those of who are not [in this position]. Some of those who are not are sitting right here now. . . . The question is, are we going to get up and move or are we gonna stay here? And the leadership should answer that question and answer it now.

Representatives of the organizations involved in the United Front then withdrew to draw up a policy proposal that would be brought back to the rest of the group for discussion and a vote. In the meantime the debate between student demonstrators and Dean Barnes continued. After a while, Jack Weinberg interrupted: "I wish I could have talked before . . . [to] Professor Barnes, 'cause I would have liked to give him the chance to respond to what I had to say. . . ."

BARNES: *I'll reply. Go ahead.*

WEINBERG: *. . . With all due respect to him, I think that all of you . . . have just seen a crown example of bureaucracy and bureaucratic thinking in action. Bureaucracy works by nibbling. By taking this and that and saying, "It's not very importnat." Bureaucracy works by getting any real, honest-to-goodness concrete issues involved in legalisms, involved in channels, involved in pressures and counterpressures, and this and that—and the whole, the whole impact—of bureaucratic thinking is to keep you from looking at the prize, as they say in the civil rights song. It keeps you from looking at the issues.*

At the time . . . when the announcement was read and it was stated that eight students were expelled—and I think the type of suspension that was stated amounts to expulsion—when it was stated that eight students were expelled, I think this entire group was shocked. Then Mario got up and reaffirmed a very clear, a very strong, a very moral position. And I think that we all responded to this question as one . . . with one thought in mind.

When Professor Barnes stood up . . . he did not in any way disagree with any of the points that we stood for. He merely raised complicated, bureaucratic, confusing issues. These issues, I think, completely cloud the point. The point is simple. The point is free speech. The point is eight students have been expelled for their position. . . . Remove from your mind much of this bureaucratic thing, or look for the substance be-

hind it and only use whatever substance it may have had and forget about the issues.

I have a request from Mario for every one of you. . . . I hope that every one of you will stay here until the groups involved reach a consensus, bring the consensus back to the floor, and that we ask your opinion on each issue. I hope that you all stay here and let us know how you feel on whatever suggestions are raised.

The representatives of the United Front took considerable time to develop strategy suggestions. Meanwhile the main group continued discussing. Eventually a voice called out, "Hey, people! One announcement of historical interest as to what actually happened on this . . . that I have gotten from this fellow who has heard from the chancellor's meeting—"

At this point many voices called for quiet. The same speaker continued:

Apparently the chancellor has now admitted that the Oakland Tribune *. . . did in fact call him and asked him, apparently, if he realized that this mobilizing of students was going on on university property. So this talk, talk, talk about amorphous pressures off campus may be a little inappropriate, in so far as that pressure that Mr. Kerr is responding to is direct pressure from . . . Mr. Knowland, who is concerned with essentially a political campaign electing a man, and a private issue: his own damned newspaper.*

Eventually Dean Barnes tried again to influence the direction of the decision students were debating:

. . . How would you, in effect, change a university community? You change it in three ways. You first of all change it over a period of time . . . by the graduates of this university going out into the community as a whole and indicating what the nature of a university is. . . . You may sometimes have to remind Regents, administrators, and faculty what the nature of those values are—and, by the way, this is an extremely important form of direct attack.
. . . The university . . . is essentially the whole community, including you. The elements of power involved are considerably different, and the real basic power in the university are those people we call the Re-

gents. . . . The powers that motivate them tend to be powers largely outside. This is one of the problems in a public university.

Secondly . . . you change a university from within. By the powers of persuasion. By the powers of discussion. By what's been going on in here tonight, in essence. Working on faculty and working on administration. And [what is] involved is nothing like a monolith. The university is an incredible community in this way. It is already 50% committed to almost any point of view anybody takes. Outside society is almost 100 % against most any new idea. Universities do, in fact, change. They change from the whole workings of these internal pressures. And that's the second way you change it.

The third way you change a university—and perhaps even in the long run the most effective—is by indicating the ultimate responsibility that you are willing to take, either in defense of the legal position of the university or else in the moral position against it. And I'm not going to argue that, as I've said to you earlier.

. . . You can do it either way. . . . This is essentially a question of tactics.

. . . I think the least effective tactics are these mass demonstrations . . . going against rules and regulations which, even though you may not consider them as being reasonable, may very well fall in the future if you use the power of your moral suasion.

. . . Every university has its own problems, its own environment in which it has to survive, and its own . . . criteria for solving its problems. This one has specific ones. . . . It is a university where the power is given into the hands of the Regents.

A voice interrupted, saying, "Once the university backs down in such a way that ruins its purpose, once the purpose of the university is sacrificed for the university's existence—"

BARNES: *Where do you—*
VOICE: *Then the university—*
BARNES: *Where do you—*
VOICE: *No longer has the reason for existence!*
BARNES: *Where do you get off so categorically?*

And so the debate continued until Art Goldberg returned, presenting the United Front proposal. Students would set up *large* tables, with perhaps five chairs behind them, on the campus the next day, instead of the small card tables they had been using. Sign-up sheets for manning the tables on a half-hour basis would be circulated, and people were asked to sign before leaving. The tables would be manned directly in front of Sproul Hall. Students at the tables would solicit donations to help the eight who had been suspended or to promote some social cause.

Demonstrators shouted for a discussion of the proposal. Someone asked what the United Front would do if the administration repeated its tactic of taking only a few names. Other students asked what would happen in a few days when they ran out of volunteers to be cited.

Members of the United Front replied that they would seek support from the Central Labor Council in Oakland and from the Bay area's United Freedom Movement. They would ask the American Civil Liberties Union for support in a legal fight and would conduct rallies to attract additional students. They might rent a sound truck to tell their story to bystanders on the streets of Berkeley.

A long-time activist, Barbara Garson, urged the group to use people sparingly at the tables and to focus on a series of rallies to embarrass the administration. Jackie Goldberg objected:

They won't respond to rallies—or to sit-ins—or they already would have. They want a few to pick off. Tomorrow, mass people on those tables! You confront them with everyone at once. You eight had the courage because we signed that petition. It's now up to us to sit there—and force their hand. No negotiation will work. It's direct action now.

Mario Savio combined the two suggestions into a single motion: there would be a massive rally at Sproul Hall tomorrow with individual tables set up throughout the day. The enthusiastic response from the assembled students made it clear that the issue had been decided.

One question remained: What should be done when the deans came up to the tables? After some debate the students decided that no one would give his name or any identification the next day. The university either would have to back down or would have to act against all of them.

By now it was 2:00 A.M. The sit-in broke up as clusters of individuals scurried off to prepare handbills and posters, to find tables, and to do the other jobs necessary before the "direct action" could begin on the following day.

five
CAPTURING
THE CAR

Students entering the campus the next morning were greeted by a variety of handbills prepared by volunteers during the early morning hours after the sit-in broke up. One, whose typing showed the effects of the late hour at which it had been prepared, was headlined: "8 Students Suspended! Free Speech Rally—Noon—Sproul Hall." It went on to describe, from the demonstrators' standpoint, what had happened the day before and concluded as follows:

. . . shortly before midnight they were told of Chancellor Strong's suspension of the eight students on the "blacklist." The students then decided to leave Sproul Hall and resume the protest today.

If we allow the administration to pick us off one by one in this manner we have lost the fight for free speech at the University of California. This technique was used when Dwinelle Plaza was closed to free speech and when the Daily Cal *was muzzled. Only by solidarity and by positive action can we maintain our basic freedoms!*
TODAY! NOON RALLY TO PROTEST ARBITRARY SUSPENSION—SPROUL HALL

Another handbill only sketched the incidents of the day before. It concentrated, instead, on suggestions for follow-up action:

It's YOUR *fight, too!*

Last night, the Administration of the University of California suspended indefinitely eight students. These students were among hundreds who had the courage to protest the University's restrictions on freedom of speech by manning tables against University "regulation." WE CANNOT LET THEM STAND ALONE.

THE TABLES WILL BE UP TODAY.
HUNDREDS HAVE DECLARED THEIR WILLINGNESS TO SIT AT THESE TABLES. JOIN THEM IN THIS FIGHT:

1. Come to the tables anytime you can.
2. Attend the protest rally at noon today at Bancroft and Telegraph.
3. Ask your professors to support this fight by:

> *a. Openly declaring their willingness to teach all students suspended for protesting.*
> *b. Demanding that the administration reinstate the eight students.*
> *c. Demanding that the administration lift its ban against political advocacy on campus.*

THESE EIGHT HAVE PUT THEIR EDUCATION ON THE LINE IN DEFENSE OF OUR RIGHTS. DON'T LET THEM STAND ALONE.

The radical, liberal, and conservative campus groups are united in protest against the administrative action.
    Labor donated.

The *Daily Californian* carried the headline, "Williams Refuses Demands; 700 Sleep in Sproul Hall." The front page included a description of the day's events, Chancellor Strong's statement at the time he announced the indefinite suspension, and the reactions of the students in Sproul Hall to this announcement.

At 9:00 A.M., tables for SNCC and Slate appeared in their locations of the day before, at Sather Gate. By 10:30 A.M. three tables had been set up on the lower landing of the wide steps leading to the entrance of Sproul Hall.[1]

A KPFA radio reporter recorded a number of arguments that occurred around the tables during the next hour—whether this was or was not an issue of free speech, and whether political advocacy was appropriate on a state university campus. Points were made with less sophistication than the night before, but roughly the same ground was covered by both sides.[2]

While these things were happening, the members of the administrative staff were trying to decide how best to meet this new challenge to their authority. The first memorandum was written to Dr. Strong and Dr. Sherriffs at 8:15 A.M.:

Dick Hafner telephoned to say that the students acting under suggestions from their leaders took off a little after 2:40 this morning. Everyone left, inside and outside, except for two students who remained on the front steps of Sproul. One of them said he was spending the night there because he has an eight o'clock class and it would be easier to make it from there.

Other than that, what the Daily Cal *says this morning is pretty much what the situation was/is. "There is a desire on the part of the students to meet with the Chancellor and there is no gathering at Sproul this morning."*

akiko

Sherriffs' memoranda began about 9:00 A.M. The following is a memorandum to files:

1. I called A. Williams at 9 o'clock. He had just gone home to shower, so gave the following message to his secretary: The Chancellor wants the Dean of Students representatives to do the actual talking to the individuals setting up tables in violation of the University's rules— or any of the violators, to come to the Dean of Students office immediately—not to tell them to come into office at later time in day, etc.

2. Hump Campbell will order the windows overlooking Sproul steps (the balcony) to be permanently shut by wire or otherwise.

During the morning a variety of suggestions flowed into the office. A message from Campbell's office said that two deans would make an arrest "if they get the right table. They will not touch the eight expellees." Campbell has reported that he warned them to act before the noon-hour crowd arrived, but that was not written down at the time.[3] Another person called to suggest that steps be taken to prevent further trouble at the Joan Baez concerts on Friday and Saturday nights, "Joan Baez being one of these liberals who start inflammatory things here."

At 11:45 A.M. Kitty Malloy, Chancellor Strong's administrative assistant, wrote the following memorandum:

Kerr called Strong and told him of Brown statement at the conference today [4] and after this Moskowitz [5] called with an appended statement that Brown wants law and order upheld. Kerr wants this in the Daily Cal *and said Earl Bolton [6] would send it over along with a civil code re: fund-raising on state government copy which might be useful. Kerr again stressed that the controversy was not a matter of freedom of speech and there were no new rules—just putting into effect old rules.*

Strong told Kerr the plan of identifying students—and if person at tables did not identify himself the police would pick him up. ES told him we were not touching speechifying at this point.

Strong told him of the efforts of Fretter in talking to various people such as Reynolds. Humphrey is nervous about situation and wondered whether to cancel—we told him not necessary to cancel.

KCM

After this call from President Kerr to the chancellor, members of the dean's staff went out to confront the students on the Sproul Hall steps. The following account is quoted from the KPFA tape.

REPORTER: *And now, at 21 minutes of 11, the tables are moving— two of them now—in front of Sproul Hall.*

Here there is a break in the sequence. The tape recorder comes back on as students are shouting, "Here they are, people!"

DEAN MURPHY: *Are you prepared to remove yourself,* and *the table, from university property?*

The members of the dean's staff had walked over to the CORE table, the one nearest the south entrance to Sproul Hall, from which they emerged. Dean Murphy was talking to Jack Weinberg, who was seated in the middle at the table. In answer to Dean Murphy's question Weinberg replied, very quietly, "I'm not prepared."

MURPHY: *Are you aware that by not doing so you are subjecting yourself to probable disciplinary action?*

WEINBERG (still more quietly): *I—uh—I'm aware that you're going to do what you'll try to do.*

MURPHY: *All right. Will you—uh—identify yourself?*

WEINBERG: *No.*

MURPHY (in a dead-pan voice, almost as if he were reading a script instead of talking to a particular person): *I must inform you if you are a student you are violating university regulations and if you are a non-student you are violating the trespass law. Will you identify yourself?"*

WEINBERG (even more quietly): *No, I will not.*

MURPHY: *You leave me no alternative but to ask Lieutenant Chandler to arrest you.*

Here voices in the background call, "What did he say?" and "Boooo!"

MURPHY: *Lieutenant Chandler, would you please arrest him.*
CHANDLER: *You come with me, then, please.*
VOICES: *Take their place!*

A male student breaks in, speaking with great politeness to a member of the dean's staff: "Mr. Van Houten—uh—would you like to see our reg cards, sir? We'll be very glad, each one of us, to volunteer them to you and show it to—" Here he is interrupted by a crowd of voices, shouting, "NO!"

DEAN: *I'm talking to him.*
A SECOND MALE VOICE: *You're talking to all of us!*
CHANDLER: *You, as of now, are under arrest, and* [speaking more quickly] *either you'll come with me peacefully or we're gonna take you, either one which—whichever you want to do.*

At this point a chorus of voices break in. They seem to be calling, "Take all of us!"

CHANDLER: *I'm talking to this person right here!*
VOICES: *All of us! All of us!*
CHANDLER: *Do you understand?*
VOICES: *All of us! All of us!* [One voice calls, "We're all managing the tables!"]
CHANDLER: *I think you can cause your group a great deal of—*
VOICE (interrupting): *Don't pick on me!*
CHANDLER (continuing): *Unnecessary—*
WEINBERG: *Don't be so pious. Will you arrest me?*
CHANDLER: *I am arresting you. Now you're either going to come with me or—or we're gonna take you. All right.*
OUTCRY: *All of us! All of us!* [There is also a series of other, undecipherable shouts.]
CHANDLER: (apparently to the radio reporter, who is thrusting a microphone in his face): *Will you step back please.*
REPORTER: *I'm with the press, Lieutenant.*
CHANDLER: *I can't help it.*
REPORTER: *I'm with the press, Lieutenant.*
CONTINUING OUTCRY: *Let's all go to* jail *with him!* "*Right!*"

Here a number of voices break in, and there is general hubbub. Apparently the police officer left at this point to get assistance. There is a sudden hush as Mario Savio comes to the table.

SAVIO: *Greeting, Dean Murphy.*

MURPHY: *Hello, Mario.*

SAVIO: *Hello.*

JACK WEINBERG: *I'm under arrest.*

SAVIO: *Oh, is that right? That's really terrible. This fellow's under arrest!*

WEINBERG (to the crowd): *While we're waiting, can I tell you a little bit about the university that—* [There is a burst of laughter.] *I made a speech a couple of times yesterday.* [Shout: "Stand up!"] *No, I want to sit at the table. I made a speech a couple of times yesterday. They haven't charged me with anything yet. I'm under arrest.*

I want to tell you about this—uh,—knowledge factory, that we're all sitting here now. It seems that certain—certain of the products are not coming out to standard specifications. [There is a small laugh from the crowd.] *Certain of the products are not coming out to standard specifications, and I feel the university is trying to purge these products, so they can once again produce for the industry exactly what they specify.*

This is a knowledge factory. If you read Clark Kerr's books, these are his precise words. The knowledge factory takes certain assignments. They take—uh—orders from industry: they want so many of these, they want so many of these, they want so many of these. . . . The university very willingly obliges and, in fact, turns out exactly what they are ordered. These are not on-campus groups, by the way, that put these orders in. These are off-campus groups. They put in orders that they want certain kinds of products. This is mass production. No deviation from the norms are tolerated.

Occasionally a few students get together, and they decide—that they are human beings. Some students get together, and they decide that they are not—willing to be products. They decide they're not willing—to be another thing produced by the university. And they protest. And the university feels obliged—I'm sure all these gentlemen here feel—very morally upset about this; uh—they're not cruel men. [Laughter and an undecipherable call in the background.]

But they feel obliged—

VOICE: *Tell us about advocacy and action!*

WEINBERG: *I'll tell you about that in a minute. It might take them a while to arrest me.* [Chuckles from the crowd.]

They feel obliged—to purge these nonstandard products. Now this is very unfortunate. Why do we stand—why do we advocate social action at the university? It's very simple. We wanna see social change—in the world in which we live. We wanna see this social change because we are—human beings—who have ideas. We think, we talk, we discuss. And when we're done thinking and talking and discussing, well, then, we feel that these things are vacuous unless we then act on the principles that we think, talk, and discuss about. This is as much a part of a university education as anything else. And let me tell you I don't think there's anything wrong with learning to become a port of industry or learning a trade or whatever else. But this can only be one part of the university.

These gentlemen, here, are university graduates. As I say, they're not evil men. But they are products, and they are acting like the product that was produced. They're doing the job that they were made for. I don't feel anger at them. I feel sorry for them.

We—I'm a member of Campus CORE. Campus CORE stands for certain principles. We of Campus CORE feel there are certain things going on in this nation of ours which are totally and completely intolerable. We feel that we, as human beings first and students second, must take our stand—on every vital issue—which faces this nation and, in particular, the vital issue—of discrimination, of segregation, of poverty, of unemployment. The vital issue of people—who aren't getting the decent breaks, the decent breaks that they as individuals deserve.

Here some people start to break in. Others call, "Let him talk!" One voice demands, "Tell us how you were singled out."

Weinberg starts to explain. "I was singled out because I'm on the right [7] and these people—" Now he is interrupted by a babble of excited voices.

OFFCIAL: *Will you move back this way so we can—*

CROWD: *Don't move!*

REPORTER: *There are four officers from the University of California police force, led by Lieutenant, badge No. 5—*

A student prompts Jack Weinberg: "Ask them what you're under arrest for." Weinberg complies.

LIEUTENANT CHANDLER: *If you were a student, and identified yourself, you would be disciplined by the dean's office. You're not identifying yourself. We're arresting you because you must be an outsider, then.*

WEINBERG: *What section?*

CHANDLER: *602-L. That's trespassing.* [There is a mild hubbub for ten seconds as students repeat the charge.]

VARIOUS VOICES: *Now, look, I'll tell you what—*
Will you swing over so we can get him?
No rough stuff.
Stay in your seat.
You get ready to get in his place and I'll slip down into this seat.

POLICE: *Will you come with us?*

GENERAL SHOUTS: *NO!!! BOOOOOOO!!*

The shouting goes on for twenty seconds. Then someone says, "One person has been taken away—Jack Weinberg, a member of Campus CORE. Jack Weinberger."

The noise swells so that his next sentence cannot be heard. Then the reporter shouts in surprise, "The entire group is sitting down!" (This is fifteen seconds after the loud shouting began when the police moved to take Weinberg away. The sound dies within another five seconds.)

The reporter continues, "The entire group which was standing there is sitting, blocking the way, locking arms in the traditional nonviolent—" Here shouts of "Booo!" begin again, presumably after people have found their seats.

The reporter goes on: "Two plainclothesmen from the Berkeley police, Inspector O'Meara of the Berkeley Red Squad, and the chief of police assisted in the arrest, wearing plain clothes." (At this point the tape ran out of Burton White's recorder, so that there is a break in the continuity while he turns over the reels. When he turns on the machine again, we hear: "Why can't we stay here if we want to?"

REPLY: *I would not do that!*

BURTON WHITE: *There's a group of students, both in front and in back of the car* [8]—*some dozen in front, some fifteen in back.*

The crowd begins to sing, "We Shall Not Be Moved." A newspaper reporter goes over to the police car and talks with Jack Weinberg: "You're not a student, are you?"

WEINBERG: *Pardon me.*
NEWSMAN: *Where were you, in front of the table?*
WEINBERG: *That's correct.*
NEWSMAN: *SNCC table?*
WEINBERG: *Campus CORE table.*
NEWSMAN: *You're a member of CORE: you're an officer of CORE in Berkeley?*
WEINBERG: *I'm a* member *of* [the] *campus chapter of CORE.*
NEWSMAN: *You're not a student, though, are you? A graduate—*
WEINBERG: *I'd rather not answer that question.*
NEWSMAN: *What's your name? I forget your name.*
WEINBERG: *My name is Jack Weinberg.* [He spells it.] *I've met you.*
BURTON WHITE (into the microphone): *And now the entire group, bit by bit, seems to be sitting.* [This announcement comes 40 seconds after the statement that there are a dozen persons in front and fifteen behind the car.] *The group which before was a dozen in front has become some 50, 75.*

The demonstrators begin singing, "We're fighting for freedom, we shall not be moved." White continues, "And as the singing goes on, more and more students pour in, sitting before the car."

Forty-five seconds after the last estimate of the number sitting down, someone shouts, "Has anyone seen Mario Savio?" Another voice replies, "Yes, he's right over here." (Other demonstrators later reported with great amusement seeing Savio come out of the Student Union building while they were sitting down, looking completely dumbfounded by what he saw.)

The demonstrators now begin singing "The Star-Spangled Banner." Within thirty seconds Mario Savio has climbed onto the police car. We can hear him talking to a policeman who protests.

SAVIO: *Would you like to arrest me?*
POLICEMAN: *I will. Sure. Very easily. I'm asking you to get off the car. Would you?*

SAVIO: *I may get off of it, but I'm not going to get—I'm not going to get—I'm not going to get away from in front of it.*

POLICEMAN: *O.K. You stand in front of it. You get off that car.*

People nearby begin shouting, "Who are you?" to Jamie Burton, a chemistry student who has appeared at the window of the dean of students office.

BURTON: *I'm one of the people who was downstairs! I'm upstairs talking to Dean Williams now. We're trying to get things settled so that we can get what we want!* [There are some shouts.]

SAVIO: *Let me tell you what's going on, folks.*

BURTON: *We can't help things as long as things are noisy down here, and as long as there's trouble down there we cannot talk up here in good faith!*

VOICE: *Talk! Talk! Talk! Talk! Talk!*

SAVIO (in a loud voice, as if giving a speech): *In a perfectly reasonable way this person, on his own initiative, has decided to act as a go-between between us and them. However, you know the conditions were this: that while they were talking up there we would be reasonably quiet down here, and so—some of us had agreed that we would, you know, just hold a nonnoisy rally at 12 o'clock. We didn't anticipate that while they were talking up there, in bad faith they would send their lackeys down here to arrest somebody.* [Cheers.] *Under those circumstances—*

BURTON: *This was* not *something that was done directly the dean's office. Dean Williams—*

VOICES: *Let the dean stop it!*

There is general shouting; then a voice cuts through, saying, "—a compromise proposal: Let the guy—release the guy. Don't bother people on tables until the end of negotiations, and we'll *quietly* disperse after the end of negotiations." (The speaker is drowned out by shouts, some cheers, and clapping.) Again, Burton calls for quiet while they are talking.

SAVIO: *We're staying right here until this guy is released.* [There are shouts of agreement with this sentiment.] *We will let the police car through only if he is first released from arrest. Now you* [garbled] *that!*

BURTON: *You're a bunch of fools!* [Boos.] *Look! You're asking too much!*

He is interrupted by various shouts: "NOOOO!" "So was the United States Constitution asking too much!" "Is the First Amendment too much?" "How about these people who were expelled?"

SAVIO (to the KPFA reporter): *I don't know his last name—Jamie Burton. He's a graduate student who on his own initiative—he says— has been acting as a go-between with the dean to try to reach a decent—*
VOICE: *Is he with Students for Goldwater? Or other—*
SAVIO: *He has not said, so far as I know.* [He shouts, happily.] *Folks! You know something! We were going to hold a rally here at 12 o'clock.*

The group begins chanting, in football game style, "LET HIM GO! LET HIM GO! LET HIM GO! LET HIM GO!" Gradually people begin clapping as they chant. This continues for thirty-five seconds. There is a burst of applause as Mario Savio takes off his shoes and climbs up on the car. Says the radio reporter, Burton White, "The officers are letting him up."

A number of persons claim to have been the first to sit down around the car. A foreign student who was making a film of scenes on the campus happened to have her movie camera in the Sproul Hall Plaza at the time of the incident. Unfortunately her single print of this film was lost in the mail a few months later, so that I have been unable to study it in detail. One faculty member who saw the film, however, believes that a nonstudent named Lennie Glaser began the capture by rolling under the car. (Lennie Glaser had gained local notoriety as a public advocate of the legalization of marijuana, and was considered something of a hophead by his critics. These perons saw the event as the reaction of excited students to the suggestion of a drug-influenced provocateur.) The accounts I have gathered from other students who sat down around the car within the first few seconds leave me skeptical of this explanation, though I do not doubt that Lennie Glaser was among the first to sit around the car.

Here is an account I gathered within the first two weeks after the event from Richard Roman, a graduate student in sociology, who believes that he provided the impetus.[9] I suspect that more than one person went through a process somewhat similar to that reported by Roman. His account may help make understandable this sudden decision by a number of students.

Dick Roman reports that he had not become involved in the controversy up to that point, though as a member (and former national chairman) of the Young People's Socialist League he had heard about it and had been totally sympathetic to the students. He had a luncheon date that day, and was walking across the plaza when he saw police arresting Jack Weinberg, with a crowd of between twenty and fifty people gathered around to watch. He saw uniformed policemen and two middle-aged men clearing a path for the policemen. (He assumed these men were administrators, but they must have been the Berkeley police chief and the "Red Squad" inspector.) The sight made Dick Roman angry. He says, "I thought, 'It's a pretty rotten thing for the university to expel and arrest someone.' It made me mad to see the university pulling this trick to punish a few—"

Dick Roman reports that he immediately thought of Bayard Rustin, the Negro civil rights and peace movement leader, whose sense of strategy Roman had come to admire when he had been in New York City a few years previously. What would Bayard Rustin have done in a similar situation? Immediately the words "collective displacement" came to him. Rustin used this term to describe a tactic he advocated when demonstrators believed that the police were moving unfairly against an individual in an effort to intimidate the rest. Rustin would urge the group to confront the police as a unit, so that the latter would have to deal with all of them, rather than with just a few people.

At this point, Roman recalls, he spoke out, suggesting that people step into the path of the police, rather than getting out of the way. He had nothing specific in mind except to refuse to cooperate with this act by the police. After he made this suggestion, he was shoved "by a fraternity type" and got angry. "Why don't you mind your own business!" he exclaimed. At this point, he says, two middle-aged men reached him and started shoving him aside.

Roman yelled, "Don't move out of the way!" Shoving, the police pulled Jack Weinberg through the crowd to the car. (He had gone limp in classic civil rights style.)

Roman thought, "Arrest everyone or no one!" He ran toward the front of the car while the policeman put Weinberg in the car. He began yelling for people to sit down in front of the car, and some obeyed him. He ran around to encourage others to do the same, waving his arms to motion them down. A few other people were also urging others to sit down. For example, he noticed a graduate student, whom he didn't know by name but recognized as being from the same department, encouraging people to sit down behind the car.

Given the events of the preceding day, I suspect that similar thoughts occurred to several people, who may have acted independently. At any rate, once the proposal was made by word and demonstration it was immediately imitated, first by about twenty-five persons, then by several hundred within a few minutes. One of the first persons to sit down described the incredulous expression on the face of the policeman at the wheel, who looked up just as he was about to turn the key in the ignition to start the car. Dick Roman, in contrast, remembers no noticeable police response at the time.

Here is an attempt to recreate the experience, recorded by Mike Rossman. He became a leader in the Free Speech Movement, which grew out of this event.

I was . . . present on the plaza . . . when Jack was arrested. The kids said . . . that they were going to put the stuff [the tables] back up the next day. . . . I figured that there was going to be some action, and, being a born sensation lover, I wanted to be present at the action. So I got there about 10:00, hung around. . . . I was waiting outside, sitting and chatting with a friend, I think. Perhaps with my sister.

. . . There was commotion and excitement, and somebody said, "They're arresting somebody." And then this car came up; there was a crowd arond it. I couldn't even see. I was somewhere north of where the car eventually was. . . .

They had got him [Weinberg] in the car, and the car was just starting to move, I think, so I sat down. I remembered San Quentin in 1960;[10] we sat down around the car then—20 of us—it was probably the first car sit-around on the coast, in recent times, and I was one of them. I hadn't sat around a car for four years.

I was not the first person to sit down. There were maybe ten people on each side of the car, seated, at the time I sat. . . .

I came over because (a) there was action there, to see what was going on; (b) they said they were arresting somebody, and here was this car, and they shouldn't arrest people—on the campus. . . . There was a big, confused scene. A lot of people standing up, moving walking. . . .

I was reacting; I wasn't thinking. There is a level of subthought that goes on. This is an accurate report of that level of subthought. Here was something that was happening, and time had to be stopped. If they took the kid away, whoever it was, then the kid would be taken away. The event would have been concluded, and you would have had to deal with the aftermath. One did not know whether you should let him be taken away or not. You didn't know what to do, so you wanted to halt time in order to figure it out. I've been in a couple of situations before when things have happened fast—like that first sit-around the car in 1960— and it's very unpleasant for things to happen fast. I would rather think than react. And so you want to stop time. The only possible way to stop time in that circumstance was to sit down around the car. . . . Just fix everything! Don't let anything move. In that sense, it wasn't so much "don't let them take Jack away"; it was "hold on a second, to figure out."

After a few minutes of sitting around, I started getting madder and madder. The word spread among the people who were sitting around, many of whom hadn't been there at the scene of the arrest, exactly what had transpired, what they had done. They had arrested a student. . . . Somewhere between ten seconds and two hours after we blocked the car—I'm sure it'll vary from person to person—it was no longer a question of stopping time. . . . At this point, Jack was in the car. One realized that it was crap that they were arresting him; furthermore, that they couldn't arrest him unless they could get that car out of here; and that they couldn't get that car out of here as long as there were x thousand people around the car. . . . We didn't know what we were going to do after that, but sitting around the car had been transformed from an arresting-time action to a positive action.[11]

A freshman girl reports:

I was in it from a few minutes before Jack was arrested, because of pressure from friends. . . . My boy friend and I were at the table when Jack was arrested. We were among the first to sit down, because John was already actively involved. I was rather dubious until sometime Thursday afternoon, the first day.

I didn't know the leaders or anything about them. I was impressed by some of the speeches they made, their rational logical analysis of the situation.

Normal procedures hadn't done anything, and it didn't look as though they were going to. Besides, they were too slow. I thought something had to be done immediately. I thought the administration's action was despicable. This was a wrong which had to be righted immediately because it would set a precedent for denying more and more rights.

I decided a few hours later that I had to participate, myself. . . . I decided that, if I believed in students' and citizens' rights, I was morally obligated to fight for them. . . . [I considered the possibility of] arrest, expulsion from school, difficulties in getting a job because of an arrest record, difficulty in getting into another school because of expulsion. But it didn't seem very likely at first. . . . It was a gamble whether any action would be taken, but if action was taken, the penalties seemed inevitable.[12]

A junior majoring in political science, a girl who had come to the campus the preceding spring, reports that she sat down because she saw it as an opportunity "to stop injustice *before* it began." She had joined the sit-in the preceding night and had decided at midnight (when the eight students were expelled) that she herself would have to participate. As she put it, action was necessary because "normal procedure was injustice." [12]

A graduate student in biochemistry reports that he acted on impulse when the administration ordered the arrest of Jack Weinberg. He wanted "to show the administration they couldn't get away with arbitrary action. . . . It was evident that the administration abandoned normal procedures, leaving the students little choice. . . . The administration was attempting to squelch the student protest by arrest and intimidation." [12]

A graduate student in nuclear engineering sat down as soon as he saw a small group surrounding the police car. He described the situation as:

an unfair arrest, a major crisis for student rights, an opportunity to assert our protest against coercion. . . . I decided to participate immediately—"bodies" were needed. People were needed then. If you used normal procedures, Jack Weinberg would have already been in jail by then. I considered the possibility of arrest, but considered it a gamble—somewhat likely, perhaps 4 : 1 odds. I decided I was going to play it by ear. . . . Students have the right of free speech.[12]

Many more people, of course, joined the seated demonstrators as the noon hour went on. Two accounts follow:

I intended to go to the noon rally. Then the cops brought a car to the plaza. I knew exactly what happened because I saw the arrest. . . . I decided to particpate when . . . Mario Savio . . . explained the background of the arrest. . . . I didn't consider any possible penalties, at first, but began to later.[12]

I came out, and here's this huge rally going—just thousands of people—I've never seen so many people in my life—and in the middle there's this big bump, but you can't see what the hell is there, you know —everybody's standing up beside it. You couldn't really see the bump; I guess I imagined it more than actually remember it. I asked somebody, "What the hell is going on?" and he said, "There's a car in there." And I said, "What's the car doing there?" and he said he didn't know. I thought maybe somebody'd driven it onto campus as a rallying thing, or something. So I walked out there to see what the hell it was, and there was that police car. I was sitting there for a couple, three hours—I walked out, I sat down, I met some chick there, or something, and I was listening to what the people had to say. Some of them appealed to me, some didn't. . . . I wanted to know what the hell they were saying. They said they were holding the police car until they let those people back in school; see, in the middle of the night they kicked those people out of school, and before all they'd said was they were being sent in for disciplinary action. . . . I thought, "If we hold out, maybe we can get them off and get something changed"—see. Now we had this police car, we had a double weapon. Well, I sat there, and I got more excited about the thing. . . . At this time I was real clean cut; white levis, button-down shirt, my hair was combed all the time.[13]

A freshman girl, who planned to major in art, wrote:

The night before, I participated in the vigil. I was dragged there by a friend, but was interested in the event, not just in the friend. . . . [When I got there on Thursday] there were already several hundred. People around me said, "Sit down; you're in the way." After listening to speakers, talking with friends on the scene, and thinking about it awhile, I decided to act. . . . I couldn't say "no". . . I was jazzed on the idea of hijacking a police car—such glorious irreverence! I was hooked on listening to the speakers. . . . The situation was made pretty clear almost immediately. . . .[12]

A sophomore in electrical engineering reports that he came over because he saw a large crowd and assumed a fight was going on. When he saw the surrounded car and the people sitting down, he joined them, without quite knowing why. After he talked with others there, he decided to stay, because he wanted to protest against the university.[12]

A new graduate student in library science writes:

I had been following the controversy. I went to Sproul Hall to see what was going on. I felt I had to stay when I heard the speakers. I thought their sincerity was unquestionable. I had no opinions about specific persons at that time. I was standing around a group of seated demonstrators. The speaker said, "Sit down if you are with us." I knew I was with them, so I sat down.[12]

When Mario Savio climbed on top of the car in Sproul Hall Plaza, the capture became a focused rally.

SAVIO: *We were going to hold a rally here at 12 o'clock. And we were going to have to shout our lungs out to get people. I'm so grateful to the administration of this wonderful university. They've done it for us! Let's give them a hand.* [Shouts of "Yea!"]

We must really feel very, very sorry for these poor policemen here, you know. Good men. They're fam-ily men, you know. They have a job to do! That's right, they have a job to do.

VOICE: *Just like Eichmann.*[14]

SAVIO: *Yeah. Very good! It's very, you know, like Adolph Eichmann.*[14] *He had a job to do. He fit into the machinery.* [Cheers and shouts of "Very good!" As Savio is talking, some sort of missile flies over his head but misses him.]

We are asking the following. We will not stop direct action against —against the administration of this university unless they accede to the following very simple and reasonable demands.

Number one: They must immediately, that is, the chancellor— Chancellor Strong, seeing as he's the one who did it—must immediately say that no students have been suspended from the university! [shouts of "Hooray!" Whistles and applause.]

Number two: Chancellor Strong—Chancellor Strong must agree to meet with representatives of the off-campus political organizations to discuss with them reasonable regulations governing freedom of speech on this campus, which means no arbitrary restrictions of any kind on freedom of speech on this campus! He must agree to such a meeting. That's demand number two! [Cheers and applause.]

Number three: The final demand is—the chancellor must agree that no disciplinary action will be taken against anyone setting up tables or speaking here until, at the very, very least, that meeting is held! ["Yea!!!!!" Whistles and applause.]

And I am right now publicly serving a notice of warning, and—I should say — a threat to this administration, that they—, they—they will be subject to continuous direct action by us, and it's going to be damned embarrassing for them. We're going to get foreign press, we're going to get domestic press, we're going to get all sorts of organizations against them until they accede to these legitimate demands! [Applause and cheers.]

Now, folks, here's what it is. A fellow who said that on his own initiative, which I have reason to doubt, [he] has been acting as a go-between between the administration and us—this fellow has now gone up to his friends in the administration—and he told us he's going to see if he can get them to drop charges—against this student who stood up for all of us. All right? Now, let us suppose that does not happen, and there's a good likelihood that it won't happen. All right, if that does not happen, I propose that everybody at this meeting, or as many as can fit, get into that damn building, get into Dean Towle's office, into Dean Arleigh Williams' office, into the offices, and just sit at the desks, just sit right in the chairs, just sit right on the floor, and make it absolutely impossible for them to conduct their work! [Cheers and applause.]

We can't really ask for too much more, can we?

At this point individual students begin asking Mario Savio questions about who he is, how he became the leader of the demonstration, who is in the car, and so forth. Savio identifies himself by name and explains that he is twenty-one years old and a junior in philosophy. He refuses to identify the person in the car, explaining:

. . . We can't tell who was arrested because he has refused to give his identification. I'd like to explain that, because there is really some legitimate difference of agreement as to whether the person should have given his identification. And I think there is a perfectly legitimate rationale for his not having done so. And it's this: There is on those reg

cards, and by general agreement people have—you know—been acceding to the demands of the university to identify themselves. Yesterday we did that. Over at Sather Gate, people sitting at a university Friends of SNCC table identified themselves in accordance with the demands, perhaps ill-considered and unjustified [demands] of the administration. And do you know what they did? They used that as a tool, as weapon to take eight . . . [Here the police radio comes on, blotting out Savio's voice.]

. . . They ignored 409 others who said they were doing the same thing. And so to protect ourselves—it's a simple matter of self-protection —we cannot accede to this demand that we identify ourselves until this administration is prepared to deal with us in a nondiscriminatory manner. . . .

All right. Now the question is, Why was *he arrested? All right, we can answer the question in two ways—at* least! *The police say he was arrested for—for violation of a trespass ordinance. All right. See?* [Chuckles from students sitting near Savio.] *I'll tell you why he was arrested in* my *opinion. He happens to be a person—and for reasons we don't need to go into right now, he happens to be a person—who has been quite outspoken in his disagreement with what the administration does. Furthermore, the people that they axed the other day were likewise people quite outspoken in their disagreement with what the administration does . . .* [The police radio drowns him out again] *. . . other people both today and yesterday who were violating the same regulations and laws. They happened to pick upon those people who are the most outspoken.*[15]

You know there's a story told—it appears in one of the tales that Herodotus tells . . . about the Persian Wars. He said—uh—it was this: A person wanted to know, how can we take over a particular city or country in the most effective way, and the following—the following parable was told.

Have you ever seen a wheat field? You see how there are some stalks of wheat that stand up above the others? It's very simple: don't cut them all down; just cut down the ones that stick up the highest. And you've won! Well, that's precisely what they did. They're smart to that extent, at any rate. That's why they arrested him! [applause.]

A light tenor voice interrupts, saying, "Mario, let me speak."

Savio replies, "We believe in freedom of speech. I don't know what this fellow wants to say, but I'd like to have him say it." As Charles Powell, the student body president, climbs up on the car beside Savio, sarcastic voices call out, "Our e—lect—ed rep—re—*sent*—a—tive!"

"Oh, I know who this person is," says Savio. "You know, I didn't recognize him at first!" The crowd laughs and shouts. Someone calls, "This isn't Monday!" (At the picketed convocation Powell had received an award for being an outstanding student.)

POWELL: *I'm Charlie Powell, ASUC president, and I'd like to try to serve somewhere in the in-between.* [Shouts of approval and disapproval, and calls of "Let him speak!"]

I would ask those who are fighting for this just cause, I think that you have real reason, and I think that I see that your reason is just. [Applause and shouts.] *I think that you believe in what you stand for. I think the Senate—the Senate in the last four or five years—has never taken a more determined and definite stand than it has this year!*

HECKLER: *It wasn't* very *definite!*

POWELL: *So I propose this. You'll let me speak for you. I will go to Dean Williams and Dean Towle and ask that this one boy, here, be allowed to go free.*

VOICES: *What about the other eight?*

POWELL: *Just a minute, I'll get to the others. This one is the immediate problem, all right?*

VOICES: *No!*

POWELL: *Just a minute.*

WEINBERG (leaning out of the police car): *I'm not the immediate problem. We're all together!* [Cheers.]

POWELL: *"All right, I'll speak to the—* ["Yea!!!"] *I'll speak for the freedom of this boy right here!* [Shouts of "Speak for all of them, for all the other eight!"] *All right! I'll propose, at the same time, to ask why the other eight were singled out, to ask what can be done to free them also. All right! At the same time while I'm asking for the freedom of these nine, I ask all of you to allow the Senate, which is now considering what can be done* [laughter]—*what should be done for the interest of the entire student body—"* [He is interrupted by laughter and applause.]

I ask that you give the Senate a week's time— [Boos, whistles, and a voice near at hand asking "Why don't you want a year?"] *A week's time to consider—*

VOICE: *You've got two more minutes.*

POWELL: *To consider several things. The administration will not allow soliciting of membership and funds; we will ask, we will look into the possibility of buying the Bancroft-Telegraph entrance* [Shouts of "Sather Gate!"], *which can now be done.*

VOICES: *It's not the place—it's the principle! We want this a free university, not just a part of it!*

POWELL: *At the same time I promise to you that we'll look into— that we'll investigate as thoroughly as possible and farther than any Senate has gone before—* [shouts from hecklers] *into the possibility of allowing solicitation of members and of funds in the nine different places that are specified.* [A small round of applause.]

Now it seems to me that my demands are reasonable enough, compared with Mario Savio's. Now I ask you—

VOICES: *No!!*

POWELL: *I ask you, I ask you to give me a chance to speak with the dean's office about these nine people.* [Shouts of "Go ahead! Sure!"] *And at the same time, give me the chance, give the Senate the chance, within a week to come with something that will be satisfactory.*

Some people shout, "Go ahead!" Others shout, "No!" Powell's statement brings a general vociferous response.

POWELL: *Will you let me do this?*

VOICES: *Why don't you take Mario? Trying to divide the campus?*

POWELL: *Mario will go with me!* [Burst of applause.]

SAVIO: *Ah, I hope, one second. First—uh—there is one thing I want to announce. That one condition I hope Mr. Powell is willing to consider. It's fine. I love to talk with people, I really do, and—uh—I'll be glad to go. Well—I'll go with Charlie Powell to see these people. All right, but—I want it understood that until this person in this car is placed, you know, out of arrest, nobody will move from here.* [Applause, shouts, cheers.]

Savio announces that Weinberg wants them to know his case remains tied to the other eight and then says, "Now, look. I'm going to go with Charlie Powell *now.* While I'm gone there's someone else with a slightly different point of view who would like to speak: Hal Draper." The crowd cheers.

As Charlie Powell and Mario Savio left the scene, Hal Draper climbed up on the car and gave a brief resumé of his review of Kerr's book. The definition of the situation had been set.[16]

SIX
ESCALATION

Mario Savio and Charlie Powell were gone from the police car for about an hour, talking first with the deans and then with Chancellor Strong and Vice-Chancellor Sherriffs. There is no detailed account of the latter meeting in the chancellor's files, but it apparently began with a discussion of rules governing student use of university facilities. Strong insisted that no rules had been changed—that, in fact, their "clarification" on Monday had, if anything, made them more liberal. Savio strongly disagreed. The conversation that followed did not bring them any closer to a meeting of minds.[1]

In the meantime the rally from the top of the car continued. Hal Draper presented his critique of Clark Kerr's educational philosophy, likening the university to a factory and explaining the immediate events in terms of this model. Then Dick Roman described how the police car capture had begun. He stressed that the university was trying "to break the back of protest" and urged students to stick together so that "next time they will have to arrest all of us or none of us." Roman invited an opposition speaker to come forward, so that the car could be turned into a genuine "free speech forum." [2]

Eventually opposition speakers did present themselves. An informal debate, which continued over an hour, followed. The first of the opposition speakers, Don Hackett from the university Young Republicans, began his remarks with these words: "Conservatives are against the actions of the university, too! We will protest their actions by all *legal* means. . . ." As the debate went on, the argument remained within these boundaries. It considered, not whether allegations against the administration were correct, but whether the capture of a police car was a proper means of response to the wrong.[2]

Savio and Powell returned from their meeting with Chancellor Strong about 1:45 P.M. They reported the chancellor had said that the university would not yield to pressure, that the suspensions would stand, and that a meeting was possible only if the demonstration ceased. Powell again asked the demonstrating students to allow the ASUC to consider the matter, asking for a week's time. When his proposal was refused by the shouting crowd, he left.

The impromptu rally continued throughout the afternoon from the top of the police car. The debate went forward sporadically. Eventually folk singers with guitars appeared, including a few professional singers who lived in Berkeley. They sang freedom songs.

During that first afternoon two additional personalities emerged as leaders of the demonstration. Dustin Miller, a former fraternity member with a strong sense of humor and the advantage of *looking* like a Greek-letter man in his white levis and button-down shirt, became an informal master of ceremonies; his humor was well received. About 4 P.M. a girl decided to speak, because she felt some of the other speakers were losing sight of the reasons why the police car had been seized in the first place. It took her about half an hour to get up enough nerve, but once she climbed up on the car her style—which reminded many faculty members of that common among radical speakers of the nineteen thirties—had a militancy that struck an instant response from the demonstrators. This girl, whose name was Bettina Aptheker, remained on top of the car much of the time for the rest of the demonstration. Her presence as one of the leading spokesmen for the demonstrators added a further element of controversy to the exchanges that took place, for her father is Herbert Aptheker, one of the leading Communist intellectuals in this country. Her prominence in the demonstration led a number of observers to speculate that it might be a Communist-inspired riot.[3]

As the afternoon wore on, students began a deliberate "escalation," which was to lead to a number of unexpected repercussions. About 2:30 P.M. Mario Savio suggested that, if the administration would not meet with them, the students might well force their way into Sproul Hall: "I recommend that 500 of you stay here around this auto and others join me in taking our request back to the deans." Savio then led about 150 students into Sproul Hall, where they sat outside the office of the dean of students.

About 4:00 P.M. Jackie Goldberg decided to enter the dean's office to

make an appointment with Dean Towle or anyone else who would talk
with her. Here is how she later described the encounter:

*. . . As I walked up and tried to make an appointment with Dean
Towle, or Dean Williams, or any other of the deans that I knew, I
walked up to the front. People were seated. There were aisles and everything else, we weren't blocking, no sit-in or anything. They were just
waiting, and I walked up and I was just ready to enter the dean's office
when there were about three policemen and four secretaries standing
behind them. And the policeman told me that if I tried to enter the office I would be arrested for assault and battery against the secretary.
And at that point I did one of the most irrational things! Like I say, I
just did something very irrational. I just said, "Well, if you're not going
to let us in, we're not going to let you out!" And that's when I asked
people to block the doorway, for which I was later cited. We kept them
blocked for quite a while. . . .*[4]

With that a "pack-in" of the Sproul Hall corridor outside the office
of the dean of students began, students moving tightly together to prevent anyone from entering or leaving the office. (The *Daily Californian*
estimated that about 400 students took part in this event.) This pack-in
created a far more explosive situation, because of a series of reactions it
triggered.

A group of faculty members in the Sociology Department in nearby
Barrows Hall noted the renewed sit-in and decided it provided an opportunity for them to serve as negotiators between students and administration. Meeting in Professor S.M. Lipset's office at the urging of Professors Nathan Glazer and William Petersen, the group proposed that
students leave Sproul Hall as a "gesture of good faith." This would
allow the faculty to intercede with Chancellor Strong to set up a meeting with the belligerents. Most of the faculty members present went to
the chancellor's office, where they had a two-hour meeting with three of
the vice-chancellors.

John Leggett, a young assistant professor in the Sociology Department, was given the task of telling the students what had been decided,
while the others talked with administrators. After the other faculty
members left Lipset's office, Leggett began to wonder what would happen if Chancellor Strong refused to meet with his colleagues. Leggett's
sympathies lay heavily with the demonstrators; consequently he went to

Sproul Hall and urged them to remain inside until they received word that the faculty group had successfully arranged a meeting with members of the administration. The students agreed to this proposal, and John Leggett returned to his office.

While the students inside Sproul Hall waited for word that the faculty had been able to talk with members of the chancellor's staff, administrators waited for word that the students had left Sproul Hall. Thus each side was inadvertently provided with "tangible evidence" of the "intractable bad faith" of its opponents.[5]

About 6:00 P.M., when no sign of withdrawal was seen, the police in Sproul Hall were ordered to close the building, and they began locking the doors. Demonstrators, aware that this was not the normal closing time, rushed to jam the doors so that the building could not be locked. Students linked arms to prevent the police from removing them from the doorways. In the melee that resulted, several students were stepped on by police trying to get through. As the police and students struggled, one girl's hair was pulled painfully and she screamed loudly. A group of male students then grabbed a policeman, pulled him down, and took off his boots. As he struggled to free himself, someone bit him in the leg. (The police reported the assailant was Mario Savio.) Students remained in Sproul Hall, and the doors stayed open.[6]

This riotous behavior added a very sour note, however, to the attempted negotiations in progress in the chancellor's office. The faculty group had met with the vice-chancellors for two hours; then S.M. Lipset and William Kornhauser talked with Chancellor Strong for another two and a half hours. At first Strong was receptive to their suggestion that Weinberg be set free, but he changed his mind after Joseph Lohman, dean of the School of Criminology at Berkeley and his police adviser, warned that the campus police would be badly demoralized if he took such an action. Lipset and Kornhauser left Strong's office, unsuccessful in their quest, about 9:00 P.M.[7] When the faculty members returned to Sproul Hall and explained what had happened, the students voluntarily withdrew from the building.

By coincidence, the first Interfraternity Council meeting of the year had been scheduled for Thursday evening, October 1. Dean Louis Rice, who had responsibility for relations with fraternity groups, was late to the meeting because he had to leave the dean's office by climbing out over a roof. As he ate supper in the kitchen of the fraternity house where the meeting was scheduled, a number of the boys asked why he was late and laughed with him about the lack of dignity involved in such an exit. A few minutes later the meeting began, attended by the president of every fraternity on campus.

The first item on the agenda was a talk by Sergeant Skeels of the Berkeley Police Department, who had been invited to speak about the importance of cooperating with the police and having respect for law and order within the fraternities. Next came a series of reports from standing committees, including an announcement of preparations for Family Day on campus two days later, when parents would be invited to visit. After a number of other items (the Interfraternity Council-Panhellenic retreat, the election of fraternity representative for student government, the IFC's Big Brother project, Fall Rush, and a report from the Interfraternity Council president, Rod Maricin) Dean Rice was asked to report on the situation on campus. Members of the Interfraternity Council then discussed briefly how the council might be of help to the administration in this crisis. Dean Rice said he wanted the fraternity system to know that the university had appreciated their general support of the administration: "We have had many calls from fraternities and fraternity men asking, 'How can we help?' We welcome your responsible involvement."

The group decided that its Executive Committee would reach other campus organizations, seeking ideas for constructive programs to help resolve the crisis. The IFC president urged the various house presidents to keep communication channels open among themselves so that they could call meetings rapidly in case new developments made joint consultation helpful. After the meeting ended about 8:30 or 9:00 P.M.,[8] Dean Rice returned to Sproul Hall, remaining outside in the plaza to watch the demonstration.

Shortly before 11 P.M., Arleigh Williams received a call from the campus police that large numbers of male students were gathering at Channing Circle; this was the traditional signal for a fraternity-based collective outburst at the university. He hurried over, hoping to dissuade them from adding further tension to the scene. By the time he arrived, however, the circle was empty.

It is difficult to reconstruct what happened next, for later campus reactions to the events left few people willing to talk about their roles in

the affair. Dean Rice believes that three groups of male students converged just outside the Bancroft-Telegraph entrance to the campus.
One group apparently came down from Channing Circle, another from
Larry Blake's, a popular fraternity drinking place, and a third from the
Monkey Inn, another beer-drinking spot popular with fraternity members. (These are hearsay reports, rather than firmly documented descriptions.)

Dean Rice reports he saw a large number of persons coming down
the mall toward the seated demonstrators, shouting, chanting, and hol-
lering. They quickly encountered a wall of people standing on the edge
of the demonstration; the new arrivals spilled around toward Sproul
Hall, climbing the steps and forming a half-moon to the east of the police car demonstrators. They did not try to enter the area occupied by
the seated demonstrators. Dean Rice recognized many fraternity men in
the crowd, including some of the "bigger boys"—athletes and other
men from a wide range of houses. His impression that the preponderance of these fraternity men came from the rougher houses may well
have been influenced by the fact that some members of these fraternities
were among the loudest hecklers. At any rate Dean Rice recognized fraternity men from the north side of the campus as well as the south side
(near Channing Circle), but noted also that a number of persons with
them were not fraternity members.

(Not quite 3% of the male students included in Kathleen Gales's
spring survey reported that they had actively opposed the police car
demonstrators. This low percentage holds for all groups except apartment dwellers majoring in the humanities or the social sciences and fraternity men. Neither apartment dwellers nor fraternity men from the humanities and the social sciences reported taking part. Thirteen per cent
of the fraternity men with other majors said that they had participated.
We have no basis on which to judge the accuracy of this self-reporting.)

Dean Rice noticed that there seemed to be two or three nuclei within
the crowd of hecklers. He circulated from group to group, talking with
them and debating the appropriateness of their action. He reports that
some of the fraternity presidents were doing the same thing.

A KPFA tape made on October 1, 1964, begins about a half hour
after the antidemonstrators had gathered. In the meantime, the station's
reporter informs us, the antidemonstrators had been shouting to get the
car moved. "They wanted to get the car out."

A professor of history, Charles Sellars, temporarily had calmed things when he climbed on the car and talked to both groups, but it is clear from the background noise on the tape that the situation had become heated again.[9] At one point a member of the antidemonstration grabbed the microphone after a scuffle with a person speaking from the top of the police car and said:

. . . Listen. I am a student here at the university, obviously, and so are most of us. Now, you people that are sitting down are for this demonstration. The people that are standing up are against it. Now it seems to me—Listen! Listen! It seems to me that if this is a student demonstration, if this is a student body as a whole speaking, the people sitting down are outnumbered! [Shouting] I think they ought to give up and go home!

By now a small fight had broken out on a nearby rooftop, which was crowded with observers trying to see what was going on. After a period of confused yelling, the police car demonstrators started chanting, to each other and to observers, "Sit down, sit down, sit down, sit down" and then "We want freedom! We want freedom!"

After a short while the tape records the sound of people moving, much talking, and some singing. The narrator reports that some of the people in the police car demonstration have moved to the Sproul Hall steps and are arguing with the antidemonstrators.

An excited student with a shrill, high-pitched voice took the microphone and introduced himself as a freshman.

I'm not gonna say that I'm for or against you in the back or that I'm for or against you in the front! Now, what you guys are doing back there is stupid! If you want to get your point across—I'm not saying that I'm for them—but if you want to get your point across, send somebody up here and get your point across against somebody from this side!

Don't—don't sit there. Just a second. Don't—don't sit there, don't sit there and give cheers. And don't sit there—you, here—and don't sit there and sing songs. And you don't sing songs. But get—get together here! Send one man up, and have one man—have your best man come up and debate it here! Not songs. One second—one second

—one second—one second! You're not—you're not fighting, one group against the other group! Send one man up! . . .

A graduate student who was a dormitory counselor presented a polished and reasoned challenge to the position being taken by those around the police car. But it is clear from the heckling in the background that not even the antidemonstrators were with him.

Savio tried to rebut the graduate student's position but was shouted down by the opposition. Then a student got up on the car who, judging from the shouts of approval in the background, stated the situation as seen by many of the antidemonstrators.

Hey, wait a minute, fellows. Hey, look! [Whistles.] *Hey! O.K., I'm a Freddie, so you can hiss and you can cheer. A lot of us—a lot of us Freddies—are down here because it's a hot Thursday night.* [Police car demonstrators shout, "Right!"] *All right.* [Antidemonstrators shout, "Shut up!"] *Hey, wait! Hold it. In a way this is wrong. It's—all right, some of them are down here because they say they've got an issue. I've been here for five years trying to get out of engineering school. I've seen 'em all the way from the time they were picketing ROTC. The thing that makes me personally sick—and this is our side of the issue—it seems like it's always the same people.*

I don't know whether you're students or not. But it looks like it's always the same people with a cause, every week!

Here the hecklers begin to shout approval and to applaud. The speaker continues: "This is—this is part of the issue! All right! This is a minority part of the university. The Greeks are still a minority. I think they've got maybe, 10%. That's not a very big majority. They don't represent the university either." There is a moment of silence, followed by cheers and applause from the seated demonstrators.

But listen! You talk about free speech and freedom! Well, we can always find a—we can always pick a rule. You can't get up in a movie theater and yell, "Fire." So this is freedom. We could come down here and picket about that, too.

The fact that this car is here! This car is checked out to an officer. He's an American. He ought to have a right to drive it out of here if he wants to! [Cheers and applause.]

This car has been damaged! Maybe it will be paid for, and maybe it won't. [Seated demonstrators yell, "It will!" A reply is shouted: "By WHOM?"] *But the first time this car was bought, it was bought with taxes!*

At this point a number of people break in, yelling a variety of replies. The KPFA reporter interviews demonstrators, and part of the speech is lost. But we can still hear the following: "The administration and the secretaries shouldn't have to leave through a back window to get out of Sproul Hall! [Cheers in the background.] That's how Dean Rice got out of there, too! That isn't right. That isn't freedom, either. I hope they give the police back their car!"

At this point the tape ran out, and some time was lost in putting a new one in the recorder. When the new tape begins,[10] the seated demonstrators are singing, "We Shall Overcome," which seems to have become their theme song, expressing their sense of unity with the civil rights movement.

There is general excitement as a fire truck drives onto the plaza, and antidemonstrators begin chanting, "Hose 'em! Hose 'em!" Speakers on top of the car urge demonstrators to remain calm. The fire truck, it develops, was answering a false alarm, and it soon leaves.

The KPFA reporter announces that students outside the crowd of seated police car demonstrators have begun throwing eggs, fruit, and vegetables. Mario Savio urges people who are "part of the demonstration for freedom of speech on this campus" not to speak, but to remain absolutely calm.

There is shouting in the background, and one loud voice cuts through the others, asking why they chose to stop the car and to keep it there. Mario Savio begins to explain the position of the demonstrators, but there are shouts from the opposition: "Buy the car from the university and *then* stand on it!" (By this time, the weights of successive speakers on top of the car have caused the top to buckle.)

Savio tries to continue with his explanation: "We told Dean Towle that we had been doing these things for many years. We asked her—."

A heckler interrupts: "You may have masturbated for many years, too! We don't care!"

Finally Savio interrupts his explanation to ask the hecklers, "What do you want?"

There are shouted replies: "The car!" Other speakers try to continue but are shouted down. "All we want is let the policemen have their automobile!"

Savio points out that the demonstrators voluntarily withdrew from Sproul Hall as a symbol of their respect for law and order, and that they expected the administration to make a response.

VOICES (shouting): *Give up the car! Yes or no?*
SAVIO: *It's not as simple as that.*
VOICES: *It is!* [Continued heckling in the background.]

Savio begins a complicated philosophical defense of the demonstrators' position, saying, ". . . Think a little more deeply." He is answered by more shouts: "Get off the car!" Savio pleads with the crowd to listen to him.

VOICE: (shouting): *If you don't like Cal, go someplace else!* [Cheers from antidemonstrators.]
SEVERAL VOICES: *Hey! You got a reg card?*
SAVIO: *Look—the only reason that I took part in this is that I like Cal very much. I'd like to see it better. I'm not here to destroy something! We're all here to try to* build *something! Why don't you help us?* [He asks the police to explain their position to the antidemonstrators.] *Listen! No one of the police is asking me to get off.*
ANGRY VOICE: *You know they can't do that without the administration's approval! You know that! You're not an idiot! You know that!*
SAVIO: *O.K., what about a representative from the administration?*
VOICE: *Get off the car and we'll listen!* [Someone suggests that the policemen might be willing to provide a table for the speakers to stand on.]

Savio begins telling about Thoreau, who opposed the war that would make free territory belonging to Mexico slave territory belonging to the United States. He says that Thoreau felt so strongly that he committed civil disobedience as a witness against the war. There are chants from the background: "We want Thoreau! We want Thoreau!"

Asks Savio, "Do you agree that there are times when questions of conscience exceed questions of law?" Something is thrown at him.

Savio, in a somewhat shaky voice, leads the demonstrators in singing, "We Shall Overcome." The crowd in back begins chanting, "We want the car!" Then, as the SNCC theme song continues, the opposition begins a song of its own: "M-I-C-K-E-Y M-O-U-S-E! Mickey Mouse, Mickey Mouse—" (This is the theme song from a children's television show.)

At this point a number of policemen emerge from Sproul Hall, standing behind the antidemonstrators on the steps and observing the scene. Savio announces, "We're going to all get off the automobile and stand around, and only one person, the person speaking, be on at a time." There is a shout: "WE WANT THE CAR!" People in the middle of the crowd begin pushing into the sitting demonstrators.

Dustin Miller than gets on the car and, combining humor and sarcasm, tries to tell the antidemonstrators why those sitting around the police car have lost faith in the university administration. As he talks, eggs fly, and one hits a policeman. Miller invites a speaker from the opposition to come up and debate. Instead, a bystander who claims to side with neither group tries to talk to both sides. He is rebutted by a third-year law student who is in the demonstration and who insists that those surrounding the police car are upholding law and order:

We stand on the highest law. We stand on the First Amendment, the Fourteenth Amendment, of the Constitution of the United States. That's the law we stand on. . . . We have the car surrounded, correct? It's force; we know that. You have us surrounded, and you're standing there. You're not able to get to us. We're going to stay here all night. You know that. The issue is joined. We have offered—again and again, recognizing these facts, recognizing where we are located—we have offered to have you send a representative up here to debate the issue.

Jerry Goldstein, vice-president of the student body, then climbs on top of the car and says, "It is a very, very disappointing thing. As an elected representative of the students—my name is Jerry Goldstein. I'm first vice-president of the student body. I'm a member of a fraternity and have been in good standing—"

HECKLER: *Oh, boy! The Hebrew Hilton!*

GOLDSTEIN: *At this moment I am more ashamed of being vice-presi-*

dent of this student body than I could be of anything in the world. I cannot get off here when there exists a potential danger at this moment that could cause many people to be hurt seriously. . . . The idealism of a cause is being fought for. Whether this be the correct means or not is one issue. But violence is not the way to correct it.

He tries to persuade both sides that they will be injured and that there will be arrests if the encounter continues. There are shouts: "Jerry! Get off the car! All we want is the car!"

GOLDSTEIN: *The police have asked me to come up here. . . . Heckling and violence are not going to solve this problem. These people couldn't get this car out of here if they had to, with all of you around. Oh, incidentally, the car is also broken. It couldn't be moved.*

VOICE (shouting): *Who broke it?*

Jerry Goldstein tries to reason with the antidemonstrators and the seated students alike, urging them all to go home. It is clear from crowd responses that he is getting nowhere. Goldstein asks the police to clear a path between the two groups and then turns back to the antidemonstrators, saying, "I am willing to negotiate—and move the car, yes. But negotiations can't proceed when you guys are kicking everybody here and forcing them closer."

There is a call: "We're going to GET the car if you don't move it!" Jerry Goldstein replies:

You're going to get the car? And maybe happen to kill a few people in the way, huh? Yeah, really good, that's excellent. Are you kidding me? These are college students. These are University of California college students. [Shouting begins in the background.] *I thought you were going to give me a few minutes to negotiate. How about starting to clear this path so I can do it?"* [Shouts from the background: "Negotiate!"]

A lighted cigarette is thrown into the crowd of seated demonstrators. General conversation breaks out; then applause is heard as a priest pushes his way through the crowd and climbs on top of the car. As a deep silence settles over the crowd, Father Fisher of Newman Hall begins to speak. He speaks slowly, as if giving a sermon. The crowd remains absolutely silent. The priest introduces himself and says:

I'm not a student. I once was. I don't whether I'm the only impartial member of this crowd. I think I know some of the issues that are involved. But the right of free speech, great as it is, and the right of authority, greatly as it must be respected, should not be brought into conflict if a human life is going to be endangered.

John Kennedy once asked, "Do not ask what your country can do for you, but what you can do for your country." And what you can do for your countrymen is to respect their differences without bloodshed. And hatred begets bloodshed. The kind of catcalling that's going to go on here will get worse as the night goes on, unless somebody calms down.

He who hates his brother is a murderer. And those who begin in hatred and resort to abuse, are going to produce murder. It is easy in a crowd to get carried away. It's a lot harder to face yourself in the mirror in the morning.

I'm not sure of all the issues involved. But I am convinced that in a free society rational men can discuss and solve their differences without bloodshed. You presumably have come to this university because you are rational men seeking to perfect your rationality. Tonight is your chance to prove it.

I have nothing more to say.

Father Fisher was greeted by applause lasting thirty-nine seconds. Listening to the tape, one assumes that the crowd will disperse at this point. Then someone calls, "Get off the car now, huh?" Another voice issues a challenge: "Can I ask a question? What basis is there for rationality if it is not within a framework of law?"

With this, a chorus of voices shouts, "Hooray!" Taunting questions are again directed to Jerry Goldstein: "Are you going to move the car? Very simple, yes or no."

Someone in the seated crowd of demonstrators shouts, "No!" Those around him respond, "Shhhh!"

The antidemonstrators turn the question to Mario Savio: "Ask fuzzy. Which one, fuzzy?" [The comment refers to his haircut.] There is silence from the demonstrators, except for a chorus of "Shhh! Shhh!" One demonstrator tries to speak, but his companions shush him. For three minutes and forty-five seconds there is no sound from the demonstrators except a continuing chorus of "Shhh, shhhh," admonishing one another not to reply.

Antidemonstrators continue to heckle and debate in the background and to applaud one another's points. Gradually their calls become more subdued and finally sound almost plaintive: "Has Slate ever given in? Has Slate ever compromised?" They are greeted by silence, except for the continuing chorus of "Shhh! Shhh!" among the demonstrators seated around the car.

Then Dean Rice climbs on top of the car and says, "My name is Rice. And I'm a member of the administration. And I know *most* of you fraternity men out there. And I'm not up here to answer any questions. I'm up here just to ask you to cooperate with us and to request you to go home."

He is answered by shouts from the background: "If they'd at least take the car out, we'd *go!*" "Ask *them* to go home!" "O.K., you requested it." "Dean Rice, you tell *them* to go home."

For a minute thereafter the silence from the seated demonstrators continues, broken only by occasional heckling and answering "shhhh's." There is a shout: "If the Berkeley police think it's fair for CORE to have a car and Slate to have a car, give us a car, too, and we'll go home! [Cheer.] IF THEY HAVE A CAR, TOO, WE WANT ONE OF OUR OWN!"

The seated demonstrators continue to admonish one another, "Shhh! Shhhh!" This goes on for another sixty seconds; then the KPFA announcer reports:

There is still a hard knot, but large numbers of people have just drifted away, one by one. The police are moving down the steps. As they come in, the people they stand next to, leave. There is quiet from the demonstrators. Two hundred people stand on the Student Union balcony, watching.

A minute later, the announcer reports that the loudest group has left for the corner of Bancroft and Telegraph. Within another half minute only about twenty people are left from the antidemonstrators, and perhaps twenty or thirty standees remain with the seated demonstrators. On the tape the sounds of a crowd leaving can be heard in the distance. Within another half minute everything is very quiet. There is only the sound of subdued conversation and an occasional "shhh."

The demonstrators remained around the car. Nothing had been settled.

The police car capture drew newspaper and television coverage far beyond the San Francisco area.[11] The events of the day and the evening led a number of persons to issue public statements that night.

From California Governor Edmund G. Brown:

I support fully the stand of U.C. President Clark Kerr and Berkeley Chancellor Edward W. Strong.

This is not a matter of freedom of speech on the campuses. I and President Kerr and the Regents have long fought to maintain freedom of speech and an Open Forum policy on all campuses of the University.

This is purely and simply an attempt on the part of the students to use the campuses of the University unlawfully by soliciting funds and recruiting students for off-campus activities.

This will not be tolerated. We must have—and will continue to have —law and order on our campuses.[12]

From Berkeley Chancellor Edward W. Strong:

Because two facts respecting University policies on students and student organizations are still being misunderstood or misrepresented by some persons, I want again to emphasize these two facts:

1. The University's policy prohibiting planning and recruiting on campus for off-campus political and social action, and prohibiting also the solicitation or receipt of funds for such purposes, is now and always has been the unchanged policy of the University.

2. The University has not restricted or curtailed freedom of speech of students on campus by any change of its own Open Forum policy.

No instance of a newly imposed restriction or curtailment of freedom of speech on campus can be truthfully alleged for the simple reason that none exists.

Freedom of speech by students on campus is not the issue. The issue is one presented by deliberate violations of University rules and regulations by some students in an attempt to bring about a change of the University policy prohibiting use of University facilities by political, social, and action groups.[12]

From Charles Powell, ASUC president:

The facts are these:

The prohibition on the solicitation of funds and membership on campus for partisan issues is not a ruling of the Chancellor or of President Clark Kerr. It is, in fact, a State law.

Therefore, the only rational and proper action at this point is to seek changes in the law. Those opportunities are not here on the campus—but in the houses of the State Legislature.

In a conference with President Kerr, I have been told that mob violence and mass demonstrations directed at the Administration will, in no way, do anything to alleviate the problem. In fact, we are indeed losing support among the Regents for concessions which have already been made.

I am certain, and President Kerr has confirmed this fear, that if demonstrations such as today's continue, we will lose the Open Forum policy. This is a tradition for which all students and President Kerr have fought long and hard, and one which we need not lose.

I appeal to my fellow students. I ask that you not oppose the Administration—the Administration can do nothing to meet the demands being made. But this I do ask: write your state legislators, then give your full-hearted support to the ASUC Senate which will ask the property at Bancroft and Telegraph be deeded to the City of Berkeley for municipal administration.

Above all, I ask you to discontinue demonstrations which are endangering lives, property, and the Open Forum policy which the entire University community enjoys.[12]

From Mona Hutchins, vice-president of the University Society of Individualists, which had been part of the United Front:

The conservative groups fully agree with the purpose of the sit-ins in Sproul Hall. Individual members of our organizations have expressed their sympathy by joining in the picketing on the steps of the Hall, and will continue to do so.

However, our belief in lawful redress of grievances prevents us from joining the sit-on. But, let no one mistake our intent. The United Front still stands.[12]

seven

CLIMAX

Late in the evening of October 1, President Clark Kerr returned home from an all-day meeting of the American Council on Education in San Francisco.[1] He found calls waiting for him from administrators on the Berkeley campus. One would gather, from memoranda to the files written in the chancellor's office the next day, that Kerr communicated a strong request to clear up the situation on the plaza, to book the man in the car and then release him, and to prevent any further sit-ins in Sproul Hall.

Later—Strong called the President, and CK said he didn't think the time to act was with thousands around—but he said—he wanted it done by 4 o'clock in the morning—so all cleared out by Family Day. (AES on other phone.) He said he had been trying to get moving on authorization of National Guard but Governor is in Los Angeles with Humphrey.

Strong expects Kerr to back him up on this as it is the only way to own responsibility to have him bring in the number of police officers required to remove the demonstrators tonight when the smallest group is there. Lohman said—we have a program now and will proceed.

Strong expects Kerr to back him up on this as it is the only way to get them out.

. . . During the day October 1 the President was asked to put national guard on 45 minute alert.[2]

Joseph Lohman, dean of the School of Criminology, and O.W. Campbell, vice-chancellor in charge of campus police, immediately went into action, consulting the various police chiefs in the area.

The unanimous opinion of all these people was that 4:00 A.M. was the worst time to get these people out. . . .[3]

October 2, 1964
7 A.M.

MEMORANDUM FOR FILES:

Stopped at Sproul Hall on way to work—crowd very quiet. Wood-ward estimates it at about 200. The attached is being handed out.

Woodward says that the latest idea is that the students will formally and grandly offer the car back to the police at 12 o'clock today. When I asked why this gesture he said he supposed that the car had "served its purpose."

I asked him whether it had been possible anytime during the night to get the car out of [the] plaza without violence. He said they had worked on this all night—and that the leader of the fraternity boys had tried to work out an agreement with the leader of the sit-downers, but that noth-ing was possible. I wanted to make sure on this point, since Kerr will want to know, no doubt, why we didn't get the car out.

I left Woodward, and he said, pitifully, "I hope this day brings some good decision."

Kitty [4]

Meanwhile, a variety of "neutral bodies" were offering their services as mediators of the dispute. After a series of meetings between Protes-tant, Catholic, and Jewish student religious groups and leaders of the demonstration, Rabbi Joseph Gumbiner arranged an appointment with the dean's staff and with Dr. Saxton Pope, an assistant to Vice-Chancel-lor Sherriffs. The religious leaders tried to present the *grievances* of the demonstrating students, without endorsing their actions around the car; they offered their help in mediating a possible settlement.[5]

While this meeting was going on in the offices at 201 Sproul Hall, a short distance away in Room 221 police chiefs from the Bay area were gathering to plan their strategy for removing the demonstrators. Dean Lohman and Vice-Chancellor Campbell worked out plans with them. Earl Bolton, a statewide University of California vice-president asked by Clark Kerr to keep an eye on happenings that day, and Ron Mos-cowitz, an administrative assistant to Governor Brown, came to the campus, learned of the conference of police chiefs, and sat in on it. A plan was devised, to be put into operation at 6 o'clock that evening. Chancellor Strong would read a prepared statement requesting the dem-onstrators to disperse. If they refused, several hundred policemen would

remove them bodily from the area. The plan was relayed to President
Kerr and Governor Brown by their assistants.[6]

On Friday, Joseph Garbarino, chairman of the Committee on Academic Freedom of the Academic Senate at Berkeley, wrote Chancellor
Strong as follows:

> . . . *As you may know, a petition asking that the Committee on Ac-
> ademic Freedom and the Committee on Educational Policy inquire into
> the dispute and report to the Senate, has been forwarded to us by the
> Secretary to the Berkeley Division in advance of its being presented to
> the Division.*
>
> . . . *I have had an informal meeting with Professors Dempster and
> ten Broek, two of the other four members of the Academic Freedom
> Committee.*
>
> *In addition to expressing our concern with the gravity of the existing
> situation, we would like to indicate to you that the Committee is ready
> to participate in any way that we would mutually agree would be help-
> ful in resolving the situation in the best interests of all concerned. . . .*[7]

Meanwhile, unaware of administrative plans or mediation efforts by
other groups, the Barrows Hall faculty members continued to discuss
what they might do to avoid a riot on campus. At noon they gathered in
Professor Lewis Feuer's office; they were now twelve in number and included a few persons with offices in Dwinelle Hall, as well as persons
from Barrows. After they met, Nathan Glazer wrote the following memorandum to Alex Sherriffs:

> *I have a different formula to propose from the one that hung us up
> yesterday.*
>
> *(1) The student demonstrators agree to accept the principles of law
> and order on campus, to use lawful means to press their case, and thus
> to release the car and the prisoner, and to follow constitutional means
> of action on the suspended students.*
>
> *(2) The administration agrees to immediately set up a board of fac-
> ulty, student leaders (including leaders of the demonstration), chaired
> by someone like Frank Newman, to have* public *hearings* on *all aspects
> of political activity on hearing, empowered to get testimony from
> whoever is relevant, to examine the way this is done at SF State or*

UCLA, etc., and to make recommendations to the Chancellor on the regulations and their administration.

. . .

Explanation: I am convinced the students want to be heard, *want a forum for their case in which they don't talk only to each other but also to faculty and administration. I think this course will lead to peace on campus. This exchange may not go through—it may require a private agreement not to press charges and to lift the suspension (which on the other hand would be understood if the students agree to go back to lawful means).*[8]

Professor S. M. Lipset, who was not part of this conference, had gone in the meantime to the chancellor's office. Here is a memorandum describing his visit:

Friday, Oct. 2, 1964
12:50 P.M.

(Lipset wandered into the Chancellor's office—the door was closed, but not locked. He asked me if any of the vice-chancellors were around, but before I could get up to answer him, he saw EWS and walked in—ao)

Marty [Lipset] said that he had just been talking with a small group of students who he took to be the leaders of the demonstrations. They transmitted a proposal to Lipset (not endorsed by Lipset) that they would call off further demonstrations for the time being if the Chancellor would lift the indefinite suspensions placed upon the eight students or announce a limited duration of the suspension.

Marty asked if he should go back or just let the proposal drift away. I said to let it drift away.

EWS[9]

Malloy
Sherriffs

Shortly thereafter, the faculty delegation from Barrows Hall arrived in the chancellor's office.

October 2, 1964
Afternoon

MEMO TO RECORDS:

Meeting in Chancellor's Conference Room: Kornhauser, Petersen, Smelser, Matza, and Glazer of Sociology; Seabury, Scalapino, and Haas of Political Science; Radner and Rosovsky of Economics; Schorske of History; Tussman of Philosophy.

I was called into the Chancellor's office and asked if I could meet with the group on Friday afternoon, primarily because I did not know anything and would be freer than the Chancellor to talk. We had an animated discussion in which this informal group, which was entirely self-appointed, discussed the situation, their fears of violence primarily between students and students, offered 4 proposals as a possible basis for some kind of "cease fire," and essentially offered themselves as intermediaries between administration and the demonstrating students. These proposals were essentially those finally embodied in the Kerr agreement as published. After I had discussed these proposals with them in some detail, pointing out as far as I could the possible difficulties involved, I acceded to their strong request that I ask the Chancellor to come in. The Chancellor did come in for a few minutes, went over each of the proposals, pointed out how far he could go and what things were outside campus authority, emphasized his responsibility for maintaining law and order on the campus, and then had to leave, presumably for a meeting in the President's office at 4:30 P.M.

After his departure, Tussman stated that the Chancellor's statement had left nothing with which the faculty members present could go back to the students, with whom they presumably were in contact, and departed. Schorske also left the meeting, saying he had a group of students somewhere, but said he would be back and, in fact, did return in a few minutes. I talked to the group for some time trying to convince them that the Chancellor had indeed gone as far as he could on each of the points indicated. I also tried to show that his cautious statements such as emphasizing the lack of any punitive desire would make it possible to accede to most of the substance of the proposals, but that on such a thing as the suspension, the Chancellor had always followed the recommendations of the faculty committee on student conduct and was not free to make the ultimate decision. To most of those present this did not seem unreasonable, although some said that they agreed with the students; others seemed to be simply interested in getting order restored and adopted a position of ostensible neutrality.

The discussion went on for some time and I suggested that they might wish me to withdraw since, after all, I was there as a representative of the administration, but they urged me to stay, and I felt that this was not inappropriate. Eventually [someone], I think it was Petersen, asked me if I would call the President and I said no, that it would not be appropriate for me to do so. Someone then asked me if I thought they should call the President, and I said I did not think it was proper for me to give advice of this kind. Seabury, I think, said he thought that as faculty members they would feel that they had not really discharged their duty unless they had made an attempt to get in touch with the President, and asked if it would be possible to call from the Chancellor's office. Rosovsky was finally delegated to call, and I can't remember now who told me that the telephone at the end of the conference room should be used. Rosovsky did call and a few minutes later came in to ask for a copy of the proposals, and either said, or I inferred, that these were read to President Kerr over the telephone and presumably recorded at the other end. The discussion continued and some time later Rosovsky came back into the room. As I recall his statement it was something to the effect that he had never heard Dr. Kerr so depressed in the time he had known him, that he appreciated their efforts, but that it was too late and that all his work over the years was going down the drain. The group began to talk about what they should do, and I stated it was clear that I should not be present. I excused myself and left.

LC 10

Meanwhile, the demonstration in Sproul Plaza went on much as before. Students surrounding the car sang, continued their "town meeting" discussion, or talked quietly among themselves. Some slipped away to sleep, while others took their places.

The demonstrators were sure that a major confrontation was in the offing: they were convinced that the university could not afford to allow them to remain in the plaza on Saturday, when families would be visiting. A number of students, including those in the political clubs, called legislators or any other influential citizens they knew, urging them to intervene with President Kerr to arrange a meeting between the demonstrators and the university administration. There was a strong sense of impending crisis.

At about 4:15 P.M., demonstration spokesmen asked to meet with President Kerr. They did not receive a favorable response. Then, as we have seen, specific proposals for discussion came to him from the faculty group. Kerr then agreed to meet with the students at 5:00 P.M., provided that representatives of the student government, the student newspaper, the campus religious organizations, and the faculty were also present.

At 4:45 P.M. police officers from Oakland, Alameda County, Berkeley, and the California Highway Patrol began marching onto the campus, taking up positions at the north and south ends of Sproul Hall and on Barrows Lane, the street immediately behind Sproul Hall, which separates it from Barrows Hall. Some 500 officers, including more than 100 motorcycle police, were on hand by 5:30 P.M., some armed with riot sticks.

The *California Monthly* reported:

As the police arrived, onlookers and protest sympathizers swelled the crowd between Sproul Hall and the Student Union to more than 7000. Spectators lined the Student Union balcony and the roof of the Dining Commons.

As the possibility of police action against the demonstrators increased, protesters were instructed on "how to be arrested" (remove sharp objects from pockets, remove valuable rings and watches, loosen clothing, pack closely together, do not link arms, go limp) and were counseled on their legal rights (give only your name and address, ask to see your lawyer, do not make any statements.) All persons with small children, those under 18 years of age, noncitizens, and those on parole or probation were advised to leave.[11]

And, as six campus police officers penetrated the periphery of the crowd—in an effort to reinforce the stranded police car—the demonstrators packed themselves solidly around the car.

At about 5:30 P.M., the demonstrators were informed that the meeting between protest leaders and University officials was in progress at University House, and that President Kerr had promised no police action until after that meeting. . . .[12]

A tense two hours followed for persons waiting in the plaza.

Down at University Hall, Clark Kerr had taken careful precautions to see that nothing went amiss. He instructed Earl Bolton to call O. W. Campbell, Joseph Lohman, and Richard Hafner with strict instructions that the police were not to go into operation until they had word from him. As an extra precaution, he insisted that Edward Strong remain with him at University Hall, even though Strong was not participating in the final negotiations taking place. (The police plan called for arrests after Strong read a prepared statement, asking the students to disperse.[13])

Several participants in the conference have described to me their impressions of what took place. The students who came down from the demonstration were gathered hurriedly, but included Mario Savio and representatives of several organizations active in the United Front, including the Young Democrats and Young Republicans, Slate, and socialist and civil rights organizations.

There was a long argument over the wording of the first point in the faculty proposed agreement: "the student demonstrators promise to abide by legal processes in their protest of university regulations." The students did not trust the motives of the administration and wanted to reserve the right to act again if the university, in their judgment, resorted to terror tactics to suppress opposition. Finally they agreed to an amended statement: "the student demonstrators shall desist from all forms of their illegal protest against university regulations." To the students, the change of wording to "desist" was important, because they felt it did not bind them indefinitely for the future, should other parts of the agreement turn out to promise less than they hoped. The import of this change apparently escaped Clark Kerr, who considered the revision an equivalent expression of the same idea.[14]

The students debated whether or not to sign the agreement, because it provided no final *settlement* of the dispute but merely offered channels for dealing with it. Demonstration leaders met separately from the other persons present and argued for almost two hours. Every few minutes, they report, someone would come in to urge them to sign the agreement, saying the police could not be held off indefinitely. Mario Savio and some of the others argued that they should not sign it, that they should insist on a settlement of the issues before they surrendered the police car. But Jackie Goldberg insisted that, whether the agreement was good or bad, they had to sign it. She said later:

> I have never known terror as I did that night, sitting in that room trying to negotiate and every 15 minutes having a secretary come and tell me she wasn't sure how long the cops could be held and she had no idea what would happen if they moved in. . . .
>
> It was no bluff. Cops can't be held indefinitely. You know, they were infuriated that they couldn't move in and—here, picture the scene. Picture this mass of people who haven't had any sleep for 32 hours; up there are the Freddies, see, with their lit cigarettes throwing into the crowd, just dying to get into a melee which we had just barely prevented the night before by a priest coming down. . . . And all these cops with their night sticks and high boots on and helmets, ready to just club their way through to the car. And about three or four thousand spectators sitting there, just like watching the gladiators and the Romans, watching to see who would get killed on an open pavement where anything goes and no photographers. . . . Well, it would have been a

riot. It would have been not only a riot, but you know who would have been hurt.

. . . I said this after every sentence I said in our caucus. I couldn't get through to them. I got through to them, but they didn't want to believe it. They finally signed the thing. I will say that if Sandor Fuchs and I had not been there they might not have signed it.

I look at things this way. In a revolution there are going to be deaths, but this was no revolution. And there is no excuse for deaths where there is not a revolution. Those guys wanted to believe . . . it was a revolution; and, by God, it was a rebellion—inside, purely within the limits of the status quo. We never got anywhere near to advocating taking over the university and running it ourselves, nor could we have possibly effected that. It was a nonrevolutionary rebellion. . . .

. . . People would either have been killed or seriously maimed from that. . . . I had no doubt in my mind. I wasn't going to leave there until we signed that agreement. I didn't care how bad it was. That's the way I felt.

. . . I knew I couldn't live with myself if I had been responsible for something like that. I don't think they could have, either. . . . I'm just saying that they couldn't believe it would happen.[15]

At 7:20 P.M., the student protesters and Clark Kerr signed the following agreement:

1. The student demonstrators shall desist from all forms of their illegal protest against University regulations.

2. A committee representing students (including leaders of the demonstration), faculty, and administration will immediately be set up to conduct discussions and hearing into all aspects of political behavior on campus and its control, and to make recommendations to the administration.

3. The arrested man will be booked, released on his own recognizance, and the University (complainant) will not press charges.

4. The duration of the suspension of the suspended students will be submitted within one week to the Student Conduct Committee of the Academic Senate.

5. Activity may be continued by student organizations in accordance with existing University regulations.

6. The President of the University has already declared his willingness to support deeding certain University property at the end of Telegraph Avenue to the City of Berkeley or to the ASUC.

(*signed*)	*Jo Freeman*	*Clark Kerr*
	Paul C. Cahill	*Jackie Goldberg*
	Sandor Fuchs	*Eric Levine*
	Robert Wolfson	*Mario Savio*
	David Jessup	*Thomas Miller*

Then all of them hurried back to Sproul Hall Plaza. At 7:30 P.M. Mario Savio climbed on top of the police car and read the agreement. He spent about ten minutes interpreting what he understood it to mean and then said, "Let us agree by acclamation to accept this document. I ask you to rise quietly and with dignity, and go home."

The demonstration was over. (Unknown to the demonstrators or to the people in University Hall, the police had actually begun to leave about 7:00 P.M., for the various chiefs had decided they could not keep their men on duty any longer.) [16] As the students slipped away, they left behind the battered remains of the police car. But they left far more than this tangible symbol of their stay—they left behind a tangled skein of unresolved issues still to be dealt with by opposing sides who had lost faith in the integrity of their adversaries. Moreover, the demonstrators emerged from what had been a harrowing emotional experience, where they had faced the possibility of physical violence and arrest, for what they believed was the defense of the constitutional rights of all Americans. Many said later that they left the demonstration feeling "committed" for the first time to their heritage as Americans. But they also left the plaza wondering about the moral integrity of the persons in authority over them and about possible relationships between, on the one hand, vested interests and, on the other, the police and even the news media that had reported their crusade.[17] The crisis of authority had temporarily been resolved. But the crisis of legitimacy had not.

From the diverse vantage points of the demonstrators, counterdemonstrators, administrators, and faculty, events of the past two weeks —and particularly of the past thirty-two hours—looked very different. Each set of participants saw quite different casts of heroes and villains, and a different set of issues at stake. Yet each vantage point was similar in perceiving its own behavior of the immediate past as reasonable and necessary in the face of irrational or badly motivated actions by others.

part iii

THE CONFLICT DEEPENS: ROUND TWO

eight
NEGOTIATIONS

Although the pact of October 2 left the issues in dispute basically unsettled, it did establish new ground rules for proceeding. The events of the thirty-two hours preceding the pact however, had left both sides with a deep distrust of their opposition.[1]

Chancellor Strong set to work on Saturday, October 3, to implement the terms of the agreement as he understood it. He, of course, had not been present for the discussions before it was signed, but he wanted to make sure that no one took advantage of the agreement by continuing to violate university regulations. Mario Savio, in presenting the pact from the top of the police car on Friday evening, had announced a Monday rally on the steps of Sproul Hall. Strong did not believe that a suspended student had a legal right to schedule a rally on university property without authorization from the administration. A memorandum by Strong's administrative assistant, Kitty Malloy, summarizes the chancellor's position that Saturday:

Saturday, October 3
11:30 A.M.

STRONG CALL TO KERR:

He said he believed that we are going to have a test case on Monday when and if Savio gets up and speaks on Sproul Hall steps. Strong said we shall have to arrest him—not entitled to speak as suspended. Kerr said O.K.

Kerr wants three things checked out in D.C. [the Daily Californian] statement—Committee is appointed by the Chancellor and is advisory to him. The Student Conduct Committee is advisory to the Chancellor —the man in car was booked and released—we are not pressing charges but further disposition of the case is in the hands of the D.A.

Strong told Kerr he was going to have the police officers to dinner to thank them for all their work—Tuesday night.

Kerr said that George Beadle had gone through a similar situation (sit-down in his office and had to make a decision whether to act immediately or wait it out—if had to do over again Beadle would have acted immediately).

KCM [2]

Mario Savio, for his part, was skeptical of the intentions of the administration. In the organizing meeting of the Free Speech Movement, held on Sunday, October 4, he said:

We have to be realistic. We won't get much from the negotiations. . . . The most we will get from them will be what publicity we give them. Everything must be completely public.

There has been war between the State of California and the students. We must see that the police incident can't recur.[3]

The weekend was a time of hectic activity at Berkeley. The demonstrators met on Sunday to form a permanent organization to represent them in the negotiations. After some deliberation they decided to call themselves the Free Speech Movement. A rather elaborate organizational structure was created for FSM, as it came to be called: a large Executive Committee would vote on policy decisions, and a Steering Committee would meet daily to plan negotiating strategy. Elected to the Steering Committee were persons who had assumed leadership in the police car incident—Mario Savio, Art Goldberg, Jack Weinberg, Brian Turner, Jackie Goldberg, and Bettina Aptheker—and three students active in socialist and civil rights organizations—Syd Stapleton, Dave Freeman, and Tom Miller.[4] Within a day or two the Steering Committee was expanded to include representatives from the independents (i.e., students who were not members of organizations participating in the United Front), from graduate students, and from the more moderate political clubs.

At 11:15 P.M. on Sunday, faculty members who had learned of Strong's plan to have Savio arrested if he spoke from the Sproul steps the next day summoned the FSM Steering Committee to Barrows Hall.[5] They asked students to hold the rally on city of Berkeley property. The FSM leadership replied that the University was taking advantage of a technicality in order to harass them. The discussion lasted far into the night, and even included 4:00 A.M. phone calls to members of the administration.[6] Finally, the faculty suggested that one of them (Nobel prize winner Owen Chamberlain) would read a statement for Savio on Monday. But the FSM decided that Savio should speak.

On Monday morning campus administrators debated the wisdom of making a new arrest.[7] When Savio spoke, no arrest occurred. At the rally statements of support were read, including one signed by forty-three political science and economics teaching assistants, who commended the demonstrators' goals.[8]

In view of the weekend's events Monday's *Daily Californian* announcement that the Faculty Committee on Student Conduct would review the suspensions produced an immediate protest from the students concerned: this was not a committee of the Academic Senate, but an advisory body to Chancellor Strong. Demonstrators also were troubled that Strong had appointed the entire negotiating committee, whereas they had understood that faculty, administrators, and students each would select their own representatives.

After a number of days spent in protesting the constituency of these committees, the Free Speech Movement issued a newsletter presenting its side of the dispute. One page of this paper urged students in general to testify against the "rigging" of the committees:

AN OPEN HEARING OF THE "STUDEY [sic] GROUP"—ATTEND AND TESTIFY:

The Chancellor's so-called "Study Committee" will hold an open hearing Tuesday, October 13, at 7:30 P.M. in Room 2000 L.S.B. The purpose of this hearing is to advise the Chancellor concerning which students HE shall allow to sit in HIS "study group" to make recommendations for modifying HIS regulations on campus political activity.

We insist that no committee be constituted until it is made clear that this committee is able to have some meaningful effect on the real world. We must demonstrate the support of the students with the Free Speech Movement. Every student who is aware has an obligation. HE MUST ATTEND THE MEETING, HE MUST SIGN UP TO TESTIFY, HE MUST STATE THAT HE CAN MAKE NO RECOMMENDATIONS ON THE COMPOSITION OF A COMMITTEE WHOSE LEGITIMACY HE DOES NOT ACCEPT.

Sign up to testify. Notice must be given to Prof. R. Williams, Room 229, Molecular Biology Bdlg. [sic], extension 2237. We must all testify. We must all come, EARLY.

Eli Katz's story is probably one of many hidden in Chancellor Strong's files. Katz had been an acting assistant in the German department last year, and he applied for an appointment as assistant professor.

On January 6, he was interrogated by Chancellor Strong about certain questions he had refused to answer before the 1958 HUAC hearings. Katz refused, "telling Strong that he had signed the Levering Loyalty oath in good faith and that he was not a Communist."

The University administration took the position that it could not process Katz's application unless he agreed to answer the questions verbally.

Katz is no longer at Cal.[9]

Meanwhile, more general support of the Free Speech Movement position was crystallizing on the campus. On Tuesday, October 7, the ASUC Senate passed a resolution asking its president to meet with President Kerr "to determine whether the Administration has violated the spirit of Friday's agreement. . . ."[10]

On Wednesday, Dean of Men Arleigh Williams received a petition signed by about 650 members of 37 fraternities and sororities, asserting that FSM was "composed of responsible students" and declaring support of its goals.[11] On October 12 a petition signed by 88 members of the faculty and urging reinstatement of the suspended students was presented to the chancellor.[12]

On the same day the Steering Committee of the Free Speech Movement met with Chancellor Strong to call for suspension of activities by the Study Committee, contending that it was illegally constituted. Chancellor Strong said he would seek the advice of the committee itself on the propriety of suspending its activities. He also explained that he had referred the cases of the suspended students to the only existing appropriate committee that could have been meant by the agreement of October 2.[13]

That week the Free Speech Movement handed out a leaflet on campus, which summarized its view of what was happening:

THE ADMINISTRATION: BUNGLING FRIEND OR DELIBERATE ENEMY?
The issue is free speech.

Early this semester we were confronted with Administrative rulings drastically reducing political activity on campus. The rights to solicit members, to collect funds, to advocate action in off-campus projects, rights students have always had at Cal, were abolished by Administrative fiat. The rulings were the response of a single individual, Chancellor Strong, to right-wing political pressure. They had absolutely no basis in law, reason, tradition, or general Regents' policy.

Administration officials frustrated all our attempts to explain that these rulings were unacceptable restrictions on our freedom of speech. Rights unexercised are lost, so we finally disregarded the new restrictions and continued normal campus political activity. In retaliation, the Administration singled out eight participating students and suspended them. When Chancellor Strong ordered Jack Weinberg's arrest, our protest spontaneously grew to a massive sit-in around the police car. Under the pressure of this demonstration, Clark Kerr finally agreed to meet with student representatives, and thirty-three and one-half hours after Jack's arrest an agreement was signed.

In order to understand the meaning of that agreement, it is essential to consider the circumstances under which it was reached. The Administration had repeatedly announced to the press, even while the negotiations were in progress, that it would not accede to the students' demands, and that it would not compromise on any aspect of the new restrictions. Our minimum demands were that the eight suspended students be reinstated, that Jack immediately be released, and that the Administration meet with us to discuss the new rulings. The Administration could not meet our demands without losing face; we could not accept the new rulings and the Administration's punitive actions without betraying our commitment to free speech. However, the situation of Friday evening was explosive. Hundreds of policemen, armed with clubs, were ready to move in on the crowd of demonstrators and make mass arrests. An agreement had to be reached.

Since the Administration could not lose face, the agreement had to be worded to allow intermediate agencies to make the concessions we demanded. Thus the cases of the eight students were to be turned over to the Student Conduct Committee of the Academic Senate and acted on within a week, Jack was to be booked but then released, and a joint Faculty-Student-Administration committee was to be set up to review the new restrictions and make recommendations to the Administration. President Kerr assured us that he would consider carefully our recommendations for members to sit on this committee, and told us that we had to have some trust in the Administration.

Now, what has happened to this agreement? The cases of the suspended students were supposed to be referred to the Student Conduct Committee of the Academic Senate, but no such committee of the Academic Senate exists. In fact, the cases were referred to a committee appointed by Chancellor Strong. The duration of the suspensions was to be decided within a week. Almost two weeks have passed and the students have not had a hearing before any committee at all. President Kerr promised to consider student recommendations for the joint Faculty-Student-Administration committee, yet when the Free Speech Movement tried to contact him during the weekend with its recommendations, he was consistently unavailable. Monday morning the names of the committee members appeared in the newspapers.

President Kerr has demonstrated bad faith even before this. As the students, in compliance with the agreement, dispersed from around the police car, Kerr was holding a press conference. He smeared and red-baited the entire Free Speech Movement. He said the students used "Communist tactics" (they were, of course, students suspended by the Administration). He even was quoted in the *Examiner* of October 3 as saying that 49% of the students "followed the Mao-Castro line"! [14]

President Kerr told us that we should trust the Administration. His statements and actions, from the moment the agreement was signed, have betrayed our trust.

The agreement is broken but our demands remain. How can we achieve them now? It is ridiculous to think that an Administration-appointed committee, whose recommendations will finally be approved or rejected by the Administration, will upset the Administration's rules. Why then has the Study Committee been set up?

The answer is simple. Committees mean delay, and delay, even for so short a time as until midterms, means the death of large-scale student protest. Furthermore, because the joint committee has no power and is ostensibly a neutral, objective body, it serves as a buffer between the students and the Administration. The recommendations of a committee two-thirds composed of Administration and Faculty will be a compromise of our demands. The Administration will then compromise with this compromise. We cannot sit back and allow a third party, however neutral, to negotiate in our behalf. We cannot settle for less than our full rights as citizens.

As long as we allow the Administration to maintain the initiative, any concessions to free speech will be a dispensation, not a restoration of our rights. We therefore cannot afford to participate in their committees, under their rules and their control.

The issue is free speech.

The faculty's Academic Senate met twice that week and devoted major attention to the controversy on campus. The chancellor presented his side of the dispute; the faculty appointed a special ad hoc committee to deal with the student discipline questions and appointed additional members to represent it in the negotiations. In addition, its Academic Freedom Committee questioned the chancellor about the decision not to renew the contract of Eli Katz, who had refused to answer questions about his political activities after having signed a loyalty oath.

Approximately 300 students attended the first public meeting of the

Study Committee on Campus Political Activity, held at 7:30 P.M. on October 13, in Harmon Gymnasium. The committee heard testimony from fifty students, all but one of whom followed the FSM newsletter's suggestion of testifying that the committee was illegally constituted and should be disbanded.[12]

During this time Jackie Goldberg tried to set up an appointment with Clark Kerr to discuss the administration's implementation of the October 2 agreement. She was referred to Earl Bolton, the university vice-president, who was Kerr's administrative assistant. Bolton suggested the FSM Steering Committee should meet with him and then talk with Kerr if the two parties reached some mutually acceptable position. The administration, he reported, was as uncomfortable with student efforts to reinterpret the first clause of the agreement "to desist from all forms of illegal protest" as the students were with the administrative appointment of committees.

Before the meeting could be arranged, however, Jackie Goldberg was voted out of the FSM Steering Committee. As the Free Speech Movement members came to feel that they had been tricked in the October 2 agreement, considerable bitterness developed toward Jackie Goldberg, whom they held responsible for their decision to sign the agreement. Therefore Dustin Miller replaced her in negotiations with Earl Bolton. About 4:30 P.M. on Tuesday, October 13, Miller telephoned Bolton to arrange a conference. The suspicious students tape-recorded the call, but the microphone picked up only Miller's part in the conversation.

Miller was very angry. The conversation bogged down completely on the sixth point that Miller had been authorized to discuss, which was the order of agenda for the meeting. Here are the instructions Miller had when he went to the phone:

f. agenda
(1) Violation of point four by administration.
(2) If Bolton refuses, we offer to discuss point two first!
(3) If no, we ask permission to see Kerr for permission to go to the Regents.[15]

After the phone call the student who was keeping notes wrote:

Bolton agreed on almost everything except beginning meeting with point four or point two. He wanted to discuss "interpretation" of Octo-

ber 2 agreement. Feeling is that this is a delaying tactic obviously filling up the whole 2 hours available Wednesday. Then . . . would [be able to say] "I have a variety of exhibits to prove. . . ." [15]

After this phone call Earl Bolton dictated a memorandum summarizing his impressions of the conversation. He had understood that the students were willing to discuss only points two and four, whereas he believed that the entire agreement should be discussed point by point, since the students were talking about beginning direct action again unless the administration met their terms. He concluded that the students were not really interested in having a conference at that time. [16]

Each side, thus, was convinced from this call that the opposition did not intend to enter a serious discussion of the points at issue. Although the FSM Steering Committee was convinced that Bolton had no intention of dealing with its concerns, some members were uneasy about the style in which the phone call had been conducted by their own representative. Shortly thereafter Dustin Miller decided to devote greater time to coordinating "Independents for Free Speech" [17] and to raising funds. [18] He was replaced by a quieter-mannered student, Ron Anastasi, for future contacts with the administration.

A few hours after the Miller-Bolton phone call, the Steering Committee went to a lawyer's home to ask advice about legal questions that were likely to confront it in the days ahead. [19] While the members were there, one of them produced what seemed to be documentary proof of why the administration had acted as it did. Bettina Aptheker described this episode to me later in these words:

> *. . . When we walked into this meeting, somebody—I really don't remember who—shoved this letter into my face and said, "Read this." I read it and almost dropped dead.*
>
> *I was told at that time—I didn't pursue it, because I didn't really want to know—that some secretary in University Hall had swiped the letters, and was with us, and would give us further information if and when she could.* [20]

This "documentary proof of administrative plans" consisted of two photocopies of letters, dated October 13, 1964. Neither letter was signed, but one bore the typewritten name of Clark Kerr and the other the typewritten name of Thomas Cunningham, the university's general counsel. Both appeared to be letters to the Board of Regents, recommending changes in university rules on political advocacy.

The letter with Kerr's name typed at the bottom included the following statement: "University facilities may not be used for the purpose of recruiting participants for unlawful off-campus action." [21] The second letter, with Cunningham's name at the bottom, was addressed to the Regents' Committee on Finance and headed, "Authorization for General Counsel to Prepare Legislation Making Certain Conduct on the Campus of the University of California a Misdemeanor." [21]

The students were sure that "unlawful off-campus action" could refer only to civil rights protests, whose legal status was not yet clarified by the courts. After all, several hundred students had been arrested in San Francisco just a few months previously for civil rights sit-ins. In fact, no other kind of off-campus action that could conceivably be considered illegal had been advocated by student groups. Since the students were convinced that William Knowland had forced the university to stop their activities at Bancroft and Telegraph because he objected to a student picket line outside his newspaper plant, they were doubly sure that the whole argument about political advocacy centered around civil rights pressure campaigns.

(The students were correct in assessing the *practical* issue at stake in the maneuvers and countermaneuvers that had taken place during the fall. However, some people who were insisting on the need to regulate "unlawful" advocacy personally favored the civil rights campaigns. While approving of student pressure tactics for this purpose, they wanted to make sure that civil police would not be brought onto an American campus because the university lacked any means to regulate abuses in its own midst. These persons were joined by others who were strongly opposed to the student campaign.)

Given the *context* of the debate and the coupling of the "unlawful off-campus action" letter with one requesting new legislation on misdemeanors, it would be difficult for student advocates of moral pressure campaigns not to assume that what *really* was at issue was the right to pursue unpopular civil rights actions whose legal status was not clear. Moreover, the letters reached the FSM leaders while they were at the home of a civil rights lawyer to discuss the constitutional issues involved in such demonstrations and the constitutional protections afforded citizens who wished to participate in this kind of activity.

Thus it appeared that the university administration was about to make its own policy on the questions in dispute, without seriously consulting the parties to the negotiating agreement. It appeared, furthermore, that the administration did not intend to recognize the complex constitutional questions involved in the civil rights tactics controversy, and that it wanted new laws to punish student activity. If this were so —and were the letters not documentary proof of these intentions?—it was no wonder that Earl Bolton did not seem anxious to talk with them before the Board of Regents met.

The students, therefore, immediately planned to mount a pressure campaign against the administration before the Regents meeting took place on Thursday and Friday. At their daily rallies they announced plans for a vigil on the Davis Campus outside the meeting place. They threatened to renew civil disobedience. They also sent a letter to the Board of Regents, requesting permission to speak. (The request was denied because the Regents have a policy of accepting only written communications from persons who are not members of the Board or its staff.)

At this point the Academic Senate began to intervene directly in the dispute, and a compromise was reached shortly before the Regents meeting took place. The students and President Kerr separately agreed to accept an enlarged negotiating committee. The FSM would have four representatives, the administration would appoint an additional two representatives, and the Academic Senate would nominate two persons to represent it.[22] The Regents took no official action on the controversy at their October meeting.

The *Daily Californian,* in reporting the agreement, stated:

Following the [Regents meeting] President Kerr held a news conference and reiterated his belief that some of the demonstrators "had communist sympathies."

In a statement issued at 12:30 A.M. today the FSM Steering Committee stated: "The FSM has every hope that the negotiations we are entering into with the administration can be productive.

"However, we hope that President Kerr's attack upon us is not an indication of an unhealthy attitude with which the administration is entering these negotiations.

"It is regrettable that the President has resorted to such attacks and that the Board of Regents has permitted President Kerr's attack." [23]

The expanded Study Committee on Campus Political Action began meeting on October 20. On the same day the office of the dean of students warned a student scientific research organization, Particle Berkeley (which publishes a student journal), that it would lose its on-campus status if it joined the Free Speech Movement, as it was planning to do.[24] Six days later Chancellor Strong refused a request from the Ad Hoc Academic Senate Committee on Student Suspensions that he reinstate the eight suspended students during the course of the committee's hearings.[25] Two days later, when the FSM's negotiators recommended that the First Amendment of the U.S. Constitution be the only policy regarding political expression on campus, the proposal was rejected. The FSM Steering Committee's notes made at the time indicate that Mario Savio wanted "to go to war over this issue" but that Jack Weinberg calmed him down.[26]

All of these events were to be expected from persons motivated by the aims the FSM leaders had projected for their opposition. With advance warning of "administrative plans" and current evidence of continued efforts to destroy opposition, the FSM did not hope for much to come out of the negotiations. The members used the sessions to try to make their points and waited for the administration to tip its hand.

On October 31, Jack Weinberg gave a long explanation of his philosophy of approach to this kind of conflict, trying to assure members of the Executive Committee of the FSM that he was not a "sell-out" in urging them to continue with the negotiations. Basing his examples on the student civil rights movement tactics in the Bay area during the preceding year, as well as on civil rights successes and failures in other parts of the country, he argued for a long-range strategy in which negotiations would be a step toward mobilizing wider campus support for the goals of the movement, rather than a way of compromising differences of principle between students and the administration. He argued that for the FSM to be successful ". . . the enemy must be viewed as monolithic. This is not a rational *conclusion,* but a tactical decision." He pointed out instances when the civil rights movement was defeated, crushed between management and union maneuvers, when it "tried to be reasonable."

> . . . *Therefore they* [*the opposing forces*] *must be approached as monolithic. We must resist the temptation to be reasonable, because if we don't we are sucked into the enemy's structure and destroyed. There-*

fore, for survival of the movement, we must treat *the enemy as mono-lithic. This philosophy has carried over for the southern civil rights movement and has been fantastically successful.*

*. . . What is a successful mechanism? It must . . . force a crisis.
. . . The enemy knows it will build; therefore is more likely to give in early. . . .*

What do you do in the civil rights movement? You either give in, develop interim tactics, or go all the way and maybe get smashed.

Weinberg went on to apply this philosophy to the current situation, and especially to the Study Committee. He pointed out that the normal response would be to handle the situation in such a way as to let both sides save face.

But there is this other civil rights philosophy at work. . . . Here is the monolithic theory at work. (1) We know we cannot win in open revolt against the state of California. (2) Our most effective weapon is the threat of just that kind of absolutely massive demonstration that they want least. We must make them believe that we are willing to go all the way. . . .

Our decision, as I see it, is we either win or lose. If we chicken out, we don't win. If we go ahead, we should be escalating the situation. Then more and more people who are closely at hand become directly involved.

We can always cap escalation with a student-faculty strike. In fact, this is the direction I feel we should head in. We must maintain unity to do that. At the right moment, we can call for a general strike. We can say we just thought of it. Many people are with us in spirit, but against our methods. It is very tense in an escalating situation. They would join the strike to relieve the tension.[26]

The Executive Committee decided then to step up pressure. Rallies began hinting that massive demonstrations might be necessary unless the Study Committee recognized the U.S. Constitution as its guiding principle.

But there were also counterpressures. On Monday night, November 2, the ASUC Senate passed a resolution urging students to support efforts of the "Hearing Committee" to reform university regulations and condemned "verbal threats on the part of leaders of the Free Speech Movement to resort to open demonstrations again." [27] And on November 4 the Interfraternity Council, after long debate, passed a resolution that it said represented "the approximately 2,000 male undergraduates who are fraternity men on the Berkeley campus." Although the resolution did not side with the previous position of the university administration, it criticized the stance of the FSM. It expressed disapproval of "unlawful and disorderly tactics in settling disputes" and its belief that "such illegal and disruptive actions as have been used and as are threatened by various demonstrators are destructive to the best educational atmosphere on this campus." [28]

Meanwhile, negotiations within the Study Committee continued. By Wednesday, November 4, all parties were in agreement that advocacy of off-campus political action should be allowed on campus. They remained divided, however, in regard to actions that might not be "within the limits of the law." On November 4, Earl Cheit, a professor of business administration and a faculty representative on the committee, proposed a university policy that "permits free expression within the limits of the law." Students expressed concern, however, about civil rights actions, whose legal status was not yet clear. Stanford Kadish, a professor of law, then rephrased the proposal to deal with these objections:

The advocacy of ideas and acts which is constitutionally protected off campus should be protected on the campus. By the same token, of course, speech which is in violation of law and constitutionally unprotected should receive no greater protection on the campus than off the campus. [29]

The students and faculty on the Study Committee seemed satisfied with this amendment, but administration representatives felt the statement was not strong enough on prohibiting unlawful action. The committee adjourned for an hour while Kadish, Frank Kidner (university vice-president for educational relations), and attorney Malcolm Burnstein for the students attempted to find a way to state this prohibition that would be acceptable to all parties. They returned with the following proposal, jointly drawn up and acceptable to all three representatives:

If, as a direct result of the advocacy on the campus, acts occur in violation of U.S. or California laws, the University should be entitled to take appropriate disciplinary action against the speakers and their sponsoring organizations, to the extent that the person or organization can fairly be found to be responsible for the unlawful acts.[29]

Mario Savio was quite upset. He argued that the compromise would, in effect, give the administration the right of prior restraint, because it left the interpretation of unlawful acts up to the university.[29] The meeting adjourned.

Comparing notes, the FSM Steering Committee members decided that the revised wording, as agreed on by the three representatives after Kidner's objections, was identical to that in the letter with Clark Kerr's name on the bottom, which had been given to them on October 13. They considered this final proof that the administration had been using the committee as a front while it led it to the conclusions the university already had reached. At this point the FSM got in touch with the *Daily Californian.*

The next morning the student paper ran a story headlined, "Kerr Refutes 'Letter Proof.'" The story reported the letters, including the proposed addition to university regulations in the "Kerr letter": "University facilities may not be used for the purpose of recruiting participants for unlawful off-campus action." The story went on to say that Kerr denied he had written the letter. Thomas Cunningham, according to the paper, said he had written both of them and stated that the "Kerr letter" had not been given to the Regents, although his own, requesting authorization "to prepare legislation making certain conduct on the campus of the University of California a misdemeanor" had been transmitted to them:

They told me to go ahead and study the problem and report back to them. I am. There has been absolutely no legislation prepared at all, and I am still studying the problem. My letter has nothing to do with University rules.[30]

Were the students, in fact, facing an administrative "plot" systematically designed to destroy them and to undermine the agreement of October 2? The sequence of events made such a surmise plausible. An examination of the documents that led to the various actions, however, shows this was not the case. It should not be surprising that administrators felt hostility toward those who had publicly attacked them and disrupted the campus. The "harassing actions" by administrators, however, like many of the events preceding the police car capture, grew out of their attempts to be scrupulously correct in administering rules—attempts to make sure that the *framework* of rules continued to be respected during the period when some of their *content* would be under examination.

Chancellor Strong, who, it will be recalled, had not taken part in the final discussions leading to the October 2 pact, attempted to put its provisions into immediate operation. The agreement stated that the suspensions would be reviewed within a week by the Student Conduct Committee of the Academic Senate. Since no such committee existed, Strong referred the suspension decision to the existing faculty committee on discipline, which in fact was administratively appointed and was advisory to him. Strong then followed "normal procedure" in appointing the Study Committee, so that it could be ready to operate at once. He appointed, as student representatives, the student body president, a senior who had received an award for outstanding leadership, and two representatives from the police car demonstrators (to be chosen by that group itself). Apparently it did not occur to him that his purposes would be questioned. This self-confidence may have stemmed in part from Strong's long-standing reputation among the faculty as a political liberal. He had been one of the leaders in the faculty opposition to a required loyalty oath some fifteen years earlier. Moreover, he served as a board member of Stiles Hall, the YMCA branch that made its building available to controversial speakers denied access to the main campus.

What about the threat to arrest Savio if he spoke on Monday? The administrative staff of the Berkeley campus questioned Strong's judgment on Monday morning and decided not to proceed in this manner. Once again, however, the decision had been technically correct by university administrative rules. It was an *understandable* reaction from a man who had observed Savio's power to mobilize thousands of students into what Strong saw as a "lawless mob" that attacked the chancellor's administration over "fake" issues. But this attitude, while understandable, did little to create a climate of mutual trust.

When Strong was challenged on each of these decisions, he conceded that he might be wrong. He agreed to stretch the rule technicalities on

Monday to avoid appearing arbitrary. As we have seen, when FSM leaders challenged his right to appoint the Study Committee, he said he would ask its membership to decide whether it had been properly constituted, rather than making the judgment himself. He explained to the Academic Senate his reasoning in sending the suspension cases to the existing judicial body and accepted the Senate's appointment of an ad hoc committee to handle the matter.

But what of the warning letter to Particle Berkeley? And why was the ad hoc committee's recommendation of interim reinstatement turned down? Once again, what appear as major strategic errors resulted from an attempt to be scrupulously correct and impartial in applying university regulations during a period of controversy. By the Kerr Directives of 1959, organizations engaging in political activity were not entitled to on-campus status, no matter what their other functions might be.

The decision to reject the recommendation for temporary reinstatement was made only after consultation between Strong, Sherriffs, Kerr, and Cunningham. In a memorandum dated 2:22–2:38 P.M., October 23, 1964, the Berkeley administration summarized its understanding of a three-way phone conference between Sherriffs, Strong, and Kerr. Here are excerpts from this memorandum:

> . . . *The Chancellor said that he had discussed the letter [from the ad hoc committee] with his staff, and that the staff recommended that the request of Heyman's committee be acceded to, and that by not acceding to the request, it would put the administration on the spot.*
>
> *Kerr reminded EWS that the Regents have formally requested that they be kept informed of the work of the two committees, and that the Regents have an opportunity to study the reports and recommendations before any changes in campus rules or procedures are made.*
>
> . . . *Kerr said, . . . "My view is that it is impossible for you to accede to this request. To do so would be terribly unfortunate. . . ."*
>
> *Kerr also said he thought the basic argument could be made that if the suspended students were reinstated, that would be to make decision prior to trying the cases. . . .*[31]

Following up this conversation, Thomas Cunningham drafted the following letter, which Chancellor Strong signed before sending to the committee:

October 26, 1964

Professor Ira M. Heyman, Chairman
Ad Hoc Committee on Student Conduct of the Academic Senate
356 Boalt Hall
Campus

Dear Professor Heyman:

*The Board of Regents has requested that the Administration confer
with the Board about any recommendations from your Committee. I understand that the recommendations and report of your Committee may
be available this next Friday or shortly thereafter.*

*The President has informed me that, upon receipt of your recommenda-
tions and report, he will request that a special meeting of The Board be
convened as soon as reasonably possible to consider them.*

Sincerely yours,

E. W. Strong

cc: President Clark Kerr

bcc: Edward Carter, Chairman of The Board of Regents
bcc: Vice-President Thomas Cunningham, General Counsel

EWS:dp [31]

Thus each of these "harassments" from the Berkeley administration
resulted from attempts of campus officials to follow literally the organizationally prescribed procedures. While persons closer to the immediate
events (i.e., the chancellor's advisory staff) occasionally recommended
that Strong let the regulations "bend" to accommodate immediate exi-
gencies, those in higher administrative positions consistently advised
that he remain scrupulously within the framework of organizational
procedures for such emergencies. In short, advisers subject primarily to
pressures and information from the immediate campus called for flexibility of response. Those who were open to criticism from both directions for handling a politically volatile dispute, and who had come to
question the judgment of the local campus administration,[32] however,
called for circumspect adherence to bureaucratically prescribed action.
However unsympathetic the Berkeley campus administration may have
felt toward the claims of the Free Speech Movement, it proceeded

within strict interpretation of the rules, encouraged by the university-wide administration to maintain this posture whenever it was inclined to "give" with the situation.

Was the university-wide administration, then, proceeding with its own "plot" to destroy the student movement or at least to ignore it in decision-making? The FSM leadership, as we have seen, were convinced that it was. The aborted efforts to talk with Bolton, Kerr, and the Regents, the "purloined letters" recommending policy *before* the negotiating meetings were held, the refusal to accept the First Amendment to the U.S. Constitution as the basis of university policy, and now the compromise amendment inspired by Kidner's objections reasserted the "purloined letter" position and fit into the pattern.

Because the university-wide administration does not keep detailed records of every phone call and conversation, the evidence for appraising the accuracy of these claims is less complete. I am convinced, however, that this so-called plot holds up no better than the conspiracy theories concerning the student radicals or the Berkeley campus administration. Let us consider each piece in the puzzle.

First, there was a loosely worded agreement, referring student grievances to a nonexistent committee. This pact, however, was based on a proposal by an ad hoc group of faculty members during the crisis period on Friday. Chancellor Strong, who might be expected to know the administrative structure of campus committees in some detail, did not participate in the discussions that negotiated the final version; it is unrealistic to assume that President Kerr would carry in his head a detailed picture of the committee structure of one campus.

Student efforts to "talk with the top" were foiled during this period. It is normal procedure for assistants to the president to clear preliminary detail in order to save his time. The replacement of the FSM contact (through no fault of the administration) led to mutual misunderstanding regarding motives and resulted in a canceled appointment. This event, however, was documented in some detail. The suspicious students, as mentioned previously, tape-recorded their end of the conversation with Bolton, and both parties wrote their impressions of what had happened immediately after the conversation. Moreover, the FSM was sufficiently displeased with the style of its intermediary to replace him for all further contacts with the administration. It seems clear that this was a case of botched communication, which might well have been rectified had not the "purloined letters" arrived to give the act a different implication. (The refusal of the Regents to hear an FSM spokesman in October had no relation to the immediate situation. The Regents for years had refused all requests to have oral presentations by non-Regents or staff at their meetings; this was a device to avoid real estate salesmen, politicians, and others who might request extensive time and prove embarrassing to refuse on an item-by-item basis.)

The "purloined letters," of course, suggest a more serious and hostile motive. The *Daily Californian*'s report that Thomas Cunningham, legal counsel for the Regents, had written both letters is reinforced by two incidental details: first, the photocopy letters were unsigned; second, they came from a single source within the office building of the university-wide administration.

The students had no way of knowing that before all Regents meetings a series of possible positions for the board to endorse is drawn up by various staff members in University Hall. In October, six or eight such proposals were drafted in various offices concerning possible recommendations to the Regents. They were presented to a meeting of chancellors of the various campuses the day before the Regents met, and it was decided then that the Cunningham draft of the "Kerr letter" would not go to the board.

Cunningham's own letter to the Regents' Committee on Finance was forwarded directly to them. Cunningham reported the committee had authorized him to study the situation and to prepare proposed legislation for the state legislature if it seemed necessary.[33]

Did the administration actually have a policy position to which it was committed during the meetings of the negotiating committee? Members of the administrative team, including Frank Kidner, insist that they did not. Kidner's letter from Clark Kerr, requesting him to serve on the committee, gives no instructions and suggests no guide lines or limits to decision-making on his part.[34] Shortly after these events, however, Kidner was chosen to represent the University of California as its legislative "lobbyist" in Sacramento. In this post, he constantly would be called on to make policy statements for the Regents regarding the acceptability of various bills that legislators were planning to introduce. Thus, while the president or the Board of Regents had authority to overrule his policy decisions, in fact he would be called upon to commit the university on a wide variety of legislative issues every year. In the two years that Kidner served in Sacramento while Kerr was still president of the university, Kidner reports, the Regents never overruled a policy position that he took in their name.[35] Thus this representative to the committee was a man in whom President Kerr placed considerable trust.

Moreover, there was little reason to assume that Kidner would need specific instructions *unless* a policy decision already had been reached. (And it seems clear that at this point no such position had yet been placed before the Board of Regents.) The final evidence supporting Kidner's explanation is the fact that the Study Committee had been specifically set up to be advisory; thus President Kerr was not bound to follow its recommendations in reporting to the Regents. Kidner reports that he discussed developments with Bolton daily and with Kerr two or three times a week as one friend to another. He reports that both gave reactions, but that neither issued instructions. Unless one holds a conspiracy theory (as the FSM did), few objective reasons appear to explain why Kidner should have had specific instructions from the president.

A conspiracy theory, of course, can be employed to explain the actions of either side. Those with a conspiracy view of the administration were convinced that policy decisions already had been made, and that the explanations given were merely covering lies. They could cite many verifying incidental details.

On the other side, there was "ample evidence" of a Marxist conspiracy if one wanted to make this assumption and to look for confirming details. Slate had published a call to revolt *before* the table-location issue had arisen publicly. As the university had modified its position in September, the student demands had shifted. Within a few hours after the police car had been captured, the daughter of one of America's leading Communists was acting as a major spokesman for the demonstrators. Moreover, she was serving as a negotiator for the Free Speech Movement and was on its Steering Committee. And the students were accelerating their pressure as the negotiating committee seemed to be approaching agreement.

But it is clear, when one reads through the minutes and the logs of meetings that the FSM Steering and Executive Committees held during this period, that Bettina Aptheker was not masterminding the decisions —in fact, the advice that carried the day was often given by persons who had been criticized publicly by members of the W.E.B. DuBois

Club just a few months earlier during the campaigns of the Ad Hoc Committee Against Discrimination in San Francisco. Moreover, Slate leadership in FSM was not particularly strong after the police car incident. Brad Cleveland, who wrote the letter calling for militant action, did not know the FSM decision-makers well and was not welcomed into their circle.

Of more interest than the truth or falsity of these conspiracy theories is the way in which "evidence" becomes organized according to their cause-and-effect hypotheses. Few of us seem committed to look for negative evidence—or to know how to find it—once we are predisposed to favor claims set before us. Thus the "accident" of sequential inputs and the chance availability of verifying procedures become far more important than might otherwise be the case. Once an appealing hypothesis calls the *motives* of actors into question, any negative evidence that these actors themselves may furnish merely engenders suspicion of calculated diversion.

I am not trying to suggest that real issues and principles were not at stake, nor that the controversy was just a regrettable accident, caused by incomplete (and occasionally incorrect) information. But the secret-conspiracy theory—which each side used to account for unwelcome acts of the opposition—worked at times to make impossible a straightforward resolution of differences.

THE BEGINNING OF A DISASTROUS STRATEGY

Although discussions within the Study Committee on Campus Political Activity were constantly narrowing the points of disagreement, all parties to the dispute had become increasingly uneasy about the intentions of opponents during the preceding week. Daily FSM rallies became increasingly militant in language.

On October 29 Chancellor Strong wrote to President Kerr, warning of probable militant action by the students and requesting a common policy for meeting it. His letter said, in part:

. . . *there is growing evidence that a new student demonstration of major proportions will almost certainly occur in the very near future.*

We must prepare our actions in relation to such an event with great care. We need to know reliably and far in advance exactly how we are to use law enforcement and police officers. I need urgently to know your position and the degree of concurrence which it will receive from both Regents and Governor.

We must develop careful and fully coordinated plans giving maximal consideration to their human consequences. We wish, therefore, to establish a committee for the development of strategy . . . [including] persons of your choosing and persons from the Berkeley campus selected by me.

. . . We shall also need a small task force to represent us in operations and enabled to act in the unhappy event of an actual incident.[36]

A phone call between the two men that day reflects their common concern about continuing violations of university rules. The conversation set in motion a strategy that, within a month, created such explosive repercussions as to shake the campus to its foundations. Here is Strong's summary of the conversation:

Thursday, Oct 29, 1964
2:20–2:30 P.M.

TELEPHONE CONVERSATION, EWS AND CK:

Kerr called to say that he has just returned from a trip East and wanted to know how things were going. . . .

Kerr said that he is expecting a possibility of a Regents meeting very soon . . . and asked if we are doing anything about further violations by the students.

Strong said that he had talked with John Landon [on the university legal staff], who said that Heyman's committee should have only the violations up to September 30, the day of the suspension, that while the committee was not exactly a court of law he was sure that there would be legal objections to bringing in subsequent violations. Strong said that he checked this point with Tom Cunningham also, and that Tom agreed with John.

Kerr insisted that these further violations should be brought to the attention of the Faculty Committee on Student Conduct—the Degnan committee [to which Strong originally had sent the September suspension cases], as Kerr refers to this committee. He said that the students should be called for infraction of rules. He said that this should be done "right now."

Kerr said that charges brought against "them" should be brought to the Degnan committee, mentioning specifically Savio and Goldberg, who have further violated rules. The appropriate action would be to have the Dean of Students call them in. "I think it will be help to have them called in in advance of the Regents meeting."

EWS said that he hopes Kerr would tell Tom Cunningham what we are doing because "I don't want . . . to put him in a difficult position."

Kerr: "We ought to have the other charges brought before the Degnan committee before the report comes down from the ad hoc committee; otherwise they might think that we didn't like the recommendations from the committee and, consequently, [were] making other charges." Kerr expressed his opinion that the Heyman committee "may go pretty light."

Kerr's point, when Strong said that Tom Cunningham insisted that we should separate the two sets of charges, was that "they could go before two committees at the same period of time." Kerr said, "I would do it as soon as possible . . . it involves only a couple of them, doesn't it, not all." Strong mentioned Savio and Goldberg.

Kerr said, "Move in on the loudspeaker thing real quick. Start calling the students in right away."

Strong agreed that Kerr had a point and said he would tell Alex to get the Dean of Students to act right away.

Kerr repeated again and again that, if we wait until the Heyman committee makes its report, they will say that we didn't like the recommendations and are therefore taking further action.

Later in the day, after Sherriffs had seen Strong's memorandum of the telephone call, the vice-chancellor wrote a long note to Strong. He pointed out that some of the eight students dismissed on September 30 were involved in the current violations. Since the administration had refused to reinstate them, the dean of students was hardly in a position to summon them for further university discipline. Moreover, Sherriffs opined, to refer additional violations to the Faculty Committee on Student Conduct would offer the FSM an excuse to begin immediate resumption of demonstrations:

. . . demonstrations are to be expected when the FSM thinks it has the trigger to set them off. This trigger would be one to our disadvantage.
. . . What happens if students or dismissed students refuse once

again to be interviewed by Arleigh Williams, if once again they arrive on the second floor of Sproul Hall with a large body of sit-inners, and if once again you have to make a decision on disciplinary action to be taken? Students already in dismissed status could not be dismissed again, although some might be expelled by you and Clark. Students newly charged with violations of rules present the same problem we had earlier of how to proceed in dealing with them and with the demonstrators and sympathizers who will rally to their support. Demonstrations are already being planned.

ACS [37]

On November 4 Strong and Sherriffs met with the Ad Hoc Faculty Committee on Student Conduct to discuss a letter Strong had sent, asking whether the committee wished to receive a report of further violations by students who had been suspended on September 30. Judging from a confidential memorandum Strong dictated after that meeting, the committee told administrators that they did not want reports of further violations and that they were unhappy about administrative efforts to influence their decisions. ". . . I said the letter was not intended to influence the committee in any way," Strong stated. "I noted that . . . a total of some 12 further violations were listed for Savio and Goldberg. Mr. Turner had also further violated university rules."

The conference apparently continued with some discussion of the nature of further violations and of the administration's intentions to follow them up. The question of whether additional violations were criminal acts or fell within the jurisdiction of university regulations was also discussed.

Strong assured the committee that its report would be referred to the Regents. In answer to a question from the committee chairman, the chancellor said new proceedings might be brought against the three students—Savio, Goldberg, and Turner—at any time, dealing with violations since September 30. Members of the committee urged Strong not to take action before their report was issued, citing two reasons quoted in his memorandum:

. . . *(1) The Senate would consider doing so an affront; and (2) the suspended students may wish to bring in the report of the Ad Hoc Committee in deliberations of the new committee. I agreed that I thought it desirable to have the report first and in fact would like to have the Committee on Political Activity finish its work before anything is done to disturb the campus tranquility. . . .*

EWS [38]

Faced with these two conflicting requests, from a campus committee of the Academic Senate and from the university president, the Berkeley administration decided to press charges on the subsequent violations but to wait until after the ad hoc committee (known popularly as the Heyman committee) had submitted its report.

REACTIONS

Administrators were not the only people becoming uneasy because of the FSM rhetoric. A survey of student attitudes taken during this period suggests that the general student body also was becoming uneasy about the course the FSM leadership seemed to be taking. Fifty per cent of students interviewed before November 2 expressed approval of both the goals and the tactics of the FSM. From November 2 through November 8, however, the proportion of persons stating such support dropped to 22%. Since a similar cross section of students was interviewed during each of these periods, the decrease in favorable reactions is not likely to have resulted from chance combinations of respondents.[39]

The survey also shows a noticeable decline in optimism about the work of the negotiating committee. One third of the respondents interviewed between November 2 and November 20 thought there was a good chance that nothing would come from the negotiations, and that real harm might result. Before that time, the students interviewed had expressed considerable hope that the committee would produce some workable results.

NEGOTIATIONS COLLAPSE

The Study Committee on Campus Political Activity did not meet on Friday, November 6. On November 7 its members reached an impasse. Frank Kidner, representing the statewide university administration, proposed to the committee an amendment alternative to the one which had held up the committee earlier. His statement read:

If acts unlawful under California or Federal law directly result from advocacy, organization, or planning on the campus, the students and or-

ganizations involved may be subject to such disciplinary action as is appropriate and conditioned upon a fair hearing as to the appropriateness of the action taken.[40]

A heated discussion between Kidner and Savio ensued, during which Kidner expressed the view that an act would not have to be proclaimed unlawful for the administration to take action.[40] This, of course, was the heart of the problem as the students saw it, for they did not attribute impartiality to the administration. There was little positive response to Vice-Chancellor Searcy's appeal that "the administration is made of men of good will," and the Kidner amendment failed.

The students offered their substitute:

In the area of First Amendment rights and civil liberties, the University may impose no disciplinary action against members of the University community and organizations. In this area, members of the University community and organizations are subject only to the civil authorities.[41]

Kadish offered a substitute amendment, defining the notion of collective responsibility. It failed by one vote. The student motion was then defeated by vote of the faculty and the administration.

When it was clear that no compromise between the two positions was acceptable to the contending parties, Earl Cheit suggested the students prepare a statement on the nature of their disagreement and present it to Chancellor Strong and to the university community. Mario Savio agreed that they should make the disagreement public. After discussion, the committee agreed to report no final conclusions until they were agreed on all the relevant points.[41] The meeting adjourned.

Members of the FSM Steering Committee were sure that they had reached the end of the line in negotiations. The administration appeared adamant in its insistence on the right to censor student political action whether or not clearly stated laws were at issue. In short, it seemed committed to stopping the student civil rights movement. The Steering Committee members believed they had final proof in Kidner's statement, which struck them as corresponding word for word to the "purloined letters" of October 13.

On Sunday, November 8, therefore, the FSM issued a statement announcing its intention to end the moratorium on direct-action civil disobedience. This statement said, in part:

. . . Although we continue to be a party to the Campus Committee on Political Activity, we feel that we must lift our self-imposed moratorium on political activity because the committee is already deadlocked over the issue of political advocacy and appears headed for a long series of radical disagreements. . . . We must exercise our rights. . . . Many students and organizations have been hampered in their efforts in the past election and in civil rights activity because of the moratorium.

After outlining the points of deadlock at Saturday's meeting, the statement continued:

. . . The Free Speech Movement proposed an amendment which is the position of the American Association of University Professors and the American Civil Liberties Union. . . .

The AAUP has declared that "students should enjoy the same freedom of religion, speech, press, and assembly, and the right to petition the authorities that citizens generally possess." The Free Speech Movement intends to exercise those freedoms on Monday (Nov. 9).[42]

In the meantime, the FSM had been preparing a "report on past campus repression" through a volunteer committee organized by Mike Rossman, a graduate student in mathematics. The Steering Committee decided to run off 3000 copies of this report to distribute when the FSM set up tables again on Monday.

As soon as the FSM statement of intent to lift the moratorium on direct action was announced, reports came to them of plans for reprisal. A lawyer said he thought Kerr would "respond with clubs." He reported that Kidner had come to the Saturday meeting directly from Kerr's office, and that Oakland and Berkeley police were on twenty-four-hour stand-by orders to come to the campus. A reporter from a national magazine called to say that he had spent the day at University Hall and that the administration was making tactical plans for Monday. He had heard they planned to use mass arrests and suspensions if necessary, and probably would get the leaders first.

At 6:20 P.M. general panic broke out when a student who helped with FSM work reported that a police car had drawn up outside. The Steering Committee expected to be arrested immediately and consulted its lawyer about procedure. No arrests occurred, however. For the rest of the night rumors flowed in, while volunteers worked feverishly to hide tables at various spots on the campus so that they would be ready the next morning. They began making calls to arrange bail money and in general to line up battle strategy.[43]

nine

ESCALATION

On Monday, November 9, massive rule violation began again. The attention of the campus had been kept focused on the Study Committee's activities through daily rallies by the Free Speech Movement. Using loudspeakers from the steps of Sproul Hall during the noon hour,[1] supplemented by an occasional newsletter and mimeographed hand-outs at the entrance to the campus, FSM members had created maximum exposure to their claims among the student body. Topics addressed at rallies had remained fairly constant: the demand for freedom of political advocacy, the October 1 and 2 demonstrations, and the unsatisfactory implementation of the October 2 pact through committees. Each new event was set within this framework. Now the deadlock in the committee was used to justify collective action once more.

Members of the FSM Executive Committee were in general agreement with the Steering Committee regarding the duplicity of the administration.[2] But there was a major split in the group concerning the appropriateness of breaking university regulations *at this time*. Splinter groups lobbied feverishly to try to block this escalation. The dissidents saw no time limit that made immediate action necessary and feared the movement would be discredited.

Within the FSM the disagreement was seen as *ideological*. Slate, the Young Democrats and Republicans, and the Young People's Socialist League formed the main opposition to immediate escalation, whereas SNCC, CORE, and the more radical political groups urged this course. Although ideological differences may have played their part, the line-up split to a considerable extent between organizations dependent on day-to-day fund raising and project recruitment and those with a longer-range operating program. In other words, many groups urging confrontation faced immediate crisis if their activities were curtailed; this was not true for the opposition.

At a showdown vote on Tuesday morning (after the tables had been up for one day) the dissidents were outvoted, 27 to 19. Reactions to the efforts to block escalation that weekend led to reconstitution of the Steering Committee to remove the more moderate tacticians, who were regarded as sell-outs. Thus persons with a commitment to radical direct action came increasingly to dominate the Steering Committee for the next month.[3]

On November 9, when FSM first set up tables again against university regulations, hand-outs were given students as they entered the campus. One long statement, justifying the renewed action, said in part:

We want to explain why we have decided to begin to exercise our rights again.

(*1*) Why we have set up the tables. *The meetings of the Committee on Campus Political Activity have not been negotiating sessions. . . . Since the committee is at best advisory, and has proclaimed itself deadlocked on the only issue it has considered yet, there is no indication that its further sessions will help restore this right. . . . Already many organizations have been seriously hurt by this restraint. . . .* Rights not exercised die away. . . .

(2) Why we have begun to advocate again. . . . *The Administration . . . demands the privilege to usurp the prerogatives of the courts, to prejudge whether an act of advocacy is illegal, and to punish offenders before they have been found legally guilty.*

Our program. *We ask for our full civil liberties as citizens, and maximum freedom of expression on campus, unrestricted by the Administration's capitulation to outside pressures. . . . Our platform . . . is based on three principles: (1) arbitrary harassment and restraints on free speech and expression must not be tolerated; (2) the Administration must not usurp the prerogatives of the courts; (3) it is impossible for an individual's civil liberties to be adequately protected unless he has a voice in the formulation, interpretation, and enforcement of all regulations governing his conduct. . . .*

We have no way to negotiate about our rights. We see no way to get them, at this point, other than to exercise them publicly. We ask for no more than our rights; we will not settle for less. We ask your understanding and support.[4]

That same day, on the campus as a whole, approval of FSM goals and tactics sank to a new low. Fourteen per cent of those interviewed for Somers' survey that day still gave complete support to the FSM. Others were more skeptical. The majority of students interviewed, however, continued to agree with the FSM stand that collection of funds and recruiting of members should be allowed on campus.

Of at least 3000 potential supporters (i.e., those who had taken part in the police car demonstration) approximately 200 of those who showed up for the supporting rally on Monday, November 9, sat down in the plaza to signal that they supported the FSM action.[5] (As a symbolic link with the police car demonstration, speeches were made from atop a chest of drawers, while sympathizers sat surrounding it.) About 400 stood watching; compared to the earlier crowds, the turn-out was small.

Seventy-five students manned tables and gave their names to members of the deans' staff for violating university regulations. In view of the experience of late September, when deans had last taken students' names for a similar offense and the university had ended up suspending eight students and arresting a ninth demonstrator, this citing of students had noticeable impact on those who watched. The Graduate Coordinating Committee, a subsection of the Free Speech Movement that had been organized to represent graduate students on the Executive Committee, announced that teaching assistants and research assistants would man the tables on Tuesday; the group claimed the university would not dare to expel its teaching staff.[6]

On Tuesday 196 graduate students set up a number of tables and collected funds. No one came out to take names. (Members of the deans' staff reported later that no one went out from their office because they saw what looked like a "wagon train" of tables set up in the plaza; to them the set-up looked like a trap to lure another captive.) To demonstrators, the failure of the deans' staff to appear was confirmation of their theory that the administration would act only against the more defenseless members of the community.

Graduate students manning the tables then sent a list of students "who should be cited" to the office of the dean of students. Within a few days this list grew to over 300 names. Dean Towle sent back a letter to each student, indicating that she would consider the "citation" an error unless she heard from him again. A number of students who had not manned tables then sent letters to Dean Towle, claiming they also should have been cited and requesting that she do so. Within the next several days a total of 710 students had issued this challenge.[7] Although a sizable response, it represents a considerable decline in the number of persons actively "taking on" the campus administration. About four times this number of students had participated in the challenge of October 1 and 2.

ABORTED EFFORTS TO SOLVE THE CRISIS

Monday morning's *Daily Californian* had carried a warning from Chancellor Strong: "If the FSM returns to direct action tactics, this will constitute a clear breach of the agreement of October 2. Students and organizations participating will be held responsible for their actions." [8]

That evening President Kerr and Chancellor Strong jointly issued a statement, which said in part:

FSM has abrogated the agreement of October 2, and by reason of this abrogation, the Committee on Campus Political Activity is dissolved. . . .

We shall now seek advice on rules governing political action on campus from students through the ASUC and from the faculty through the Academic Senate, . . .[9]

Within the FSM Executive Committee, a group of students who had been out-voted on Tuesday morning in regard to the table manning decided the time had come to reappraise strategy. They believed that the Steering Committee was more interested in confrontation and national publicity than in making positive gains on the campus. They had begun to feel that the radicals were alienating the moderates in much the same way that the university was alienating the students, and the events of that weekend only cemented their attitude. The University crisis seemed to them to be replaying itself in microcosm. This group also felt, however, that an open split would probably do more harm than good, by providing ammunition for the administration.

After the crucial vote in which they lost, five members of this group went to a local restaurant to talk about what could be done. They feared that the Steering Committee was deliberately headed on a collision course and that the administration would play into its hands, with the students as innocent pawns in the game. Frustrated at their inability to communicate with the FSM radicals, they decided to get in touch with faculty members who knew President Kerr personally, to see whether they could learn how the administration intended to respond. One of these professors, S. M. Lipset, arranged for this group to meet directly with Clark Kerr.

Two meetings with Kerr were arranged that week.[10] The first was an exploratory meeting held on Tuesday night at Lipset's home.[11] The parties arranged to meet again at Kerr's office the following afternoon. The dissidents set as a precondition of negotiations, however, that students manning tables in the current escalation not be disciplined. If Kerr and the moderates could come to an agreement on campus regulations, they promised to try to obtain approval for it from the rest of the FSM Executive Committee.

When the parties met again on Wednesday, the splinter group from FSM had put into writing its own proposals: (1) Advocacy of off-campus action should be permitted on the campus. (2) There should be no discipline of a student for advocating that others undertake a legal act (such as picketing), even if the demonstration later involved actions that led to arrests. (3) There could be discipline by campus authorities for advocacy of actions that were unlawful. (4) All such cases, however, would be decided by a tribunal of faculty members nominated by the Committee of Committees of the Academic Senate.[12] (5) The university administration would retain responsibility for nonpolitical discipline but would not be responsible for the outcome of political cases.

Kerr was not very happy with some of the demands, particularly that discipline be handled by the Academic Senate. To the students, Kerr's attitude seemed quite different from what they had perceived it to be the night before. The group, expanded to include Young Republicans and Goldwater supporters, caucused in a conference room near Kerr's office. They unanimously decided that they were being used and angrily concluded that the negotiations were a farce. They were particularly distressed to hear a news report that the office of the dean of students had mailed letters citing the students who had manned tables on Monday. Since amnesty had been an absolute precondition for the present negotiations, the students denounced this action as double-dealing and left. They did not mention the negotiations at the FSM Executive Committee meeting that followed, for they considered the effort worthless.[13]

Some months later, Lipset tried to explain to me why amnesty had not been granted as agreed:

When the announcement was made—which infuriated them—well . . . I felt that Kerr is just too good a politician to do a thing like this —not the moral question—so I tried to get hold of him. . . . [After trying a number of places] I called at about 9:00, and I got hold of him—and I told him about it, and he said, "My God, that was the note!" Well, then he told me that at about 5:00 or 5:30 somebody had given him a note, and he had looked at it and put it in his pocket, and when he pulled it out it was about this thing. I think it was from Hafner [Richard P. Hafner, public affairs officer for the Berkeley campus], saying that they were going to issue this statement. Somehow it hadn't clicked. He had looked at the thing and put it in his pocket, and the implications of it hadn't struck him. And he hadn't done anything.

So then he said, "Look, it's out already." So he said he would call Strong and see if they could issue some statements about it. . . . I think [the statement] said something to the effect that they [the students manning tables] would be called before the dean, but there wouldn't be any punishment. . . . But the damage of this had been sort of done. Well, then, that was about it. That was the end of the moderate negotiation.[14]

The students, unimpressed by this explanation, thought they knew a better reason for the failure to honor the agreement. At noon that day the faculty representatives to the Study Committee held a meeting in Pauley Ballroom of the Student Union building to report on the status of discussions at the time the Committee had been dissolved. The students believed that Kerr had decided the faculty was offering him a better deal, since its position had been closer to that of the administration. Hence these students decided they had been used and were extremely bitter.[15] And so the demonstrations continued.

A NEW VOTE OF CONFIDENCE

On Friday, November 13, the Academic Senate Ad Hoc Committee on the suspensions released its report.[16] The members recommended that six of the eight suspended students be reinstated as of the date of their suspensions. They recommended further that Mario Savio and Art

Goldberg be given six-week suspensions, to begin on September 30 and end on November 16. (Thus they recommended that the suspensions for these two leaders should end in three days.) Spokesmen for the FSM hailed the report as a vindication of their position.

Thereafter, approval of the goals and tactics of the FSM shot upward. As mentioned previously, on November 9, when tables were set up again, only 14% of the students interviewed by Somers' methods class expressed unreserved approval of the FSM. During the four-day period that followed, while the administration was canceling the Study Committee on Campus Political Activity and beginning disciplinary action against those who manned the tables, approval rose to 28%. And in the week that followed the release of the report by the Ad Hoc Committee on suspensions, 47% of the students expressed unreserved approval of the demonstrators' goals and tactics.[17]

ten **SPIRITUAL** **ENCOUNTER**	THE HEIGHTS With the Free Speech Movement and the Berkeley administration clearly at an impasse, the tripartite Study Committee dissolved, the *sub rosa* negotiations with the university president abandoned, and an escalated challenge from supporters of the FSM, the conflict appeared

beyond solution by the parties most immediately affected. The next meeting of the University Board of Regents, however, was scheduled for Friday, November 20, at Berkeley. This group seemed then the one hope for resolving the problem.

The FSM announced plans for a massive vigil to take place outside the Regents' meeting place during their Friday deliberations. Permission was requested to appear before the board and "formally present the platform of the FSM, which consists of a carefully formulated body of proposed regulations to govern student political activity on campus."[1] In response, President Kerr indicated that the Regents would prefer not having anyone speak, but that they would receive written proposals.[1]

As FSM leaders wondered how to ensure a large crowd on Friday, someone remembered that Joan Baez had spoken approvingly of the police car demonstration while giving a concert in the campus Greek Theater on Friday, October 2. Through a sympathizer of their cause they contacted Ira Sandperl, Joan Baez's close friend. Eventually Joan Baez agreed to come from her home in Carmel, California, to give a free concert from the steps of Sproul Hall at noon on Friday as a recruiting device for the vigil.[2]

But Friday, November 20, was the day of the Big Game Rally as well as of the Regents meeting. The college pep organizations had scheduled a "Beat Stanford" rally for Sproul Plaza, and for the same noon-hour period that FSM had scheduled its Baez concert and vigil-recruiting rally. Two large, and quite different, crowds collected in the plaza. One, consisting of sympathizers of the FSM, was facing east toward the Sproul Hall steps. The other crowd, wearing blue and gold (the university colors) and dressed in the style of the collegiate subculture, was facing south, toward the Student Union steps.

Before the FSM could begin its rally, cheerleaders of the other group began leading a "Beat Stanford" yell. For a while things were tense, for it was clear that neither rally was going to give way to the other.

Then Steve Weisman, a member of the FSM Steering Committee, had an inspiration. He led the FSM crowd in a "Beat Stanford" yell. The cheerleaders responded with a "Free speech" yell. Gradually the two rallies blended, the crowds mingled, and the tension dissolved. The cheerleaders made their rally a short one, so that people could hear Joan Baez. The head cheerleader ended his pep talk to the crowd by saying, "Now I want all of you who are with me to bring a candle to the bonfire tonight." Turning to the FSM ralliers, he said, "And I want all of you to get a black arm band to wear to the vigil!"

With this gesture, the boundaries between the two crowds were broken, people turned east, and the FSM rally began in earnest. Because of the double scheduling of the area and the publicity about the free concert, the group had a very large crowd. Also, thanks to the implicit endorsement of the head cheerleader, the Free Speech rally had been made "legitimate" for the entire crowd.

The speeches were short and simple. The FSM had an American flag beside the microphone and talked about the importance of defending the U.S. Constitution. Joan Baez gave a brief talk about nonviolence. After singing an antiwar song, "With God on Our Side," she asked the crowd to join her in the Calypso version of "The Lord's Prayer." A hush settled over the crowd as she began; then subdued and reverent voices joined in the chant-refrain, "Hallowed-ah be Thy name." It was a powerful emotional experience, rhythmic, the entire group singing, led by one of the country's most talented artists.

At the end of the song an FSM leader announced, "And as Joan Baez leads us in singing, 'We Shall Overcome,' we will march, six abreast, with the American flag in front of us, to the Regents meeting. I hope you will all join us."

The FSM Steering Committee and the people at the front marched around behind the crowd and then north, toward the main drive of the campus. Monitors moved forward among the crowd, motioning people to join the line six-abreast. It was soon apparent that almost the entire crowd was falling into the singing, marching line.[3]

As the crowd moved through Sather Gate, north past the library and classroom buildings to the main campus drive, a number of people who had not gone to the rally but had crowded along the edge of the pathway to watch the march fell into line at the end. I noted persons in the crowd of marchers who before the rally had assured me they were not going to become involved in this controversy.

The marching maneuver of circling the crowd effectively broke up the sense of spatial separation that allows persons on the edge of a crowd to remain uninvolved. Since ardent supporters, normally at the front of a crowd, now were moving all around one, it required conscious effort to remain separate from what was going on.

The *Daily Californian* estimated that 3000 students took part in the vigil; the FSM leaders thought there were 5000. I am sure that there were not less than 2000, judging from the spacing of the line of marchers, and they may well have been more. After marching north to the main campus drive, the demonstrators proceeded down the hill to University Hall at the west edge of the campus, where the Regents were meeting.

Students who first joined an FSM action at the time of this vigil seem to have been strongly impressed by the moral tone of the rally, as the following essays indicate:

I decided to participate when it became obvious that talk alone did not do any good. . . . I do not decide merely on a tactical *basis. The moral argument speaks for the* whole *man, the tactical argument for his intelligence only. . . . I believed in freedom of speech and of petition. Because of the arbitrary power of the Regents, this was the only thing that could be done.*[4]

I was impressed by the order and sincerity of the demonstration—the purpose was to get a hearing and this was clear. . . . An action had been chosen behind which the whole campus could unite, unlike previous actions like sit-ins or manning tables.

. . . The people behind changes in rules would realize the issue had mass concern; it didn't just affect a few radicals. I thought, naively I guess in retrospect, that that meeting would wish to comply with the feelings on campus. I sort of thought rules would be liberalized then, but didn't have really concrete ideas about what I expected.

I decided to participate when the lines went by me because I saw some friends in it and they called me to join. I thought the action was an acceptable one, and I was influenced by my friends. . . . I was unconvinced about the FSM in general, but supported this particular action [4]

While the Regents met, FSM sympathizers sat on the lawn across the street. Joan Baez continued to sing and to talk.

THE DEPTHS

Defeat by the Regents

A five-man delegation from the FSM Steering Committee was given reserved seats in the spectators' gallery of the Regents Conference Room. Eventually the delegates returned to report to the crowd. The Regents had approved the following recommendations, submitted by President Kerr and Chancellor Strong:

1. That the sole and total penalty for six students be suspension from September 30 to date.

2. That the other two students be suspended for the period from September 30, 1964, to date and that they be placed on probation for the current semester for their actions up to and including September 30, 1964.

3. That adjustments in academic programs be permitted for the eight students on approval by the appropriate Academic Dean.

4. New disciplinary proceedings before the Faculty Committee on

Student Conduct will be instituted immediately against certain students and organizations for violations subsequent to September 30, 1964.

5. That rules and regulations be made more clear and specific, and thus, incidentally and regrettably, more detailed and legalistic; and that explicit penalties, where possible, be set forth for specific violations.

6. That the Berkeley campus be given sufficient staff in the Dean of Students Office and the Police Department so that as nearly as possible all students involved in violations be identified with the fullest possible proof, since the incompleteness of identification of participants and collection of full proof have been held against the university; also that the general counsel's office be given sufficient staff so it may participate, as necessary, in the legal aspects of student discipline cases, particularly since a more legalistic approach is being taken toward student discipline.

7. That the right and ability of the university to require students and others on campus to identify themselves be assured by whatever steps are necessary.

In addition, the Regents revised university policy on political action. The Regents' resolution, introduced by President Kerr, read:

1. The Regents restate the long-standing University policy as set forth in Regulation 25 on student conduct and discipline that "all students and student organizations . . . obey the laws of the State and the Community. . . ."

2. The Regents adopt the policy effective immediately that certain campus facilities, carefully selected and properly regulated, may be used by students and staff for planning, implementing, or raising funds or recruiting participants for lawful off-campus action, not for unlawful off-campus action.[5]

If my notes made at the time are accurate, the FSM Steering Committee reported to the vigil, in regard to item 4 of the first resolution, merely, "There will be new disciplinary proceedings against students and organizations for subsequent violations, to be handled by the faculty committee." No date was mentioned for the time period to be considered. One would assume, from the context in which it was said, that this meant discipline for any actions in the future.

Since item 4 became centrally important in the days that followed, I later asked several members of the FSM Steering Committee if they had heard the statement that discipline would be instituted for events of October 1 and 2, and if so why they had not reported it at the time. Apparently they were so upset by the announcement that Strong and Kerr were asking *heavier* penalties than the ad hoc faculty committee had presented that they did not hear the dates involved for "new disciplinary proceedings." [6] (The FSM Steering Committee, incidentally, was as surprised as the rest of the campus by the events that followed.)

There was general consternation among the vigil participants when the section of the meeting dealing with discipline was reported. Mario Savio announced that the policy had been decided by Kerr in mid-October, although the Regents had just now acted on it. Savio continued, ". . . I'm serving notice on them now. We're going to be ready for them. We're not going to take this sitting down. If they try to enforce these unconstitutional regulations, they're going to suffer for it. . . ." [7]

Then Michael Rossman spoke. Unlike the others, who sounded angry, Rossman spoke in a deep, moderate voice:

I am disappointed. I gather that you're all disappointed, too. It looks like that if we want to keep this up—if we want to continue fighting for what we began fighting for—there's going to be a long and bitter battle ahead. The time, parenthetically, to start that battle I think will be Monday.

They did not hear the delegation of five we sent in. . . . They have disregarded the recommendations of the Heyman committee and in addition intend to institute disciplinary proceedings against how many more of us? Seventy more who were cited? The two hundred graduates whose names were sent in? The eight hundred who signed the list? How many?

They disregarded at least three separate proposals from the faculty. They disregarded the proposal from the student body as represented by the ASUC and, so far as it represents the student body, the proposal of the FSM—which I do trust represents these people here.

Instead they listened to their legal counsel, for the best way to get around what we want. "We" being the faculty, the students. In one or another form, we have expressed our wishes. They have been denied. We have no voice. We have never had a voice. They are not giving us a voice now. They will fight to the last—delicately, professionally, discretely; by memoranda, by legal counsels, but they will fight to the last bitter end not to give us any voice.

I do not want to say anything inflammatory about it now. This is something that everyone should, I think, take home and ponder for himself. Ponder it for the weekend. Maybe have it pondered by Monday because—well—I do not know what Monday will bring. I do not know if anybody knows what Monday will bring. Monday will bring one thing, certainly: the graduate students.

Another graduate student, Michael Abramovitch, said, "Young people are giving their lives, their youth, to bring this issue to the courts. The Regents are side-tracking this into their closet."

Steve Weisman, chairman of the Graduate Coordinating Committee, announced there would be a Monday rally to decide what to do next. Then the crowd sat in silence for fifteen minutes. At the end of that time, Joan Baez began singing, "We Shall Overcome."

Weisman, normally the calm voice in the FSM, arose, obviously quite agitated. He proposed a sit-in in the Regents building across the street. Dustin Miller immediately supported the suggestion.

It was Mario Savio's turn to be a calming influence. He urged restraint, pointing out that there was room for ambiguity and interpretation of the ruling. "Let us not lay ourselves open to discrediting."

Reginald Zelnik, a young faculty member in the History Department, spoke next.[8] He said the faculty had been slapped by this decision, just as had the students. There was a meeting of the Academic Senate on Tuesday. He urged restraint in the meantime.

A student came to the microphone to urge a sit-in as a test case. Savio replied that the students needed a test case, but not one of disturbing the peace. He called for a show of hands regarding the sit-in. There was an overwhelming "no" vote. The meeting adjourned until Monday noon.

In its Monday issue the *Daily Californian* reported the following conversation with Clark Kerr:

Kerr was asked after the meeting who would decide the illegality of advocated action. "In the usual case you'd wait for the courts to decide," he said. "It would then go to the Faculty Committee on Student Conduct."

Asked if the new policy was more stringent than the old, Kerr replied, "That's absolutely not true."

Specific regulations were not set down, he said, because "the question of writing rules and regulations is pretty complicated. The Regents prefer to make general policy statements."

"General counsel for the University will probably make up the specific regulations," he added, "and the Board will take a look at them."

The Regents did not allow the ASUC Senate or the Free Speech Movement to address the Board orally, but said they would consider all reports carefully before the next meeting.[9]

On November 21 the question of legal versus illegal advocacy of action was underscored when Art Goldberg and David Wild, both students at the university, were two of eight persons arrested while picketing the Oakland *Tribune* and booked for trespassing and disturbing the peace for sitting-in at the *Tribune* offices. Goldberg, who had just been reinstated by the Board of Regents and had been placed on probation, said that more than 5000 leaflets advocating a picket of the *Tribune* had been distributed on campus Friday.[9]

Many months after the events I asked Clark Kerr how the decision was reached to bring those two particular resolutions to the November meeting of the Board of Regents. Kerr said he had learned, after the earlier blow-up in the fall, that recent Supreme Court rulings had made the university policy prohibiting political advocacy out of date— that the direction of recent court decisions was to extend protection of freedom of speech into the area of advocacy as well. He had learned, furthermore, that Stanford University had quietly changed its regulations in the spring to conform to this new development, and that San Francisco State had made the change somewhat earlier. He therefore had decided that the university policy should be changed as well. But he was aware there would be opposition to such a change on the part of some Regents, and that there was considerable feeling about the capture of the police car.

Kerr reported being surprised that the Heyman committee had not covered events of October 1 and 2. He said that Chancellor Strong believed firmly some disciplinary action should be taken for violation of university regulations at that time and that he was aware several Regents also felt strongly about the matter. To Kerr the crucial thing was to get a change in policy passed by the meeting. He expected liberal Regents to back the change and hoped to avoid resistance from more conservative members of the board. Therefore he decided to include both recommendations together, assuming that any discipline which resulted would be in the nature of a reprimand for misbehavior. It did not occur to him that anyone would take the second item seriously.[10] He was soon to learn how deeply he had miscalculated the mood of the campus.

Those who supported the policy position of the Free Speech Movement left the vigil distressed and angry. The FSM Steering Committee met nonstop for forty-eight hours, trying to decide on a course of action. Toward the end of that time they were utterly exhausted, angry, confused. They were united in their judgment that the Regents had slapped the students and faculty in the face, and that the new liberalization of university rules did not resolve the basic issue in dispute. They felt something had to be done but could not agree on what it should be. Mario Savio, who had remained calm at the vigil, became more and more angry as he thought about the situation. He believed the students should hold a sit-in in Sproul Hall on Monday to register a moral protest of the decision. Others sympathized, feeling they were being harassed by the administration, but considered the time was not ripe: it was not yet clear to the general student body what the administration intended to do, for the disciplinary statement was ambiguous. If the FSM acted too soon, it would lose the great body of support gained through the vigil. The vote went back and forth, no one really satisfied with any outcome. Finally, in the early morning hours of Monday, November 23, the exhausted Steering Committee voted, 5 to 4, to have a sit-in in Sproul Hall that afternoon.[11]

Collective redefinition fails: the "abortive sit-in"

On Monday, a very large crowd gathered for the noon rally. The event began with a series of antiadministration songs, sung to the tune of Christmas carols. The lyrics were clever and so popular an expression of the mood of the time that the tape recording of these songs was made into a record which sold widely on the campus. The themes of the songs were the administrative distrust of students, overly protective dormitory rules ("Womb with a View"), the impersonal treatment of students, and the political maneuvering of the university president.

Tape recordings of the rallies held during the fall show the issues of discontent gradually widening as the controversy progressed. Beginning with concern about rights to a small strip of territory, the students had shifted their focus to freedom of expression and advocacy on the campus as a whole. After the arrest of October 1, they began to talk about the proper purposes of the university. A great deal of rhetoric described the university as a factory where students were considered less important than the IBM cards they handed in at various windows. Much attention was given to bureaucratic responses from administrators and staff members who dealt with students. Little by little, as the controversy deepened, more and more issues became united. By December 3 it was apparent that the very nature of the university itself was at stake. But we are getting ahead of the story.

On November 23 speakers denounced President Kerr and Chancellor Strong for ignoring the Heyman committee's recommendations. Then, in the midst of the rally, Vice-Chancellor Alan Searcy came out the main doors of Sproul Hall with a portable lectern and his own public address system. It was the first time that a member of the administration had appeared at a rally to challenge claims being made by leaders of the Free Speech Movement. Searcy read a statement by Chancellor Strong that said, in part:

The new policy provides opportunities for direct political action requested by 18 off-campus student organizations on September 18, and by the ASUC Senate on September 22.

. . . Activities of students in disobedience of the laws of the State and community are punishable in the courts. The University maintains jurisdiction over violations of its rules including those which prohibit use of University facilities for planning and recruiting for actions found to be unlawful by the courts. There will be no prior determination of double jeopardy in matters of political and social activities organized on the campus by students and staff. The demand of the FSM that the University permit the mounting of unlawful action on the campus without penalty by the University cannot and will not be granted.

Most of the items in the report of the faculty group of the Committee on Campus Political Activity are subject to action by the Chancellor. I will take appropriate action upon consultation with the Student Affairs Committee and through that Committee with the ASUC Senate. . . .[12]

Searcy went on to point out that the students really had no idea of what the administration intended to do. He asked them to wait twenty-four hours to see what the specific application of the Regents' new policy statement would be.

At the end of his short speech, Searcy turned to leave. Mario Savio took the FSM's public address system microphone and called, "Hey! Get back here!"

The vice-chancellor returned to his microphone but refused to debate with Savio. He soon left.

The FSM orators called the chancellor's statement "another stall," and claimed that the new policy gave the administration the power to crush off-campus social movements at the moments when they would be most needed.[13] Mario Savio called for students to sit-in at Sproul Hall then and there. He explained that, since the Steering Committee had been split over what to recommend, he was asking people to join him inside as a *personal* witness.

Steve Weisman, a member of the Steering Committee, then took the microphone to argue against the "personal witness" sit-in on tactical grounds.

Art Goldberg invited speakers to come forward "for five or ten minutes of advocacy" to test the new regulations. A spokesman for the Oakland *Tribune* picketing project, the business agent for the East Bay Municipal Employees Association, and representatives from DuBois, Slate, and other organizations came to the microphone to stress that their groups were not afraid to carry out such a test.

Mario Savio then read from the *Tribune* an editorial entitled, "Who Runs the University?" (In view of the student beliefs about *Tribune* influence on university policy, the editorial sounded ironic.) Marty Roysher, a member of the FSM Steering Committee, read a mocking reply to a letter Dean Towle had sent to students who manned tables earlier in the month.

Debate over the appropriateness of a sit-in at this time continued until 2:00 P.M., with members of the Steering Committee publicly disagreeing about the appropriateness of the tactic. Eventually, from the rather large crowd that had come to the rally, several dozen protesters began walking inside the building. Finally, about 300 persons went inside. Some of them told me that afternoon that they had come in, not because they were convinced it was a good idea, but because they didn't want the administration to think the FSM had no following.

Meanwhile, outside the building the debate over tactics continued. A boy went to the microphone and said, "Fifteen hundred to 2000 people left. I think this demonstrates this is a mistake today."

A girl replied, "We must stand united."

Eventually one of the song writers angrily took the microphone and stated, "The leadership has pulled a shit-trick. But we have no choice but to go in and join them."

Several people began proposing alternative action to support the students inside instead of joining them: they might ask for individual appointments with the dean, they might write letters, they might undertake a systematic breaking of the rules.

Marty Roysher took the microphone to defend the action of those who had gone inside: "We are making a moral witness by sitting in that inhuman hall this afternoon. . . . we cannot be put off day after day." Eventually Jack Weinberg came to the window and urged people to come inside, stressing that the unity of the movement must be maintained.

Inside the building, a spirited debate was going on, while many people milled about quietly. Mario Savio insisted that majority decisions were not binding on minority points of view. "You cannot bind individual consciences. Those who want to go are not, therefore, finks."

Weisman came inside to report: "Those of us downstairs think the meeting should be broken. It is a meaningless, dispirited group. I can't handle them. I think no one could. They won't come in. I won't either."

The argument about proper procedure continued with some heat. Barbara Garson,[14] who edited the FSM newsletter, spoke militantly:

Five thousand people were ignored, Friday. When I think of this action, I think my intention is a moral one, also. My intention is to win!

The Regents gave an honest answer: "We're not listening to the faculty; we're not listening to the students. We decide. We run the show."

I would disrupt the functioning of this building! I do not say in this that the minority should act without the majority. But they will listen only when they see it is not worth their while to suppress us! It is the only tactical, the only logical, position.

A small group near the improvised speakers' stand applauded enthusiastically.

Meanwhile Bettina Aptheker, who had opposed the sit-in when it was voted on earlier, rounded up the Steering Committee and insisted that they vote again. After some discussion, it was decided, by a 6–5 vote, that the group should leave by 5:00 P.M., having stayed inside long enough to save face but not long enough to discredit themselves completely.

Shortly before 3:30 P.M. Jack Weinberg tried to present this decision to the students sitting in. It soon became clear that the group was not united. There was much background noise, and milling through the building. Also, an undercurrent of hostility within the group, which had not been noticeable on earlier occasions, was perceptible. As students argued, many began by citing their credentials: what they had done in the Free Speech Movement, how many civil rights arrests they had, and the like.

In advocating the decision of the Steering Committee, Weinberg said, "Let us not override this decision, even though I voted against it. We must not split the movement. I want to know your pleasure."

He was immediately challenged by a number of hostile demonstrators: "No Steering Committee decision is final for individual actions!"

Weinberg excitedly interrupted: "Wait a minute! Here's WHY we decided: a lot of us came in here against our better judgment to support others. We cannot ask others to continue."

He was shouted down. It seemed clear that the Steering Committee no longer had control of this group. Then Bettina Aptheker climbed up on the card file in the second-floor lobby where the argument was taking place. She spoke with militancy and apparently unshakable confidence: "We're in this thing to win!" She was greeted by shouts of approval and applause from the dissidents.

We are a political movement! We are fighting the administration and the Regents! Every move should be geared to win. [Shouts of approval.]
If we're gonna win, we gotta stick together! Damn it, if we're gonna win, you've got to stick by a decision of the Steering Committee, no matter how badly split that vote was! [Loud applause.]

Then she announced a 9:30 meeting of the Executive Committee, open to any members of the movement, to be held at Hillel Foundation. (There was more applause.)

Several people then spoke of the need for the Steering Committee members to get some sleep, so that they could begin to think clearly. Finally a girl called, "Let's have no more speakers. Let's just sit down."

"Yeah," said Savio, "that's not a bad idea. But I just want to say one thing because some of the things I've heard make me sick." He paused, and there was silence.

The problem of disorganized people—leadership needs some kind of organized legitimacy. ORGANIZATIONS. GRAD STUDENTS. INDEPENDENTS.

I've been criticized because they say mass democracy is dishonest. I've watched Fidel Castro, and I agree. But I—we—have tried to feel what those who commit themselves on the line are feeling. I have really tried. [Quiet comments: "That's right."]

*I voted against leaving, but I urge you to abide by this, for there are good reasons on the other side. I must urge—*INSIST*—that you leave. I hope you will consider that with some friendship.*

Some of the more militant demonstrators refused and directly challenged Savio's leadership. Finally one of their spokesmen climbed up on the card file and shouted: "Why did we come here in the first place? If we leave will we remain a vanguard or become an institutionalized political party? We've committed suicide if we leave."

A shout came from the side: "Somebody tell us to stay!" There was a call for a show of hands of those who wished to stay. Only a few hands went up.

It was a badly demoralized and split group. Bettina Aptheker led the students in singing "We Shall Overcome" as they finally left Sproul Hall.

The meeting at Hillel Foundation that night was morose, and found no new direction. A number of persons on the Executive Committee, as well as friendly observers of the movement, opined privately that the FSM was dead.

The final blows

At the Academic Senate meeting the next day Lawrence Levine [15] offered a motion on the "free speech" controversy. He asked the Senate to support the establishment of a faculty committee that would have "final jurisdiction on questions of political rights and free speech." He argued that such a resolution would solve the current controversy about advocacy of unlawful acts: it would be able to give fairer judgments because it would not be subject to external pressure, and it would have more cooperation from students because they had greater faith in the faculty.

The motion was defeated when it was attacked by History Department Chairman Henry May: "I do not think it is proper or wise for the faculty to take over the responsibilities of disciplining students." May claimed that this was an *administrative* function.[16]

For the remainder of the meeting, the Academic Senate devoted its energy to condemning the administration "for its disregard and contempt" for the Senate in the handling of the Eli Katz case. The motion, passed by a vote of 267 to 79, commended the Academic Freedom Committee for urging "prompt implementation" of the recommendation by the Privilege and Tenure Committee that called for Katz's reinstatement at the university. The *Daily Californian* summarized the situation as follows:

The Freedom Committee had objected to a statement from Chancellor Strong which maintained "no action" would be taken with regard to Katz until the Committee had issued a report on the general policies and procedures involved in the Katz case.

Since the Privilege and Tenure Committee had already made a judgment on the Katz case, the Freedom Committee claimed the Chancellor's request would have one Academic Senate Committee reviewing the findings of another.[16]

That day Katherine Towle denied Slate's request for permission to show "Un Chant d'Amour" on campus. This film by Jean Genet concerns homosexuality in prison. Said Dean Towle, "A public showing is not compatible with the educational purpose of the University of California." (The film already had resulted in considerable public controversy in the area. There had been a threat of possible police action if it were shown in Berkeley.)

As the students left for the Thanksgiving recess, advocates of the Free Speech Movement were dejected. They had experienced defeat by the Regents, dissension within their ranks, an "abortive sin-in," further "evidence" (i.e., the Academic Senate censure) that the administration was not to be trusted in political matters, a refusal of the faculty to endorse the FSM position, and, finally, censorship by the dean's office of the content of an art form. The vulnerability of the university to public criticism and outside pressure seemed clear, but its possibilities for successful resistance to such forces were not apparent.

eleven
THE SHOWDOWN

Over the Thanksgiving recess, to the complete surprise of the Free Speech Movement leadership and indeed of the campus at large, disciplinary letters were sent to four students for violations of university regulations during the demonstrations of October 1 and 2. Most observers had assumed this period was covered in the ad hoc faculty committee's report.

Vigilers a few days before had not heard the directive from the Regents, ordering administrators to draw up disciplinary charges for events occurring after September 30. But this action had, in fact, been ordered.

During the week after the Regents meeting, therefore, Edward Strong and Thomas Cunningham's staff went to work, documenting charges against students who had been involved in the pack-in and the police melee on the afternoon of October 1. They considered only cases where there was clear, documentary evidence of violations. On Saturday, November 28, Strong sent out letters of citation to Brian Turner, Jackie Goldberg, Art Goldberg, and Mario Savio.

The letters charged the FSM leaders with entrapping a university police car and an arrested person:

On October 1 and 2, 1964, you led and encouraged numerous demonstrators in keeping a University police car and an arrested person therein entrapped on the Berkeley campus for a period of approximately 32 hours, which arrested person the police were then endeavoring to transport to police headquarters for processing.

In addition, Savio's letter charged him with leading demonstrators into Sproul Hall for a pack-in that blocked doorways and passageways:

. . . disrupting the functions of that office and forcing personnel to leave through a window and across a roof. . . .

You led and encouraged demonstrators forcefully and violently to resist the efforts of the University police and the Berkeley city police in their attempts pursuant to orders, to close the main doors of Sproul

Hall on the Berkeley campus. On October 1, 1964, you bit Berkeley city police officer Phillip E. Mower on the left thigh, breaking the skin and causing bruises, while resisting Officer Mower's attempts to close the main doors of Sproul Hall.

Art Goldberg's letter had this charge:

You threatened Sgt. Robert Ludden of the University police by stating to him, in substance, that if police reinforcements attempted to remove the prisoner from your control and that of the demonstrators, he, Sgt. Ludden, and other police officers stationed at the entrapped police car, would be violently attacked by you and other demonstrators.

The letters ordered Savio and Goldberg to attend a hearing by the Faculty Committee on Student Conduct: "You may be represented by counsel at the hearing. The recommendation of the Faculty Committee on Student Conduct will be advisory to me." [1]

Dean Katherine Towle considered the action most unwise and voiced her strong disapproval before the letters were sent out. She was overruled, however, on the grounds that the Regents had ordered disciplinary action for events occurring after September 30.[2]

Word of the letters spread quickly. The FSM Steering Committee reconvened as soon as possible, holding an emergency meeting Sunday at 4:00 P.M. Bettina Aptheker since has stated her reaction, which was shared by many others on the Steering Committee:

I knew that was it. That's what we were waiting for—for the final atrocity. . . .

I was sick and tired of hanky-pankying around with their negotiations, and not knowing what they were going to do. . . . Kerr was a great maneuverer. He was much smarter than we were, in terms of that. The thing he didn't have was support. But we did. I was much more comfortable in mass action than in any of these kinds of negotiations.[3]

At 8:30 P.M. on Sunday the Steering Committee issued a statement:

The Administration sees the free speech protest as a simple problem of disobedience and refuses to recognize the legitimacy of the students' needs. . . . By again arbitrarily singling out students for punishment, the Administration avoids facing the real issues.

Its action violates the spirit of the Heyman Committee report and can only be seen as an attempt to provoke another October 2. We demand that these new charges be dropped.[4]

When reached by the *Daily Californian,* Chancellor Strong would not confirm that disciplinary letters had or had not been sent: "Out of concern for the students, no matter what the occasion, the Chancellor's office makes no announcement of students being called up for disciplinary action." [4]

Members of the Steering Committee were sure they knew why the university had acted. They were convinced that the November 23 sit-in had persuaded the administration that the FSM was weak and demoralized and that now it could get away with such action.[3]

The FSM battle plan was simple: its members would issue an ultimatum, demanding that the university withdraw charges against Savio, Turner, and the two Goldbergs. If the administration refused, as they expected it would, they would begin a sit-in in Sproul Hall on Wednesday, December 2. They would remain in the building overnight, hoping to be arrested. They were sure that a large number of arrests would lead to a general student strike, which the graduate students in the FSM had been encouraging. If the administration ignored the sit-in, they would call a strike for Friday, anyway, hoping to have engendered enough sympathy in the meantime to get a large response.[3]

On Monday, November 30, Chancellor Strong rejected demands that the charges be dropped:

The Heyman Committee limited itself to charges of misconduct up to and including September 30, and declined to consider charges of violations after that date. . . . These further charges have been referred to the Faculty Committee on Student Conduct for hearing. . . .

. . . In threatening to engage in direct action if the charges are not dropped, those who make such threats demand a decision based not on facts but on intimidation. The charges, properly, will be subjected to the test of evidence.[5]

The Graduate Coordinating Committee of the FSM announced a meeting on December 1 "to plan for a T.A. [teaching assistant—that is, a graduate student who assists in the teaching of courses] strike." Rumors spread over the campus not only that four FSM leaders had been cited, but also that eight organizations affiliated with FSM were facing disciplinary action. Administration spokesmen refused to comment on the charge.[5]

The next day, December 1, a letter from President Kerr, dated November 30, appeared in the *Daily Californian:*

Relying on the Daily Californian *as a medium of information is like relying on smoke signals. You can gain an impression that something is being said, but you can never be quite sure what. My current concern is the continued unwillingness of the Editors to quote what I actually said in an item which has been discussed within the University community from time to time, with the* Daily Californian *being the chief carrier of misquotations.*

Now I realize that misquotations may be more interesting than quotations and the Daily Californian *succeeds in being interesting. With the hope that it might also be accurate, I am turning to the Icebox [6] as a last resort, hoping it may be open also to the cause of accuracy as it is to so many other and sometimes quite contrary causes.*

Herewith are two actual quotations which are a lot less interesting than the misquotations:

1. At a press conference held in conjunction with a speech before Town Hall in Los Angeles on October 6 and in response to a reporter's question, I said:

"Experienced on-the-spot observers estimated that the hard core group of demonstrators—those who continued as part of the demonstrations through the night of October 1—contained at times as much as 40 per cent off-campus elements. And, within that off-campus group, there were persons identified as being sympathetic with the Communist Party and Communist causes."

2. On October 2 at a press conference in San Francisco following a meeting of the American Council on Education, I said:

"I am sorry to say that some elements active in the demonstrations have been impressed with the tactics of Fidel Castro and Mao Tse-Tung. There are very few of these, but there are some."

The *Daily Californian* answered President Kerr's letter with the following statement:

Early in the Bancroft-Telegraph "free speech" dispute President Kerr was quoted as saying that 49 per cent of the student demonstrators were Mao-Marxists.

The Daily Californian *never ran that so-called quotation at any time because we understood it was not accurate.*

We believe that we acted for the "cause of accuracy." [7]

There was no mention in Kerr's letter of the current dispute. It was printed the day that the FSM Steering Committee made a formal ultimatum to the administration, backed up by an announcement from the Graduate Coordinating Committee that teaching assistants would strike on Friday, December 4, "if conditions warrant."

The FSM ultimatum was printed as a handbill and circulated. It said, in part:

A SPECTRE IS HAUNTING THE UNIVERSITY OF CALIFORNIA—THE SPECTRE OF STUDENT RESISTANCE TO ARBITRARY ADMINISTRATIVE POWER.

The Board of Regents has used Chancellor Strong to attack leaders of the Free Speech Movement:

Chancellor Strong has summoned Arthur Goldberg, Mario Savio, and Jackie Goldberg before his Faculty Committee on Student Conduct. These three students have been singled out—from among thousands— for their participation in the demonstrations of October 1st and 2nd.

The Administration has also initiated disciplinary action against these student organizations. Campus CORE, Young Socialist Alliance, Slate, Women for Peace, W.E.B. DuBois Club, University Friends of SNCC.

WE DEMAND THE FOLLOWING ACTION BE TAKEN BY WEDNESDAY NOON:

That disciplinary procedures against Arthur Goldberg, Mario Savio, Jackie Goldberg, and the student political organizations be halted. That the Administration guarantee there will be no further disciplining of students or organizations for political activity that occurs before a final settlement is reached.

That freedom of political activity be protected by revision of present University policy so that:

—Only the courts regulate the content *of political expression.*

—Faculty, students, and Administration jointly determine and enforce all regulations governing the form *of political expression.*

—All regulations which unnecessarily restrict political activity be repealed.

Two missing ingredients for collective response had now been added, one by action of the administration, the other by action of the Free Speech Movement. First, the disciplinary action and the refusal to comment on rumors of further discipline against political organizations provided compelling "evidence" that the claims of the FSM about the meaning of the November Regents meeting and the intentions of the university administration were well founded. Second, the FSM ultimatum,[8] with its twenty-four-hour deadline, provided a time limit that sharpened the fuzzier deadline implied in the administrative letters requiring students to report for a disciplinary hearing.

That evening the ASUC Senate passed a "demonstration resolution":

(*1*) . . . *the FSM no longer has the extension of on-campus political rights as its goal, and . . . its present plans for civil disobedience are directed solely toward meaningless harassment of the University.*

(*2*) . . . *the ASUC Senate encourages all responsible students to avoid the scheduled sit-in December 2nd. . . .*

(*3*) . . . *the ASUC Senate . . . encourages department chairmen . . . to make preparations to accommodate students . . . [if] any teaching assistants neglect their classes.*

(*4*) . . . *the ASUC Senate encourages all students to continue to attend their classes . . .*

(*5*) . . . *the ASUC Senate shall fully investigate the manner in which the administration has pursued prosecution of students involved in demonstrations throughout this semester.*[9]

Clark Kerr was out of town when the FSM ultimatum was delivered to his office. After telephone calls and staff conversations it was decided that no response would be made to the ultimatum.

Noon on December 2, 1964, was the deadline the FSM had set for a reply to its ultimatum. By 12 o'clock a very large crowd—perhaps four or five thousand people—had assembled in Sproul Hall Plaza to see what would happen. Joan Baez had returned to lead singing for the rally and sit-in.

The ASUC had set up loudspeakers in the Student Union Plaza, one level below and just to the west of Sproul Plaza, and was conducting its own rally. In contrast, it was poorly attended.[10]

The FSM rally of December 2 had a quality different from any which had preceded it.[11] Speakers were far more excited; their voices were strident and harsh. There was an urgency in striking contrast to the pace of FSM rallies in the past. Previously some speakers may have been militant, and speaking styles varied widely, but there had been an element of rational discourse, of charm of expression, in most of the rallies. On December 2 this was gone. The tone, the rhythms, the tense, searing timbre of voices were similar to those heard during an altar call in a major religious revival campaign. The crowd felt the tension. The speakers made it clear that in their view anyone who did not enter Sproul Hall was deserting his fellow students, leaving them to the mercies of the police and an untrustworthy administration. A number of people turned to their neighbors, talking loudly, breaking the spell.

Early in the rally Charles Powell, ASUC president, had appeared in fraternity garb (bleeding madras sport shirt), to ask the students not to sit-in. Mario Savio called him a traitor and a fink.

There is little need to present the order of speakers or their messages, for the definition of crisis had been set earlier, along with the action that would be needed to resolve it. All that was required at this rally was a reminder, along with pressure to act in response to the crisis.

Savio gave a speech that day which became a classic, one frequently referred to on the campus thereafter. He said, in part:

We have an autocracy which runs this university. It's managed. We were told the following. "If President Kerr actually tried to get something more liberal out of the Regents . . . why didn't he make some public statement to that effect?" And the answer we received from a well-meaning liberal was the following: he said, "Would you ever imagine the manager of a firm making a statement publicly in opposition to his Board of Directors?" That's the answer.

I ask you to consider: if this is a firm, and if the Board of Regents are the Board of Directors, and if President Kerr in fact is the manager, then . . . the faculty are a bunch of employees and we're the raw material. But we're a bunch of raw material that don't mean . . . to be made into any product, don't mean to end up being bought by some clients of the university. . . . We're human beings.

And that brings me to the second mode of civil disobedience. There is a time when the operation of the machine becomes so odious, makes you so sick at heart, that you can't take part; you can't even passively take part, and you've got to put your bodies upon the gears and upon the wheels, upon the levers, upon all the apparatus and you've got to make it stop. And you've got to indicate to the people who run it, to the people who own it, that unless you're free, the machines will be prevented from working at all.

Joan Baez told the demonstrators:

. . . The only thing that occurs to me, seeing all you people there—I don't know how many of you intend to come inside with us—but that is that you muster up as much love as you possibly can, and as little hatred and as little violence, and as little "angries" as you can— although I know it's been exasperating. The more love you can feel, the more chance there is for it to be a success.

As Joan Baez sang, "We Shall Overcome," demonstrators began filing up the Sproul Hall steps and into the building. They came in groups, a steady stream, somewhere between a thousand and fifteen hundred people.

As the crowd poured in, Joan Baez sang, "Oh, Freedom." Then Dustin Miller, in a hoarse but rhythmic, almost sing-song voice, defended "what have been called Marxist tactics." He urged a mass sit-in, saying that the more people participated, the less danger there would be of reprisal.

The pressure built up. Mario Savio called the people inside the building persons "committed to the cause of free speech. Those sympathizers outside are less committed." He urged them to man a sympathy picket line if they were afraid to go inside, and to cooperate with the student strike when it came. Jack Weinberg hoarsely urged all present "to defend freedom of speech by going inside."

Savio said, "Some of our best faculty were forced to leave in the 1950 loyalty oath controversy. Some of our best students may be expelled now." (There was scattered laughter in the crowd.)

Bettina Aptheker came out to announce that there were 1500 demonstrators in the building. "There is now no danger of reprisal," she said and called on more students to join them.

People continued to enter (and some to leave) Sproul Hall all through the afternoon. The building was officially closed down and staff members were sent home.

Here are two students' explanations of why they entered Sproul Hall. The first was written by a mathematics major, a sophomore in his third semester on the Berkeley campus. He had joined the vigil of September 30 but did not sit down around the car.[12]

My attention was attracted by the mass demonstrations that took place from September on. I became active once I decided that the Regents were very wrong in their decisions. The student protests were a natural result of the Regents' actions. . . . I decided to participate in the December strike and sit-in (before arrests) because I was convinced that the students were right. It took me that long to decide that they were. . . . The Regents wouldn't listen. The normal channels were tried in vain by other students. I don't know the details. . . .

No one encouraged me, personally, to act. . . . Mario was eloquent. I found the moral arguments most persuasive. I was also persuaded by Jefferson and de Toqueville.[13]

A freshman girl, planning to major in art and living in a college dormitory, had followed earlier FSM activities sympathetically but had not become involved until she joined the December sit-in.[14] She writes:

The situation influenced me. It seemed the only way. I joined when I came to the self-realization that I had not acted on what I believed in, in the past. I had not acted on a principle I believed in. It was a major crisis for me. I was aware, generally, of what other people around me thought. I wouldn't have been there, otherwise.[13]

Inside Sproul Hall, a myriad of activities went on through the afternoon and evening. The FSM had announced that they would conduct a Free University inside Sproul Hall. Each floor of the building was devoted to a different kind of activity so that people could locate themselves by preference for how they would spend their time. There was a study hall, a discussion area, a sleep area, and square dancing and movie areas. Laurel and Hardy movies were shown. (Rumors spread around the community that the banned Genet film had been shown.) A Jewish Chanukah service, attended by about four hundred demonstrators, was conducted on the first floor. Joan Baez sang and led folk singing. A Peace Corps trainer conducted a Spanish class in one area of the building, a sociology faculty member discussed the theory of conflict in relation to Clark Kerr's handling of the Free Speech issue, a Quaker addressed a class on civil disobedience. Spirits were high.[15]

At 7 o'clock the doors to Sproul Hall were locked. Anyone who wanted to leave was allowed to, but no one was permitted to enter. A number of students gained admittance, however, by means of a rope tied to the second-floor balcony, and baskets of food were brought in by the same method. Many students had left before the doors were locked. Others continued to leave to go to evening classes or on other errands. Some apparently were convinced that the sit-in would last indefinitely without action by the university and settled down for a long stay. Others became uneasy when the doors were locked and decided it was time to get out.

That night the university Young Republicans formally withdrew from the FSM. Warren Coats, their president, said, "What the FSM is asking, in effect, is that the administration cease to be an administration.[16]

Inside Sproul Hall, the sit-in continued. At 11 P.M. Joan Baez decided that nothing was going to happen that night, and left. Unknown to the students, it was at that precise hour that things began to happen in earnest.

Earlier in the evening Clark Kerr had called an emergency meeting of key members of the Board of Regents. Beginning at 7:30 P.M., he met with Edward Carter, the chairman of the Board of Regents; and Donald McLaughlin and Theodore Meyer, the chairmen of the Regents' two principal committees, Finance and Educational Policy, at the Hilton Inn near the San Francisco Airport.[17]

President Kerr brought these Regents up to the minute on developments in the controversy and proposed a simple procedure. The building would be sealed off so that no one else could get in. Lights and water would be left on, and any person who wished to leave would be allowed to do so with impunity, simply by identifying himself. Identification would be asked in order to provide a basis for dealing with what were believed to be a large number of nonstudents in the building. Then, at 10 o'clock the next morning the entire matter would be reviewed again with the Governor. (Governor Brown was attending a banquet in Los Angeles, and Kerr had been unable to reach him.) The plan covered that night only and did not extend past 10:00 A.M. the next day.

The Regents at the meeting indicated that the situation was a matter for administrative, rather than Regents', decision. The meeting ended about 9:15 P.M.

Vice-President Earl Bolton, who had gone with Kerr to the airport, kept in touch by phone with Vice-Chancellor O.W. Campbell and Police Chief Frank Woodward on the Berkeley campus. The campus officers were aware that the meeting was taking place.

After the meeting ended, Earl Bolton drove Clark Kerr to the president's home in El Cerrito. As they reached the house, the call that Kerr had been trying to make to the Governor came through. After talking with Governor Brown, Kerr came out to tell Bolton the Governor agreed with the plan. Bolton then went to Dwinelle Hall to talk with Chancellor Strong and inform him of these developments.

At about 11:05 P.M. a call came through the Dwinelle switchboard for Bolton from President Kerr. The Governor had called Kerr back to say he had changed his mind. As Bolton remembers the conversation, Kerr said that the Governor felt it was necessary to ask the law enforcement officers in Alameda County to clear the building, in order to keep peace in the state. Brown ordered the State Highway Patrol to implement the plan.

Although Governor Brown ordered the building cleared, he did not order the arrest of the students. When the local law enforcement officers planned their strategy, however, they decided the only practical way to implement the order was to arrest the demonstrators for trespassing.

The arrests began at 3:05 A.M. on December 3, after Chancellor Strong had gone from floor to floor with a bull horn, saying,

May I have your attention. I am Dr. Edward Strong, Chancellor of the Berkeley campus. I have an announcement.

This assemblage has developed to such a point that the purpose and work of the University has been materially impaired. It is clear that there have been acts of disobedience and illegality which cannot be tolerated in a responsible educational center and would not be tolerated anywhere in our society.

The University has shown great restraint and patience in exercising its legitimate authority in order to allow every opportunity for expressing differing points of view. The University always stands ready to engage in the established and accepted procedures for resolving differences of opinion.

I request that each of you cease your participation in this unlawful assembly.

I urge you, both individually and collectively, to leave this area. I request that you immediately disperse. Failure to disperse will result in disciplinary action by the University.

Please go.[17]

Outside the building approximately 635 policemen had been assembling for nearly an hour. They were members of the Alameda County Sheriffs Department, Oakland Police Department, Berkeley Police Department, University Police Department, and California Highway Patrol.

Inside the building students had been aware that arrests were imminent. The FSM Steering Committee wanted the entire campus to see the arrests. Therefore members advised students to go limp; if each person had to be carried out, the job could not be finished before other students would be returning to the campus. They were sure that these other students would strike when they saw police carrying the demonstrators off the campus.

The Steering Committee decided that Steve Weisman should leave to coordinate the graduate teaching assistants in striking the next day. Although the campus police had announced earlier that anyone could leave the building simply by identifying himself at the door, the Steering Committee was not at all sure that this blanket permission would extend to leaders of the sit-in. Consequently they lowered Weisman from a second-story window by means of a rope.

Meanwhile a number of students were trying to decide what to do. One student, who left just before people on his floor were due to be arrested, described to me how he walked up and down the halls, trying to make up his mind. He would go down the stairs to the front door, see someone he knew, become ashamed, and go back up the stairs. Finally caution overcame his sense of shame, and he left. Another student called home to tell his parents that the police were about to start arrests; he was having trouble deciding what to do. When his parents ordered him to leave the building, his mind was made up: he returned to his seat on the floor and was arrested. Although a number of people did leave as the arrests took place, 773 persons stayed and were booked.

The first person arrested was the civil rights attorney, Robert Truhaft.

All arrested persons were given the choice of walking or being carried. If they went limp, they were charged with resisting arrest. Truhaft said this was the first time civil rights demonstrators had been charged with resisting arrest for going limp.

There was a small scuffle when the police tried to confiscate the FSM's public address system, which had been set up in the second-floor lobby; otherwise the arrest procedure was relatively efficient. The police cleared the fourth floor first, and then moved to the third. They interrupted their efforts there to begin removing students from the second floor after people from the first and the third floors began piling together on the second floor. Apparently many who had been on the third floor hoped to avoid being carried down an extra flight of stairs. On the other hand, some originally on the first floor wanted the arrests to take longer. The police seemed to consider this movement to the second floor to be a "jam-in."

Most of the people who were arrested early in the procedure report that they were handled carefully and fairly gently by the police. As the morning wore on, however, treatment apparently became rougher. Altogether it took the police twelve hours to clear the building. That weekend several students on the second floor told me that as the police got tired they began to be less careful how they carried people down the long marble staircase. Some students reported having their heads bounced on the steps; others said that their hair was pulled, their arms were twisted, and the like. There were many charges of "police brutality" by the students, many of whom had previously never been arrested or faced handling by the police.

The students were taken to the university police station in the basement of Sproul Hall and booked. They were then put in paddy-wagon buses belonging to Alameda County, for transportation to various jails and eventually to the Santa Rita Prison Farm operated by the county. For many of the middle-class university students, being treated as a criminal came as a severe shock. They knew that they were going to jail for a cause they believed in, but they were not prepared for the impersonal discipline they received.

When the students were released from jail, widespread tales of brutal treatment at police hands circulated on the campus. Lawyers representing the students urged them to report all injuries. The Berkeley chapter of the American Civil Liberties Union began working with the lawyers and the arrested students, trying to document cases of police brutality. No charges were ever brought in court, however, in spite of many hours of poring over pictures of the arrest and obtaining sworn testimony from various students. Therefore, although the police were probably quite rough toward the end of the period of duty (and some officers may have been less than courteous to students as their backs grew weary and their tempers short), it is unlikely that "brutality" in the normal *police* understanding of this term occurred often, if at all. To the students and their friends, however, such technicalities were unimportant. They were shocked at the treatment that "moral witnesses" had received from those who considered them to be "criminals." Reaction across the campus was severe.

twelve
CHAOS

THE STRIKE BEGINS

As the arrests continued through the night and into the morning, an angry crowd of students congregated outside Sproul Hall, trying to see what was going on. A cordon of police blocked off Barrows Lane behind Sproul Hall, forming a human wall that separated the watching students from those who were being arrested. Some bystanders came up to the policemen outside, and were then arrested. So, the students thought, this was how the authorities responded to protests of unfair treatment!

Anyone entering the campus early Thursday morning was handed the following leaflet:

STRIKE!

LAST NIGHT CHANCELLOR STRONG READ THE RIOT ACT. GOVERNOR BROWN AUTHORIZED STATE POLICE TO BREAK UP OUR MASSIVE SIT-IN. AS YOU READ THIS, OUR FELLOW STUDENTS ARE BEING DRAGGED OFF TO JAIL—OUT OF SIGHT BEHIND SPROUL HALL.

YOU MUST NOT STAND BY AND DO NOTHING. YOU MUST NOT GO ON AS IF NOTHING WERE HAPPENING. IT DOES NOT MATTER WHETHER YOU SUP-

PORT A PARTICULAR TACTIC—THE MATTER IS THAT THE POLICE ARE ON
OUR CAMPUS SENDING STUDENTS TO PRISON FARMS IN AN ATTEMPT TO
CRUSH THE FREE SPEECH MOVEMENT AND ALL IT STANDS FOR. THERE
ARE ONLY TWO SIDES. YOU MUST CHOOSE YOURS—AND DEFEND IT.

SUPPORT YOUR FELLOW STUDENTS. JOIN THEM IN A MASSIVE, UNIVER-
SITY-WIDE STRIKE. DO NOT ATTEND CLASSES TODAY.

STRIKE!

About 6:30 A.M. students carrying picket signs began marching at the
entrances to the campus.[1] At first some teamsters delivering goods to
the university honored the strike, but when they learned that no organized union had called it they went through the line.

Large pieces of cardboard, bottles of black ink, and poles were
spread out in Sproul Plaza. As people came through, saw the police,
and talked to others, they began picking up pieces of cardboard and let-
tering their own picket signs. All morning, as word of the arrests
spread, people came flocking to the Sproul Hall area. A woman wheel-
ing her grandchild in a stroller joined her graduate student sons in the
picket line at Bancroft and Telegraph. Other nonstudents came to
watch, and some to picket. A great crowd had gathered on the Student
Union roof and balcony, as well as in the playing field above Sproul
Hall across Barrows Lane and on the plaza itself. It was an extremely
angry crowd. "Strike" signs were visible in the hands of many picketers
in the crowd.[2]

I estimated that perhaps five or ten thousand people might be
crowded together on the plaza by noon, looking through the Sproul Hall
windows, trying to see what was happening inside while rumors of police brutality passed through the crowd. At most rallies each person
placed himself so that he had at least a small perimeter of space around
him, anywhere from six inches to three feet. That morning, people were
pressed shoulder to shoulder, chest to back. There were no boundaries
of personal territory. You could *feel* the breathing rates of people
around you. As you craned to see between people, you became aware of
a sea of outraged faces. You could feel tense bodies surrounding you.
Some people were shouting at the police, while others muttered to
themselves or their neighbors.

Then, about 12:30 P.M., there was a ripple of interest and relief as
someone began pushing through the crowd carrying loudspeakers for a

public address system. Steve Weisman appeared and announced eight demands:

1. That the university withdraw charges against organizations and the four students.

2. That there be no further charges until the Free Speech controversy was ended.

3. That there be no restrictions on free discussion, except for such regulations as might be needed for traffic reasons.

4. That there be an end to police brutality.

5. That there be an end to police interference.

6. That Chancellor Strong resign.

7. That President Kerr resign.

8. That the university not press charges against the students being arrested now.

After Weisman was given a prolonged ovation, Paul Jacobs, a visiting faculty member spoke: "This is the saddest day on the campus. Kerr and Brown are my friends. We have had profound disagreement in the past. We have profound disagreement about what happened in Sproul Hall!"

A group of policemen came to the window of Sproul Hall to listen, and people shouted and booed as they caught sight of them. Jacobs continued:

DO NOT BE PROVOKED BY THE POLICE! [Applause.] *The police were introduced to the campus last night in a way not becoming to the university or to the Governor of this state. The university, eventually, will have to start again becoming a university.*

You will have to demonstrate just as much patience . . . [as you can]. You must maintain your patience and humor.

The rally continued for two hours with prolonged applause for several speakers. Reginald Zelnik, for example, received an ovation when he said, "This is a sad day, but it's still a good university. Some day it's going to be a great university, because you are going to make it so."

THE FACULTY MUTINIES

In the meantime Nathan Glazer, chairman of the Social Sciences Integrated Program and a member of the Sociology Department active during the police car demonstration, had posted signs around campus announcing a faculty meeting in Wheeler Auditorium at 1 P.M. More than 800 professors and instructors attended. A number of teaching assistants also were there, but were asked to stand in the side aisles and not vote, since they were not members of the Academic Senate.[3]

Glazer began by trying to make clear the nature of the impromptu meeting:

This meeting is not to be construed as a meeting for support. It is hard to decide whether the administration or students are more inept, obstinate, impossible to bring to reason.

We are here, not to take sides, but to protest the action of today. This is not an official faculty meeting.

Leo Lowenthal, vice-chairman of the Sociology Department, and Robert Scalapino, chairman of the Political Science Department, came forward to speak.[4] Scalapino expressed reservations about the student actions in calling a strike but said he was concerned about the university, which is supposed to be a citadel for truth and learning. He announced a meeting in Barrows Hall for the chairmen of all departments, to establish a working committee to provide leadership in the crisis. He expressed doubt that any meaningful vote could be taken in the Wheeler Auditorium meeting.

Lowenthal then recommended that classes be temporarily suspended so that faculty could spend their time in resolving the present crisis. He explained that his recommendation involved neither endorsement nor disapproval of the student action.

Henry May, chairman of the History Department, read the following resolution:

3 December 1964

In view of the desperate situation now confronting the University, every effort must be made to restore the unity of our campus community, and to end the series of provocations and reprisals which has resulted in disaster. With this purpose, the faculty members here assembled urge that the following actions be taken immediately:

1. That the new and liberalized rules for campus political action be declared in effect and enforced, pending their improvement.

2. That all pending campus action against students for acts occurring before the present date be dropped.

3. That a committee selected by and responsible to the Academic Senate be established, to which students may appeal decisions of the Administration regarding penalties for offenses arising from political action, and that decisions of this committee be final.

Henry F. May

Chairman, Department of History

Speakers rose to defend and to attack the motion. Someone suggested it be dropped. Reginald Zelnik replied, "There are twice as many faculty here as attended the last Senate meeting. This is a crisis situation. Not to vote would be intolerable. May called for a vote. . . . The overwhelming majority wish to vote!"

The argument continued, with more conservative faculty members defending the right of the Governor of the state to clear the building. Then Franz Schurmann, professor of history and sociology, spoke, setting the tone for the rest of the meeting:

I have not been an active participant, but events of the last few days have changed my mind. The faculty are largely to blame: in a sense we have *become a factory, dependent upon a bureaucracy for leadership. I support the resolution as a symbolic act by which faculty begins to take leadership to provide moral guidance.* [Enthusiastic, prolonged applause.]

Of all inept groups on this campus, the faculty is most inept. We have the first opportunity to take action. I ask that we express our views on the current crisis, for example, holding classes.

Students have brought us to the point where issues should be settled in a court of law. But the first man carried out [Robert Truhaft] *is a lawyer.*

I agree this is an achievement. Many of us support some of the issues drawn by the students . . .

A zoologist spoke in support of the resolution: "This is today, not yesterday. Not students, but police, occupy Sproul Hall. The university is dead today. We should support the resolution."

And Herbert McClosky of the Political Science Department said:

Many of our best, most sensitive-conscienced students are concerned. There are a few agitator types, but mainly honest concern. [Warm applause.]

For reasons of prudence, realism, leaving aside the question of where virtue lies, any question of regulating student conduct off campus is impossible and should be avoided whenever possible.

McClosky offered two additions to Henry May's resolution:

1. Retraction of the Regents' decision that the university could prosecute students for advocating illegal off-campus action.

2. A demand that no student be prosecuted by the university for participating in any off-campus activity.

Voting began on the May resolution. Glazer tried to avoid a vote on the McClosky amendments but was shouted down; they were overwhelmingly approved.

May moved that the meeting adjourn. Before it could, however, John Reynold of the Physics Department, chairman of the Berkeley chapter of the American Association of University Professors, read a resolution passed unanimously by the executive committee of the association, and asked faculty members present to support it. The resolution stated the belief of the AAUP executive committee that "the present crisis cannot be resolved until: (1) there is complete amnesty for past offenses in the free speech controversy; and (2) there is a new chief campus officer who will have the confidence of the campus." The resolution was greeted with widespread applause.

Another motion was made to adjourn but was voted down. Then Roger Stanier of the Bacteriology Department read the text of a telegram a group of faculty was planning to send to Governor Brown and asked for signatures.

The undersigned members of the faculty of the University of California at Berkeley strongly condemn the presence of the State Highway Patrol on the Berkeley campus. We also protest the exclusion of faculty members, including at least one member of our Committee on Academic Freedom, from Sproul Hall, at a time when the police were admitting newsmen and photographers. Punitive action taken against hundreds of students cannot help to solve our current problems, and will aggravate the already serious situation. Only prompt release of the arrested students offers any prospect of restoring the unity of campus life and of a return to normal academic functions.

The statement was received with great enthusiasm, and 361 persons signed it.

John Searle of the Philosophy Department introduced a motion calling for the suspension of all classes until there was a favorable atmosphere for learning and the faculty could devote its attention to teaching. "The presence of mass police destroys the atmosphere of teaching," he said. "We should suspend classes out of respect for, rather than contempt for, academic process."

Nathan Glazer insisted on adjourning the meeting before a vote was taken. A number of faculty headed for the courthouse to raise bail for arrested students. Bail had been set at $166.00 to $276.00, depending on the number of offenses with which a student was charged.

As the faculty left Wheeler Auditorium, someone projected a question on the screen at the front of the auditorium: "If policemen arrest 1,000 students, how long before they arrest you?"

At the end of the meeting I asked Glazer why he had insisted on adjourning the meeting without a vote on Searle's motion. He said he had done so in order not to alienate the conservative faculty with a vote for suspending classes, which would drive them to the right. "A great deal has been accomplished already," Glazer said. "Leave the departmental chairmen with some sense of responsibility so they will not meet in reaction to faculty mob action."

The faculty had, for practical purposes, deposed the chancellor. They had decided to provide their own administrative leadership in the form of the Council of Departmental Chairmen. Thus the mass arrest of several hundred students had brought results more extreme than the FSM planners could have hoped. Not only did it spawn a strike that paralyzed the campus (as they had intended); it also led to a faculty "mutiny" that repudiated the campus administration and created a temporary faculty organization to act in place of the administration in these matters.

THE STUDENT STRIKE IS ORGANIZED

Meanwhile, students began organizing the strike in earnest. A "strike central" was established on campus. Several departmental offices were turned over to the students by sympathetic faculty chairmen; the teaching assistant offices and research assistant offices provided additional services, telephones, and the like. Ironically, many of the leaflets were run off on a mimeograph machine in the office of the Social Sciences Integrated Program, which was headed by Nathan Glazer and Lewis Feuer, both of whom were deeply disturbed by what they felt was a mob response. Feuer, who had been active in radical student politics during the nineteen thirties, was even more disturbed by what he saw as parallels to the rise of the Nazi movement in Germany. (A number of emigres on the faculty shared this concern.)

There could not have been a more ideal location than the Berkeley campus in which to turn several thousand people loose to their own inventive ingenuity. Almost every student seemed to have developed his own specialty, for which he took responsibility. The activity was madly chaotic, directed in only the most elementary senses, and yet remarkably coordinated.

Students in the ASUC Senate, trying desperately to halt the strike before the university would be closed down, were convinced that their phones were being tapped, as were a number of faculty members and administrators.[5] The FSM established a "rumor central," to coordinate all rumors flowing around and to try to discover what the faculty chairmen were up to. Many hundreds of dollars, often from contributions made on the spot by the students involved, were spent. Seeing the remarkable amount of organized activity going on around them and its clearly sizable expense, some members of the student government became convinced they were the victims of a tightly organized, externally financed and directed, Communist plot.[6]

How widespread was the strike? Thanks to the presence of the police through the morning and the early afternoon of December 3, which kept a crowd gathered to watch them, and to the faculty meeting in the afternoon, not many classes met that Thursday. Friday was a better day to test the effectiveness of the organized effort. Saturday newspapers appeared with headlines stating that the strike had been ineffective. Several newsmen told me later they had based their stories on information received from the university public information office. Since the university does not keep attendance records, the number of students out of classes was difficult to gauge. Several news stories reported accurately that the strike seemed limited primarily to students in the College of Letters and Science; few went on to report, however, that this group made up the greater part of the student body.

On Friday I made spot checks in some of the main classroom buildings used by the humanities and the social sciences. Between 11 and 12 o'clock in the morning, for example, normally a time of full capacity for most rooms in Dwinelle Hall, the building had forty-one empty classrooms. Most of the twenty-seven rooms where classes were meeting seemed one-third to one-half full. Through open doors I could hear classes discussing the strike. Some, however, continued with their regular lessons.

On Friday afternoon the Graduate Coordinating Committee met to evaluate the effectiveness of the strike. Reactions of faculty and teaching assistants in forty-six departments were reported, via graduate students who supported the strike and tried to evaluate its effectiveness in their departments.

Table 4 summarizes their reports that afternoon. It shows that teaching assistants were somewhat more favorably disposed to the strike than they thought faculty were, but that for about two thirds of the departments considerable agreement was *reported* to exist between these two levels of instruction.

These reports are subject, of course, to the biases of the student informants, all of whom favored the strike. A number reported great pressure being placed on them by faculty members, however, so the picture was not slanted entirely in one direction.

What were student responses? Some students picketed actively, others stayed away from all classes but did not picket, and a third group attended classes selectively, skipping those that were cancelled and going to others where they were having academic difficulty or whose instructor they expected would oppose the strike. (In one widely circulated rumor some students were reported to have sat holding their picket signs while they took a mid-term examination that one angry professor had scheduled.)

Still other students carried antistrike picket signs, urging students to

TABLE 4 | **december 4 reports of the graduate coordinating committee concerning faculty and graduate student responses to the strike**

Reported reactions of faculty

Reported reactions of graduate teaching assistants ↓	Number of departments with				Total number of departments reporting each reaction from graduate teaching assistants
	Great support for the strike	*Moderate support*	*Little support*	*Unknown support or no report made*	
Great support for the strike	13			4	17
Moderate support		5	4	2	11
Little support			9	5	14
Unknown, or no report made	2		2		4
Total number of departments reporting each reaction from faculty	15	5	15	11	46 departments reporting

attend classes. Feelings were high between the two groups, and there were a few fist fights.

Kathleen Gales's spring survey asked students to describe their behavior during the period of the strike. If we project the responses found in this survey onto the total campus population, an estimated 10,500 students probably took part in the strike. About 4800 actively picketed, about 1900 more struck—in the sense of attending no classes, though they did not man the lines—and an additional 3750 cooperated partially. In contrast, about 3500 students actively opposed the strike, and about 8100 ignored it. (These students came predominantly from fields outside the humanities and the social sciences.) [7]

How did the FSM elicit so widespread a response? Partly, of course, it was the shock of seeing police troops on the campus. Partly, it was the sheer effort at organization. Volunteers from the FSM tore apart student telephone directories, handed out a page per volunteer, and asked each to call the list to urge students to stay away from classes until something was settled. Some students literally telephoned all night, waking the people on their list and urging them to strike. But this could not have been effective without the impressions created by watching the police in operation.

A number of students who stood peering into the windows of Sproul Hall during the arrests were convinced they were witnessing a truly brutal scene. Here are a few essays, written several months later, in which students tried to recapture their initial responses:

What attracted my attention? Screams of people from the upper floors of Sproul Hall; breaking glass; cordons of policemen. I did not really know what had happened. I arrived after most of the arrests had taken place, during the frantic balcony last-stand.[8] The press info was conflicting; all I knew was I was afraid. . . . The tension of all present was clear.

. . . I was at the rally which led to the December 2 sit-in. For personal reasons I decided not to participate. I left and went to work. In the morning I heard of the arrests, and picketed.

I decided to participate after hearing screams, shouts, crashes from second floor of Sproul; students being arrested. I was infuriated by this. I was emotionally involved; that morning was a crucial dividing point. It called either for active support or active denial because of the danger.

I felt that the strike was the only means left to the students which would impress the administration with the seriousness of intent; in fact, the only means left at all.[9]

The Regents laughed—scoffed—at all our "normal" procedures. . . . When I saw 600 police—an army—on Bancroft Way at 3:00 A.M. it was just clear that the time for discussion was past. It was now time to act.[9]

After seeing the cops pushing and striking students in Sproul Hall (I was watching from outside), I felt there was no choice but to support the students. Students were being treated like hardened criminals, not just protesters. . . . I became involved, with no qualms.[9]

I had not thought much about the Movement until I saw that people were willing to be arrested for the sake of what they believed. . . . At first they were a bunch of beatniks. I was unconcerned. Then when they began to drag *people out of Sproul, that was it. . . . You saw this cop standing there with his shiny badge, and you realize that the people who sent him there did not care in the slightest for democratic principles.*

The actual hour in which I made the plunge was just after hearing what Krech said to the class [on Friday]. He was the man on campus to whom I held the highest value. After hearing him speak, I was certain that it wasn't just a bunch of "beatniks" rioting, but people who were really willing to pay a high price for their ideals.[9]

The police stopped me from entering the campus my usual way. I wasn't sure what had happened, but I soon found out that people were being carried out of Sproul Hall. . . . The police were no solution. . . . The sit-inners had very legitimate grievances. They needed my help because they had given their bodies for my rights.

A friend of mine was picketing when I left an 8:00 class. When the FSM and a friend active in FSM needed my help passing out literature, I decided to join in. Things had gone too far.

"Normal" procedures hadn't worked for months.[9]

The thing that attracted my attention was the viciousness of police in arresting Sproul Hall demonstrators. . . . The strike was against this police brutality and against the violation of the university's integrity by the use of police. . . . I hoped it would show the depth of student concern to faculty, the public, etc. I expected public anger at police brutality. . . . The injustices stated above were flagrant.[9]

I had attended rallies and signed petitions, but the strike was the most open and active demonstration I took part in. . . . I already heard of the arrests on the radio before getting to school, but hadn't decided what to do until I got there. . . . I was outraged. . . . When I'd gathered information from bystanders, seen and talked with police, I picketed for the strike. I wanted to bring the strike to the attention of those who didn't know what was happening. . . . Attention had to be brought physically *to the situation. . . . We had to show the public that the student community backed the arrested students.*[9]

Many of the students pinned IBM cards to their shirts or blouses. Some of the cards had been punched to spell "F S M" or "Free Speech." Others read, "I am a student: do not fold, spindle, or mutilate." [10]

thirteen

DRAMA

It was a frenzied weekend. The arrested students' sympathizers raised bail money, phoned students urging them to continue the strike on Monday, and tried to find out in talks with the faculty what the departmental chairmen were doing. The group of faculty members who had produced the motion Herbert McClosky introduced at the ad hoc faculty meeting on Thursday continued their efforts to create a workable policy statement that could end the crisis. Soon this group was attracting 200 faculty members to its meetings and was drawing up petitions to present to the Academic Senate as a policy position that would recognize the grievances of the Free Speech Movement. Student religious organizations began issuing letters and statements in support of the arrested students.

Friends of the administration were also busy. They rounded up speakers to tour the dormitories, cooperatives, fraternities, and sororities urging students to return to their classes. (These speakers often were faculty members from fields socially and spatially far removed from the humanities and the social sciences, where the ferment was centered.) The FSM immediately began recruiting faculty and graduate student teams to counter the administration advocates. In several of the dormitories the two teams arrived at the same time and had a debate.

On Saturday night, December 5, Edward Strong had an acute gall bladder attack and was hospitalized. He asked the hospital to screen all inquiries for him, letting administrative phone calls through, but keeping out the press.[1] Soon rumors were circulating that he was being kept a prisoner in the University of California Medical Center to keep him from taking further repressive acts against the students, that his disappearance was part of a clever plot, that he had been emotionally ill and was now hospitalized.[2] No detail seemed too small to escape attention, comment, and speculation by the excited campus.

The departmental chairmen, aware that they were now the *de facto* government on the campus for the next few days, spent many hours—as a group and through a smaller steering committee—trying to hammer out a solution to the crisis that would be acceptable to their assorted sentiments and also to Clark Kerr and that could be presented to the faculty and students on Monday. Robert Scalapino, who had called the meeting of departmental chairmen in the first place, had been elected chairman of their steering committee.

The ASUC Senate issued statements condemning the strike and held emergency meetings to rally support for its position. With the active help of the Alumni Association staff, the Senate set up a counter-FSM organization, named University Students for Law and Order.

The big news on Sunday, however, was President Kerr's announcement that all classes would be canceled between 9:00 A.M. and noon on Monday. Faculty would meet by departments from 9 to 10 o'clock on Monday morning to discuss a proposal "to inaugurate a new era of freedom under law," unanimously approved by 73 departmental chairmen on Saturday. From 10 to 11 o'clock the faculty would meet by departments with graduate students to explain the plan to them. At 11:00 A.M. there would be a meeting in the Greek Theater on campus to present the plan to the general student body.

The *California Monthly* reported: "Kerr's announcement came after he had spent four hours in discussions with Governor Brown, members of the Board of Regents, and faculty members. President Kerr previously had announced he would speak to the students on his return from Chicago, Tuesday or Wednesday." [3] (He had canceled a trip to the Midwest.)

The plans were carefully arranged. Monday morning would be spent in building up support for the proposals, which would be announced at 11:00 A.M. At the Greek Theater university service employees in their "Sunday suits" would usher and do the work of crowd control normally assigned to the campus police. Uniformed police would be stationed nearby, ready to respond if trouble developed, but only plain-clothes-police would be at the site of the meeting. Under the circumstances, it was believed, the presence of uniformed police could be inflammatory.

During the noon hour, the ASUC would hold a rally in the Student Union Plaza to back the proposals. The afternoon would be spent in discussing the proposals within departments, with faculty holding "open house" for students who wanted to come in and talk between 2 and 4 P.M.

Meanwhile, the FSM Steering Committee was keeping well informed of developments, thanks to the ingenuity of a graduate student striker who had "a hot line to Kerr." [4] Much of the committee meeting on Sunday was taken up with reports of what "the enemy" was planning and with plans for an FSM counter-rally in Sproul Plaza to follow the one in the Greek Theater. Committee members decided to picket the Greek Theater meeting and, if possible, to have a group of "minstrels" who would precede Kerr. They expected their own rally to be attacked physically by strikebreakers and tried to map a strategy to cope with such action if it came. [4]

Not all departments followed the recommended schedule of faculty meetings, to be followed by graduate-and-faculty meetings on Monday morning. In departments that did, results varied. An explosive session was held by the Sociology Department. [5] A number of its faculty rose to attack the departmental chairmen's proposal, saying it was inadequate to meet the crisis. Graduate students said they considered the proposal inflammatory, given the tensions on the campus at the time. They asked faculty members to intervene to make sure that some FSM spokesman also could be heard—preferably Steve Weisman, chairman of the Graduate Coordinating Committee and a member of the FSM Steering Committee. These sociology graduate students said they felt that a one-sided presentation could be dangerous under the tense conditions prevailing.

At the end of the meeting Philip Selznick, chairman of the Sociology Department, announced he would not sit with the other departmental chairmen in the Greek Theater because he could not endorse the proposed resolution of the dispute. Then, just before the meeting broke up to allow people to go to the Greek Theater, an impassioned graduate student pleaded to have Steve Weisman on the platform: "Because if no one from the FSM is up there, all hell's going to break loose at 11:30!" [5]

As soon as the sociology meeting ended, a group of faculty members compared notes. They decided Kerr and Scalapino should be told that the FSM wanted a speaker and was threatening trouble if it did not have one. S.M. Lipset then tried to contact Kerr but found that the president already had left for the Greek Theater. Lipset hurriedly left a verbal message with Kerr's office staff and rushed up the hill toward the ampitheater. A few moments later the University Police Department received a call from the administrative offices, warning it to be ready for trouble. Some men were immediately dispatched up the hill to guard the stage.[6]

DRAMA AT THE GREEK THEATER

The outdoor theater was jammed with an estimated 16,000 people. The crowd was arranged in layers: fraternity and sorority students who planned to support the departmental chairmen's statement arrived an hour or two early, so that supporting students would be visible to the television cameras. They sat in the lower levels of the theater. The FSM students who had been arrested, at the other extreme, were at the very top. They had been among the last to arrive because of their legal arraignment that morning.

Before the convocation, Mario Savio, accompanied by Bettina Aptheker and Tom Miller, went backstage. Savio asked for an opportunity to speak. Scalapino, who was to serve as chairman, told Savio that the meeting was "structured" and was not an "open forum." *No one* was to speak except Scalapino himself and the president. Savio then asked whether he could at least make an announcement of the FSM rally. Scalapino refused, pointing out that the rally was already well publicized. (The same ruling was applied to the ASUC officers when they arrived about the same time to request permission to announce their post-theater rally in support of the resolutions.)

Savio angrily told Professor Scalapino that the meeting "usurped the authority of the Academic Senate," which was scheduled to meet the next day. The departmental chairmen, Savio claimed, were trying to provide a *fait accompli* before their colleagues had a chance to present their own ideas. John Leggett of the Sociology Department sided with Savio in this debate. Scalapino, however, stood firm in his ruling.[7]

Savio and the small group with him walked out on the stage of the theater as they left the argument with Scalapino. As soon as they were recognized by the crowd, a cheer went up. Bettina Aptheker and Mario Savio looked at each other. It seemed clear that the crowd was with them, and Savio decided he was going to speak. The group sat down front, in the press section of the audience, debating tactics. Bettina Aptheker advised Savio to be direct about it: "Just walk up to the microphone. No one will stop you." [8]

In the meantime the convocation had begun. It had a certain Olympian quality—the setting in the outdoor Greek Theater, the vast crowd, arranged in tiers of differing sentiment, and President Kerr, flanked by the departmental chairmen. Robert Scalapino opened the meeting, explaining it had been convened solely on the initiative of a small number of faculty members, and presented the chairmen's proposals as "our maximum effort to attain peace and decency."

I will quote the account of this meeting carried in the *California Monthly,* which prepared the official university chronology of these events.[9] Comments from my field notes have been added in brackets.

President Kerr, flanked by all the Berkeley campus department heads on the Greek Theater stage, publicly accepted the proposal presented to him by the Council of Department Chairmen and announced the terms:

1. The University Community shall be governed by orderly and lawful procedures in the settlement of issues; and the full and free pursuit of educational activities on this campus shall be maintained. [About half of the audience at the lowest levels of the theater applauded. The crowd on the grass at the top of the theater booed loudly.]

2. The University Community shall abide by the new and liberalized political action rules and await the report of the Senate Committee on Academic Freedom.

3. The Departmental Chairmen believe that the acts of civil disobedience on December 2 and 3 were unwarranted and that they obstruct rational and fair consideration of the grievances brought forward by the students. [The boos became deafening, from my location near the top of the theater.] [10]

4. The cases of all students arrested in connection with the sit-in in Sproul Hall on December 2 and 3 are now before the Courts. The University will accept the Court's judgment in these cases as the full discipline for those offenses. [The FSM and the more liberal faculty had been demanding not only campus amnesty, announced here, but intercession by the university with the courts to drop charges against the students. This partial concession was received with great disapproval by the crowd at the top of the theater. Those below seemed mixed in their reaction.] *In the light of the cases now and prospectively before the courts, the University will not prosecute charges against any students for actions prior to December 2 and 3; but the University will invoke* *disciplinary sanctions for any violations henceforth.* [The divided reactions continued.]

5. *All classes shall be conducted as scheduled.*[9] [A few "STRIKE" signs were raised in the air.]

The *California Monthly* account continued:

During the meeting, Savio sat approximately 15 feet from the edge of the stage. As President Kerr spoke, he shook his head and muttered, "Hypocrite." A reporter asked Savio if he was going to speak. Savio nodded and said, "I'm going to speak."

. . . Professor Scalapino provided background on the Council of Departmental Chairmen's proposals. Scalapino praised President Kerr for the "courage and vision" in accepting it. Scalapino also said, "No one would claim that we are presenting here a panacea—a perfect and final answer. We are offering the possibility of an orderly and fair atmosphere in which to reassess our problems, a possibility that demands for its success the good will and the good faith of all the members of the community." [9]

My notes of the rest of Scalapino's speech, made at the time, are as follows:

There are a small number of people interested in fomenting [loud boos from the top of the audience and clapping from the bottom] . . . *utopia. They are not a reflection of the majority.* [Boos, clapping.] *A few wish to destroy the university, on the ultra-left and the ultra-right.* [Shouts of "Ohhhhhhh!" from the audience at the top.] *No one wants the university shielded from external criticism. The greatest challenge is, Can we preserve and enhance freedom under law?*

When Scalapino finished speaking, a number of the people sitting in the lower levels of the theater stood up to applaud the speech. A group of students began singing, "Hail California." They were shouted down with calls of "Quiet!"

Kerr was introduced again. Although there was some booing, the audience generally was quiet.

This setting seems operatic, theatrical. [There were quiet chuckles.] *Today seems theatrical thanks to the* audience *that's here.*

Today we must decide to move ahead, productively, in peace, or to continue anarchy. [Moderately loud hissing began.] *We have one group's proposal for a new beginning. . . . The chairmen deserve commendation.* [The group seated near the bottom of the theater applauded.]

As President of the University, I welcome it and endorse it and shall present it to the Regents of the University at their next meeting. In the interim, until the Regents meet next week, this proposal is in full force.

The *California Monthly* account continues:

As President Kerr neared the end of his remarks, Savio rose and walked to the far left (south) end of the Greek Theater stage, and stood there for two or three minutes while President Kerr completed his remarks. At the conclusion of the President's address, Chairman Scalapino moved to the rostrum and announced the meeting's adjournment.

Simultaneously, Savio moved rapidly across the front of the stage to the rostrum, clutching a scroll of paper in his hand. As he reached the rostrum, two University police officers grabbed him and pulled him away from the rostrum. [They seized him by his coat and tie, dragging him backstage.] [11]

There was a general gasp of disapproval; then pandemonium broke out in the theater. The crowd of standees at the top surged forward, shouting disapproval and struggling to see what was going on. Art Goldberg, who had been at the top of the theater with the other arrested students (but who was an athlete in excellent physical condition), vaulted down to the stage, dashed backstage to where Savio was being held, and demanded that he be released. A number of other people had rushed up on stage and were milling around. In the meantime, Bettina Aptheker, who had come to the edge of the stage with Savio, began leading a chant that almost the entire audience, including many of the earlier applauders, seemed to take up: "Let him speak! Let him speak! Let him speak; let him speak!" Then came the cry, "We want Savio! We want Savio!"

Savio was returned to the rostrum, and the microphones were turned back on. The crowd hushed. Savio said, "I just wanted to announce a rally at Sproul Plaza following this meeting. Please leave here. Clear this disastrous scene, and get down to discussing the issues."

In terms of winning general support for the proposed policy, the meeting had been a disaster for the administration. Among those who viewed the scene, however, sentiment was not unanimous, by any means. Some of the seated supporters of the administrative position had begun shouting angrily at Art Goldberg when he had tried to speak before Savio returned to the microphone. (Goldberg had shouted, "The administration has not acted in good faith! When the opposition comes up they have no rebuttal!") As the crowd left the amphitheater, I overheard someone comment, "Such a Communist tactic! Mob rule. . . ." It seemed clear that reaction among those at the theater was divided, though a number of persons who previously had supported the administration now seemed shaken. One thing was clear: the meeting had not settled anything.

President Kerr was quite upset about the incident. He said:

There had been some indications of threats to disrupt the meeting. . . . The police were prepared. Apparently, they weren't aware the meeting was over. . . . Whether we have a new start seems somewhat doubtful.

. . . We wanted to walk one additional mile. There are those who think we've walked too many miles already.[12]

(I had been at the meeting where Lipset thought he was getting word of an FSM plot to disrupt the Convocation, and I had reached the same conclusion. At 11:30 I had looked at my watch and waited to see what would happen. It was approximately at that moment that Savio came to the stage, and so I assumed that his action had been arranged in advance. I was highly skeptical, in consequence, when members of the Steering Committee of FSM assured me individually, a few days later, that the move had been Savio's own spontaneous reaction. I also was skeptical when the graduate student who had made the "warning comment" insisted that he knew nothing of such a plan beforehand and that he had assumed the meeting would be over by 11:30. It has been particularly interesting, therefore, to read through the log of topics discussed at FSM Steering Committee meetings during the weekend in question. I find no reference to such a plan, although it is possible, of course, that this omission was deliberate. The log I was allowed to read was not intended for public perusal, however, even by members of the FSM Executive Committee or by other Steering Committee members. Moreover, it includes details of strike reports coming in to FSM that could have resulted in criminal charges against some of the strikers had they become public at the time. Thus there is little reason to assume that the writer of the log was being careful or was protecting the Steering Committee in his note taking.)

After the convocation nearly 10,000 people jammed Sproul Plaza for the FSM rally, according to reporters who estimated crowd size at the time. In contrast, about 375 persons went to the lower plaza to hear the ASUC rally, despite the louder public address system being used down there.

The crowd in Sproul Plaza seemed about evenly divided between supporters and detractors of Savio. There was a great deal of vocal reaction in the form of booing of persons or viewpoints with which particular individuals in the crowd disagreed. The FSM announced that the strike would continue, but that the graduate students probably would vote that afternoon to suspend it at midnight, so that there could be an atmosphere of calm for the faculty meeting on Tuesday afternoon, which would have to resolve the issue. The FSM leaders called on the faculty to support their demands.

COLLECTIVE RESPONSE

The strike on Monday was a continuation of the one begun on Thursday. Over the weekend a group of graduate students in statistics, distressed by newspaper reports that the strike was ineffective, had organized several volunteers to make a statistically reliable check, systematically, each hour of the day on Monday. They covered thirty-two buildings scattered over the campus, walking through each hour to see how many classrooms were in use and whenever possible counting the number of students present.[13] (A number of nonstriking faculty members, seeing a striking student peering into the classroom, angrily reported that the strikers were trying to intimidate them.)

The report on class meetings, compiled from records made by the group of volunteers, is given in Table 5. I have not included their figures for times other than 8 A.M., noon, 1 P.M. and 2 P.M., because all classes were canceled between 9:00 A.M. and noon, and the departmental chairmen had recommended an open-house discussion period between faculty and students in each department between 2:00 and 4:00 P.M. The attempted class boycott was most successful during the noon rallies, but a good part of the campus was idled by the strike at other times as well. Before the Greek Theater meeting, social science and humanities classes were much less likely to meet than classes in other disciplines. Thereafter students in all courses behaved similarly during the rallies and the early afternoon.

TABLE 5	percentages of regularly scheduled classes not held on Monday, December 7, 1964			
Building	*At 8:00 A.M.*	*At Noon*	*At 1:00 P.M.*	*At 2:00 P.M.*
Humanities and social science	61% (125)	70% (112)	40% (122)	41% (147)
Others	37% (76)	70% (50)	38% (142)	49.5% (93)
All	51% (201)	70% (162)	39% (264)	44% (240)

The numbers in parentheses indicate the numbers of classes normally scheduled for a particular hour.

These attendance statistics for Monday suggest the weekend lobbying in dormitories had done little to weaken the strike—a not surprising finding since the core of resistance was coming from apartment dwellers. In the absence of new events the definitions of Thursday and Friday apparently held fast.

fourteen

REVOLUTION

Immediately after the meeting in the Greek Theater on December 7, a rather shaken Clark Kerr went with Robert Scalapino to the latter's office in Barrows Hall. Professor Paul Seabury of the Political Science Department and Professor Hans Mark, chairman of the Nuclear Engineering Department had arranged a meeting there between the president, departmental chairmen, and members of the Senate Committee on Academic Freedom. Perhaps fifteen to eighteen faculty members were involved, meeting at first in separate rooms according to their official roles.

Seabury was convinced that the Greek Theater incident had discredited the chairmen's solution and that some capitulation to demands now was necessary in order to preserve the university. He picked up from the table a mimeographed copy of the McClosky proposal, prepared for the ad hoc faculty meeting on December 3, and began to argue that the university needed to buy time. He believed this proposal could provide a breathing period in the controversy.[1]

Later the members of the Academic Freedom Committee joined the discussion. Their views were rather different, for they had been participating in what came to be called the Committee of 200, a group of faculty who came together during the crisis to support the principles of unrestricted speech and advocacy on campus being demanded by the Free Speech Movement. The Committee of 200 had been meeting over the weekend to draft a resolution which the Academic Freedom Committee would introduce at the meeting of the Academic Senate scheduled for Tuesday, December 8. These persons began talking with Kerr shortly before noon; then some of the faculty left in order to speak at the noon rally in Sproul Plaza.

Some who left the conference early understood Clark Kerr to say their new proposals looked interesting and might be workable. Those who remained for the rest of the discussion, however, were aware that Kerr was not at all comfortable with several points of the proposed policy statement, particularly with its implications for the Regents' authority. The representatives of the Committee of 200 decided, however, to present the resolution as it stood: the policy statement reflected the overwhelming sentiment expressed at the informal faculty meeting held in Wheeler Auditorium a few days earlier.[2] That evening the Academic Freedom Committee formally endorsed the resolution drawn up by the Committee of 200.

The next day, from shortly after noon until almost 2.00 P.M., President Kerr talked by phone with representatives of the Committee of 200, who were gathered in Scalapino's office. The conversation apparently revolved around changes that Kerr wanted made in the resolution to be submitted that afternoon.[3] When the Academic Senate meeting was held, however, the faculty members submitted the resolution in its original form and argued against making any amendments to it.

THE FACULTY MEETS

Almost a thousand members of the Academic Senate turned out for the December 8 meeting. In advance of the session the FSM had mimeographed copies of the Report of the Committee on Academic Freedom (i.e., the proposal drafted by the Committee of 200).[4] A crowd of several thousand students gathered outside Wheeler Auditorium, the site of the faculty meeting, to listen to the proceedings being broadcast by means of loudspeakers.

In the following account I quote from a transcript of radio station KPFA's recording of the meeting,[5] which convened under the chairmanship of Professor Richard W. Jennings of the Department of Law. The first speaker was Professor Joseph Garbarino, chairman of the Academic Freedom Committee of the Academic Senate.

GARBARINO: . . . Let me remind you that on October 13 the Berkeley Division passed a resolution calling on the Committee on Academic Freedom "to enquire immediately into the recent university rulings on student political activity in the Bancroft-Telegraph area, the students' protests against these rulings, and the larger problem of students' rights to the expression of political opinion on campus and in the living and dining halls. . . ." Two days later, on October 15, the Division took further action concerning the dispute when a resolution that resulted in the reconstitution of the tripartite committee that was established by the October 2 agreement between the administration and the students was passed by this body. With the activation of this latter group, which came to be called the Committee on Campus Political Activity, the Committee on Academic Freedom interpreted its charge to involve a basic review of the problem of student political activity while the tripartite group concerned itself with trying to reach a settlement of the immediate controversy. Proceeding on this basis, the Committee on Academic Freedom laid its plans for a deliberate consideration of the long-range problem of developing a coherent philosophy to serve as a guide for a policy that would encourage the responsible exercise of maximum political freedom on the Berkeley campus. The succession of events that have occurred during the last three weeks, however, have given this issue an urgency which called the original plan of operation that had been adopted by the committee into question. . . . With this in mind, we propose the following motion. There is a brief preamble: in order to end the present crisis, to establish the confidence and trust essential to the restoration of normal university life, and to create a campus environment that encourages students to exercise free and responsible citizenship in the university and in the community at large, the Committee on Academic Freedom of the Berkeley Division of the Academic Senate moves the following propositions:

1. That there shall be no university disciplinary measures against members or organizations of the university community for activities prior to December 8 connected with the current controversy over political speech and activity.

2. That the time, place, and manner of conducting political activity on the campus shall be subject to reasonable regulation to prevent interference with the normal functions of the university. That the regulations now in effect for this purpose shall remain in effect provisionally pending a future report of the Committee on Academic Freedom concerning the minimal regulations necessary.

3. That the content of speech or advocacy . . . should not be restricted by the university. Off-campus student political activities shall not be subjected to university regulation. On-campus advocacy or organization of such activities shall be subject only to such limitations as may be imposed under section 2.

4. That future disciplinary measures in the area of political activity shall be determined by a committee appointed by and responsible to the Berkeley Division of the Academic Senate.

5. That the Division urge the adoption of the following—of the foregoing—policies, and call on all members of the university community to join with the faculty in its efforts to restore the university to its normal functions.

Before closing, let me refer back very briefly to section 2. The language in section 2 reads "that the time, place, and manner of conducting political activity on the campus shall be subject to reasonable regulation to prevent interference with the normal functions of the university." The approach that is embodied in this section and in the following section 3 is viewed as one of permitting a broad range of problems connected with freedom of political activity as far as the content of activity is concerned, while regulating the "time, place and manner" of its exercise, so as not to interfere with the primary functions of the university. It is this area of problems that remains to be dealt with and which will be the subject of a later set of recommendations. Mr. Chairman, I so move.

CHAIRMAN: You've heard the motion. Is there a second? Professor Tussman?

TUSSMAN: I'm Joseph Tussman. I am the chairman of the Department of Philosophy—

CHAIRMAN: Are you making a second?

TUSSMAN: I'm making a second—and one of the working committee of five chairmen which acted recently on behalf of all the chairmen on the Berkeley campus. I wish to second the motion which the Committee on Academic Freedom has placed before us. The crisis through which we are passing involves at least three sets of problems. First, there are problems resulting from recent attempts to resolve what is essentially a moral and spiritual crisis by the use of radically inappropriate means, the attempt to deal coercively and punitively with problems of mind and spirit. In this field, we may hope, I believe, that the spirit of amnesty will now prevail. Second, there are problems arising out of the quality and scope of university regulations governing speech, assembly, and political or social action by members of the academic community. And, third, there are problems arising from fundamental defects in the living constitution of the university, in the relations between students, faculty, and administration, in the general structure of authority. Permanent peace and health will not be easily attained, but the propositions before us are a good beginning. I think they are all necessary.

I will comment only upon point 3, which provides "that the content of speech or advocacy should not be restricted by the University. Off-campus student political activity shall not be subject to university regulation. On-campus advocacy or organization of such activity shall be subject only to such limitations as may be imposed under section 2." This rule will obviate most of the difficulties in this sensitive area. It is a sensible rule, but I think we should regard it as more than just a sensible rule, as more than a way of avoiding tough administrative problems, and even as more than a rule which protects important rights. We should regard it and support it as symbolizing the fundamental commitment of the university to its own essential nature, for it expresses the conviction that ours is an institution whose proper mode of dealing with the mind is educational, not coercive. We are not the secular arm. If we have forgotten this, we should be grateful to those who are now reminding us. I hope the Senate will pass this motion; it is badly needed, it has been very carefully considered, it has the support of many members of the academic community. It is, I suppose, public knowledge that it is strongly supported by chairmen of departments. Nevertheless, it is a good motion. [Laughter.]

Professor Herbert McClosky of the Political Science Department then explained that the resolution had grown out of discussions held by 200 faculty members, who had met as an ad hoc group since the informal faculty meeting of December 3. He described a petition handed him in support of the resolution, which had been signed by 80 individuals from 20 university facilities on the campus, and added:

It is my hope . . . that we can now put aside our differences and that we can all manage—students, faculty, university officials, and Regents—to strike an attitude of generosity and magnanimity so that the damage might be repaired and so that we can all return to work. It is in this spirit, Mr. Chairman, that I wish to second the motion for the adoption of this resolution.

FEUER: My name is Feuer, Departments of Philosophy and Social Science, and I am introducing an amendment and speaking in defense of this amendment. The amendment is to paragraph 3 of the proposed motion, first line of paragraph 3, to alter it as follows: "that the content of speech or advocacy on this campus, provided that it is directed to no immediate act of force or violence, should not be restricted by the university," and then in the last line of paragraph 3 to alter "as may be imposed under section 2" to "as have been heretofore stated."

I should like to explain why I have moved this amendment. It does not strike at the philosophy of the Free Speech Movement as I understand that philosophy, as it has been expounded by some of its proponents. Insofar as the Free Speech Movement is sincerely committed to nonviolence, it has nothing to fear from this amendment, which is aimed to keep from university, from advocacy on university premises and grounds, those who are advocating the immediate commitment of acts of force and violence. The particular resolution which we will enact will probably become a model for many of the universities from here to the East Coast and including the state of Mississippi. As this resolution stands now, without an amendment, it would allow a student Ku Klux Klan chapter to organize itself on campuses to carry on meetings at which they would advocate planned and organized actions for defacing Jewish synagogues, Negro and Catholic churches, and they would claim the protection of the university sanctuary for these acts of speech, advocacy, and organization. Unless we had a provision, some amendment which will make it clear that we do not condone this sort of action or behavior, we are opening the way for every extremist and crackpot organization which can then enter upon this campus, advocate its most immediate measures, without fear of any action on the part of the university, and then the Federal Bureau of Investigation and other police agencies will be able to claim with some show of force that, since the university is not carrying out the most minimal safeguards of democracy, they have the right to infiltrate our premises with their agents. We will then truly become a police university.

Now it seems to me that, if this resolution as it stands now were to be enacted, we would be embarking upon the kind of situation which helped destroy freedom and democracy in the universities of central Europe during the thirties, and many of us recall those days. At that time, Nazi students organized their attacks on the outside community, on Jews, on liberals, on Democrats, on Socialists, and they claimed immunity; they claimed immunity from the university authorities, which could do nothing. And at the same time, they claimed immunity from the police. And this very type of resolution became an instrument, not for the safeguarding of democracy, as Professors Tussman and McClosky suggest, but for its destruction. It seems to me, then, to safeguard the future of the university, its autonomy as its own self-governing institution, and democracy here, such an amendment as I have presented should be passed.

CHAIRMAN: Now with that amendment, it would then read: . . . "That the content of speech or advocacy on this campus, provided that it is directed to no immediate act of force or violence, should not be restricted by the university. Off-campus student political activity shall not be subject to university regulations. On-campus advocacy or organization of such activity shall be subject only to such limitations as have been heretofore stated." Is that your amendment, Professor Feuer? [Pause.] You have heard that amendment. Is there a second to the amendment to the main motion?

Professor Nathan Glazer, who had been chairman of the informal faculty meeting on December 3, seconded the Feuer amendment. He argued that the university must retain the right to act in response to circumstances that are outrageous and detrimental to free speech and democracy. . . . I think it is not too difficult to envisage a situation where, without trying to raise anybody's hair, force and violence is directly organized on the campus, and the campus has—and the administration or the student committee governing this has—no recourse at all in such a situation either in terms of forbidding such activity or in terms of disciplining anyone involved in it.

CHAIRMAN: Professor [Jacobus] ten Broek [of the Political Science Department, a specialist in constitutional law].

TEN BROEK: Thank you, Mr. Chairman. On behalf of the Committee on Academic Freedom, I should like to express our opposition to this proposed amendment. The framework of the resolutions which we have presented is carefully designed to do a simple thing: Render unto Caesar that which is Caesar's, and render unto the university that which belongs to the university. As to content, as to the substance of what men say, this place should be absolutely free. So far as the university is concerned, this is an educational institution; we are engaged in the business of education. That function carries us into lots of areas of thought and even some areas of activity. We are concerned with knowing ourselves, with discovering knowledge, with spreading knowledge, with developing among our students some sense of morality and some capacity for self-government in a democracy. All of this requires that we adhere to standards which permit people to say what is on their minds; we should not forbid them to say anything.

On the other hand, this is an educational institution; we've got to conduct our business and consequently it is necessary to have regulations which will deal with the time, place, and manner of what is said. It is necessary to prevent the use of loudspeakers which interrupt classes, it is necessary to see to it that people can use the paths which lead to the library and even occasionally lead to classrooms, where students sometimes want to go. It is necessary to take care that the procedures and the mechanics of conducting political activity and operating a system of free speech be so regulated, so reasonably regulated, as to enable this institution to continue to carry on its major function.

Now, if you're going to talk about limiting the content of speech and advocacy, then it seems to me the very minimum that you should do is to use the language which after many years of experience the Supreme Court has developed in this field, and I'm not sure that even then they're talking about the content of speech and advocacy. You have here an expression which is that the content of speech may be limited if it is directed to an immediate act of a certain kind. Well, what speech is directed to an immediate act of violence? Suppose a person advocates violence; then suppose he does it in a context in which there is not the slightest danger that that will come about. Is there any reason why you should stop that even if your concern is violence? All right, now, our concern is not violence. This is the concern of the civil community. This is the concern of the FBI. And if Professor Feuer thinks that the FBI does not now have a right to come on this campus, he better think again. They have a right to come on this campus; they are on this campus very frequently. Other police are on this campus; our own police force is an adjunct of the police force of Berkeley. We should leave all these matters of restriction of content to the society where constitutional restraints will be imposed on those who act to invade freedom of speech.

We should be concerned with the intellectual and spiritual task of running a university where anybody can say whatever is on his mind, and other people can listen to him and think about it and make up their minds whether they agree or not. This resolution is not just a declaration of principle; this proposal that Dr. Feuer is making opens up to university regulation what we are here saying should not be regulated by the university in any manner, shape, or form. What other people do by way of regulation belongs to their jurisdiction and not to ourselves. The committee on Academic Freedom is opposed to this amendment to our resolutions.

Here Professor Johannes Proskauer of the Botany Department asked whether the Academic Senate had the right to pass such a resolution as the one proposed or whether this matter lay with the Regents.

CHAIRMAN: I am going to recognize Professor Carl Landauer. . . .

LANDAUER: Carl Landauer, Economics. I would like to support the Feuer amendment. I fully agree with what has been said about the necessity of an amnesty. Mistakes have been made from all sides, and the only conclusion we can draw is no further penalties. But as far as number 3 is concerned, I think Professor ten Broek is wrong when he says that the resolution of the Academic Freedom Committee gives Caesar that which is Caesar's. And I'm not so much worried about Caesar's well being as I'm worried about the fact—the likelihood—that Caesar will take that which is his if we don't give it to him. The position that we can permit the organization of any lawless action on the campus—that is, the campus organization of any lawless action in the community—is in my opinion tenable only if at the same time we recognize the moral right of the police to come to our campus and suppress this activity. This moral right I'm not willing to concede to the general law-enforcement agencies. I cannot prevent them from coming to our campus in certain contingencies, but I want to minimize these contingencies. And consequently I must draw the conclusion that we ourselves must have a possibility in outrageous cases of lawlessness which are advocated or organized on the campus to interfere with our own academic means. Nobody wants to regulate the content of speeches or other expressions when it is a matter of nonviolence; any philosophy can be advocated by students, by faculty, by anyone. We have made great progress in this respect as far as outside speakers are concerned. We are now much freer than we used to be.

But, members of the Academic Senate, I have made a—I have some experience in fighting interferences with academic freedoms. People who are of my age and who are here will remember the oath question. We were in the oath question. We were not successful by any means. We had at the very best a quarter victory. But we had a quarter victory only because our position was fully defensible. And that was finally recognized by a number of groups or institutions, including courts, which were of decisive importance for the outcome. I would not hesitate to fight the Regents—as we probably will have to when this resolution is adopted—to fight the Regents on a defensible cause. We have done that before; we shall in all probability have to do it again. But I do not want the Academic Senate to put itself into a position in which the fight cannot be conducted from a basis which is inherently not defensible.

CHAIRMAN: Professor Rynin had his hand up first. Will you please stand instead of holding up your hand. Remember that the debate is on Professor Feuer's amendment to the main motion presented by Professor Garbarino. Professor David Rynin, Speech Department?

RYNIN: Philosophy. [Laughter.]

CHAIRMAN: After this, I'll ask each person to state his name and rank.

RYNIN: I find it very regrettable that we're putting ourselves in the position where we have to declare ourselves against force and violence. No one is in favor of force and violence. But . . . if we begin debating this matter and pass this resolution, this will mean one thing to the people who have been most active in this struggle, people whom I honor and respect despite their shortcomings, and who I think have done a great service to the university, the Free Speech Movement. They will understand this only in one way: namely, that this vague language about advocating action directed towards force and violence, or however it is stated, as once again putting them in the position in which if they prepare boycotts or sit-ins or picketing against the outside community in the name of civil liberties and preserving and safeguarding the rights of minorities, that they are again subject to the same kind of punitive threats and actualities as has led to this miserable situation in the first place. . . .

CHAIRMAN: Professor [Owen] Chamberlain [of the Physics Department, a Nobel laureate].

CHAMBERLAIN: Mr. Chairman, I wish to speak against the amendment. I have the feeling that there are some things that the students have been trying to tell us that are relevant to this question. In particular I want to try to distinguish between these two things that are discussed: on the one hand, force and, on the other hand, violence. There are strange happenings on our campus these days. There are meanings to be read from them. I think the students have attempted to be articulate in explaining them to us; I think they have had real difficulty. On the matter of nonviolent civil disobedience, the students are quite proud of their use of the method called civil disobedience. They have used it under some of the most trying conditions, particularly in the South. They are proud of its feature of putting high value on the human lives of others and at the same time low value on the rules of men, which seem at times rather arbitrary, especially to the young people.

In commenting on civil disobedience, from my own point of view, I want to say that I tend to disagree with the students. I feel that I have great investment in the continued existence of any orderly society. In fact, I could not feed myself or my family except as I have the cooperation inherent in an orderly society. But, if we are to convince the students that they too have a vested interest in preserving order, we probably must convince them that they have at their disposal other tools—tools that are more suitable for all, but fully effective.

On the right of social action: the students are not well impressed by the world as they see it. They see much is wrong, and I am sure many of us do. They feel it their privilege, indeed their responsibility, to take steps, to make change in an undesirable pattern.

The necessity of being heard: the students, particularly those most active politically, feel the necessity of having their views heard, yet feel that within the spectrum of methods their elders would recommend to them there is little that would allow them the effectiveness that they feel their conviction warrants. It is all very well for a committee of the faculty to say that the recent disorders have hindered the consideration of student proposals, yet I for one do not believe it. The students feel that they have had no legitimate channel open.

On the matter of paternalism: while it is the claim of this university that it exists for the purpose of helping young people to become skilled and responsible citizens, the administration and faculty have very often taken a rather paternalistic attitude towards students. The students may rightly say that there can be no sudden transition, the day they receive their last academic degree, from dependent children to independent adults. They're insisting they *are* young adults; they are insisting they do carry responsibility. They are showing us that even such a simple matter as law and order on our campus depends upon them. They are asking that we recognize their views not just as the view of youth, but also as the view of adulthood.

Intellectual integrity on both sides: many of us have noticed the distortions in the FSM literature. I take it I do not have to count comment on that. Yet all has not been well on our side. We insist on demeaning the students by reference to the "new liberalized rules." I grant that in the technical sense the rules have been liberalized. I think a person who reads the old rules and the new rules would agree. But this should not obscure the fact that the meaning of a rule is inexorably tied to its customary interpretation. In terms of the interpretation of the old rules during the last academic year, I believe the logical interpretation of the new rules is that they are more restrictive. I urge that we do not too often refer to the new rules as "liberalized."

Mr. Chairman, I feel that many of the actions that our students would be most proud of might run into difficulty with the Feuer amendment. I regard the occupation of Sproul Hall as a use of force, but not a use of violence. I suggest that the amendment is not proper as formulated; I suggest that we reject it. Thank you.

Professor Bernard Diamond of the Law and Criminology Schools spoke, opposing the Feuer amendment and urging the Academic Senate to stay out of the area of criminal law. He argued that the relation of civil disobedience to criminal law was complex, and that current laws were sufficient to deal with the situation. "We should restrict ourselves to the spirit of the principle of free speech."

CHAIRMAN: Professor [Albert] Lepawsky [Political Science Department].

LEPAWSKY: . . . Professor Chamberlain spoke of nonviolent civil disobedience. I submit that we have seen and continue to see here on this campus during this crisis period violent uncivil disobedience. And if we do not face up to the question of whether we will bow in one form or another to this pressure, we are not meeting our main obligation here this afternoon. I am not myself concerned about many of the details we are going to get into this afternoon, but I hope, Mr. Chairman, we will get a good expression of opinion on what I think is our basic question—and not these technical questions of how to phrase regulations.

The students have obviously found a good thing. They have discovered a means of not only debating but achieving some consequences resulting from that debate, which in my judgment are enormous. The implications are great, not only for this university or for the university systems of this country and abroad. Speaking of abroad, I always used to be proud of the fact, when I went to Latin American universities, that we didn't have such things, and I am afraid that we are going into a period of our history, unless we put our foot down on this major issue here this afternoon, and not ask the courts to enforce some minor regulations, or to engage in some major Constitutional thinking on this question. This is our responsibility; indeed, this is the final opportunity for the university, and the faculty has the honor of facing up to that opportunity directly. That it has refused to face up to; indeed it has capitulated to forces which destroy that responsibility up to this point.

The main reason that I would at least favor the amendment, but certainly not adopt the provision as it is now suggested, is that the new constitutional system, or system for constituting policy-making and decision-making efforts, is being imposed upon us by, not nonviolent civil disobedience, but, as I have said, by an uncivil disobedience. The young man who grasped that microphone yesterday after the president laid down rules for orderly conduct is a man of great capacity. He and his colleagues I hereby give the grade of A+ to in how to administer certain things, and I won't mention those things. And if we are going to condone in any manner whatsoever by our action here this afternoon the kind of behavior represented by that final act of defiance on the part of brilliant Mr. Savio yesterday, we are not merely passing judgment on a minor aspect of a student movement, we are enacting a new system for making decisions and arriving at policies at a major American institution. Indeed, it may affect our democracy as a whole.

I will tell you one final anecdote about my own life, and then leave the podium, Mr. Chairman. I came from a university in the South; I must say I was very proud of my graduate students there. They were all, if I may use that term in a way in which you'll understand it, liberals to the core. They were not the typical southerners that you think about or hear about when you hear about southern colleges or universities. I was proud of them, but I was not proud of our president. Because our president, Mr. Gallilee, at one time ordered the police on the campus to use violence upon the students in the following form. He said, "Don't shoot them too high: shoot them in the legs!" And we called him, "Shoot-'em-in-the-legs Gallilee." I do not want the University of California, which I have the greatest respect for, and which is an institution that is having an effect on world affairs as well as scientific and educational affairs of great moment—I don't want this institution to remind me of my experience with "Shoot-'em-in-the-legs Gallilee," and if I am not crude, Mr. Chairman, I want to end my remarks by saying [that] I do not want to substitute for "Shoot-'em-in-the-legs Gallilee," "Bite-'em-in-the-leg Savio."

CHAIRMAN: It has been suggested that . . . two more speakers from each side be recognized. I recognize Professor Selznick.

SELZNICK: Philip Selznick, professor of Sociology. . . . Our problem is to find a policy that is tenable, that can be defended, that can be implemented, that can find its way into a series of regulations and governing provisions that we can all live with and that are proper to a university. The university has all the resources it needs to deal with disorderly behavior on this campus. It can deal with disorderly behavior by invoking its own rules, it can deal with disorderly behavior by invoking the rules of the civil authority. It retains the right to file charges against anyone who breaks the law.

Our problem is not the control of acts but of speech. And we are moving here—I sincerely hope we shall conclude here—a movement toward a policy that protects the content of speech and that assumes the risks of that protection.

I am not unmindful of the great issues and problems raised by Professors Feuer and Glazer. I know that political abomination has existed in the modern world and may yet be with us again. How shall we deal with political abomination in an educational institution? It is not a tenable policy, it is not a defensible policy, it is not a workable policy to deal with such abominations by attempting to introduce the sorts of restraints envisioned by the amendment. This amendment is unworkable, as Professor ten Broek has suggested. This amendment is not consistent with the basic spirit and aims of a university. We want to invoke the new policy, the policy we should have had all along, the policy we are adopting not out of concession to pressure, not out of submission to outside forces, but because I think at long last we are ready to adopt a policy that should have been with us through all these times. We adopt this policy not only because it is consistent with the Constitution of the United States. We adopt this policy because it is the most fitting policy for a great university. I sincerely hope that we will vote down the Feuer amendment and give our full support to the Committee on Academic Freedom.

CHAIRMAN: I recognize Professor [Daniel] Arnon.

ARNON: Arnon, Cell Physiology. . . . We are told that the mob is waiting outside. We are told that, unless we do as we heard yesterday—those of us who were at the rally—unless we vote right, we will never solve this problem. . . . We have students who are determined to fight for their principles no matter what, no matter whether they destroy the university, no matter whether they bring destruction on themselves and on the university. From this they will not budge. But we the faculty, we must vote not according to our principles, but according to the danger which these students present. I submit that this is not an honorable alternative—choice—for this faculty, no matter what the issue and no matter how grave. . . .

Professor Selznick . . . has told us that the university has great resources for enforcing its regulations, that the university can always call on the civil authorities to help them. . . . Have we seen during the last week that this very point which he invokes has any semblance of reality? I submit it has not. . . .

If the university becomes the place which receives the greatest protection in our community for positions for advocacy leading, in the phrase of the amendment, to immediate acts of force and violence, are we not becoming, . . . *ipso facto,* the place from which such attacks will be launched and mounted? . . . And above all I submit that this body must at this moment, which is of tremendous importance to this university and all universities in the country, vote on principle, but not under duress.

CHAIRMAN: We have now been debating for about an hour and ten minutes. I would like to suggest that the chairman of the Academic Freedom Committee select a speaker to close and that Professor Feuer either [speaks] himself or . . . selects a speaker on the amendment as the closing. Professor Stampp is speaking as a member of the Academic Freedom Committee.

STAMPP: I'm Kenneth Stampp of the History Department . . . the propositions of the Committee on Academic Freedom were not addressed to expediency, but to high principles. I agree that the Feuer amendment sounds reasonable enough because, as has been said before, none of us believes in force and violence. But I also believe that the proposed Feuer amendment would change the whole nature of the propositions that have been submitted to this body today by the Committee on Academic Freedom. It would to a considerable extent put the university once again in the business of regulating speech and advocacy, and I think it would get us back to where we were before this meeting today.

Now the question has been raised, What rights can the Board of Regents delegate to our students and what rights do our students have? I don't think the Board of Regents can delegate any rights to our students. These rights they have under the Constitution of the United States and under the Constitution of the state of California. The Regents neither delegate these rights nor are empowered, I think, to take them away.

Now the propositions that we introduced today may prove in practice to have weaknesses and shortcomings, but these propositions can be amended by this body when it deems [the situation] appropriate to do so. But we still hold as a general proposition that, while our students are accountable to civil authorities for violations of the laws of the state and of the community, and responsible to the faculty of this university for the violation of regulations concerning the time and place and manner of speech advocacy, our students can properly expect of the university that it will respect their Constitutional rights and will protect them in their exercise. Thank you.

CHAIRMAN: Professor Feuer yields to Professor Petersen to make the closing argument on the amendment to the motion presented by the Committee on Academic Freedom. Let me say while Professor Petersen is coming up here that I greatly appreciate your attention and also the very high level in which this very crucial debate has been carried on.

PETERSEN: My name is William Petersen, I'm a professor of sociology, and I speak for Professor Feuer's amendment. . . . Phrases that would be edited out of any campaign speech as too platitudinous to include are an issue in this body. I merely feel that Professor Rynin pointed to precisely the issue. We are threatened by a group which has found a mode of behavior that permits a group of irresponsible true believers to dictate what they want, and the solution that is offered by the opponents of this amendment is that this group is so powerful that, if we offer even platitudinous opposition to their force and violence, . . . we must expect as a result force and violence. I submit that this is blackmail, that it would be undignified to submit to. And I ask further, Where does this stop? If we submit to this, then what?

I think that I can point to one example. The T.A.'s [teaching assistants] on the campus wanted to strike; unfortunately there is a law that if you strike against the state government you are by that act dismissed. In a number of departments the TA's presented this dilemma to the faculty. In a number of departments the faculty and the TA's conspired on how to break the state law without the TA's incurring any inconvenience from this act. I submit that this is no function for a true teacher. If there is a bad law—and this may be a bad law—and if there is someone with the courage to break it and test it in court, if I agree with his moral position I will support him. But I will not support a faculty which refuses to come out for the law in general against force and violence in general and moves from this position under the pressure of a bunch of rowdies into conspiring with the students to break other laws as well.

At this point the chairman called for a standing vote on the amendment proposed by Feuer.

SECRETARY: Mr. Chairman, the vote on the amendment is 284 aye, 737 nay.

CHAIRMAN: I declare the amendment to the motion as lost. Are you ready for the question on the main motion? All right, I recognize this gentleman here. I think he has a right to speak. . . . We are now directed to the question on the main motion presented by the Committee on Academic Freedom.

ZEMACH: Charles Zemach, Physics. Mr. Chairman, we have heard in the last few days that the action of the Committee of Chairmen was an interim measure. We may wish to believe that the motion before us is a final word on some of the subjects it treats. I suggest that this motion is an interim measure—this motion is as interim as anything else. Look, for example, at point 4. This says that "discipline on political activity is to be done by a Senate committee." I hope that the Senate has enough imagination to realize what the potentialities are. Let us suppose that under new enlightened rules a discipline case comes up. The committee members may be told by the people whom they are considering the discipline of that they are breaking the rules, that they are violating an agreement, that they are betrayers. They may be confronted with massive sit-ins at their meetings. They may be confronted with massive sit-ins in their classrooms, in Sproul Hall, or anywhere else. They may be asked to share their heavy responsibilities with student representatives, because this is what a university is supposed to be—to have faculty and students working together towards truth. They should not be surprised to hear the loudspeakers of Sproul Hall blare forth that they are trying to crush the civil rights movement or that they are creatures of a scheming president or that they are honest and sincere but need student support to withstand the pressures of the Oakland *Tribune* and right-wing businessmen, or that they are power-mad, or that their wives have long been intriguing for their increase in power. These are all phrases I have heard from FSM leaders in the last two days, either in public speeches or in serious negotiations. The bit about somebody's wife was by an FSM leader in serious negotiations. To those of you who do not like to hear these things on loudspeakers or read them in the newspapers, I suggest you keep off that committee. I might even say that those of you who don't enjoy that sort of conflict the way the FSM leaders enjoy that sort of conflict, you might keep off that committee.

Let no one believe that questions of law and order and discipline are being solved by the motion before us. We are changing the battlefield. The terrain of the new battlefield will also be difficult. Now, then, there is something very fine and noble about a community like this going forth to take on responsibilities. Not haggling over whether one is forced to do so, or whether the responsibilities might be left on someone else. There will also be something comforting about being able to look back on one's work and being able to say, "I did my duty; I did my best." This is particularly true if you reach one of these situations where there is nothing else to be comfortable about.

Finally, there is the hope—and much depends on this—that students who love the university will be able to find something final about this measure. And I say that again. There is the hope that—and much depends on this—and everything depends on this—that students who love this university will find something final about this measure. In the spirit of these sentiments, I shall vote wholeheartedly for this motion, but let's not kid ourselves that the future is all peaches and cream. Thank you. . . .

There followed a rather complicated series of questions, explanations concerning parliamentary procedure, and an additional amendment, which was defeated.

CHAIRMAN: I would like to say that there is some unhappiness by people who feel that there should be an opportunity to vote on the main motion, and I'm going now to put that main motion so that anyone can, without any question, know that a vote was taken on it. That is, the motion which is now unamended, presented by Professor Garbarino, chairman of the Academic Freedom Committee. I ask that all those in favor of the motion please indicate by saying "aye." [Ayes heard.] Contrary, "no." [No's heard.] The motion is carried. If there is a call for a division, we will have a count. All right, we have heard the call. Will the secretary please announce the vote.

SECRETARY: Mr. Chairman, the vote is 824 aye, 115 nay.

Outside the building, students burst into cheers and wild applause. The Academic Senate went on to pass a second resolution, which stated, in part:

> . . . The present grave crisis in the life of the University demands that the Berkeley Division of the Academic Senate offer leadership to the campus community, and whereas, the existing organization of the Division is not well adapted to the exercise of such leadership under the emergency circumstances now prevailing, therefore be it resolved . . . that an Emergency Executive Committee . . . be constituted to represent the Division in dealing with problems arising out of the present crisis during the remainder of the present academic year, reporting its actions regularly to the Division, and convening the Division when necessary. . . .[6]

The Academic Senate, normally a consultative body to the campus administration, had taken over important aspects of the government of the campus. As the faculty members walked out of Wheeler Hall, they passed through a crowd of several thousand cheering, applauding students, who formed an honor guard lining either side of the entrance. The ovation lasted until the last faculty member had left. A number of people were crying.

THE STUDENTS AND THE REGENTS REACT TO EVENTS

On Monday and Tuesday, December 7 and 8, aside from the strike and the Greek Theater drama, the students had been carrying on a quiet revolution of their own. For these were the days of the ASUC student election.

The Daily Californian gave almost no coverage to the candidates' positions before the election. Therefore knowledge of candidates' platforms depended on hand-outs and posters or on word-of-mouth presentations. The *context of events,* however, gave clear positions to the incumbent ASUC government and to Slate. The ASUC officially had condemned the strike, working actively with the administration to try to stop it and even setting up a counterstrike organization. Slate, in contrast, was an active part of the Free Speech Movement.

On Wednesday, December 9, the *Daily Californian* carried a kicker headline over its masthead: "Slate Sweeps Into Office; No Runoffs." For the first time since the graduate students had been removed from student government, Slate had won an election. Moreover, every Slate candidate had been elected. The interests represented in the current ASUC leadership had been repudiated. The turnout vote was 5276, which the *Daily Californian* reported was almost double the usual total.[7] Two FSM personalities, Brian Turner and Dustin Miller, had been elected, along with Tom Meyer, Bob Nakamura, Gary Feller, Shirley Arimoto, Marston Schultz, and Stephen Cornet. Although half the current ASUC officers would remain in the Senate, student government clearly was not going to be a "company union" in the months ahead.

Comments of the losing candidates, together with Slate's victory statement, strongly suggest that "free speech" and "company union" were the dominant themes of the campaign. Here are excerpts from the statements of two of the losing candidates:

The ASUC will have a new direction. I call upon all students to assess this direction by understanding and participating in the issues of next semester.[8]

The election results are clearly a mandate for an active ASUC in the arena of student politics and willing to lead in the implementation of student interests. . . .[8]

Slate officials said, "Slate promises to immediately implement its program upon taking office, including full freedom of speech on campus, a co-op ASUC store, low-cost student apartments, and the readmission of graduate students [into student government]." [8]

Unfortunately, the only spring survey with reliable sampling methods and good return rates did not ask about voting in the December election. Circumstantial evidence, however, suggests that the most active pro-FSM strikers (those manning picket lines) may have voted out of proportion to their numbers on the campus as a whole. They were outside, near voting booths, during the first day of the election. Some strike coordinators, speaking to picketers over electronic bull horns, reminded people of the student government election and urged them to vote.[9] In addition, the crowd listening to the Academic Senate meeting being broadcast over loudspeakers on Tuesday afternoon stood only a few feet from one set of voting booths.

Approximately 3200 undergraduates manned the picket lines during the strike. The most popular Slate candidate-at-large received 2716 votes. (The least popular Slate candidate polled 2475 votes, as contrasted with 1705 for his highest-running non-Slate competitor.) Again, for the student government seat representing apartment dwellers (the commuter-independent representative), the Slate candidate polled 1652 votes, as contrasted with his opponents' showing of 304 and 50 votes, respectively. Approximately 2000 of the picketers were undergraduates living in apartments. These figures do not *prove,* of course, that the picketers voted in large numbers, but it is clear that both the context and the physical location of voting booths should have helped to mobilize potential support for the Slate position.

All in all, December 8 had been quite a day. Supporters of the Free Speech Movement had been given control of student government; the faculty had passed a resolution basically supporting the position the FSM had been advocating all fall; and the faculty had taken charge of the campus governing machinery.

The major headline on Wednesday's *Daily Californian* read, "Faculty Plan—Peace Near? Regents Decide Next Week." [7]

The chairman of the Board of Regents was considerably less pleased with the turn of events than were the students. On December 9 he issued the following statement:

The Constitution of the State of California clearly charges the Regents with full and ultimate authority for conducting the affairs of the University of California. This they exercise principally through their appointed administrative officers and by delegation of certain specific but revocable powers to properly constituted academic bodies.

It now appears that on the Berkeley campus these traditional methods have proved inadequate to deal effectively with the extraordinary problems created there by regrettable recent incidents. Hence, the Regents will consider this whole matter directly at their next meeting now scheduled to be held on December 18 in Los Angeles.[10]

HOW MUCH OF A REVOLUTION HAD IT REALLY BEEN?

A number of faculty members said later that, when they walked out of Wheeler Auditorium after the meeting of December 8, saw the cheering students, and realized that they had endorsed the position of the FSM, they wanted to turn right around and change their votes. But it was too late.

The Committee of 200, of course, was overjoyed at the outcome. Its members immediately met to choose a slate of candidates to run for the newly created Emergency Executive Committee. They decided to vote as a block, to make sure that persons who were committed to the principles of the resolution were on this committee.[11] All their candidates made it into the run-off election, which was held on Monday, December 14, but only one, Carl Schorske, was finally elected to the Emergency Executive Committee. The others elected were Raymond Bressler, professor of agricultural economics; Earl Cheit, professor of business administration; Arthur Ross, chairman of the Department of Business Administration; and Robley Williams, professor of molecular biology. Richard Jennings, professor of law and chairman of the Berkeley Division of the Academic Senate, had an ex officio position on the committee.[12]

Although the students and some of the Regents did not realize it for some months, the election of December 14 was as crucial a decision for the Academic Senate as had been its vote of December 8. The faculty at large turned its back on the group that had given leadership in the academic freedom dispute, except for one-man token representation. The other persons elected were part of the on-going committee structure of the Senate, and were regularly called on for the traditional administrative work of university committees. They were far from a radical elite. With the exception of Carl Schorske, few members of the Committee of 200 received many more than 200 votes in the run-off, despite the fact that in the first balloting this slate of candidates had been given the highest number of votes. The immediate crisis that had produced the nearly unanimous faculty resolution vote was past: classes were in session, the police were no longer on campus, the FSM had ceased to threaten massive disobedience. Thus the context that existed on December 8 had become less salient by the time of this vote.

In addition, major lobbying to defeat the Committee of 200's candidates had taken place as soon as the first balloting showed this group to have the highest number of votes. For the faculty, the final outcome reflected traditional voting alliances rather than any collective response to crisis. On the basis of the election it appeared that the bulk of the Academic Senate membership shifted to a considerably more conservative position in the week after the meeting in the Greek Theater.

In the week following the faculty resolution members of the Academic Senate worked tirelessly to interpret their position to the public and to the Regents. While the Emergency Executive Committee met with the Regents on December 17 "for a frank discussion," other Berkeley faculty members were lobbying for a statement in support of their position by the Academic Council of all the University of California campuses.

At the Regents meeting of December 18, held in Los Angeles, the board did not accept the Berkeley Division of the Academic Senate's proposed solution to the crisis. Instead, the board adopted the following motion:

1. The Regents direct the administration to preserve law and order on the campuses of the University of California, and to take the necessary steps to insure orderly pursuit of its educational functions.

2. The Regents reconfirm that ultimate authority for student discipline within the University is constitutionally vested in the Regents, and is a matter not subject to negotiation. Implementation of disciplinary policies will continue to be delegated, as provided in the by-laws and standing orders of the Regents, to the President and Chancellors, who will seek advice of the appropriate faculty committees in individual cases.

3. The Regents will undertake a comprehensive review of University policies with the intent of providing maximum freedom on campus consistent with individual and group responsibility. A committee of Regents will be appointed to consult with students, faculty, and other interested persons and to make recommendations to the board.

4. Pending results of this study, existing rules will be enforced. The policies of the Regents do not contemplate that advocacy or content of speech shall be restricted beyond the purview of the First and Fourteenth Amendments to the Constitution.[13]

The Regents also issued a statement to the university faculty:

1. The Regents express appreciation to the Academic Council of the University-wide Senate for its constructive proposals and analysis of recent developments,[14] *and welcome the continuing discussion taking part in the divisions of the Academic Senate on the several campuses.*

2. The Regents reaffirm faith in the faculty and student body of the University, and express the conviction that this great academic commu-

nity is in the process of finding the means to combine the freedom with responsibility under today's new circumstances.

3. The Regents respect the convictions held by a large number of students concerning civil rights and individual liberties.

4. The Regents reaffirm devotion to the First and Fourteenth Amendments to the Constitution, and note that University policies introduced in recent years have liberalized the rules governing expression of opinion on campus. The support of all the University community is essential to provide maximum individual freedom under law consistent with the educational purposes of the University.[13]

The *California Monthly* reported that Edward W. Carter, chairman of the Board of Regents, had stressed that the board was standing firm on its resolution of November 20, which provided that students could plan lawful off-campus political or social action, with the Regents retaining the right to regulate such activities on campus.[13]

Here again was an ambiguous resolution of the issues. The statement could be interpreted to mean either that the Regents were accepting the position of the students and faculty or that they were planning to reject it.

After the Regents meeting the newly elected Emergency Executive Committee of the Berkeley Division of the Academic Senate issued a statement that said in part:

. . . The positive attitude of the Regents, their resolution on advocacy, and the current development of new regulations by administrative and faculty committees working with students at Berkeley, make it possible for the campus to return to its primary functions of teaching, learning, and research.

We believe that the base is being established for full political freedom with academic order, and we call on all members of the University community to join in strengthening it.[13]

In contrast, the FSM leaders interpreted the Regents' action very differently. In a prepared statement Steve Weisman said:

We are shocked that the Regents refused [the faculty's] recommendations. . . . Despite the efforts of students and faculty, the Regents have decreed that there shall be no change in the policies repudiated by both students and the Academic Senate.

The students, as in the past, will continue to defend the rights of the academic community. The faculty, we hope, will stand with us in this fight.[15]

Thus at its meeting of December 18 the Board of Regents took three actions which became important. First, it stated publicly its commitment to upholding the First and Fourteenth Amendments to the U.S. Constitution. (Thus it recognized publicly the concern that had underlain support for the Free Speech Movement all fall. It was the first time that an administrative body of the University had publicly affirmed its position on this crucial issue in the dispute.) Second, the Regents set up a committee, under the chairmanship of Theodore Meyers, to look into rules for student discipline. Third, while Clark Kerr was out of the room, they set up a committee under the chairmanship of Regent William Forbes to investigate the series of crises that had arisen through the fall and to make recommendations to the board concerning possible changes in the structure or policies of the university.[16]

On December 28 the Committee on Academic Freedom of the Berkeley Division of the Academic Senate released a report recommending a new basis for regulating student political activity.[17] The report was finally presented to the Academic Senate on January 5, 1965. In the meantime, wishing to have the matter settled before classes began after the Christmas recess and also not wanting to bind the Academic Senate in advance, Chancellor Edward Strong announced on December 31 that the Committee on Academic Freedom's recommendations would go into effect "provisionally" on Monday, January 4, the first day of classes after Christmas.[17]

There was an immediate outcry that Strong's "provisional" implementation showed he was trying to undercut the Committee on Academic Freedom. His statements and actions since December 8 were considered provocative to students who had participated in the demonstrations.

On January 2, two days after Strong's announcement, at an emergency meeting of the Board of Regents, the chancellor was relieved of his duties.[18] The public announcement by the board, however, stated that Strong had been granted a leave of absence "to recuperate from his recent illness." Martin Meyerson, Dean of the College of Environmental Design on the Berkeley campus, was named to replace him as acting chancellor "for an indefinite period." [19] (Meyerson had been on the

Study Committee for Campus Political Activity and had been one of the more sympathetic proponents of student concerns within the administration during the fall controversy. A few days earlier he had agreed to be the vice-chancellor of the Berkeley campus.[20]

The revolution, it appeared, had been completed. The chief campus officer had been removed; the Academic Senate had defended the legal position of the student demonstrators; student government would represent the voice of the student protesters; the Regents had bound themselves to uphold the First and Fourteenth Amendments of the U.S. Constitution; the new political action rules were favorable to the concerns of the student demonstrators; and the new chief administrative officer of the campus was sympathetic to the concerns of the students. Moreover both the students and the faculty, through the elections and resolutions of December 8, had indicated that they expected to be directly involved in decisions concerning future policy on the campus. It had been an expensive struggle, and the possibility of jail sentences still hung over the heads of almost 800 demonstrators, but it seemed to have reached a successful conclusion. Within a short period the FSM Executive Committee and Steering Committee announced plans to disband until such time as they might again be needed. The energies that had been devoted to the campus struggle were redirected to issues in the surrounding community and nation. As the semester ended, it seemed to be an amazing victory for the small band of civil rights activists who had taken on the university administration.

part iv

THE FINAL ROUND: REACTION SETS IN

By the time the new school term began in January 1965, the Free Speech conflict could be said to have passed through five phases. The first, beginning in July and ending on September 29, 1964, was spent in defining issues and maneuvering for positions. Then had come the second phase—a series of massive confrontations, lasting three days from September 30 through October 2, 1964. These encounters resulted in a re-establishment of authority, but in no resolution of the problems that had led to the original challenge.

A third phase of the conflict occupied the month of October. It was a period of mutual testing of the intentions of opponents, the development of conspiracy models of the opposition, and what might be called "defensive escalation" by both sides. Then, in the first three weeks of November came the fourth phase—a new period of direct confrontation, this time much more ritualized. This period ended with the November Regents meeting, where the board attempted to settle the issues that had remained in controversy when authority was re-established in October. By the time the policy statement was made, however, authority once again was in question, and the "settlement" was, in fact, no settlement at all. Decisions made at this meeting led, within a week, to the most serious confrontations of the fall.

This fifth phase produced what amounted to a revolution, deposing the chancellor, making an internal settlement of the policy issues in dispute, and providing major access to student government for the radical critics of the university. As we have seen, this fifth stage, "the revolution," appeared to have been won by the students; it was in fact won by the faculty. And it was more nearly a palace *coup* than the kind of value-oriented revolution that some students were advocating.

The spring semester and the following summer, in turn, might be described as having four phases. January and February were a "honeymoon" period between the student and faculty revolutions (the first phase), watched uneasily by a group of skeptical dissenters on the faculty and their supporters in the Board of Regents and the state legislature. In March came an explosion that produced an attempted "Restoration," in the nineteenth-century sense of the term (the second phase).[1] There followed a ten-week period of prolonged conflict (the third phase), in which the campus rocked from crisis to crisis as the new administration and the Board of Regents clashed increasingly with students. For a while the continued tenure of the university president came into question, this time from actions not of the "revolutionaries" but of "counterrevolutionaries" among the Regents. In the summer came a rounding of the conflict (the fourth phase), as Regents attempted to deal with some of the issues which had been raised, but not settled, by the year's events.

THE "HONEYMOON"

January and February, 1965, produced an amazing transformation at Berkeley. Martin Meyerson, the new acting chancellor, spoke with appreciation of the concerns that motivated student protesters. He announced an interim period of minimal rules for political activity, in which the campus jointly would explore ways to implement the "time, place, and manner" details of the faculty resolution of December 8. He appointed Neil Smelser, a faculty member not directly involved in the dispute but highly regarded as a teacher and scholar (he was the university's expert on collective behavior), to be his special assistant for political affairs. Thus the new administration would by-pass both the dean of students and the vice-chancellor for student affairs in dealing with political issues on the campus. Meyerson also spoke about the need for educational reform at the university, actively encouraging faculty members and students to explore this area more seriously.

This change of climate produced four immediate results. First, the Free Speech Movement officially disbanded "until such time as it might be needed again." The Steering Committee, which had been meeting daily for three months, and the Executive Committee, which had gathered once a week, held no meetings at all during a two-month period. Students who had been arrested in the December sit-in formed an organization to represent their interests in their trials on charges of trespass and resisting arrest, which occupied much of the spring,[2] but only a few of the FSM leaders played an active role in this organization. Others turned their energies to the causes that had motivated them to challenge the administrative rules in the first place.

Second, there was a renaissance of political activity on the campus. A *New Yorker* staff writer, visiting Berkeley in February, described the political activity on the plaza as giving it a carnival atmosphere.[3] Not only was there a mushrooming of "cause" tables all over the Sproul Plaza area, but also student demonstrations in the surrounding community took on a new importance. The Oakland *Tribune* picketing project had ended officially in early February.[4] A week later Campus CORE and Oakland CORE began picketing restaurants in Jack London Square, a fashionable entertainment area of Oakland. The CORE groups claimed certain restaurants had refused to upgrade Negro employees. On the weekend of February 12 about 200 demonstrators took part in the Jack London Square picket. Five persons, four of whom were students at Berkeley, were arrested for "disorderly conduct." Rallies on campus that week presented the arrests as one example of a number of instances of police harassment experienced by the picketers. An appeal was made to the federal government for protection from the Oakland police. Students were urged to resist efforts to discourage them from using newly won rights to advocate social causes. The next weekend approximately 3800 persons took part in the CORE demonstrations in Jack London Square, and eventually the campaign spread to other downtown eating places in Oakland.[5]

At the same time that political advocacy on campus and direct social action off campus were being revitalized, the student government was introducing a series of controversial legislative proposals that could affect its relationship to the university. Probably the most important of these concerned the readmission of graduate students to the ASUC. On February 24 graduate students voted 1876 to 1193 in favor of rejoining the student government. An undergraduate election to accept this proposal then was held; and an amendment to the ASUC constitution, allowing graduate students to participate, passed by a vote of 3345 to 1293.[6]

Students also began to enter more vigorously into the *intellectual* dialogue inherent in political positions. A number of graduate students who had helped to tutor members of the FSM having academic difficulties at the end of the first semester established a Free University off campus. The Free University planned to offer courses not included in the Berkeley curriculum, subjects that these students thought necessary to provide "socially relevant" training.

Another group of students, most of whom had been active in Slate and the Free Speech Movement, founded a brassy student publication entitled *SPIDER Magazine. SPIDER,* said its editors, stood for the central concerns of today's college students: sex, politics, international communism, drugs, extremism, and rock and roll.[7]

Coupled with the political renaissance so strikingly evident on the campus came a third phenomenon—an artistic renaissance that left some viewers enchanted, others dismayed. Strolling folk singers and informal concerts became common on the plaza. Poets would produce verses for their audience on the spot. New and exotic styles of dress appeared as it became "in" to "express yourself." All this meant that persons not employed by the university or registered for classes were flocking to the plaza area, either to perform, to engage in the artistic and political arguments taking place there, or simply to savor the atmosphere.

In contrast to the formal disbanding of FSM, the political upsurge of activity on the campus, and the artistic bloom, came a fourth, more conservative response. A group of faculty members who had voted against the December 8 resolution, who felt that the wrong man had been removed in December,[8] and who believed that a laissez-faire policy on the campus was producing a genuine state of anarchy acted together in what came to be called a Truth Squad. They began writing magazine articles and letters to newspapers critical of the changes at Berkeley. Some of these persons were reported to be contacting sympathetic Regents and members of the state legislature about what they believed were daily excesses occurring at the university.

What kinds of things disturbed them? They were concerned, first, with what they saw as a dishonest glorification of the Free Speech

Movement and an elevation of political manipulators to sainthood. They were distressed by efforts of part of the faculty to have charges dismissed against students who had been arrested in December. They believed that lenient policies, such as granting "incomplete" grades to students who had been too busy demonstrating during the fall to complete their course work, amounted to rewarding students for insurrection. In addition, they felt that the "no rules" period was producing a state of anarchy, in which the moral standards of the community were coming into disrepute.

In February, a faculty member who was particularly active in some of these efforts talked to me in great distress about two incidents that he saw as proving the extent of corruption developing on the campus. First, a student had taken a chair from the plaza for use behind a political recruiting table. According to this report, the missing chair was located in the student's room, but he was not punished. (His excuse that he had taken it home for the night because the building from which he got it had closed reportedly had been accepted at face value, allowing him to perpetrate theft without punishment.) Second, and more disturbing to my informant, was the decision of a new ASUC Slate Senator to send letters to university health services across the country, asking for their policies on the dissemination of birth control devices and information. This action produced widespread headlines and much consternation on campus, since the student had received no authorization to send the letter and had implied that Berkeley was considering a change in its own policy.[9]

In short, there were a number of instances of what these persons considered a gross corruption of community standards by those active in or sympathetic to the FSM. I have been unable to document the extent to which these faculty members were in touch with state legislators or Regents. Some natural scientists at Berkeley who were reported to be active leaders of the Truth Squad, however, had personal friends on the Board of Regents and in the state legislature. It is reasonable to presume that they shared their perceptions and concerns with these people on various occasions.[10]

Conservative faculty members were not the only persons with such friendships, and it is clear from interviews with faculty members who were not part of this group that Regents and legislators were getting informal reports of events at Berkeley from a number of sources. At any rate, what is important for our explanation is the high probability that conservative legislators and Regents were receiving word of a disquieting "series of abuses" taking place on the campus in the aftermath of the Free Speech Movement.

THE "RESTORATION" EFFORT

In February the campus held its annual Ugly Man contest, a charity drive to raise money for World University Service and for Cal Camp.[11] The Ugly Man contest involves spirited competition among many fraternities and a few other organizations on campus. In 1965 the contest was won, after a ribald campaign in the tradition of Cal Smokers,[11] by Alpha Epsilon Phi, which had sponsored "Miss Pussy Galore." This campaign had amused a number of students but had attracted little attention from faculty members, the general public, or the press.

One week later, however, John Thomson, a nonstudent who had been active in radical political circles in New York City and who had moved to Berkeley after the Free Speech Movement wandered onto campus holding a 5 by 8 inch piece of notebook paper in front of his chest. On the paper he had written the word "Fuck." He sat on the Student Union steps, near the street.

A Berkeley city policeman caught sight of the boy and the sign from his police car as he turned the corner. He reported a violation of obscenity laws, stressing the visibility of the sign to pedestrians and vehicles at least fifty feet away. Notified of the violation, campus police came out to arrest the sign bearer.[12] That was March 3.

When Art Goldberg and a few of his friends heard about the arrest, they were incensed. Why, they asked themselves, could a fraternity win the Ugly Man Contest through a highly obscene campaign, while a little guy who simply carried a small sign was arrested? [13]

The next morning Art Goldberg, Suzanne Goldberg, and a few other students went to the chancellor's office and demanded that the university drop charges against Thomson, threatening to hold an "obscenity rally" if the administration did not respond. The chancellor's staff did not give them the assurance they demanded, but instead warned them that such a reprisal could set off an explosive conservative political response across the state.[13]

Nevertheless, at noon Art Goldberg and a few friends staged an impromptu "obscenity rally" on the Student Union steps, protesting the discrimination involved in public honor for fraternity obscenity and arrest for a nonconformist's obscenity. It was a boisterous rally, one not taken very seriously by the 150 or so students that watched it, to judge from laughing reactions. Art Goldberg spoke, using the offensive term on Thomson's sign several times over a public address system. Dan Rosenthal, chairman of Cal Conservatives for Public Action, announced that his organization had ordered 1000 "Fuck communism" signs. Nicholas Zvegintov, a graduate student in business administration who was active in the Graduate Coordinating Committee during the Free Speech Movement, led a cheer spelling out the offensive word.[14]

Four more arrests were made that afternoon. A freshman, David Bills, was arrested after he sat down behind a table set up to raise money for John Thomson's court costs. Over the table was a sign announcing the "Fuck Defense Fund." When Bills was arrested, a person not currently enrolled on the campus sat down in his place and also was arrested. A small crowd followed these two into the police station in the Sproul Hall basement. Michael Klein, a graduate student in English, began reading aloud passages from *Lady Chatterley's Lover* to show that the offensive word was used in literature. He, too, was arrested for obscenity. Finally, officers arrested an Oakland City College student in the crowd after he held up a hand-printed sign bearing the word.[14]

Thereupon the battle was joined. At noon the next day the chairman of the English Department at Berkeley, Mark Schorer (who had written an introduction to one edition of *Lady Chatterley's Lover*), spoke at a rally. He condemned the obscenity controversy as not worthy of serious students. Schorer drew a sharp distinction between using questionable language in a book and reading it aloud, out of context, to flaunt it in public. Some persons at the rally disagreed with Schorer. That afternoon Mark Van Loucks, a pre-law undergraduate, signed complaints against four persons for use of obscene language at the rallies. By day's end nine persons had been arrested. Only three of the arrestees were enrolled currently at the university.[15]

The newspapers of the area gave the obscenity rallies major front-page coverage. Art Goldberg, FSM leader, was featured prominently. From many stories one would assume that the Free Speech Movement had staged the rallies and that they were being attended by large numbers of students. Soon, the abbreviation FSM was being used to describe the "Filthy Speech Movement," and wits were describing the situation as one of Freedom Under Clark Kerr.

Within a few days the state legislature played a tape of the March 5 obscenity rally as evidence of moral degeneracy on the Berkeley campus. The newspapers reported that the tape was played by State Senator Jack Schrade to a meeting "for men only." In public statements, legislators expressed shock that such things would be said in public on the state campus.[16]

No surveys of student reactions were made at this time. On the day of the first obscenity rally I heard many students who had been active in the Free Speech controversy express annoyance that people were acting so childishly in public. With continued arrests, however, these activists began to be concerned that a countercrackdown was in the offing. More generally, students seemed to be annoyed at the exaggerated accounts appearing in the press. Very few persons attended the rallies which continued for a few days thereafter. (The third obscenity rally, held in the lower Student Union plaza, was conducted by a former student named Charlie Artman. Only three persons attended the rally: a campus police officer, I with my tape recorder, and a third person who appeared to be a genuine member of the audience.[17])

The FSM Executive Committee was hastily reconvened once the arrests began and it became apparent that the press was going to link the events to the Free Speech Movement. In a long meeting at which all delegates spoke, giving reactions and advice, the FSM tried to decide what to do. On the one hand, they were united in being furious with Art Goldberg for allowing their enemies the opportunity to discredit the movement. On the other hand, they were concerned not to abandon fellow students and FSM members as scapegoats to be sacrificed by the university administration. At one point the group seemed to have decided to make a public statement disassociating itself from the obscenity rallies. Then, at the very end of the meeting, the Executive Committee decided to issue a statement demanding "due process" for those accused of illegal activity.[18] The statement, when it appeared, did nothing to challenge the press interpretation of the Free Speech Movement and the "Filthy Speech Movement" as identical. Moreover, former leaders of the FSM, speaking at rallies on the issue of student arrests, varied so greatly in their personal statements about the issue as to leave much room for selective quoting by the newspapers.

A man rumored to be part of the Truth Squad, who had written several vituperative articles critical of developments at Berkeley, spoke to me in fury about Art Goldberg's action. When I asked him why he was angry about this but not about the obscene remarks by the fraternity boys, he replied:

That was different. That was a bunch of fraternity boys blowing off steam. You know that when it's all over they're going to return to take their place as respectable members of society. But these *people are out to deliberately break every rule they can, to try to tear down society.*

This viewpoint, apparently, was shared by a number of other observers. By Tuesday, March 9, just six days after John Thomson's sign had sparked the crisis, the situation exploded.

Acting Chancellor Meyerson had called for the appropriate committees of the Academic Senate to conduct hearings against the students accused of obscene conduct. It was not clear to members of the Academic Senate, however, whether this was a political issue, involving "manner of speaking" violations, or behavior that would fall under the rubric "conduct unbecoming a student"—that is, behavior to be handled by the traditional student discipline committee. (This distinction between political and nonpolitical offenses had been a major issue in the fall.) Both of the committee chairmen involved disclaimed jurisdiction over the case.[19]

On March 9, after news accounts had noted that both faculty committees declined to handle the case, Edwin Carter, chairman of the Board of Regents, called President Clark Kerr. Although no record was kept of the conversation, Kerr apparently understood Carter to be giving him an ultimatum, ordering him to expel the students immediately. Kerr was quite upset. To him this apparent fiat raised not only the issues of due process for the students and of nonintervention by the president's office in campus affairs, but also—and more serious—the issue of meddling by the Regents in the daily operation of the university. The "ultimatum" seemed to him to exceed appropriate relationships between Regents and administrators.[20]

Kerr called Martin Meyerson, and both of them talked with Edwin Carter. Kerr recommended to Meyerson that they submit their resignations to the Board of Regents rather than accept this kind of intervention in the day-to-day business of the university. Meyerson agreed.[21]

At 4 P.M. Kerr and Meyerson called a press conference, announcing their intention to resign. Kerr and Meyerson requested that the news not be released until 6:30 P.M., so that they would have time to contact members of the Board of Regents. The story was rushed to the newspapers and to radio and television stations immediately, however, so that several Regents first learned of the announcement from the communications media. This produced considerable resentment in the days ahead.

Kerr and Meyerson issued similar statements on March 9. Meyerson then submitted a long letter of resignation to the Board of Regents on Saturday. Kerr, however, did not actually submit a letter of resignation, although he earlier had announced his intention to do so.[22] Meyerson also issued a separate statement commenting on the campus situation:

I call your attention to the state of student conduct at Berkeley. The most recent flagrant violation of accepted behavior was the display of obscenity which assailed the campus and the public last week. The four-letter-word signs and utterances had a significance beyond their shock impact; they also symbolized intolerance for the rights and feelings of others. . . . What might have been regarded earlier as childish bad taste has become to many the last straw of contempt.[23]

Reactions to the announced resignations was immediate. The Emergency Executive Committee of the Academic Senate, a number of leading members of the faculty, various groups of the Berkeley campus, and the ASUC Senate released public statements urging the president and the chancellor to reconsider. Telegrams and calls from educators across the country began pouring in.

The next day Kerr released a public statement about what he called "the filthy speech movement," a statement that made clear his disapproval of it, but that did not mention directly his concern about pressures from the Board of Regents. He said in part:

We are currently faced with a new confrontation at Berkeley potentially filled with great passion. Offenders must be disciplined but due process must have its due place. And faculty committees should not seek to avoid their responsibility for assisting in discipline because of minor questions of internal jurisdiction and doubts about the ultimate state of the civil law.

Academic institutions have traditionally set standards of moral and ethical behavior conductive to their principles. The University must

*have the right to augment civil law with rules that will protect and en-
hance educational purposes.*

*I have joined in a dramatic step, which is not my inclination. I have
done so to try to stop, to the extent I can be helpful, the continuing and
destructive degradation of freedom into license and a new confrontation
at Berkeley. . . .*[24]

Reactions from the "left" and the "right" were also immediate. The
FSM Executive Committee released a statement protesting "this latest
and most catastrophic tampering by certain Regents with campus affairs." It continued:

*Only in the recent controversy over "obscene" words can students be
said not to have acted responsibly. The FSM did not initiate or support
this controversy. We regret both that the students involved acted in an
unfortunate manner and that the police and some administrators chose
to escalate the issue and endanger campus peace rather than permit student interest in the subject to wane. . . .*[25]

After the Kerr statement became public, the FSM Steering Committee issued a second statement, which included the following comments:

*According to Kerr, "We are currently faced with a new confrontation at
Berkeley potentially filled with great passion." This statement is a lie,
and an insult to students, faculty, and local administrators. The obscenity issue died last week and is now in the courts where it belongs. President Kerr has seized upon a dead issue to avoid giving the real reasons
for his resignation. He has slandered our hard-won political freedoms
and our movement towards academic reform as "the continuing and destructive degradation of freedom into license". . . .*

In contrast, the Oakland *Tribune* editorialized on the front page as
follows: "Many observers believe the wrong man was allowed to leave
when Chancellor Edward W. Strong vacated that position. He was
looked upon as a firm force in a troubled and fluid campus situation.
. . ." [26] In the days that followed, the *Tribune* presented the case for
Strong's retention (the Regents had not acted on his resignation) and
for the removal of Kerr. The story claimed that Strong had favored a
relatively firm course of action throughout the fall but had frequently
been overruled by Kerr.[27]

On March 11, two days after his announcement of intention to resign, Martin Meyerson reported the appointment of an ad hoc committee to handle the cases of reported obscenity, thus resolving the "difficult question of jurisdiction." [28] A satirical columnist for one of the San Francisco papers described the situation as a proposal: "Let's hang them by their thumbs." To which everyone had responded, "No, let's give them a trial first. Then let's hang them by their thumbs." [29]

On March 12, the day before the Regents were scheduled to hold an emergency meeting to consider the resignations, the Academic Senate of the Berkeley campus convened. About 1250 of the 1500 voting members attended, an even larger turn-out than on December 8. The meeting was carefully organized, with speakers from every wing of the faculty giving the same message, roughly this: We must stand united against threats to the university at this time. We must do everything we can to prevent the resignations of Clark Kerr and Martin Meyerson from being accepted. If the faculty appears at all to be divided, the enemies of campus autonomy will take full advantage of the situation and will do great damage to the Berkeley campus.

On a standing vote, approximately 1100 persons rose to support a resolution asking both Kerr and Meyerson to withdraw their resignations. The resolution also condemned "the willful flaunting of obscenity on this campus" by a few students, "strongly endorsed" the administration's action to start disciplinary proceedings against the students involved "under due process," and advocated a better balance between statewide administration and campus autonomy. When the "no" vote came, only 23 persons stood up, the rest of the dissidents refraining from voting either way.[30]

The Academic Senate then passed a resolution expressing "personal affection and professional esteem" for Strong, and "gratitude for his devoted and generous service to the University." [31] Thus the Senate avoided taking sides in the now-public controversy between Strong and Kerr.

The next day was Saturday, March 13. In a carefully guarded meeting, limited to its members, the Board of Regents took no vote. Meyerson withdrew his resignation, and the written resignation of Chancellor Strong was accepted without comment. Some persons present have reported that nothing was resolved in the meeting, but that the skills of Governor Brown in chairing the meeting prevented divisions within the Board of Regents from becoming public through the mechanism of formal votes. Since minutes of executive (i.e., closed) sessions are not open for study without the explicit permission of the Board of Regents, I have been unable to verify these reports.

At the close of the meeting Kerr issued this statement:

1. After discussion with the Board of Regents, Acting Chancellor Meyerson and I have decided to withdraw our resignations pending further discussions with the Board. These resignations were made without full opportunity for Board consideration, which we regret.

2. The Regents and both of us completely disapprove of the obscene behavior which took place recently on the Berkeley campus by a few students and non-students. We applaud the condemnation of these actions by the vast majority of students and by the Academic Senate.

3. Proceedings are now under way to discipline the students involved, in an orderly and prompt way.

4. All Regents have and do fully support the orderly handling of such cases, and encourage us to proceed expeditiously, which we are doing.[32]

UNENDING CRISIS

On the Tuesday after the Regents meeting (March 16) the Berkeley administration began disciplinary proceedings against four students for actions during the obscenity rallies. Three of the students—Art Goldberg, Michael Klein, and David Bills—also were facing charges in the courts. The fourth student to face disciplinary charges on campus was Nicholas Zvegintzov, the graduate student accused of leading the "Fuck" cheer at the initial rally.[33]

Two days later, during the noon hour, representatives from the chancellor's office went out to the *SPIDER Magazine* table and forbade its sale on the campus, because the new edition made use of the offensive four-letter word that had figured in the earlier controversies. At the same time a student-written play, *For Unlawful Carnal Knowledge,* was also banned. Selling either document, the administration stated, constituted "conduct unbecoming a student." A crowd of students gathered around the *SPIDER* table to protest this action, as soon as a rally speaker announced what was happening. Despite threats of discipline if sales went on, and of the arrest of nonstudents for trespassing if any followed the table onto the campus, the group surrounding the *SPIDER* table moved it from the Bancroft-Telegraph strip onto Sproul Plaza. Mario Savio spoke at an impromptu rally around the table, calling *SPIDER* political and its banning an "infringement on free speech." The magazine sold briskly throughout the afternoon, despite numerous administration-student conferences aimed at stopping its sale.[34]

Students assumed that the banning of *SPIDER* represented a deliberate administrative decision to crack down on controversial expression on campus. There was, in fact, considerable division within the administration. The chancellor's assistant on political affairs, the staff of the dean of students, and other members of the administration met to counsel Meyerson to ignore the magazine at least temporarily, but a member of the Emergency Executive Committee insisted that action was needed.[35] Meyerson issued a temporary restraining order on the sale of the magazine, which he lifted March 31.[36]

On March 21, Meyerson announced a series of interim rules, which immediately became the subject of challenges by student groups.[37] There were daily rallies protesting infringement of the rights of free speech. An unusual situation occurred on March 24, when a group of faculty members who had supported the December 8 resolution scheduled their own rally, calling students "moral spastics" for responding to every cause, and urging them to "cool it."[38]

The next day, however, brought a Regents meeting that left things anything but cool. After a presentation by Clark Kerr, the Regents voted to set aside the graduate student vote of February 24 and the undergraduate student vote of March 2 concerning the readmission of graduate students to the student government. The action was taken after it was pointed out that a majority of the students had not voted on this matter and that it would affect the amount of fees charged them each semester. Kerr suggested that the Regents might expect some criticism from the more radical students, but that precedent would indicate the majority should not be bound to a minority decision. Guidelines for an acceptable majority of voters and for the proportion of votes necessary in the future were adopted.[39]

Rumors of plans to void the elections had circulated before the meeting, and both Student Body President Charles Powell and a representative of the Graduate Coordinating Committee had requested permission to speak on the matter. (Both planned to oppose the recommendation.) Neither student was allowed to speak, however, despite efforts by Regent Catherine Hearst to obtain permission for Powell to be heard. Some of the more liberal Regents expressed surprise after the meeting when they learned that students considered their constitutional rights to have been abridged by the decision; they had not been aware of the issues involved or of the impossibility of the standards set, so far as past experience at the university was concerned.[40]

Powell called a press conference immediately after the Regents meeting; he announced that the ASUC would not be bound by the board's ruling but would be responsible to its own constituency. The Graduate Coordinating Committee called for the election of graduate representatives to proceed as planned, with the results binding on the ASUC whether or not the required proportions of students actually voted.[41]

Mario Savio was quoted as saying that the Regents had "forgotten about the consent of the governed" and had "apparently declared war on the whole campus." He warned that the FSM was preparing for battle.[42]

The next day, March 26, the Graduate Coordinating Committee accused the Regents of "flouting all standards of legality, morality, and decency" in order to get a "rubber stamp parody of a student government." The ASUC Senate, in emergency meeting, voted to hold the election for graduate representatives despite the Regents' ban, because the election conformed with the ASUC constitution. The solid support for this resolution crossed the Slate non-Slate lines that had divided the vote on many other issues during the spring.[43]

The ASUC efforts to hold the graduate elections as scheduled were halted, however, by rulings of the Student Judicial Committee, which held that the elections would be illegal. Powell then tried to canvass graduate student desires by means of a mailed questionnaire.

The Graduate Coordinating Committee, however, announced that it would go ahead with the elections anyway, using campus voting booths for a "freedom ballot" modeled after that used by Mississippi Negroes who had been denied the opportunity to vote in the regular elections. The members also announced that, if their candidates won, they would take their seats in the ASUC Senate whether or not the administration and the Regents recognized the validity of the election.

Approximately 5000 undergraduates and 3000 graduate students voted on April 5, 6, and 7. Thirty-one per cent of the graduate students turned out for the election, short of the 50% required by the Regents but a far higher proportion of students than normally took part in campus elections. The vote was 7184 to 868 in favor of a constitutional amendment to include graduate students in the ASUC. The graduate representatives, elected by the roughly 3000 graduate students voting, were all members of the Graduate Coordinating Committee, which received a 4–1 endorsement by the voters. The opposition, a slate of candidates who called themselves the Associate Graduate Council, had denounced the freedom ballot as unconstitutional in view of the Student Judicial Committee's ruling and had urged their supporters not to vote in the election. Nonetheless, they received about 20% of the votes cast.[44]

Meanwhile, the ASUC was trying to find some way to cope with student desires and Regents requirements. Powell proposed that they resolve the dilemma by creating a "Crisis Commission," composed of the Senate plus the ten graduate students who won in the freedom ballot. Although the current ASUC would continue to be the official student government, it would agree to make no major policy decisions that would be binding in the fall. The Crisis Commission would draw up proposals for a more effective student government for the coming year and would dissolve as soon as graduates were seated in the Senate.[45]

That night, April 7, the ASUC Senate met in an atmosphere of crisis. Campus police had confiscated an FSM table during the day because the Free Speech Movement had refused to register under the new campus regulations.[46] There were widespread rumors that the campus police intended to arrest the "graduate senators" if they attempted to take their seats in the ASUC. (One graduate program at the university even scheduled a required meeting for all its students that evening in an effort to make sure they would not be arrested if police moved in on the ASUC meeting.) By the time the meeting broke up at 2:30 A.M., however, the graduate senators no longer were demanding to be seated.

So far as the "freedom senators" were concerned, the crucial decision of the Senate meeting was an amendment to Powell's proposal to create a Crisis Commission. This amendment would have made the student Senate subservient to the commission, rather than vice versa. The Slate "coalition" in the Senate split on this vote, despite great pressures from members of the Graduate Coordinating Commission, and consequently the measure lost. The GCC members then stalked out of the meeting, accusing the Slate undergraduates of selling them out and saying they would refuse to serve on so powerless a body. The Senate then passed a resolution urging that representatives of the ASUC be given speaking rights at meetings of the major Regents' committees; they also requested that all members of the ASUC Senate have nonvoting membership rights in the Academic Senate.[47]

Meanwhile, hearings for the four students charged with obscene conduct had begun amid a legal snarl. Attorneys obtained a court injunction on March 26, temporarily halting the hearings because they could prejudice the impending civil obscenity trials for three of the accused. This injunction was overruled by Alameda Superior Court Judge F. M. Van Sicklin a week later, on April 2.[48]

On April 1, mass trial began for 159 defendants in the December arrest. It was understood that this trial would set the precedent for handling the cases of all 773 arrested persons.[49]

On April 20 the *civil* obscenity trials against persons arrested in the obscenity crisis began in the Berkeley-Albany Municipal Court. The next day Acting Chancellor Meyerson announced that Arthur Goldberg had been dismissed from the university for his part in the affair, that the other two graduate students were suspended until fall, and that the freshman involved was suspended for the rest of the semester, because of "their roles in March obscenity issues." The sentences had been recommended by the Ad Hoc Committee on Student Discipline.[50] (The nine defendants in civil court subsequently were found guilty and given jail sentences.)

When the obscenity verdicts were announced by Meyerson, there was an immediate angry reaction from students. The next day, April 22, about 1500 students attended a rally denouncing the administrative action. Mario Savio announced that this decision marked "the end of our honeymoon with Marty." He tore up the permit obtained for the rally and announced that from now on students would formulate their own rules. He stated that the rally would not end at 1:00 P.M., as required in the campus regulations at that time.[51]

After the rally had continued for fifteen minutes past the designated closing time, the university cut off the power for the loudspeakers. Leaders of the protest had expected this to happen and had brought their own substitute equipment, which they immediately set up and began to use. The meeting turned into a discussion of what students should do in the face of the most recent administrative actions.

An undergraduate in sociology came to the microphone to argue against the rule violations that were occurring. As he was speaking, a campus police officer emerged from the center doors to Sproul Hall, behind the speaker and slightly to his right as the audience faced him. As the officer approached the speaker, a ripple of amusement began to spread through the crowd as person after person saw the officer and apparently began to predict what was going to happen.[52] The laughter continued until the officer reached out and tapped the student on the shoulder. Then the laughter ceased. The crowd surged forward, pushing, shoving, and shouting incoherently. A few moments later the crowd had doubled in size.

For the first few moments there was disorganized pushing and shouting, in an effort to stop the policeman from his task. Soon I noticed Bettina Aptheker and another student whom I could not identify standing slightly above the rest of the crowd on a low retaining wall. Once again, as she had done at the Greek Theater, Bettina Aptheker, accompanied by the unidentified male student, began leading a chant, which the crowd gradually picked up: "Let him speak! Let him speak! Let him speak!"

After a few moments the chanting stopped. There was silence as everyone looked at the policeman, who then spoke hesitantly and seemed nervous. He suggested mildly that the rally had gone overtime and that they would be welcome to continue it in the "Hyde Park area" of the lower Student Union Plaza. The offer was indignantly rejected by persons who had been major speakers at the rally.

The student at the microphone, who had been arguing that they should obey university regulations, looked troubled by this turn of events. Sue Stein, a leader in the Graduate Coordinating Committee and the master of ceremonies for this part of the rally, asked if he intended to continue speaking. He stood, scratching his head, trying to decide what to do. Sue Stein suggested that if he didn't want to speak he should turn the microphone over to someone else. Finally he indicated that he would continue speaking. The policeman left, the crowd fell back to its customary location in the plaza, and the student continued, "There are a lot of things wrong with this university. . . ."

He was greeted by delighted applause and shouts of amused approval. He soon gave up his attempt to persuade students to honor the rules, and the rally continued for some time thereafter.[53]

That evening the FSM Executive Committee met and decided to send a telegram to the Regents meeting in Los Angeles the next day, giving an ultimatum if the disciplinary action were not reversed. The telegram claimed that the procedure constituted "the denial of even rudimentary guarantees of due process" for the accused students and was sent in the name of a "Provisional Committee to Protest Student Rights." The telegram gave the Regents until April 28 to reverse the disciplinary action.[54]

About this time, the Emergency Executive Committee of the Academic Senate sent a letter to the Regents recommending that a single hearing officer responsible to the chancellor be appointed to handle student discipline cases, rather than assigning such duties to a faculty committee.[55]

At the Board of Regents meeting on April 23, members revoked their invalidation of the undergraduate election of March 2, but reaffirmed their decision not to recognize the February 24 graduate election as valid because too small a number of graduate students had voted. (The *California Monthly* reported that President Kerr said the ASUC was to remain an undergraduate association, pending further consideration by the board in May.) [56] The ultimatum by the FSM was responded to as a joke.

The Regents Committee to Review University Policies, headed by Theodore R. Meyer, proposed a new set of rules governing student and nonstudent political activity. The proposals were more restrictive of student activity than anything that previously had been considered at Berkeley and were planned to supersede the Kerr Directives. The proposed rules gave the chancellor on each campus power to interpret what kinds of actions would *not* be permitted on his campus, to regulate "time, place, and manner" rules on his campus, and to exercise authority over student government if the chancellor judged that its duties were not being exercised responsibly. The proposals required student governments to receive approval from the campus chancellor before constitutional amendments were voted on, forbade either voluntary or compulsory student governments to take stand on issues not directly related to the university and its operations; and prohibited nonuniversity personnel and nonstudents from distributing posters, circulars, handbills, and other documents on university property. Finally, the proposed rules noted that students convicted of violations of law were not immune from further discipline by the university community, including suspension or expulsion.

A challenge to FSM authority

While the Regents were meeting in Los Angeles, Mario Savio spoke to about 2500 persons at a rally on the Berkeley campus. He suggested that some form of direct action would be appropriate unless the Regents reversed the disciplinary action against the four students charged with obscenity. Toward the end of the rally, Brad Cleveland, who had written the letter in the September Slate "Supplement to the General Catalogue," came forward through the crowd to challenge Savio.

Cleveland demanded that Savio tell the audience what kind of follow-through on the ultimatum he had in mind. He spoke forcefully and scornfully, claiming that another sit-in would simply lead to the arrest and expulsion of a few thousand students. Did Savio intend to sacrifice them? If not, what did he intend to do?

Savio had no answer for Cleveland. (Indeed, the question of follow-through on the ultimatum had not been discussed in the FSM Executive Committee meetings.) The rally seemed about to disintegrate. It was saved as an emotional performance, however, by the arrival of the SNCC Freedom Singers quartet. They gave a brief speech linking the student struggle at Berkeley with the civil rights effort elsewhere. After the quartet sang a number of Negro folk songs, the entire crowd joined hands in a serpentine pattern and, swaying back and forth to the music, sang "We Shall Overcome." [57]

That was Friday. On Sunday, April 25, the Emergency Executive Committee of the Academic Senate issued a statement defending the handling of the obscenity discipline cases as having been in accordance with due process and the spirit of the December 8 resolutions.[58]

The next day Savio spoke again at a rally, vigorously denouncing the Meyer Report. At the end of the speech he said that he had been accused of Bonapartism, and that he was convinced if a movement could not survive without its leader it did not deserve to survive:

> *Any insurrection against educational tyranny not organized by you is not worth being organized. . . .*
>
> *Lest I feel deserving of the charge of "Bonapartism" which even I sometimes have made against myself, I'd like to wish you good luck and good-bye.*[59]

With that Savio strode rapidly away as the crowd stood stunned by the sudden announcement. The next day he explained his action in a letter:

If the student rights movement at Berkeley must inevitably fail without my leadership, then it were best that it fail. . . .

Let me add that perhaps the saddest thing about this community is the continuing reluctance of faculty to defend the rights of students. . . .

The Berkeley students have been forced to desperate acts because their professors repeatedly have failed them. . . .[60]

Savio went into seclusion, and not even his old friends knew where he was. It soon became clear that the resignation was real and not a maneuver.

Meanwhile, April 28, the deadline set in the FSM ultimatum, was fast approaching. Of the fall Steering Committee, only Savio and Suzanne Goldberg (soon to become Mrs. Savio) had remained active in the Free Speech Movement organization during the spring. The Executive Committee called an emergency meeting, which all of the other old-timers attended. It began at about 10:00 P.M. and lasted until after 4:00 A.M. the next morning, as the group wrestled with the problem of what to do now that the Regents had ignored its ultimatum. One by one it dawned on the people present that they could think of no response that would not be more damaging to the students than to the Regents. A number of ideas were suggested, but all proved unworkable as they were explored more fully. Finally, Jack Weinberg and Bettina Aptheker persuaded the others that their only hope was to form an organization for the longer-term struggle, an organization that would have a committed membership and could bargain with the administration and the Regents in the knowledge that its membership would support it through some such mechanism as a strike. (A strike by students violated no laws and thus left participants relatively protected.) The Executive Committee then voted to disband the Free Speech Movement and to form another organization, to be called the Free Student Union,[61] that would have a broadly based membership.

Hence student response to the Regents the next morning was the announcement of the formation of a Free Student Union for long-term bargaining with the administration and the Regents and for collective protection of student rights. The press, which had come to cover the ultimatum, generally described this as a face-saving gesture of defeat.

Students who had been active in the FSM immediately began an organizing campaign for the Free Student Union. By Friday, April 30, 1965, the *Daily Californian* estimated that approximately 2000 students had purchased membership cards at twenty-five cents apiece.

With student protesters putting their energy into the Free Student Union, and the Graduate Coordinating Committee having attacked the Slate ASUC senators and student government as ineffectual, the spring student government elections attracted fewer Slate supporters than they had in December. On May 3, Jerry Goldstein (ASUC vice-president, who had spoken from the top of the police car during the near riot on October 1) was elected student body president, defeating his Slate opponent by a vote of 3970 to 2078. Only two Slate candidates won seats in the student government,[62] and there was little danger that ASUC would be controlled by student radicals in the coming year.

The Regents' new challenge

Meanwhile, the campus was mobilizing to fight the Meyer Committee's recommendations on student rules for political activity. The California Alumni Council announced its support of the proposals, but the secretary to the Regents was beseiged with letters from students and faculty expressing their opposition. The Committee of 200, which had drawn up the December 8 proposals, sent a letter strongly critical of the recommended rules. The Faculty Forum, a "moderate" faculty party formed during the spring to counter the influence of the Committee of 200, also sent a letter to the Regents, criticizing the report and offering a number of alternative suggestions.

On May 10, by a vote of 192 to 24, the Academic Senate approved an amended Emergency Executive Committee resolution on the Meyer Report. The resolution made five points (1) Regulations concerning student behavior on campuses should be defined in terms of educational and scholarly objectives of the university, rather than in terms of general community standards. (2) There must be no restriction on the constitutionally protected rights of students. (3) Regulation of the off-campus behavior of students is not an appropriate concern of the university. (4) "Time, place, and manner" regulations should be made by individual chancellors after consultation with students and faculty. (5) There should be reasonable standards of due process for disciplinary measures at the university.[63]

The next day, May 11, Los Angeles attorney Jerome C. Byrne and his staff, which had been commissioned by the Forbes Committee of the Board of Regents to study the causes of student unrest and to make recommendations, released its report. The report defended the student protest, criticized the university administration, and recommended major decentralization of university decision-making procedures. Moreover, the report was highly critical of the statewide university administration and of the relationship of the Board of Regents to individual campuses. Edwin Carter, chairman of the Board of Regents, said succinctly at the time of its release, ". . . I doubt if the committee will treat most of its recommendations with much seriousness." [64]

In view of its content and the timing of its release, the report was a highly political document. The Free Student Union greeted it with enthusiasm; reactions within the Board of Regents ranged from extreme criticism to delighted praise. President Kerr immediately called an emergency meeting of chancellors from the nine university campuses to discuss the report. It was announced that within a few days Kerr would present an alternative report recommending administrative reorganization to permit the campuses more autonomy. [65]

On May 19 California State Assembly Speaker Jesse Unruh (an ex-officio member of the Board of Regents) [66] and State Senate President Hugh Burns (who headed the California Un-American Activities Committee of the legislature) announced that they might set up a joint legislative committee to investigate the state's higher education system, including the university. The next day the California Assembly voted 53 to 11 to curb "outside agitators" by giving state college officials power to throw potential trouble-making nonstudents off the campus. Unruh cast the deciding vote to give the measure the two-thirds majority it would require to send it to the Governor for signature. [67]

Thus, when the Regents convened at Riverside, California, on May 20, the controversies dividing the university community had spread far beyond the immediate institutional "family." The board's proposals to curb student political activity had encountered the organized resistance of the Berkeley faculty, indirect condemnation from the staff hired by a Regents' committee to investigate campus unrest, and the endorsement and supportive intervention of the state legislature. On one side, conservative politicians were discussing an investigation of the university; on the other side, liberals who dominated the staff investigation for the Forbes Committee not only were publicly countering the *policy* proposed by the Regents but were bringing into question the very *structure* of the university administration.

At their May 21 meeting, the Regents voted to defer consideration and action on either the Byrne Report or President Kerr's counter proposal for administrative reform. The Meyer Committee proposals on student conduct were revised considerably in light of faculty criticism. President Kerr announced that he would draft specific regulations to conform to the broad policy outlines and would have them ready by July 1.

At the opening session of the meeting Edwin Pauley cited "rumors" that he said had come to him from conservative faculty members at Berkeley. He claimed that an experimental teaching program being developed by Joseph Tussman, the chairman of the Philosophy Department, was really going to be a course in revolution, taught by Marxists. A liberal Regent, Frederick G. Dutton, contradicted the interpretation being given and expressed concern that such accusations damaged the reputations of professors.[68]

At the meeting of the Berkeley Academic Senate held on May 27, 1965, the body approved the following resolution:

Whereas the Faculty of the College of Letters and Science of the Berkeley Division of the Academic Senate has approved an experimental program of undergraduate education to be conducted by competent and respected members of the Berkeley faculty:

And whereas, certain of the Regents have attacked members of the faculty on the basis of their alleged political and social views, have irresponsibly broadcast hearsay allegations damaging to them, and have questioned an instructional program that is within the responsibility of the faculty:

Therefore, the Berkeley Division of the Academic Senate:

1. Reiterates that the content and staffing of academic programs are the responsibility of the faculty and states that these allegations should not interfere with the proposed programs' going forward as authorized.

2. Expresses its gratification that the Board of Regents refused to entertain these irresponsible allegations, and its particular appreciation of those members of the Board who showed an understanding of the proper relationship between the Regents and the faculty.

3. Asks apologies from the Regents involved for their attacks and allegations.[69]

Meanwhile rumors were widespread throughout the state that the conservative Regents had finally formed a sufficiently large coalition to depose Clark Kerr at the June meeting of the board. The rumors gained wide dissemination after the education editor of the Los Angeles *Times* (a paper controlled by the husband of an influential Regent) published a series of articles based on intensive interviews with members of the board. The reporter, who was considered the dean of educational reporters in California, claimed that Kerr had gradually offended a number of Regents by opposing their interests on various issues arising over a six-year period as the university moved into the forefront of American educational institutions. He claimed that events of the year had channeled these divergent grudges into a common cause.[70]

Thus the school year ended on a note of foreboding. The continued appointment of the acting chancellor had not been settled, and Meyerson had come under criticism from some of the more conservative Regents. There were widespread rumors that President Kerr might lose his job at the next Regents meeting. The Academic Senate had felt it necessary to defend its decision-making powers over *courses* from what it considered to be attack by the Regents. Then, on June 4, as the examination period brought an end to the school term, Jesse Unruh and Hugh Burns introduced a resolution requesting $150,000 from the state legislature for a study of the "free speech" and "filthy speech" student uprisings on the Berkeley Campus.[71] The prophets of doom were predicting the collapse of the once-great university.

ROUNDING THE CONFLICT

To the surprise of many, the summer months brought a new resiliency.

The June meeting of the Board of Regents was held on the San Francisco campus. The question of Kerr's continued tenure as president was not raised. In fact, the meeting opened with a motion by Dorothy Chandler, expressing the board's appreciation for Clark Kerr's administrative skills and approving his proposal for the reorganization of administrative relationships between the Regents and the statewide university administration, and between the president's office and the individual campuses.[72] (Dorothy Chandler had been rumored to be the key link in the coalition to oust Kerr; hence with this move the battle was ended before it began.) As subsequently adopted by the Board of Regents in its summer meetings, the reorganization plan gave each chancellor much greater control over day-to-day decisions concerning his campus and removed certain powers from the Board of Regents, while continuing to centralize key policy-implementation decisions in the office of the president.[73]

Shortly before this June meeting of the Board of Regents State Senator Hugh Burns had released his annual report on Un-American Activities in California. It was actually an attack on President Kerr, accusing him of being soft on Communists and of hiring them as his key assistants. In a news conference at the end of the Regents meeting Kerr rebutted the accusations. The Regents stood behind Kerr and his attacked assistants, as did other members of Burns's committee in the State Senate who had refused to sign the report.[73] Moreover, the appropriation asked by Unruh and Burns to investigate the two student uprisings was lost in economy moves as the annual budget was considered in the closing days of June.

Thus the legislature did not begin an investigation of the university, although through its financial power it did intervene indirectly. In what legislators termed an "economy move," the out-of-state tuition was raised. Discussion on the floor of the legislature, however, linked this measure with considerable criticism of "out-of-state agitators," whom some legislators considered responsible for the events at Berkeley. In a second "economy move," the legislators eliminated from the teaching appropriations for the Berkeley campus an amount of money equivalent to 158 teaching-assistant salaries. Legislators said publicly that this cutback had nothing to do with events on the campus. A number of students and administrators were highly skeptical of this claim, however, because the reduction equaled the salaries of the precise number of teaching assistants who had formed a union affiliated with the American Federation of Teachers to protect their jobs after they had joined the December strike. Whatever the reason, this unexpected budget cut created a major crisis for the Berkeley administrative staff. All undesignated funds were diverted into salaries for teaching assistants to try to keep the instructional program operating.

After considerable discussion with the Board of Regents over the summer, Martin Meyerson was not reappointed as acting chancellor at Berkeley. It is reported that negotiations came to an end after Meyerson demanded assurance that the board would not intervene in campus operation but would leave administration to him.[74] To replace Meyerson, the Regents hired Roger Heyns, a vice-president at the University of Michigan, who had been expected to succeed the current Michigan president upon his retirement. Heyns came to Berkeley with a widely respected reputation as an administrator at Michigan, a campus subject to many of the same currents as Berkeley.

Thus, as the fall began, the deep anxiety that had characterized the mood of the Berkeley campus in the late spring had changed to a cautious optimism. There was hope that the campus might experience a new birth of vigor as it responded to the challenges that had shaken it so thoroughly.

It is time for this account of events at Berkeley to close. The beginning of a new school year brought a new cast of characters among students and administration. Nevertheless, massive collective behavior continued to characterize the campus.

In 1966 the gubernatorial race in California brought the university under major attack from Ronald Reagan, the Republican candidate. The Republicans promised to "clean up the university"; charged it with offering courses in "drugs, sex, and treason"; announced that John McCone, former head of the Central Intelligence Agency, would conduct a major investigation if they were elected; and hinted that perhaps the president of the university should be replaced.[75] Moreover, the election campaign of 1966, like that of 1964, set off a chain of conflict between students and the Berkeley administration that led to a return of police to the campus and a second major strike, of several days' duration, during the early part of December.

At the first meeting of the Board of Regents after Ronald Reagan was elected governor, Clark Kerr was fired as president of the university.

These later events are a story in themselves. We should not close this report without mentioning them, however, for they make it clear that collective behavior at Berkeley during the 1964–1965 demonstrations had an impact far beyond the immediate campus or the original issues that gave rise to the outburst. What began as a tiny gesture, by a handful of students, turned into a tidal wave that has not yet run its course.

sixteen
UNDERSTANDING
WHAT HAPPENED

For those who went through it, the spring of 1965 at Berkeley seemed to present a kaleidoscope of crises. Seven more collective confrontations had developed during the spring. Targets of hostility had ranged from campus police and administrators through the Board of Regents and even had included "the power structure of Oakland" (the industrial city immediately adjoining Berkeley). The immediate *focus* of conflict shifted frequently—so rapidly in fact that it left many observers almost dizzy from the effort just to keep up with day-to-day crises.

For its first two weeks the controversy in the fall had centered around student rights to engage in political activity. (Students claimed that the new interpretation of rules, making former proselyting territory off limits, effectively prevented their participation in political action. They demanded a return to the old procedures allowing such activity on the immediate edge of the campus.) Once the administration shifted its rules to allow *some* kinds of political activity on the campus itself but continued to deny students the right to use the old territory in the former manner, the controversy shifted to a challenge of the university's right to restrict on campus *any* political activity that was allowed citizens in the surrounding community. By November 7, when students walked out of the Study Committee hearings, the issue for them had shifted again, to a challenge of the university's right to "prejudge" the courts. They demanded that the university pledge not to consider as "unlawful political advocacy" tactics whose legality had not yet been tested in the courts, even though arrests might have been made. (Far from being a quibble, this got to the heart of procedures then being used by the civil rights movement to pressure businessmen to hire more persons from ethnic minority groups.)

On November 20, the Regents failed to clarify this point in their new policy statement but arranged for enlarged disciplinary powers on campus. Thereupon students, although not abandoning their earlier demand, shifted their attention to the university's relation to civil strife between interest groups in the community. The students claimed that the university was not politically neutral if it offered research help to vested interests while preventing students from mobilizing support for persons oppressed by existing customs. The neutrality of the university, rather than the practical effect of particular rulings, became the issue. Then, by December 3, with mass arrests and a strike, the issue broadened again to focus on the nature of the university as an *institution* in the larger society, questioning its authority structure, its relation between "education, research, and service," and the types of experience its educational program should provide. In short, critics demanded that an institution of higher education provide moral leadership in the community.

With each shift in focus of the conflict, issues became more difficult to meet directly and to resolve—both because they were more general and because they came closer to the heart of genuine value dilemmas that higher education had failed to solve in its massive growth over the preceding twenty-five years.

Why this shift in focus? Some observers would dismiss it simply as a clever strategy to discredit an opposition. But such an explanation seems too simple. What accounts for growing student and faculty response to these charges? (Few participants took the broader issues seriously when they first arose in the controversy.) Moreover, why do other settings of prolonged conflict often produce similar patterns of shift in the focus of dispute, even when an opposition is devoid of tacticians?

I believe a better explanation is found in the changing authority levels that came to be centrally involved in the controversy. At first the dispute was with the student affairs staff of the Berkeley administration. In the September mass petition of complicity and sit-in, students directly challenged the authority of deans to enforce controversial political rules on the campus. This led to intervention by the president and the chancellor, who indefinitely suspended eight students. Demonstrators challenged this level of authority the next day, with the police car seizure; eventually negotiations re-established authority lines, after providing a way to deal with grievances. But with a second challenge to the university-wide authority structure, in the student walk-out of the Study Committee and public defiance of rulings, initiative shifted to the Regents. The December sit-in directly challenged the authority of this board, whether students so intended or not, since the discipline cases involved had grown out of a Regents' decision. Then the Governor intervened, only to be challenged in turn by a university-wide strike.

The practical question at stake for the dissidents was the right to mobilize students for coercive action in favor of the underdog. Direct challenges to higher levels of authority occurred at a "point of no return" in exchanges dealing with this specific question.

Each time personnel at a lower organizational level failed to resolve the rule/authority crisis facing them, a higher level of decision-maker became involved. And with each shift in level of authority came a more basic questioning: Why should persons at that level in the university insist that students obey rules whose constitutionality had come into question? Students asked what *commitments* persons at a given level of authority might have that would lead them to discourage student involvement in the larger civil rights struggle—rather than to ignore or to actively encourage such participation. As more of the organizational structure became directly involved in opposition to student demands, a wider range of university relationships came under surveillance. The most radicalized students had been asking these questions, of course, at the very beginning of the conflict. But their questions became relevant to a larger segment as the extent of opposition to student perspectives became clear.

Administrators, using a very different context, seem to have been unable to keep up with the shift in publicly salient issues. They consistently failed to recognize the nature of the underlying concern being raised by students and to speak to that issue directly, rather than to the broader questions of university structure and authority relationships. Administrators knew, of course, that there had been no actual attempt to pressure the university to stop civil rights campaign recruiting near its borders, as students claimed. And they knew that this had not been their *intention,* in announcing a reinterpretation of rules. Thus they found it extremely difficult to take student concerns at face value or to address them directly. They conscientiously attempted to resolve the policy questions students raised—but their slow organizational procedures could not keep pace with the continual shift in focus of the controversy. Attempts to settle "yesterday's" questions, while refusing to reassure students regarding the really central issue in dispute, served only to increase distrust on the campus and to encourage further challenges to authority.

When all levels of regularly constituted authority proved unable to resolve the crisis, and in fact came under question themselves, a previously uncommitted body intervened. Faculty members, who had no formal authority to set policy, nevertheless decreed a change in rules that could settle the dispute, by clarifying the underlying issue that had remained unsettled in each encounter with authority. In their December 8 resolutions they tried to re-establish a basis of consensus which could provide legitimacy to a formally constituted authority structure.

Many of the people who opposed the students at these various authority levels, it seems clear, did see far broader issues involved than the immediate civil rights campaigns. Why were they so unsuccessful in communicating their perspective to the general student body and the faculty?

One reason, of course, was that the Free Speech Movement kept attention riveted on its own definition of what was at issue—through daily rallies, often rebroadcast over radio station KPFA; through newsletters and frequent hand-outs; and through dramatic actions. It insisted that the *purpose* of regulations could be found in their *consequences*. Although this argument tended to confuse motive with result, it was powerful because *in fact* the consequences of a policy may be of more importance than its underlying rationale.

The same argument had been raised often before, in political harangues, without gaining widespread support. But now, thanks to state and national events, it had new meaning. It was put forward at a time when a clearly articulated conflict had emerged in the nation regarding basic orientations toward the use of power (nationally and internationally) and toward the place of minority groups in American life. The months in which the conflict crested coincided with a critical period of public choice in regard to the directions governmental policies should take.

In the preceding year, Bay area students had demonstrated that they could influence the direction of some of the issues. If the consequence of university policy, *in fact,* was to remove students from relevant action at a critical juncture in American life, and if the highest levels of university authority concurred in perpetuating this policy, something about the relationship of higher education to current power struggles was thereby revealed.

Occurring at a critical moment in time, the Free Speech controversy brought all these issues together. It focused attention on the larger university structure (which until then students had largely ignored) and its relation to power in American life.

The first massive encounter of the spring, the CORE demonstration in Oakland, in some ways seems almost like the last flicker from issues that had burned fiercely in the fall. But perhaps it was more like a dying ember that lights a new conflagration: for, to a worried section of the public, it was the first indication of what student dissidents intended to do with their new-found freedom. Thirty-eight hundred demonstrators, pressuring local business establishments, must have been an awesome sight to many.

The second "indication" of new directions for student energy was reported by the press two weeks later. News reports provided little interpretive background but described a former FSM leader conducting an "obscenity rally." Reaction was swift—and powerful. The inability of the student movement to direct its own ranks laid it open to widespread misinterpretation and discredit. As issues became more local, the context that FSM supporters used became less comprehensible to the general public.

With political crusades no longer the center of student controversy, questioning of the nature of the modern university turned inward. No longer was the focus of attention on who the university serves, and why, but on proper rights and restraints within the structure itself. Who has what rights? What limits may each segment of the university properly place on others? Who makes what decisions, and for whom? To what extent can its leader be trusted to manage the enterprise in the public interest? (And for which public?)

To a great extent the controversy revolved around a definition of student roles in the new university. Does a student have *rights* as a member of the community? (If so, what rights?) Or should he be considered a temporary resident, a trainee who has only *privileges?* In other words, does "student" refer to a transient *person* or a permanent *role* in the structure (a role filled by changing personnel)?

But the debate was not limited to the student question, for the authority issue ran deeper. Eventually a Regents, study committee asked whether the university should be considered a trust, managed by Regents for the state, or a state-subsidized but independent educational enterprise, with a policy set by those most immediately concerned (or technically qualified to promote educational goals).

As the controversy widened, moving beyond particular ways the university affects political controversy to consider the basic relationships that exist among its personnel, wider segments of the public became involved. The state legislature began to consider the issues, and eventually the nature of authority relations within higher education—and their relationship to the state government—became a central issue of the gubernatorial race in 1966. Once the basic direction and authority of the university came into dispute, there proved to be no easy formula that could serve to "put Humpty Dumpty together again."

Although the university went on much as it had before, the attacks on it—from opponents at both ends of the political spectrum—became far more damaging. By the spring of 1969 conflict between youth and the Regents at Berkeley had reached the proportions of war, with deaths resulting from pitched battles between National Guard and populace. With increasing momentum each side seemed to create its own "self-fulfilling prophecies" of what opponents would do. The basis of social order within the university was far from settled.

Yet to focus only on the continuing conflict at Berkeley is to blind ourselves to other, perhaps farther-reaching, impacts that this year of conflict had, both at Berkeley and farther afield. Several years after 1965, we can point to at least five developments of more than passing importance.

First, the Berkeley example encouraged a rash of revolts against alleged administrative abuses on campuses across the country. During the spring of 1965 there were demonstrations at Yale, St. John's, Brooklyn, City College of New York, Princeton, Washington College, the University of North Carolina, the University of Washington in Seattle, Hampton Institute in Virginia, the University of Pennsylvania, Cornell, Queens, Kentucky State College, the University of Colorado, and the University of Notre Dame.[1] Some observers claimed that as many as forty campuses had similar outbursts within the year that followed, but I have found no records to document the claim. Although it is not clear that Berkeley students should be given credit for all these expressions of what came to be called "student power," the leaders of demonstrations on several campuses that spring explicitly cited the Berkeley revolt as their inspiration. Once it gained momentum, it spread so rapidly[2] that it eventually became the hallmark of the cohorts that entered universities after the events of the Free Speech Movement had taken place. From October, 1967, to May, 1969, 471 demonstrations occurred on

211 campuses (about one out of every ten schools in the country).[3] Confrontation had become almost a way of life on some campuses. As students demonstrated that forceful intervention was not a tactic available only to authorities, use of force by administrators became more extreme. The invasion of campuses by police, which had seemed so shocking in 1964, became almost routine, and on more than one occasion was superseded by the use of armed National Guardsmen. By May, 1970, students were directing these tactics not only against the university but also against the national government. On 287 campuses students struck in opposition to enlargement of the war in Southeast Asia. Several students were killed in encounters between students and police or National Guardsmen.

Second, at Berkeley itself the clearest settlement to emerge from the controversy was the establishment of student rights to engage in political activity on the campus. There was a general reformulation of rules for political behavior. These continued to be the source of much contention in the years that followed, but the general principle of unrestricted free speech and political advocacy on campus seemed no longer to be in dispute.

Third, faculties and administrators on many campuses, including Berkeley, began a sweeping reassessment of the role of teaching in a research-oriented university. Student unrest sparked a wide range of educational experiments, many of which were aimed at giving students a less passive role in the scholarly enterprise and at creating smaller structural units within large universities, so that closer interaction between students and faculty could be encouraged. At Berkeley a Select Committee on Education, made up of influential members of the faculty, spent a year examining the educational program of the university and recommending forty-two changes to improve teaching on the campus.[4] Many of the proposals were adopted, after faculty discussion, although the two that seemed most critical for the educational climate were turned down. (One would have established a new vice-chancellor's post to develop educational innovations at the university; the faculty, in rejecting this recommendation, set up a Board of Educational Development subservient to the traditionally conservative Committee on Educational Policy of the Academic Senate. This change guaranteed that innovation would be encouraged, but could not result in major pressure to change the overall educational program unless it originated with the bulk of faculty themselves. In 1969 the Regents abolished the Board of

Educational Development, in reaction against a politically controversial course it had sponsored. The second defeated proposal would have required the university to make teaching skills an explicit criterion for promotion of faculty members to tenure rank.) A number of other innovations, less fundamental to the structure of faculty relationships at the university, however, were accepted with considerable enthusiasm. An experimental college within the university was established by Joseph Tussman, who had been serving as chairman of the Philosophy Department.[5]

Fourth, the Free Speech controversy, and its successors around the country, sparked a re-examination of administrative relationships within the university. We have seen some of the questions concerning centralization-decentralization of decision-making that were raised at Berkeley. In the years that followed, the Board of Regents at the University of California adopted varying positions in regard to these matters—but a once-closed issue had again become a lively matter of concern. In some states where university regents are elected rather than appointed, student radicals began to run for these posts. Thus the question of which interest groups would be represented on policy boards for the public universities began to be raised.

Fifth, the confrontations between students and authorities, which became common after 1964, led to severe testing of the boundaries between legislatures and universities. In California, both in 1965 and in 1967 threats by conservative legislators to make an exposé investigation of the state university were circumvented by supporters of the Regents. But, it will be recalled, the legislature did intervene indirectly in university affairs in 1965 through its power to raise out-of-state tuition and to reduce the budget appropriation for Berkeley.

Traditionally touchy relations between state universities and legislatures around the country did not improve during this time. By mid-1969, moreover, the federal government was discussing more direct intervention in campuses that could not control unrest.[6]

Higher education in America, which had drifted into increasingly larger combines oriented toward research and "service," found itself pressed, both from within and without, to re-examine its role in the larger society, its priorities, and its authority structure. To an impressive extent Berkeley's drama from the year of the Free Speech controversy was being replayed on the national scene.

NOTES

ONE *Structuring the conflict*

1. University of California, Office of the Registrar, *Statistical Addenda, 1947–48/1956–57,* 1947–48 Table I: Summary of Students, pp. 3–4; Table X: Veterans, pp. 22–23.

2. *Ibid.,* Table I for each year, and *Statistical Addenda, 1917–47,* same tables.

3. California State Department of Education, *A Master Plan for Higher Education in California, 1960–1975,* prepared for the Liaison Committee of the State Board of Education and the Regents of the University of California, Sacramento, 1960.

4. Sidney Suslow, administrative analyst, Office of the Registrar, University of California, Berkeley, *A Ten-Year Survey of Certain Demographic Characteristics of the Student Population at the University of California,* March, 1963, mimeographed report.

5. Over this period 174 students were listed as officers of the following organizations: Berkeley Friends of SNCC, Berkeley W.E.B. DuBois Club, Campus CORE, Independent Socialist Club, Slate, Students for a Democratic Society, Young Democrats, Young People's Socialist League, Young Socialist Alliance. It has been possible to trace the major field of study for 125 of these officers from other university records. Seventy per cent of the group majored in mathematics, economics, political science, sociology. English, and history. Another 8% were concentrating in other departments in the humanities and the social sciences. Faculty advisers (which give further indication of the sections of the faculty known to the students) came primarily from the Political Science and Speech Departments, with a few from the History, Classics, Sociology, and Statistics Departments.

6. S. M. Lipset, "Opinion Formation in a Crisis Situation," *Public Opinion Quarterly,* Spring, 1953; reprinted in S. M. Lipset and Sheldon S. Wolin (eds.), *The Berkeley Student Revolt: Facts and Interpretations,* Garden City, N. Y.: Doubleday-Anchor, 1965, pp. 464–494. A reworking of the data presented in Tables 15 and 16 of this report shows the following percentages of students opposed to the proposed loyalty oath, by major area of study: students in the humanities, 78% (76); in the social sciences, 75% (113); in

the physical sciences, 64% (36); in engineering, 41% (41). Numbers in parentheses show how many students in the sample came from each area of study.

7. Hanan C. Selvin and Warren O. Hagstrom, "Determinants of Support for Civil Liberties," *British Journal of Sociology,* 1960; reprinted in Lipset and Wolin, *The Berkeley Student Revolt,* pp. 494–518.

8. Unpublished tables from the survey conducted by Robert Somers after the police car capture give the following results for the fall of 1964. Numbers in parentheses show how many students were interviewed.

Student group	Percentage approving of FSM goals and tactics	Percentage approving of FSM goals but not of its tactics	Percentage disapproving of FSM goals but liking its tactics	Percentage disapproving of both goals and tactics	
By major					
Social sciences	51%	25%	11%	13%	(53)
Humanities	39	29	14	18	(51)
Physical sciences	38	31	15	15	(26)
Life sciences	24	38	29	10	(21)
Engineering/ architecture	8	25	28	39	(36)
Business administration	0	23	23	54	(13)
By grade point average					
High (A to B +)	45	29	10	16	(38)
Medium (B to C +)	31	27	21	21	(135)
Low (C and below)	15	38	37	10	(52)

9. Data compiled from an unpublished report, a statistical survey of graduate students enrolled at the university, prepared for the Graduate Division in May, 1961, by Sidney Suslow. The histories of entering graduate students in each department for the years 1924, 1935, 1949, and 1954 are summarized in tables. I used data from the entering groups for the fall of 1949 and 1954 in the following departments (chosen because they had the highest enrollments of graduate students): social sciences—anthropology, economics, political science, psychology, sociology; humanities—art, English, history, philosophy; physical and natural sciences—chemistry, physics, zoology, mathematics. (These were the only graduate programs, in departments whose undergraduate majors are in the College of Letters and Science, that had 100 or more graduate students enrolled in 1964.) The Graduate School of Business Administration also is included for comparative purposes, as are the Schools of Public Health and Engineering, which have shorter, more carefully structured graduate programs.

10. University of California, Berkeley Academic Senate, *Education at Berkeley,* Report of the Select Committee on Education, March, 1966, Appendix I: Graduate Students Fully Supported from Official Sources, Spring, 1965, p. 226.

11. Clark Kerr had been chancellor of the Berkeley campus. When Robert Gordon Sproul retired as president of the multicampus University of California, Kerr replaced him in that role. The university-wide offices were also in Berkeley, so that Kerr (who is highly reputed as a social scientist in his own right) could easily maintain a continuing interest in the Berkeley campus despite his wider responsibilities.

12. Information obtained in an interview with Errol Mauchlan, assistant chancellor, April 22, 1966.

13. See Allan M. Cartter, *An Assessment of Quality in Graduate Education,* Washington, D.C.: American Council on Education, 1966.

14. See University of California, Office of the Registrar, *Statistical Summary,* 1964–65, Table 6.

15. Enrollment figures from registrar's office, University of California, Berkeley.

16. This is probably an understatement: figures were taken from listings of faculty on leave each year, by department, in the university catalogue. Several persons familiar with the data have warned that these catalogue listings fail to include persons who received grants after the listings were made up. Hence this estimate of one fourth of tenured faculty in the social sciences and the humanities being gone for part of each year is *conservative.*

17. The thirteen departments listed in Note 9 were used to compute these ratios. The ratios were obtained by subtracting faculty on leave for at least part of the year from total number of faculty listed in the catalogue, by department, and comparing the result to the number of undergraduate majors and graduate students listed as enrolled with that department.

Again, these figures are conservative. Freshmen and sophomores (who have not yet declared their majors) are not included. Nor do these ratios consider the number of students enrolled in the various courses offered by the departments; the ratio of faculty present for the year to students being taught by a particular department is considerably higher. These latter ratios changed as follows: for the social sciences, from 1 : 91 to 1 : 132; for the humanities, from 1 : 132 to 1 : 155; for the natural sciences from 1 : 68 to 1 : 92.

The figures given in the text, rather, are ratios of the faculty present for the year in various departments to the numbers of students for whom these departments assumed special responsibility.

18. Descriptions in this section are based on the dates at which new buildings were erected on campus, with impressions checked against occasional maps appearing in "back to school" issues of the *Daily Californian* through the years. The list of dates for campus buildings was obtained from a report issued by the Campus Planning Committee and Office of Architects

and Engineers, "Long-Range Development Plan, University of California, Berkeley, June, 1962," Appendix D, pp. 46–53.

19. University of California, Housing Services, "Survey of Residence," reports issued yearly, 1947–1964.

20. *Ibid.,* Fall, 1964.

21. Tables 2-1 through 2-3 are adapted for this report from the data gathered by William Nichols. The results of his surveys (which studied participation in student government activities on campus) have not been published. The data are available from the Data Library of Survey Research Center, University of California, Berkeley.

22. The questionnaires for this survey, unfortunately, did not specify parties other than conservative Republican, conservative Democrat, liberal Republican, liberal Democrat, and "Other." Most observers of the Berkeley scene would agree that the "Other" category would contain an overwhelming proportion of Socialists of various schools. For example, in the fall of 1964, 618 students who claimed to have sat-in around the police car in October filled out questionnaires available from an FSM table shortly after the events. They were about evenly divided between persons who reported this demonstration as their first and those who claimed to be veterans of such activity. Twenty per cent of the first-timers and 51% of the veterans identified themselves as some variety of Socialist. Survey by Glenn Lyons, reported in Lipset and Wolin, *The Berkeley Student Revolt,* Table 2: The Police Car Demonstration: A Survey of Participants, p. 524.

23. Summaries compiled from University of California, Public Information Office, biographies and additional information from business data sources gathered by Marvin Garson for an FSM pamphlet.

24. The most flagrant recent intervention of this kind was the decision of the 1965 state legislature to reduce the university budget by $678,480, an amount equivalent to the salaries for 158 teaching assistants (Errol Mauchlan interview, April 22, 1966). This action followed a review of TA utilization and performance by the legislative analyst for the 1965 state legislature. It is probably not coincidence that over 150 graduate students had formed the Union of University Employed Graduate Students on December 9, 1964, two days after a strike conducted by graduate teaching assistants (*Daily Californian,* Thursday, December 10, 1964, p. 1.)

25. Rule 17, University Regulations, The University of California.

26. *Daily Californian,* Thursday, November 8, 1934, p. 1.

27. I have chronicled these struggles in detail in "Yesterday's Discord" (written with Sam Kaplan), *California Monthly,* February, 1965; reprinted in Lipset and Wolin, *The Berkeley Student Revolt,* pp. 10–35.

28. On October 11, 1940, the Board of Regents adopted a resolution stating that ". . . membership in the Communist Party is incompatible with membership in the faculty of a state university." This prohibition of Communists from the teaching faculty came after a graduate teaching assistant in mathematics spoke before the Berkeley School Board on behalf of an appli-

cation to rent a meeting hall made by the Young Communist League. See the account in the *Daily Californian,* Wednesday, October 2, 1940, p. 1. Other details were carried on Tuesday, September 24, 1940; Friday, September 27, 1940; and Monday, September 30, 1940.

29. See accounts in the *Daily Californian* as follows: Wednesday, October 31, 1934, p. 1; Thursday, November 1, 1934, p. 1; Tuesday, November 6, 1934, p. 1; Monday, April 15, 1935, p. 1; Thursday, April 23, 1936, p. 1; Friday, April 23, 1937, p. 1.

30. San Francisco *Chronicle,* Thursday, April 28, 1938, p. 11.

31. *Daily Californian,* Wednesday, May 9, 1956, p. 1 (incl. pictures).

32. *Daily Californian,* October 7, 1957, p. 1.

33. Reported in an interview with Edward Strong, formerly the chancellor at Berkeley, June 9, 1966.

34. This information has been gathered in a variety of conversations with Mike Miller between 1960 and 1963, and with Dave Rynan, an early Slate participant, in conversations between December, 1964, and June, 1966.

35. *Daily Californian,* December 12, 1957, p. 1; March 3, 1958, p. 1; October 16, 1958, p. 1; March 10–18, 1959, p. 1; March 9, 1960, p. 1; March 15, 1960, p. 1; December 15, 1960, p. 1; March 22, 1961, p. 1; February 15, 1962, p. 1; November 13, 1962, p. 1.

36. *Daily Californian,* August 22, 1958, p. 1.

37. I base this comment on remarks made during the fall of 1961 at several planning meetings conducted by twenty-three campus organizations which met under the coordination of the Student Civil Liberties Union (an affiliate of the American Civil Liberties Union). They were negotiating with the university administration over restrictions on speakers and on the place and time of meetings, as well as on similar problems that had arisen from the summer, 1961, reinterpretation of the Kerr Directives.

38. *Daily Californian,* Friday, April 10, 1959, p. 1.

39. *Daily Californian,* Monday, May 4, 1959, p. 1.

40. *Daily Californian,* Monday, April 27, 1959, p. 1.

41. *Daily Californian,* Monday, May 4, 1959, p. 1.

42. *Daily Californian,* Friday, August 7, 1959, p. 1.

43. No separate graduate organization was proposed by the chancellor's office to replace participation in the ASUC; beginning in 1960, formation of a voluntary organization was attempted by graduate students themselves. The students who spearheaded these campaigns described the organization as a graduate students' "union"; some campus administrators expressed concern that the organization's militant demands (which frequently paralleled those made by Slate) did not represent graduate student sentiment as a whole. In the fall of 1962, three years after the removal of graduate students from student government, the dean of the Graduate Division took a poll of their desires for a representative body. In the spring of 1963, the Graduate Division asked departmental chairmen to arrange for graduate students to represent their departments in a Graduate Advisory Committee. This com-

mittee, however, did not move far beyond structural organization work into substantive giving of advice or reactions. Also, it was not structured to be self-generating in terms of active programs to reflect graduate student concerns. (Information from *Daily Californian,* Friday, September 14, 1962, and from Karen Many, representative of the Sociology Department graduate students to the Graduate Advisory Committee.)

44. *Daily Californian,* Monday, May 18, 1959, p. 1.

45. *Daily Californian,* Friday, May 1, 1959, p. 1.

46. Reported in the *Daily Californian,* October 23, 1959, p. 1.

47. *Daily Californian,* Friday, May 13, 1960, p. 1.

48. *Daily Californian,* Wednesday, May 11, 1960, p. 1; Thursday, May 12, 1960, p. 1.

49. *Daily Californian,* Friday, May 13, 1960, p. 1.

50. *Daily Californian,* Thursday, May 12, 1960, p. 1.

51. This report is based on a story by Dan Silver that appeared in the *Daily Californian,* Friday, May 13, 1960, pp. 1 ff.

52. Reported by Cecil Thomas, staff member of Stiles Hall who talked with the police chief.

53. *Daily Californian,* Monday, May 16, 1960, p. 1, and San Francisco *Chronicle,* Saturday, May 14, 1960, pp. 1, 2, 4, B.

54. *Daily Californian,* Tuesday, September 27, 1960, p. 1; Friday, September 30, 1960, p. 1.

55. *Daily Californian,* April 18, 1961, p. 1; May 4, 1961, p. 1.

56. See reports and editorials in the *Daily Californian,* Monday, May 16, 1960, p. 1; Wednesday May 18, 1960, p. 1; and Thursday, May 19, 1960, p. 1.

57. Civil rights organizations during this period began to introduce speakers by citing the number of arrests they had for civil rights activities, in a manner similar to that of academicians who enumerate academic honors when introducing guest speakers.

58. The *Daily Californian* first mentions this organization on Tuesday, November 5, 1963 (p. 1). Jack Kurzweil, an early member, reports it was formed to conduct the campaign against Mel's Drive-in Restaurant at that time.

59. *Daily Californian,* Friday, March 29, 1963; Wednesday, April 3, 1963, p. 1.

60. *The New York Times,* May 8, 1963, p. 29 : 5.

61. *Daily Californian,* May 8, 1963, p. 1.

62. *The New York Times,* June 13, 1963, p. 1 : 8.

63. *The New York Times,* August 29, 1963, pp. 29, 1 : 8.

64. *The New York Times,* September 16, 1963, p. 1 : 8.

65. *Daily Californian,* September 17, 1963, p. 1.

66. *Daily Californian,* September 23, 1964, p. 1; September 24, 1964, p. 1.

67. *Daily Californian,* October 11, 1963, p. 1.

68. *Daily Californian,* November 23, 1963, p. 1.

69. See accounts in the *Daily Californian,* March 1, 1964, p. 1; March 6, 1964, p. 1; March 14, 1964, p. 1; April 20, 1964, p. 1.

70. *Daily Californian,* March 1, 1964, p. 1; March 6, 1964, p. 1; March 14, 1964, p. 1; April 20, 1964, p. 1.

71. The editorial in the *Daily Californian,* Wednesday, May 13, 1964 (p. 12), supports the right of students to engage in massive civil campaigns. The issue of Tuesday, June 16, 1964 announces speeches by defendants to tell of their experiences. Other evidence comes from conversations on the Student Union Terrace, tape recorded in March, 1965, during the "freedom vote" crisis at the university; students explain to outsiders what the Sheraton-Palace demonstrations meant to them and why they now believe in militant pressure tactics for civil rights.

72. *Daily Californian,* March 10, 1959, p. 1.

73. *Daily Californian,* April 8, 1959, p. 1.

74. *Daily Californian,* May 16, 1960, p. 1.

75. *Daily Californian,* March 2, 1962, p. 1.

76. *Daily Californian,* October 24, 1960, p. 1.

77. Announced at commencement, June 10, 1961 (San Francisco *Chronicle,* June 11, 1961, p. 1).

78. The *Daily Californian* of March 22, 1961, reports that State Senator Hugh Burns and Assemblyman Don Mulford warned, after Slate brought Frank Wilkinson to Berkeley, that Slate would lose its campus privileges (p. 1).

The story carried in the *Daily Californian* for August 1, 1961 (p. 1), juxtaposes paragraphs referring to budget-cut problems and to the new student regulations accompanying the withdrawal of Slate's recognition as an on-campus organization.

79. San Francisco *Chronicle,* June 11, 1961, p. 2.

80. The closest thing to such an exchange occurred in a series of letters printed in the *Daily Californian* on November 16, 1961, and November 18, 1961. Two members of Slate attacked President Kerr's latest revision of the Kerr Directives (after Slate had been denied recognition as a campus organization). In his reply President Kerr angrily defended his policy as more liberal than those of his predecessors and offered to return to the earlier regulations if a majority of the students preferred them.

81. For at least three decades election years had been difficult periods for the university. Discussion of campaign issues on campus during the controversial 1934 gubernatorial campaign (in which a Socialist received the Democratic nomination for governor) led to dismissal of UCLA student body officers by President Robert Gordon Sproul and to student "strikes" at Berkeley and Los Angeles in retaliation (*Daily Californian,* October 31 to November 6, 1934, p. 1). A 1940 ruling barring political statements by university employees led to the firing of a graduate student teaching assistant after he spoke from the floor at a student discussion meeting and to a Regents' policy prohibiting the employment of Communists (*Daily Californian,* October 2, 1940, p. 1; October 12, 1940, p. 1).

After the 1948 election, which included the controversial Progressive Party, the loyalty oath fight occupied the attention of the state for two or three years. (See the *Daily Californian,* May 16, June 24, September 29–30, 1949; February 28, 1950.) Other controversies, begun in 1956 over the appearance of Adlai Stevenson as an off-campus speaker to an on-campus audience, led as we have seen, to basic modifications in the university regulations regarding the freedom of partisans to speak on campus (*Daily Californian,* May 9, 1956; October 7, 1957). Note that these controversies seem to boil over approximately every eight years; they are most likely to arise at a time when the electorate is deeply split between the alternative value choices represented by candidates for office. (In 1934, for example, the choice was between a Socialist advocating state ownership and a Republican advocating free enterprise. The 1940 election challenged the common-law limitation of two terms for the president, later made mandatory in a Constitutional amendment, and concerned the question of movement toward involvement in World War II. The 1948 Progressive Party controversy involved the support of Communists and other left-wing political parties for the candidacy of Henry Wallace. Other Presidential candidates that year included Harry Truman, the Democrat, who won the election; Strom Thurman of the segregationist States Rights Party in the South; and Thomas Dewey, the Republican. The split of the Democratic Party into three camps that year made ideological differences particularly potent. In contrast, the 1956 election was less tense; the major difference between candidates concerned Stevenson's opposition to continued atomic testing in the atmosphere. Perhaps because the issues were less divisive, the controversy that arose also was less divisive, involving fewer persons and fewer structural levels of the university.)

TWO *Opening moves*

1. This information came from an interview with Alex Sherriffs, conducted on August 16, 1966. Katherine Towle's impressions of the source of difficulty with political hawkers during the spring differs from that of Alex Sherriffs' in one important respect: he reports the problem as one *of students moving their tables onto university property after they were asked to move them,* but Dean Towle saw the situation rather differently: ". . . There was the disregard by the students of the requests of my office to keep tables in order and not to set them up in places where people had trouble getting through" (tape-recorded interview, June 14, 1965). This statement suggests that Dean Towle did not consider the students' activity a violation of university rules, nor did she carry on earlier communications with students in these terms; rather she seems to have considered the problem one of impeding traffic. Sherriffs apparently assumed that requests to move were being made on a different basis.

The problem might have been avoided by not placing plaques in the brick sidewalk to mark the area as property of the university. These were inserted, however, for a legal reason: if the area closed off for the new plaza was not formally marked by the university as its own property, and if the university did not officially close it to through traffic for at least one day per year, the site of a former street would revert to ownership by the city of Berkeley.

2. Reported to me in an interview with Hafner, July 8, 1966, and later verified through phone calls and correspondence with Carl Irving and Roy Grimm.

3. A few *members* of the DuBois Club have told me since that time that they joined the Scranton demonstration line while standing outside the convention hall. Although they were acting as individuals—and apparently were motivated largely by a desire to get inside so that they could watch what was happening—it is possible that they were recognized by someone who made the phone call.

4. Information from a memorandum in the chancellor's office, giving details of the meeting.

5. Reported to me in an interview conducted on August 16, 1966.

6. This was Dick Hafner's impression, apparently shared by Arleigh Williams (See Katherine Towle's report on his memorandum to her, quoted on pp. 54–55.)

7. Chancellor Strong's office files.

8. Tape-recorded interview conducted on June 14, 1965.

9. "Chronology of Events, Three Months of Crisis," *California Monthly,* February, 1965, p. 35. The letter to student organizations was dated September 14 and arrived in the mailboxes of their leaders on September 16.

10. *Slate Supplement Report,* Vol. I, No. iv.

11. Only 2 of the 618 students who filled out questionnaires after sitting around the police car on October 1 and 2, 1964, mentioned the letter as a factor in their decision to join the demonstration. Since this sample of demonstrating students was self-selected, there is no final proof that *other* demonstrators had not been influenced by the pamphlet. This evidence suggests, however, that it is unlikely the Slate letter had widespread impact on demonstrators before their collective act. There are at least two reasons why this may have been true. First, its call to civil disobedience had to do with demands for course improvement and new teaching methods. Second, the typography and general style of language of this long report make for difficult reading. It is probable that most students began the letter and then turned to the more immediately interesting descriptions of course prospects facing them.

The ideology of the letter, however, is a reasonable *reflection* of a general conception of the university administration held by the more active members of Slate at the time. Actually, the letter was printed as a "summer supplement" over the objections of the editors of the *Slate Supplement Report.* A majority of Slate members present at a meeting during the summer voted to print it 'because it called a spade a spade' and suggested what action could be taken (reported by former *Slate Supplement* editor Phil Roos, August 5, 1966).

12. Reported by Edward Strong in an interview, July 8, 1966.

13. Tape-recorded interview with Jackie Goldberg, May 14, 1965.

14. From the files of the office of the dean of students.

15. Tape-recorded interview with Jackie Goldberg, May 14, 1965.

16. Tape-recorded interview with Brian Turner, June 3, 1965.

17. This reasoning is most understandable, since these students thought pressure was coming from a source that liked *conservative* political activity by students but wished to stop *radical* activity.

18. Tape-recorded interview with Art Goldberg, May 18, 1965.

19. Tape-recorded interview with Jo Freeman, May 19, 1965.

20. Tape-recorded interview with Jackie Goldberg, May 14, 1965.

21. *Daily Californian,* September 18, 1964, p. 1.

22. The eighteen organizations that had formed the United Front were the following: Campus CORE (Congress of Racial Equality), Campus Women for Peace, Independent Socialists (not affiliated with any national socialist organization), May 2nd Movement (a group formed to protest the war in Vietnam), Particle Berkeley (an undergraduate organization that publishes a science journal sold on the Bancroft-Telegraph strip), Progressive Labor (a Marxist group favoring Communist China), Slate (a campus political party), Society of Individualists (a conservative study group), Student Committee for Agricultural Labor, Students for a Democratic Society, Students for Goldwater, University Civil Liberties Committee, University Friends of SNCC (Student Nonviolent Coordinating Committee), Young Democrats, Young People's Socialist League (affiliated with the Socialist Party of Norman Thomas), Young Republicans, Young Socialists Alliance (affiliated with the Socialist Worker Party, a Trotskyite Marxist group), W.E.B. DuBois Club (a Marxist organization, a number of whose leaders are affiliated with the American Communist party).

23. Taken from chronology in the *California Monthly,* February, 1965, pp. 36–37.

24. Tape-recorded interview with Jackie Goldberg, May 14, 1965.

25. Here we see clearly demonstrated the function of rumor in an ambiguous but threatening situation. Rumor provides apparently independent confirmation of claims about the reasons why a critical situation has occurred. In rumor the confirming information comes at least once removed from its source, and therefore crucial details become highly susceptible to transformation. Paradoxically, a first-hand report is usually far less convincing to a group of people. Part of the reason that rumor is powerful is that it removes control of details from those who are providing the confirmation. It thus becomes easier to shape the material to a pre-existing explanation (or to make a new explanation seem plausible).

THREE *Confrontations*

1. *Daily Californian,* Monday, September 21, p. 1.

2. Interview with Jo Freeman, May 19, 1965.

3. Letter from chancellor's office files.

4. Memorandum from Chancellor Strong's files. My interview with Clark

Kerr occurred on December 13, 1966. (He had told this version of the encounter, however, to other persons many months previously.) Katherine Towle's version of the conversation was obtained on December 14, 1966.

5. Chancellor's office files. Chancellor Strong later added an interpretation of this memorandum, saying that Vice-President Cunningham indicated he was not clear about the current legal status of the university's position on speech and advocacy because of recent Supreme Court rulings. Strong also reported that President Kerr called Sherriffs back, saying that he had talked with Cunningham, who had agreed to stand by the rules (interview, July 8, 1966).

6. Memorandum dated September 21, 1964, from chancellor's office files.

7. *Daily Californian,* September 22, 1964, p. 1. Later verified by Miss Towle.

8. *Daily Californian,* Tuesday, September 22, 1964, p. 1.

9. *Daily Californian,* September 22, 1964, p. 1. It is not clear how the reporter distinguished "activists" from "non-activists," or whether the figures are an estimate or a rough count.

10. Answers from questionnaires returned in May, 1965, by members of the newly formed Free Student Union. Unfortunately, all information about demonstrators who became active before the police car incident was obtained far after the events, and coverage is quite spotty. Generalizations are not legitimate from the data available. I quote these two accounts, however, because I believe they are typical of the range of reactions expressed at that time by demonstrating students.

11. *Daily Californian,* Tuesday, September 22, 1964, p. 8.

12. *Daily Californian,* Wednesday, September 23, 1964, p. 1. The vote was 11 to 5. The petition was as follows:

I, the undersigned, believe in the value of active involvement in our community and with the issues which confront it. Because of this, I lend my full support to the ASUC Senate in its urging of President Kerr and the Regents of the University of California to grant to students and student organizations the following privileges on the Bancroft-Telegraph corner as well as the other eight areas of political distribution on campus:

1. Permission to distribute printed material advocating student participation in political and social action.

2. Permission to distribute printed matter soliciting political party membership, or supporting or opposing partisan candidates or propositions in local or national elections.

3. Permission to receive funds to aid projects not directly concerned with an authorized activity of our university.

I believe that these requests are, by their very nature, a part of the "open forum" concept, and that the granting of these same requests in no way sacrifices the administration of our University's affairs to any political or sectarian influence.

I, the undersigned, choose not to lend my support to this petition:

13. Tape-recorded interview with Jackie Goldberg, May 14, 1965.

14. Quotations taken from text furnished by Edward Strong. Printed in the *Daily Californian,* Wednesday, September 25, 1964.

15. "We Shall Overcome" is a Negro spiritual, chosen by the Student Nonviolent Coordinating Committee (SNCC) as its theme song during its first organizing conference at Raleigh, North Carolina. During the spring vacation period of 1960 students taking part in the sit-in campaign at southern lunch counters met together to form a permanent organization, which became SNCC.

16. The single-file march from Sproul Hall to University House stretched a quarter of a mile (*Daily Californian,* Friday, September 25, 1964, p. 1).

17. *Daily Californian,* Friday, September 25, 1964, p. 1.

18. Information from a questionnaire returned in May, 1965, by a member of the newly formed Free Student Union.

19. From tape-recorded interviews with Dustin Miller and Michael Rossman.

20. Quoted in the *Daily Californian,* Monday, September 28, 1966, p. 1.

21. Reported in a tape-recorded interview with Jackie Goldberg, May 14, 1965.

22. Oratory would not be expected from Mario Savio, for he had a slight tendency to stammer in private conversations, but he had come to feel very strongly about the issues involved. Savio had joined the Sheraton-Palace demonstrations the spring before and had been arrested. While in jail he met, as a cell-mate, a former graduate student in mathematics named Jack Weinberg. Weinberg had dropped out of school that spring semester to work full time on CORE-sponsored civil rights projects. During the time that both were in jail, Savio decided to go south for the summer to work with SNCC.

When he returned in the fall, he was designated chairman-elect of University Friends of SNCC. He then became a participant in the United Front. Until the rally he had not been especially dominant in United Front activities; when he stood up before the crowd to speak about the importance of the civil rights movement and of student involvement in the issues of the day, however, he became self-assured and expressed himself powerfully. A number of other persons also spoke, but a majority of the students who described this rally afterward were most impressed by Savio (information gathered in a tape-recorded interview with Mario Savio, May 11, 1965).

23. Both quotations taken from Free Speech Union questionnaires, May, 1965. The second student had favored the civil rights demonstrations of the previous spring but had not become involved in them. He had joined one other picket line previously, manned by CORE outside the Republican convention that summer.

24. Contents of letter shared by courtesy of Edward Strong.

25. As background information for the Regents, the Berkeley campus administration prepared three documents describing the controversy. These are presented in Appendix D of the dissertation on which the present account is

based. (See Max Heirich "Demonstrations at Berkeley," University of California Library, 1967.) All of this information was given me in an interview with Edward Strong, conducted on June 27, 1966. Professor Strong still has a copy of this memorandum in his personal files, so that we were able to verify the recommendations of the Regents Committee on Educational Policy in specific detail. They are identical to the remarks made by Strong at the university convocation on Monday, September 28, 1964.

26. Copied from the manuscript of Chancellor Strong's speech.

27. *Daily Californian,* Tuesday, September 29, 1964, p. 1.

28. Quoted in the *California Monthly* chronology of Free Speech Movement events, February, 1965, p. 38.

29. Reported in a phone conversation with Jackie Goldberg, October 21, 1966.

30. There has been some confusion as to whether this meeting, which was crucial for redefining the basis of the conflict, occurred *before* or *after* the announced change in university policy on September 28. The confusion occurs because a United Front pamphlet, handed out on Monday morning, September 28, urges, "Support the students who are putting up tables at Sather Gate in defiance of the arbitrary administrative regulations denying the students free access to political literature." This implies that the decision to move tables to Sather Gate had occurred *before* this announcement. If so, the context and thus the meaning of the decision by the students would be changed.

No minutes were kept of these meetings, so that it is impossible to pinpoint the exact date with final assurance. Because its timing is so important, I have reinterviewed many of the participants in this meeting in an effort to discover its date. Memories are hazy, but the evidence available to these participants suggests that it occurred in the sequence I have reported.

The term "Sather Gate" was used throughout the controversy, even before the decision to move table locations had taken place. In fact, some students were not aware that the Bancroft and Telegraph entrance was not "Sather Gate" because of the continued use of the latter term to refer to the location of political advocacy, even after the borders of the campus changed in 1960. A student who wrote handbills during this period reports that the term was not used precisely.

My major reasons for reporting the timing in this sequence, however, are these: (1) Jackie Goldberg has a vivid recollection of the sequence of learning about the Proposition 2 mailing and the sense that the university had admitted the bankruptcy of its own position. As Jackie said, "We did very little during that period that was not in reaction to administrative moves." (2) No tables, in fact, went up until Tuesday. The United Front usually acted immediately on any decisions that it made.

The evidence for the timing is not firm, but the nature of the decision is clear, as is its consequence for what followed.

31. Tape-recorded interview with Jack Weinberg, June 11, 1965.

32. Tape-recorded interview with Jo Freeman, May 19, 1965. "Fink out" was a slang term for becoming frightened and not carrying out a promise.

33. Tape-recorded interview with Mario Savio, June 9, 1965.

34. Tape-recorded interview with Brian Turner, June 3, 1965.

35. Tape-recorded interview with Katherine Towle, June 14, 1965.

36. *Daily Californian,* Wednesday, September 30, 1964, p. 1.

37. Tape-recorded interview with Katherine Towle, June 14, 1965.

38. The campus YMCA has an open-speaker policy and consequently had become meeting-headquarters for many groups that could not hold membership meetings on campus.

39. Both Brian Turner and Jack Weinberg reported, many months later, that this talk crystallized their own conceptions of what the university was about. Jack Weinberg also stated that he paraphrased much of the content of the talk in an impromptu speech the next day. Hal Draper was a Socialist and a frequent speaker at student political meetings; he was employed on the University Library staff and edited the journal *New Politics.*

FOUR *Sit-in*

1. Tape-recorded interview with Brian Turner, June 3, 1965.

2. The five students cited at this point were Mark Bravo, Brian Turner, Donald Hatch, Elizabeth Gardiner Stapleton, and David Goins. I have been unable to learn the order in which they sat down at the table.

3. Tape-recorded interview with Jack Weinberg, June 11, 1965.

4. Some observers think that a student named Tom Miller started this petition, but no one is sure. Miller was a veteran of civil rights demonstrations from the year before; several demonstrators have commented that circulating such claims for signatures was a standard "civil rights tactic," designed to make sure that many people act together, rather than becoming isolated.

5. Lists of students by courtesy of Marston Schultz, volunteer FSM archivist, who collected as many of the documents of the period as he could find.

6. All essays by members of the Free Student Union. The answers were written in May, 1965, in reply to a question asking how students first became involved in the controversy.

7. Chancellor's files. Memorandum dictated on September 30, 1964.

8. When Arleigh Williams recounted this episode to me in June of 1965, he did not remember that he had not acted spontaneously; thus I assumed that his agreement with instructions must have been substantial at the time.

9. KPFA is a nonprofit listener-supported station, operated by the Pacifica Foundation. It is devoted to educational radio programming and accepts no advertising. Taped excerpts of the Free Speech controversy events were played over the station daily during much of the 1964–1965 school year and were followed with great interest by the larger Berkeley community. Fortunately KPFA has preserved its original tape recordings of public events during the controversy, and I have found them to be invaluable sources of data.

10. Thomas F. Parkinson is a professor of English.

11. Ronan E. Degnan was chairman of the chancellor's Advisory Committee on Student Discipline. These phone conversations were necessary because the chancellor's office is located a block away, in Dwinelle Hall. (The building normally closed at 7 P.M.)

12. Chancellor's files. Memorandum dictated on September 30, 1964.

13. This appraisal is based on interviews conducted with Katherine Towle, Arleigh Williams, Edward Strong, Alex Sherriffs, and O.W. Campbell during 1965–1966. No resolution of these differences of perception concerning the nature of the issue in dispute occurred, so far as I could judge at that time.

14. Two more students, Sandor Fuchs and Mario Savio, had been added to Art Goldberg and the five who had manned the table, because of their actions inside Sproul Hall that afternoon.

15. Information supplied by Edward Strong in an interview June 9, 1966. The memorandum summarizing this meeting was drawn up by the president's office rather than by the chancellor.

16. Reported in a tape-recorded interview with Arleigh Williams, June 16, 1965.

17. Both statements were quoted on the front page of the *Daily Californian* for Thursday, October 1, 1964.

18. All summaries and quotations of this encounter come from tapes made by KPFA on September 30, 1964.

19. Thus Barnes included in his remark the area where students had just been "cited" (by the dean's office) for carrying on such activity—the event that had precipitated the current sit-in.

20. Savio is referring to an escalation of the Vietnam conflict during the late summer of 1964. Before the Tonkin Bay resolution the Republican Presidential candidates had criticized President Lyndon Johnson's handling of the war as not sufficiently belligerent. After this decision to escalate, the conduct of the war received less attention from these candidates. See *The New York Times,* August 16, 1964, p. 68 : 1; August 18, 1964, p. 30 : 4; August 21, 1964, p. 3 : 1, 5.

FIVE *Capturing the car*

1. The account that follows is based on a KPFA tape, made on October 1, 1964.

2. Perhaps this brief excerpt from these debates will give the tone:

HECKLER: *They're not saying you can't hand out these pamphlets! It's simply saying you cannot solicit funds!*

DEMONSTRATOR: *Actually that means you cannot self-perpetuate yourself! If SNCC cannot collect funds, then SNCC better close up its table right now and leave because—"*

Here a babble of voices interrupts, then one voice cuts through the others, saying, "Then you kill an organization! Then you kill an organization by your deal. And I don't like to kill an organization.

Others call out, "Let the young lady speak. Let the young lady speak!"

GIRL: *If you're saying that people can believe whatever they want, and they can say whatever they want, but they can't give money to further this sort of belief, you're putting in a very artificial kind of bond here, saying, "Say anything you want, think anything you want, but don't help anyone to do anything concrete to carry out what you think."*

The argument continues until finally one of the bystanders asks what SNCC is. There are gasps of laughter from the demonstrators. The bystander receives a mocking answer, and someone calls "Hello Freddie." ("Freddie," it will be recalled, is a derisive term used on the campus to refer to members of fraternities.)

3. Reported in an interview conducted on February 25, 1966.

4. Both President Kerr and Governor Brown were in San Francisco, attending a meeting of the American Council on Education. Governor Brown had expressed his embarrassment at having to address the meeting at a time when the state university was faced with massive rule breaking by students.

5. Ron Moskowitz was the Governor's assistant.

6. A vice-president for the statewide University of California administration, who is also a lawyer.

7. The right side of the steps as you face Sproul Hall.

8. The police had driven a campus police car around onto the Sproul Hall Plaza, behind the demonstrators, apparently in order to save steps while carrying the arrested man, who would be booked in Berkeley rather than in the Sproul Hall police station.

9. The account that follows was written from notes made during an interview with Richard Roman, on approximately October 15, 1964. It is a close parallel to an account he gave demonstrators on October 1 (KPFA tape), but this version explains *how* Roman decided what to do.

10. This event refers to a demonstration opposing capital punishment, held during an execution at San Quentin in 1960. The vigil that preceded the decision to surround the car at San Quentin had been an early Slate project.

11. Tape-recorded interview with Michael Rossman, June 1, 1965. His memory after the event of other details of this time period is well substantiated by a tape recording he made for himself on October 2, 1964, when he returned home from the police car incident. (A transcript of the October 2 tape is available from my files.)

12. Taken from essays written for me by members of the newly formed Free Student Union in May, 1965.

13. From a tape-recorded interview with Dustin Miller, June 11, 1965.

14. Adolph Eichmann had been tried by the State of Israel in 1961, for his part in the murder of millions of Jews under Adolph Hitler. Eichmann, who was accused of being "the butcher of Buchenwald," contended that he had merely followed orders. A widely read book about the trial had appeared during the preceding year; see Hannah Arendt, *Eichmann in Jerusalem: A Report on the Banality of Evil,* New York: Viking, 1963.

15. All of the persons in the administration who have been interviewed about this arrest have insisted, individually, that they had no idea who the person at the table was and that they did not suspect when they approached him that he was a nonstudent.

16. A code quickly developed around the police car to signal whether one was taking part in the capture or was merely watching; persons who stood up were considered to be watching; those who sat down signaled by this posture that they had joined in the capture of the car.

SIX *Escalation*

1. Reported by Edward Strong in an interview June 20, 1966, and later amplified by letter.

2. Based on a KPFA tape, recorded on October 1, 1964. The *Daily Californian* for October 2, 1964, reported that by noon 300 demonstrators had surrounded the immobilized car. By 12:30 P.M., it continued, several thousand students were crowded around the car.

3. Since these rumors became widespread, it may be worth while to consider them here. I have been unable to find evidence to support the contention that Communists were particularly influential in any of the meetings of the United Front before the police car incident. Bettina Aptheker was only tangentially involved until the afternoon of October 1, although she had signed the petition of complicity and was helping to man the W.E.B. DuBois Club table when Jack Weinberg was arrested. Throughout that fall, members of the Steering Committee of the Free Speech Movement insisted that Bettina was not following a party line in their deliberations and that, in fact, hers frequently was the more conservative voice of reason in their meetings.

Edward Strong, who became the prime opponent of the Free Speech Movement, laughs when someone suggests it was a Communist front. He insists the students were too romantic, too undisciplined, too anarchic to represent a Communist organization. He says the only person who never surprised him, after his years of teaching in New York City and observing Communist Party members there, was Bettina Aptheker. He claims he was always able to predict what her responses would be (interview of June 20, 1966).

In a letter dated March 10, 1969, Bettina Aptheker wrote the following description of her relationship to decision-making groups in the Free Speech Movement that emerged from the police car demonstration:

I believe that most on the Executive Committee, and certainly the people on the Steering Committee, knew that I was in the Party. There was at the time (there still is) a campus chapter of the Communist Party, of which I was a member. That chapter met continuously throughout the FSM and repeatedly discussed the crisis and especially tactics and courses of action to follow, etc. Those discussions were of great value to me. Often, although not always, the specific positions which I took at FSM Steering and Executive

*Committee meetings reflected the discussions and ideas of my comrades.
However, our policy was, that as a member of the Steering Committee I
would carry out the decision of it, which to the best of my ability I certainly did. I would mention here that, had an occasion arisen in which the
Steering Committee came to a decision which* in principle *I could not uphold, I would have resigned from it. A "Party Line," in this instance, was
not a rigid, dogmatic thing, but a living changing one, reflecting the ongo-
ing campus situation. My point is that as a Communist on the Steering
Committee I acted BOTH as an individual and as a member of a Party
collective. I make a point in mentioning this, because there is such general
confusion about "Party Line" and the role of a Communist and so forth.*

My favorite quotation in answer to this accusation of Communist domi-
nation, however, comes from Jo Freeman, a member of the more moderate
faction of the FSM Executive Committee, who described to me in a tape-recorded interview, May 19, 1965, a period when she had come to distrust the
intentions of the more radical members of the FSM Steering Committee.
When asked whether she thought the Committee was controlled by Communists, she laughed and said:

*The [FSM] didn't start out as a good revolutionary cadre would, being able
to plan and organize [demonstrations], and set everything up so it could
happen. It was totally unplanned, disorganized, unstrategical; no concept of
the total political situation. These people who said we were controlled by
outside agitators and outside money—I'd just sit there and laugh, and think,
"God! I wish we were!"*

4. Tape-recorded interview with Jackie Goldberg, May 14, 1965.

5. This account is based on three sources: a KPFA tape made inside
Sproul Hall on October 1, 1964; scribbled notes by Nathan Glazer, which
he kept as a running record of faculty activities at that time; and later inter
views with John Leggett.

6. This account was pieced together from a KPFA tape and accounts of
the incident gained from tape-recorded interviews with Mario Savio and
Michael Rossman, both of whom were involved in the encounter.

7. Based on notes made at the time by Nathan Glazer and supplementary
information received from S.M. Lipset.

8. Dean Louis Rice, interviewed on August 20 and 27, 1966, tried to reconstruct the contents of the meeting from memory.

9. Four other faculty members had spoken from the car earlier in the
evening, well before the antidemonstrators converged on the group. John
Leggett had explained how the confusion between faculty-administration and
Sproul Hall demonstrators had arisen. Nathan Glazer, S.M. Lipset, and William Petersen had reported on their conversations with members of the administration and had urged the students to go home.

10. This KPFA tape provides the basis for the report of events that follows.

11. From this point on, both local and national news media followed

events at Berkeley. Readers may wonder at the frequency with which I quote the campus newspaper and the Oakland *Tribune* for news accounts of later events. Many episodes were covered by *The New York Times* as well as West Coast papers, by *Life, Look,* and *Time* magazines, and on local and national television news programs. All of these sources, of course, were available to Berkeley participants.

Surveys made at Berkeley during the year of the conflict show that a high proportion of the student body read the *Daily Californian* every day; thus it seems a logical source of commonly shared information. The Oakland *Tribune* became important to participants because of their assumption that William Knowland, its publisher, was centrally involved in the dispute. For this reason many partisans read the *Tribune* to see how the "conservative opposition" was describing events. These two papers thereby assumed special importance as information sources for participants.

12. These statements were reprinted in the *California Monthly,* February, 1965, pp. 43–44.

SEVEN *Climax*

1. Kerr was not scheduled to return until the next morning.

2. Unsigned memorandum to chancellor's files, written October 2, 1964.

3. Memorandum to files written by Kitty Malloy on October 2, 1964.

4. Memorandum from the chancellor's files.

5. Reported by Keith Chamberlain, acting campus minister for the Westminster Foundation (Presbyterian) that year, in a tape-recorded interview, May 12, 1965.

6. This meeting has been described to me in detail by Earl Bolton and O.W. Campbell.

7. Letter from the file of the chancellor's office.

8. Memorandum and notes of meeting from Nathan Glazer's files.

9. Memorandum from the chancellor's files.

10. Lincoln Constance (LC) was dean of the Graduate School at Berkeley.

11. It is clear that the Ad Hoc Committee Against Discrimination arrests of the preceding spring had left some students highly sophisticated regarding tactical procedures and legal rights during a mass arrest.

12. *California Monthly,* February, 1965, p. 43.

13. Reported in a tape-recorded interview with Earl Bolton, August 2, 1965.

14. The account of this negotiating meeting is reconstructed from tape-recorded interviews with Jo Freeman, Jackie Goldberg, and Mario Savio.

15. Tape-recorded interview with Jackie Goldberg, May 14, 1965.

16. Reported to me in an interview with O.W. Campbell.

17. These comments are based on remarks written by the 618 demonstrators who filled out questionnaires in October, 1964, for fellow-demonstrator Glenn Lyons, and on comments written by members of the newly formed

Free Student Union in May, 1965. There is no statistically valid measure, however, of how widely such reactions were shared by the students who took part, since both samples consist of volunteers.

EIGHT *Negotiations*

1. The minutes of the organizing meeting for the Free Speech Movement (recorded by Sherry Stevenson on October 4, 1964) show widespread skepticism about administrative motives.

2. If this memorandum from Chancellor Strong's files accurately reflects Kerr's remarks, he apparently wanted to counter the interpretations Savio had given of the pact in his final speech from the top of the police car on Friday night. Kerr wanted it to be clear that normal decision-making procedures at the university were not superseded by the negotiating arrangements. The committees would be advisory to the duly constituted policy-making groups.

George Beadle is referring to an earlier student sit-in at the University of Chicago, which had been discussed by the students inside Sproul Hall on September 30.

3. From the minutes of the organizing meeting, FSM Archives.

4. From the minutes of the organizing meeting. Before the group voted, Bettina Aptheker expressed uneasiness that Red-baiting might occur if she were selected: "I've got a last name that's dynamite. Think about that when you vote. Please represent the independents on this body."

5. The account of this meeting is reconstructed from notes kept by an FSM student and by a faculty member.

6. Memorandum from Chancellor Strong's files.

7. Memoranda in the chancellor's files and additional details reported later by Edward Strong indicate widespread discussion within the Berkeley campus administration on Monday morning about the proper procedure to be taken at noon. The administrative staff decided that an arrest would appear provocative and should be avoided.

8. See *California Monthly*, February, 1965, p. 45. The Political Science and Economics Departments had offices for their teaching assistants on the same floor in Barrows Hall.

9. Free Speech Movement newsletter, University Archives, Bancroft Library, the University of California, Berkeley.

10. Quoted in the *California Monthly*, February, 1965, p. 45. While the student government was meeting with Kerr, the FSM Steering Committee was protesting to Vice-Chancellor Searcy of the Berkeley administration.

11. *California Monthly*, February, 1965, p. 47. A fraternity man who had joined the police car demonstration had been elected to the FSM Executive Committee to represent "unaffiliated students" a few days before. Also, three days previously students who sat-in around the police car had started collecting donations to pay for the $334.30 damages done to the police car by speakers standing on its roof. Unfortunately someone absconded with

these funds, which were being collected at a table on the sidewalk at Bancroft and Telegraph; thus this gesture of "good faith" never reached the administration.

12. *California Monthly*, February, 1965, p. 47.

13. From report in *California Monthly*, February, 1965, and from summary memoranda in the chancellor's files.

14. Clark Kerr had immediately denied the *Examiner* "quotation." Kerr states that Savio quoted his denial at a subsequent rally; the president's request that the student newspaper publish his denial, however, went unheeded. The student paper had not published the original quotation and continued to ignore the matter.

15. Record of proceedings kept by a member of the FSM Steering Committee. (Point four, of course, refers to procedure for examining the decision to suspend the eight students.)

16. Reported in tape-recorded interview. Original memorandum in University Hall files.

17. This organization, made up of students who had participated in the police car capture, who were concerned about "free speech" issues, but who did not belong to any of the political clubs on campus, had the largest membership of any group in the Free Speech Movement.

18. Miller produced two phonograph records of FSM events and songs, based on KPFA tapes. Through sale of these records the FSM raised over $30,000.

19. Committee members assumed that they either would be starting civil disobedience again or else would be part of a reconstituted negotiating committee. In either case they would need legal advice about the technical issues involved. The lawyers approached were chosen because they had been active in cases involving civil rights demonstration defendants and because they were among the few lawyers whom anyone on the Steering Committee had ever met or known personally.

Information about the meeting with the lawyers comes from notes kept by a member of the Steering Committee and from later interviews with several other members who tried to reconstruct from memory what had happened during this two-day period.

20. Tape-recorded interview with Bettina Aptheker, July 2, 1965.

21. Information about the contents of these letters is taken from a report in the *Daily Californian* of Thursday, November 5, 1964. The paper carried interviews with both Kerr and Cunningham and titled its story, "Kerr Refutes 'Letter Proof.' " This incident will be discussed shortly.

22. Arthur Ross, a member of the School of Business Administration, an associate of Clark Kerr's over some years in the Institute of Industrial Relations, and a practiced labor-management mediator, acted as go-between for the Academic Senate in arranging a compromise between the FSM Steering Committee and the university administration.

23. *Daily Californian*, October 16, 1964, p. 1.

24. *California Monthly,* February, 1965, p. 48.

25. *California Monthly,* February, 1965, p. 49.

26. Quotations from notes made at the time by an FSM member.

27. *California Monthly,* February, 1965, p. 50.

28. The full text of the resolution can be found in the files of the dean of students' office.

29. *California Monthly,* February, 1965, p. 51. (It is easy to understand why the students had come to distrust the impartial judgment of the university in such matters.)

30. *Daily Californian,* Thursday, November 5, 1964, pp. 1 ff.

31. From the chancellor's files.

32. In separate interviews sometime after the events, both Clark Kerr and Edward Strong stated that the president lost confidence in Strong's administrative judgment during the crisis of October 1 and 2. Strong went on to comment that it was clear at the October, 1964, meeting of the Board of Regents that Kerr was ready to replace him as chancellor when the proper opportunity arose.

33. *California Monthly,* February, 1965, p. 51.

34. A photocopy of this letter is in my files.

35. Interviewed on December 5, 1966.

36. By courtesy of Chancellor Strong.

37. Memoranda from Chancellor Strong's file.

38. Excerpts from confidential memorandum in Chancellor Strong's file, dated 10:00 A.M., Wednesday, November 4, 1964.

39. Robert Somers' fall survey of attitudes toward the Free Speech Movement includes interviews taken during this time. I constructed these records of changing campus reactions by grouping his respondents by date of their interview.

40. *Daily Californian,* November 9, 1964, p. 1.

41. *California Monthly, op. cit.,* p. 52.

42. Quoted in the *California Monthly, op. cit.,* p. 52.

43. This account is based on notes made at the time by Ron Anastasi.

NINE *Escalation*

1. The loudspeakers were set up in defiance of campus regulations to the contrary.

2. The FSM Executive Committee included representatives from all sponsoring organizations. It met regularly—often once a week—to review actions and approve new strategies. The Executive Committee elected a small Steering Committee to handle problems arising between Executive Committee meetings and to suggest tactics to the larger group. The Steering Committee met continuously during the more hectic periods of the conflict. From time to time its membership was altered by vote of the Executive Committee.

3. This account is based on letters written at the time and later remem-

brances of Jo Freeman, Brian Turner, Jack Weinberg, Ron Anastasi, Suzanne Goldberg, Mario Savio, Mike Rossman, and Bettina Aptheker (tape-recorded interviews with each). Their individual interpretations of some events of this period differ widely, but they are agreed on the events recounted here.

4. Excerpts from Free Speech Movement hand-outs of November 9, 1964. Complete copies are in the University of California Archives, Bancroft Library, Berkeley.

5. Estimates of the number of participants and of crowd size are taken from the *Daily Californian*'s story about the rally, November 10, 1964, p. 1.

6. See *California Monthly,* February, 1965, pp. 52–53, for an account of events on November 9, 1964.

7. This count is taken from lists preserved by the Free Speech Movement.

8. *California Monthly,* February, 1965, p. 52.

9. *California Monthly,* February, 1965, p. 53.

10. This account is based on reports by Jo Freeman, S.M. Lipset, and Clark Kerr, interviewed several months after the events had taken place.

11. S.M. Lipset was a personal friend of Clark Kerr. He had been active in the faculty group trying to arrange for negotiations between students and the administration at the time of the police car capture.

12. The students included points 3 and 4 to disarm opposition from conservative elements who might oppose the new policy; as veterans of earlier civil rights demonstrations, the framers of this proposal believed "unlawful actions" could "spontaneously emerge" during a demonstration or could be suggested at off-campus locations. Thus they saw this issue as a semantic debate rather than as fundamental to the current civil rights efforts. They differed basically in this respect from the more radical leadership in the FSM, who believed that such wording involved fundamental constitutional issues.

13. Eventually, however, word of the meeting leaked out, and a copy of the proposals reached members of the ASUC. This led to bitter charges of double-dealing within the FSM inner circles and diminished still further the waning influence of the more moderate group within the Executive Committee.

14. Tape-recorded interview with S.M. Lipset, August 28, 1965.

15. Tape-recorded interview with Jo Freeman, May 19, 1965.

16. See *California Monthly,* February, 1965, pp. 82–87, for the report of the Ad Hoc Committee on Student Conduct, dated November 12, 1964.

17. Figures come from my reanalysis of Robert Somers' data.

TEN *Spiritual encounter*

1. *California Monthly,* February, 1965, p. 56.

2. Reported to me in interviews with Michael Rossman and David Rynan. In 1964 Joan Baez was probably the most popular folk singer among college audiences.

3. This account is reconstructed from field notes made at the time. A KPFA tape presents the vigil itself.

4. From essays written by members of the Free Student Union in May, 1965.

5. Reported in the *California Monthly,* February, 1965, p. 57. The account continues. "No specific procedure on discipline for advocacy of 'unlawful off-campus action' was passed. Approval for the first section was unanimous; the second section received a few 'nays.' "

6. Item 4 was possible because the Heyman Committee, appointed by the Academic Senate to consider the discipline announced by the administration, had decided to limit its attention to actions that had occurred *before* the suspension of the eight students. It did not concern itself with events of October 1 and 2.

7. From the context of his remarks one would assume that Savio expected action against civil rights demonstrators who might be arrested in the course of a demonstration and then punished by the university administration as well as the courts.

8. Zelnik had become involved in the controversy earlier through his close friendship with Keith Chamberlain, the acting campus minister at the Presbyterian student center that often housed the FSM Executive Committee meetings.

9. *Daily Californian,* Monday, November 23, 1964, p. 1.

10. Reported in an interview conducted on December 13, 1966.

11. This account is compiled from separate versions of the weekend given by Mario Savio, Mike Rossman, Steve Weisman, Jack Weinberg, Bettina Aptheker, Ron Anastasi, and Walt Herbert, a campus minister who met with them.

12. *California Monthly,* February, 1965, pp. 57–58.

13. The account of the rally and sit-in that follows is a composite of my field notes, KPFA tape for November 23, and *Daily Californian* reports summarized in the *California Monthly.*

14. A few years later, she became known as the author of the satirical political play, *MacBird.*

15. Levine was a member of the history faculty who, along with Reginald Zelnik, led a coalition of young academics seeking to resolve the dispute.

16. *Daily Californian,* Wednesday, November 25, 1964, p. 1.

ELEVEN *The showdown*

1. Excerpts from these letters, as quoted in the *California Monthly,* February, 1965, p. 58.

2. Reported to me separately in interviews with Katherine Towle and with Arleigh Williams.

3. Tape-recorded interview with Bettina Aptheker, Friday, July 2, 1965.

4. Quoted in the *California Monthly,* February, 1965, p. 59.

5. *California Monthly,* February, 1965, p. 59.

6. "The Icebox" is the *Daily Californian*'s letters-to-the-editor column.

7. *Daily Californian,* Tuesday, December 1, 1964, p. 8.

8. Quoted in the *California Monthly,* February, 1965, p. 59.

9. *California Monthly,* February, 1965, pp. 59–60.

10. When I arrived about 12:40 P.M., there were seven students dressed in coats and ties. I assumed they were to be speakers.

11. The account that follows is based on my notes made at the time, on written accounts in the *California Monthly,* February, 1965, pp. 60–64, and on a KPFA tape, recorded on December 2, 1964.

12. This student went into Sproul Hall but left before he was arrested.

13. From essays written by members of the Free Student Union in May, 1965.

14. This student remained in the building to be arrested.

15. The account of events inside Sproul Hall during December 2 and 3 is based on news accounts in the *California Monthly,* February, 1965, and on KPFA tapes made at the time.

16. In rally speeches, Savio had been saying that the university administration should "sweep the sidewalks" and that *policy* should be made by students and faculty.

17. The account that follows is based on summaries in the *California Monthly* chronology, February, 1965, pp. 61–62, notes made from KPFA tapes of the arrest, and interviews made on December 3, 4, and 5, 1964, with arrested students.

TWELVE *Chaos*

1. The account that follows is based on notes I made at the time.

2. For the first time that fall I felt uneasy about what a crowd of pro-FSM demonstrators might do. In October the police car demonstrators had been determined to stop a miscarriage of justice, but they had been good-humored for the most part. On December 3, however, the only noticeable humor appeared when I pulled out my note pad and began writing observations of the crowd. The people around me burst into a shout of laughter, and one said, "Some people just can't stop their research for anything, can they?"

3. This account is based on my notes made during the meeting, supplemented by reports in the *California Monthly,* February, 1965, pp. 62–63.

4. There already had been a small meeting of concerned faculty chairmen, mainly those of the Economics, History, Political Science, and Sociology Departments (the last represented by its vice-chairman because Philip Selznick, the chairman, was not on campus that day). The group, called together by Paul Seabury, vice-chairman of the Political Science Department, met in Robert Scalapino's office. Scalapino's remarks in Wheeler Auditorium were based on sentiments expressed at this meeting.

5. These comments are based on tape-recorded interviews made at the time with one of the leaders in the resistance to the strike.

6. The FSM leaders, in contrast, reported their consternation at the frequency with which supporters ordered supplies without authorization, in the name of the Movement. Far from being financed "with outside money,"

FSM went several thousand dollars in debt, only partially recouped by contributions and the sale of records.

7. These figures are based on my own analysis of Kathleen Gales's data.

8. There had been a brief scuffle on the second floor when the police tried to prevent those sitting-in from putting a public address system on the balcony so that people outside Sproul Hall could hear what was happening.

9. Excerpts from essays by students who had joined the Free Student Union, May, 1965.

10. Seeing this, a number of observers speculated that the students who supported FSM were reacting to the impersonality of a large university, that they tended to be the alienated and the anomic—those lacking meaningful ties to social groups on the campus. The survey data provide little support for this theory. Robert Somers already has pointed out that in November, 1964, 82% of the students in his sample reported themselves satisfied with courses, examinations, and professors, and 92% agreed that, "although some people don't think so, the president of this university and the chancellor are really trying very hard to provide top-quality educational experience for students here." (See Robert Somers, "Mainsprings of the Rebellion," in S.M. Lipset and Sheldon Wolin, *The Berkeley Student Revolt: Facts and Interpretations,* Garden City, N.Y.: Doubleday-Anchor, 1965, p. 556.) There was no difference in the percentages reporting these reactions among supporters of the Free Speech Movement and other students on the campus. The FSM enthusiasts were somewhat more likely (60%, as compared with 48% of the campus as a whole) to believe they could have little influence on administrative decisions, but there is little evidence that these students were anomic. Rather, the supporters of the FSM came from groups that had little direct tie-in to the administration of the university, whereas those who disapproved tended to come from groups that had such channels.

In her spring survey, Kathleen Gales found a similar endorsement of the university as an excellent place to be, all in all. When Gales asked the Berkeley students whether they thought the university was a factory, however, 80% agreed. Moreover, there was practically no difference, in regard to this sentiment, by major or residence group, despite the variation in reactions to the FSM along these dimensions.

The high proportion of agreement with the factory analogy, even among those with little sympathy for the position of the protesters, suggests that a sense of helplessness or impersonality within the system was not peculiar to FSM supporters; thus it is of little help in explaining differences in reaction.

THIRTEEN *Drama*

1. Reported to me in an interview with Edward Strong, December 16, 1966.

2. I collected rumors that weekend by circulating in crowds on the campus.

3. *California Monthly,* February, 1965, p. 65.

4. Quoted from student's notes of the Steering Committee meeting, held on Sunday, December 6, 1964.

5. This account comes from notes I made at the time.

6. This account is based on S.M. Lipset's retelling of this story in a tape-recorded interview August 28, 1965, with details added in subsequent letters from him, and on reports from campus policemen who were on duty at the time.

7. This account is a composite of the report in the *California Monthly*, February, 1965, p. 67, and the accounts given in tape-recorded interviews with Mario Savio and Bettina Aptheker during the summer of 1965.

8. Tape-recorded interview with Bettina Aptheker, July 5, 1965.

9. *California Monthly*, February, 1965, pp. 67–68.

10. Persons on the stage had impressions of audience response quite different from those I gained at the top of the amphitheater. Surrounded by "supporting layers" of students, they describe loud applause for Kerr and Scalapino, and no sympathy for the militants until the police incidents.

11. The two policemen had been sent to the theater to prevent violence. They apparently were trying to protect Clark Kerr. In the pandemonium backstage, Joseph Lohman, dean of the School of Criminology, Paul Seabury of the Political Science Department, and Joseph Tussman, chairman of the Philosophy Department, intervened to have Savio released. (Reported in a letter from Paul Seabury, forwarded to me on June 20, 1968.)

12. *California Monthly*, February, 1965.

13. Probably never before in history had a "revolutionary situation" been so accessible to students of political and social behavior and so well documented.

FOURTEEN *Revolution*

1. This account of the meeting in Scalapino's office is a composite of reports by Robert Scalapino and Paul Seabury in letters during 1968 and 1969.

2. Accounts of this meeting have come from several sources. All seem agreed that Kerr had made it clear by the end of the meeting that the resolution was not acceptable to him in its current form. Not all informants, however, had been aware of his feeling at the beginning of the meeting.

3. Reported to me in a letter from Robert Scalapino, dated March 10, 1969.

4. Among the chief draftsmen of this resolution were the following members of the faculty: William Kornhauser, Sociology; Leo Lowenthal, Sociology; Herbert McClosky, Political Science; Charles Muscatine, English; Howard Schachman, Molecular Biology and Biochemistry; John Searle, Philosophy; Charles Sellers, History; Philip Selznick, Sociology; Henry Nash Smith, English; and Sheldon Wolin, Political Science. There were three members, each, from the Political Science and Sociology Departments and two from English, one historian, one philosopher, one physical scientist, and

one statistician. A number of historians and mathematicians were active in the formation of this group.

5. Transcript prepared for Academic Publishing—Berkeley, a member of the Council of Campus Organizations, which provided an approximate successor to the FSM Executive Committee in 1966.

6. Minutes of the Berkeley Division, Academic Senate, December 8, 1964.

7. *Daily Californian,* Wednesday, December 9, 1964, p. 1.

8. *Daily Californian,* Wednesday, December 9, 1964, p. 1.

9. I witnessed this activity Monday, but have no systematic evidence of how often such reminders were made, or of how many students actually went from their picket line to the voting booths.

10. Quoted in the *California Monthly,* February, 1965, p. 69.

11. Reported to me at the time by William Kornhauser.

12. *California Monthly, op. cit.,* p. 71.

13. *California Monthly, op. cit.,* p. 73.

14. See *California Monthly,* February, 1965, pp. 89–90, for this report.

15. *California Monthly, op. cit.,* p. 74.

16. *Los Angeles Times,* December 20, 1964, and interview with Clark Kerr, December 13, 1966.

17. Interview with Edward Strong, December 16, 1966, while reading through his files of the period.

18. Reported to me separately in interviews with Edward Strong, Martin Meyerson, and Clark Kerr.

19. *California Monthly, op. cit.,* p. 74.

20. Information from Martin Meyerson.

FIFTEEN *Spring, 1965*

1. After Napoleon was defeated and the traditional leaders again formulated European political policy, an effort was made to "restore" authority relationships that had existed before Napoleon's rise to power.

2. Students arrested in the December sit-in were brought to trial and later given a variety of sentences, which tended to vary in severity in relation to the student's prominence in the controversy and the attitude expressed toward officials who interviewed him. "Troublemakers" received sentences of up to 90 days in jail.

3. This writer also gave the first description of what has since come to be called the New Left among student radicals—the nonideologically committed challengers of the status quo. See Calvin Trillin, "Letter from Berkeley," *New Yorker,* March 13, 1965.

4. The Ad Hoc Committee claimed publicly that it quit the picketing because of "substantial gains" made at the *Tribune;* privately, some of the leaders claimed that disagreements within the Executive Committee led to its abandonment (*Daily Californian,* Thursday, February 4, 1965, p. 1, and Friday, February 5, 1965, p. 1).

5. *Daily Californian,* Monday, February 15, 1965, p. 1; Tuesday, February 16, 1965, p. 1; Friday, February 19, 1965, p. 1; Thursday, February 25, 1965, p. 1.

6. *California Monthly,* June, 1965, pp. 52–53.

7. *Daily Californian,* Friday, March 19, 1965, p. 1.

8. They saw Strong as firm against the students, and Kerr as compromising. The following list of letters to the editor and journal articles is representative of opinions expressed by persons identified with the group: Daniel I. Arnon, letters to *Berkeley Daily Gazette,* January 4, 1965, February 1, 1965, February 2, 1965, and February 10, 1965; Lewis Feuer, articles in *The New Leader*—"Rebellion at Berkeley," December 21, 1964, pp. 3–12, "A Reply," January 4, 1965, pp. 9–10, "Pornopolitics and the University," April 12, 1965, pp. 14–19; John H. Lawrence, "The Regents Role," *Science,* June 4, 1965, pp. 1276–1277; William Petersen, "Faculty Rebellion at Berkeley" (Xeroxed) and "What's Left at Berkeley," *Columbia University Forum,* Spring, 1965, pp. 39–44.

9. The *Daily Californian* reported a slightly different version of the story and indicated that charges were being brought against the persons involved. See the issue of Friday, February 12, 1965, p. 1. For the contraceptive poll dispute see the *Daily Californian,* Tuesday, February 16, 1965, p. 1.

10. A number of faculty members, including some active in the Berkeley campus administration during the spring of 1965, believed that the Truth Squad amounted to an organized conspiracy to discredit the more liberal trends on the campus. Whether such a conservatively oriented "conspiracy" actually existed I have no idea, nor is it important for our purposes to have an answer. What *is* important for our understanding of events is to know that some faculty members became friends apparently because of their common reaction to the Free Speech Movement and its aftermath, and that this group included a number having personal contacts with members of the legislature and the Board of Regents. This linkage, whether or not deliberate, could help explain why some members of these two state bodies viewed events in March with the degree of alarm they expressed. If reports of campus "excesses" had indeed been building up over time, the legislative reactions that followed March events appear less surprising.

11. World University Service is an international, student-sponsored service organization. Cal Camp is a summer camp operated by university students for youngsters from impoverished backgrounds. The Cal Smoker was Berkeley tradition, an all-male assembly at which people smoked and told off-color stories, engaged in pranks, and the like. The Smoker tradition, associated with athletic events, had been reactivated in the fall of 1964 after some years of disuse.

12. This account is a composite of a report in the *California Monthly,* May, 1965, pp. 10–11, and June, 1965, p. 53, and an interview with William Beall, chief of Berkeley Campus Police, July 2, 1969.

13. Reported in a tape-recorded interview with Art Goldberg, May 18,

1965, and in a conversation with Neil Smelser, March 4, 1965, which was repeated in a letter dated April 21, 1967.

14. *Daily Californian*, Friday, March 5, 1965, pp. 1, 14. The student involved reported that invitations to speak to women's clubs, declined sharply after this incident.

15. *California Monthly*, June, 1965, p. 53.

16. *Daily Californian*, Thursday, March 18, 1965, p. 12.

17. Artman protested "the hypocrisy of society" and proceeded to use a coined four-letter word in the contexts normally reserved for the expression "fuck."

18. This account is based on a tape recording of the meeting that I made at the time.

19. *Daily Californian*, Tuesday, March 9, 1965, p. 1.

20. This account is a composite of newspaper stories of the time and descriptions and interpretations provided by staff members.

21. Reported to me by Martin Meyerson in correspondence dated June 17, 1969.

22. Close associates of Clark Kerr describe him at that time as weary and angry at all sides for provoking the situation. They insist the move was not chosen as a strategic power play but was an emotional expression of general exasperation. Others, as might be predicted from events of the previous months, were inclined to view it in power terms.

23. Quoted in the *California Monthly*, June, 1965, p. 53.

24. Quoted in the *California Monthly*, June, 1965, p. 53.

25. *Ibid.*   26. *Ibid.*   27. *Ibid.*   28. *Ibid.*

29. The columnist was Art Hoppe of the San Francisco *Chronicle*.

30. This account is based on my notes of the meeting, made at the time, and the account in the *California Monthly*, June, 1965, p. 54.

31. Minutes of the Academic Senate, March 12, 1965.

32. Quoted in the *California Monthly*, June, 1965, p. 54.

33. Zvegintzov was the only one of the four students who was playing a major role in campus politics that semester: he was running for graduate representative to the ASUC.

34. See the *Daily Californian*, Friday, March 19, 1965, p. 1, and the *California Monthly*, June, 1965, p. 54.

35. Reported by Neil Smelser in an interview on June 25, 1965.

36. *Daily Californian*, Thursday, April 1, 1965, p. 1.

37. *Daily Californian*, Monday, March 22, 1965.

38. Quoted in the *California Monthly*, June, 1965, p. 55.

39. The account in the text is based on notes I made at the Regents meeting, later checked against a photocopy of Kerr's letter of March 12, 1965, to Martin Meyerson regarding past policies on student fees and voting. Kerr's report to the Regents did not mention that the Berkeley campus *never* had had a majority of students voting on any issue, except for the questionnaire gathered when study lists were filed, which had been used in

1959 to remove graduate students from the ASUC. (This, of course, had not been an election in the usual sense of the term.) See Chapter 1 for an account of that poll.

40. This report is based on notes I made at the meeting, plus reports of Regents' reactions made to me by faculty members shortly thereafter. Neil Smelser, who was serving as special assistant to the chancellor for political affairs, says the decision to void the elections was made on two grounds: first, a genuine concern about university precedent; and second, a concern that, if graduate students joined the ASUC the Graduate Coordinating Committee would represent them and tip the balance to the Slate-GCC coalition, effectively presenting the administration with many challenges that did not now have to be faced because of the split vote between Slate senators and the representatives previously elected.

Two proposals concerning the problem had been prepared in University Hall before the Regents meeting. The more conservative one was chosen to present to the board.

41. *Daily Californian,* Monday, March 29, 1965, pp. 1, 5.

42. *California Monthly,* June, 1965, p. 55.

43. *Ibid.*

44. *Daily Californian,* Thursday, April 8, 1965, p. 1.

45. *Ibid.*

46. The FSM was protesting a ruling that "recognized" organizations could have as members only registered students, faculty, and staff.

47. *Daily Californian,* Thursday, April 8, 1965, pp. 1 ff.

48. *California Monthly,* June, 1965, p. 55.

49. *Ibid.*

50. *California Monthly,* June, 1965, pp. 55–56.

51. *California Monthly,* June, 1965, p. 56.

52. On the tape recording of this rally one can *hear* people "catching on" as the officer approached the speaker, for there is constant swelling in the volume of laughter from the crowd.

53. This account is based on a tape recording and notes I made at the time.

54. *California Monthly,* June, 1965, p. 56.

55. *Ibid.*   56. *Ibid.*

57. This account is based on a tape recording and field notes that I made at the time.

58. *California Monthly,* June, 1965, p. 56.

59. *Ibid.*   60. *Ibid.*

61. This account is based on notes I made at the meeting.

62. *Daily Californian,* Wednesday, May 5, 1965, p. 1, and Monday, May 10, 1965, p. 1.

63. *California Monthly,* July-August, 1965, p. 48. (Note that attendance, as indicated by the vote, had returned to more typical numbers for this group.)

64. *California Monthly*, July-August, 1965, p. 48.

65. *Daily Californian*, Friday, May 14, 1965, p. 1.

66. Unruh seems to have joined Burns in this venture in order to control the committee investigation and to avoid punitive legislative action.

67. *California Monthly*, July-August, 1965, p. 49.

68. *Ibid.* 69. *Ibid.*

70. This series of articles on the University of California appeared in the Los Angeles *Times* during May, 1965.

71. *California Monthly*, July-August, 1965, p. 49.

72. This report is based on notes I made at that meeting.

73. *Daily Californian*, Tuesday, June 22, 1965, p. 1, plus notes I made at the press conference following the June 1965, Regents meeting.

74. Personnel matters are discussed in executive session; consequently the minutes of the discussion are not available as this account is written.

75. The Republican gubernatorial candidate also suggested during his campaign that students should not be allowed to criticize American foreign policy in time of war or discuss "Black power," the controversial campaign of militant Negro organizations.

SIXTEEN *Understanding what happened*

1. Ann Arbor *News*, March 15, 1965, p. 12.

2. See, for example, Richard Flacks' account of how Students for a Democratic Society (an organization that he co-founded) belatedly came to recognize the possibilities for social change existing in the spreading campus protests, which SDS had largely ignored: "Student Power and the New Left: The Role of SDS," p. 19, paper presented at the Annual Meeting of the American Psychological Association, September, 1968, San Francisco.

3. *Des Moines Register*, July 2, 1969, p. 1; *Ann Arbor News*, May 14, 1970, p. 11.

4. See University of California, Berkeley Academic Senate, *Education at Berkeley*, Report of the Select Committee on Education, March, 1966.

5. *California Monthly*, July-August, 1965, p. 49. Tussman's experimental college was a residential unit offering a two-year core program of ungraded independent study centered around the analysis of significant crises in Western culture.

6. In a Senate committee hearing, reported by the press on July 7, 1969, Senator John McClelland of Arkansas justified such intervention on the grounds that the federal government was providing 20% of the total budget of the nation's 2300 colleges and universities (*Times-Post* Service report from Washington, D.C., July 7, 1969).